Film Review
2011-2012

Film Review

2011-2012

Michael Darvell and Mansel Stimpson

EXECUTIVE EDITOR:
JAMES CAMERON-WILSON

SIGNUM BOOKS

*In memory of Ray Norton (1928-2011) and
Denny Drinkwater (1930-2011), two good friends who worked
in the film industry and were crazy about the movies* – MD

*To George Savvides, critic and actor, because his contributions to this
annual in recent years fully deserve this extra recognition* – MS

Acknowledgements

The editors of *Film Review 2011-2012* would like to thank the following,
without whose invaluable help this book might not have appeared:
Charles Bacon, Alex Buchan, Jeremy Clarke, Peri Godbold, Marcus Hearn,
Marshall Julius, Marysia Kay, Penny Lucas, Jonathan Rigby, George Savvides
and Derek Winnert.

Frontispiece: Gary Oldman in *Tinker Tailor Soldier Spy*.

First published in Great Britain in 2012 by Signum Books, an imprint of
Flashpoint Media Ltd
22 Signet Court
Cambridge
CB5 8LA

A CIP catalogue record for this book is available from the British Library.

ISBN 978 0 956653 45 1

Designer: Peri Godbold.
Managing editor: Marcus Hearn

Printed and bound in China by 1010 Printing International Ltd.

Contents

Introduction

by **Michael Darvell**

Last year's edition of *Film Review*, volume number 66, was a catch-up issue covering 18 months' worth of film releases, because we had lost our publisher the year before. This entailed an effort to review some 700 titles, although in the end we covered around 650.

There is always a drop-out rate for various reasons: films that do not get a press screening, those that have limited runs (possibly not even in the UK), or are aimed at club screenings or television-only transmission. There are films that receive a belated release and then disappear quickly before our team of reviewers has had a chance to catch them, and also some that go straight to DVD. The perennial problem of Bollywood releases is still with us, although the films themselves seemed to be less in evidence during 2011. We have caught sight of some of them but many Bollywood titles have gone straight to their cinema audiences without benefit of press shows. This means that of the 500 or so films released during 2011, we have managed to cover all but about 30.

Having changed our production and printing schedules, *Film Review* can now cover the complete calendar year – rather than reviewing, as we did for many years, six months' worth of films from one year (July to December) and six months from the following year (January to June). We can now obtain a better overview of a full year's releases and this also ties in better with the award-giving organisations such as the Oscars, the Golden Globes, the Baftas and the Critics' Circle. We hope you approve of the new coverage, which is the first time since the early 1950s that a complete year's output in UK cinemas has been published in a single *Film Review*. This should, we hope, set the standard for future editions.

Earlier this year I happened to glance through the film listings of some 50 years ago. Of course there were many more cinemas then, even though, by 1960, the popularity of television was an ever-present threat to film-going audiences. It was from the 1950s that cinemas began to close down, well before the growth of the multiplex had even been mooted. But in 1960 there were still cinemas on practically every corner and, apart from the West End houses in London, the suburban and provincial cinemas continued to attract their audiences. If you lived in the south London district of Tooting, for example, you had a choice of five cinemas, all within easy reach of the main shopping centre. And the choice of programmes was very wide indeed. With some cinemas showing separate Sunday shows or having a change of programme twice a week, and as most cinemas then showed double-bills, you could, if you were really clever, see up to 16 films a week.

During the week of 4 March 1960 Tooting had *Odds Against Tomorrow* and *Fort Bowie* all week at the Astoria; *These Dangerous Years* and *The Man from the Alamo* at the Vogue from Sunday, with *The Curse of Frankenstein* and *Day of the Bad Man* from Thursday; the Classic had *The Little Hut* and *Let's Be Happy* from Sunday, with *Lust for Life* and *The Extra Day* from Thursday; the Mayfair had *Two Way Stretch* and *Naked Fury* all week; while the famous Granada, the most fabulously ornate cinema in the country, had *Backlash* and *The World in My Corner* on Sunday only, with *Operation Petticoat* and *The Awakening* from Monday to Saturday.

Just listing those film programmes brings back memories of what it was like to go to the pictures some 50-odd years ago. You didn't have to book in advance, tickets were relatively cheap and well within the pockets of most patrons, including

Opposite: The imposing façade of the Plaza on London's Lower Regent Street in December 1959.

Below: On sale that same month was the 1959-60 edition of *Film Review*, with Disney cover stars James MacArthur and Janet Munro.

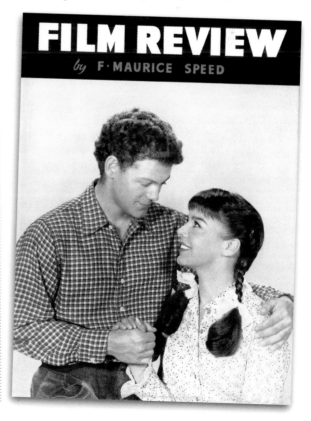

Two of the exciting 3D sensations of 1953.

children. Fifty years on cinemas may have improved in appearance (although that is sometimes debatable), but is the experience any better? In 1960, with continuous performances you could go to the cinema at any time you liked, without having to plan or book in advance. Admittedly you can now see more films at a multiplex cinema than you could have seen in the old days of single-screen houses, but it is definitely a different experience. There are no cinemas now in Tooting but in, for instance, Stratford in east London you have a choice of two cinemas, the Vue multiplex with some 20 screens and the Picturehouse with just four. During the week before Christmas 2011 you could have seen some 30 films, with only four children's films appearing at both. I know which cinema I would prefer – the small-scale, user-friendly Picturehouse. Not only because it's cheaper, but also because it feels like going to a local corner shop rather than a production-line supermarket.

In his book *The Good, the Bad and the Multiplex* (published last year by Random House), film critic and broadcaster Mark Kermode goes to town on the multiplex experience and the decline of 3D movies. His account of trying to take his young daughter to see a Zac Efron movie, *The Life and Death of Charlie St Cloud*, at a local multiplex is an eye-opening experience but one that is probably shared by many families. They don't half make it difficult for you to see a film these days. Admittedly you can book in advance online but then you have to pay extra for the privilege...

Another theme in Kermode's book is the topical one again of 3D stereoscopic films. In the days and years gone by when the cinema was trying to capture a new audience or at least keep an old one, film producers, exhibitors and distributors sought out new gimmicks. It began

in the early 1950s with 3D films. You may, like me, remember going to see *Bwana Devil* in 1952 or *The Charge at Feather River* or *House of Wax* in 1953 or *Creature from the Black Lagoon* and *Gorilla at Large* etc in 1954. The musical *Kiss Me Kate* was shot in 3D but, living as I did between Pinner and North Harrow, in north-west London, my local ABC cinemas, the Langham at Pinner and the Embassy at North Harrow, were not equipped for 3D, so I only saw the flat 2D version of *Kiss Me Kate* at the Embassy.

To see 3D films then one had to travel to Harrow, where the ABC Dominion had the necessary projection equipment. I saw *The Charge at Feather River* there and found it very exciting at the time, particularly the scene where a snake looms out of the screen and one of the cast spits at it. Interesting note: André de Toth, director of *House of Wax*, couldn't understand what all the fuss was about with 3D when he saw the rushes of his film. Ironically, he was blind in one eye so could not appreciate the three-dimensional aspect of his own film.

The 3D stereoscopic film actually pre-dated the two-dimensional film. British film pioneer William Friese-Greene invented a 3D process in the 1890s, which subsequently enjoyed a somewhat chequered and spasmodic career. The films were popular for a time in the 1950s but, as new attractions such as CinemaScope and other similar widescreen processes came along, 3D lost its novelty attraction and disappeared again.

However, it has made several comebacks over the years and, as the process became easier to control, more films were made in 3D, although they did not repeat their initial success until relatively recently. It has only been in the last few years that the process has come back into its own in a big way, much to the pleasure of exhibitors who can now charge extra for 3D screenings (plus the cost of the glasses, of course), as if it were not already prohibitively expensive to watch films at most cinemas, even in 2D. Currently, barely a week goes by when there is not a new 3D film on release. However, it has been shown that UK audiences are tiring of the stereoscopic experience and the extra costs incurred, preferring instead to watch their films in the old-fashioned 2D process. Often, quite frankly, the addition of 3D effects makes little difference to the enjoyment of most films anyway, apart from the occasional scenes where everything appears to be, as one 3D film once had it, 'comin' at ya'.

Nowadays, with home screens getting bigger and bigger and with the introduction of High Definition, plasma screens, DVDs and Blu-ray as well as the improvements in sound reproduction, it is actually possible to (almost) recreate the cinema experience at home. I have friends who have gone the whole hog and built themselves a cinema in their back garden. This means that their invited guests can enjoy their own choice of film and watch it in comfort without all the attendant drawbacks that going to the pictures involves.

October 2011 saw the 'grand' opening of the newest Essoldo in Leyton, north-east London. The Cinema Theatre Association Bulletin reported that "as a crowd (a boy walking his dog) gathered outside, invited dignitaries arrived for this auspicious occasion." This latest Essoldo is "under the personal supervision of the owner, Mr Graham Rumble, who previously ran the six-seat Essoldo Bethnal Green… Unusually, the auditorium is at first-floor level. The eight seats are of the padded, tip-up type and the auditorium is tastefully decorated in pleasing shades of brown, orange and beige. There is stepped seating but no balcony. The most up-to-date projection machine provides a steady, flicker-free image and a good view can be had from all seats." We wish it well and would encourage others to install their own home cinemas, which could be so much more rewarding an experience than viewing the latest releases in a dreary multiplex.

If you want a reminder of how cinemas used to be before the multiplex hit the UK, take a look at Richard Gray's book *Cinemas in Britain: a History of Cinema Architecture*, which he has updated in a stunning new edition published last year by Lund Humphries. It covers the growth of cinemas in the UK from their earliest beginnings in the late 19th century right up to the present day. It includes multiplexes, which have already celebrated their silver anniversary, having been first introduced to Britain as long ago as 1985. The Point, a brand-new building in Milton Keynes, was the first UK multiplex and it's still there, only now it's called the Odeon. Those that followed in its wake were, sadly, not as good, and it has been downhill all the way ever since.

Gray covers the pioneers of the industry who first showed their films in the early years of the 20th century in tiny shops converted to fledgling cinemas. Interest grew during the First World

War and purpose-built cinemas gradually began to appear. Following the introduction of talking pictures there was a huge growth in cinema building and then came the eventual rise of the 'super' cinemas. These picture palaces could seat up to 4000 patrons and were built in the 1920s and '30s, times of great hardship when a trip to the flicks afforded the pleasure of not only seeing the films, but also being in a building that was quite unlike the poor conditions that many families living in lowly accommodation had to endure. Instead, the new picture palaces offered an escapist experience in the atmospheric style of a Gothic cathedral (Granada Tooting), a Moorish palace (Astoria Finsbury Park), an Art Deco fantasy (Astoria Brixton) or a Spanish city (the Avenue/Odeon Northfields in Ealing). Both the films and the cinema buildings themselves fired the public's imagination and took them out of their ordinary, normal lives and into luxurious dreamlike surroundings.

Just glancing at the photographs of the picture palaces in Gray's book shows exactly what we are missing in today's cinema buildings. Although many of the super cinemas of the 1920s and '30s remain extant, not all of them are still used for showing movies. However, there are over 120 cinema buildings that have now acquired listed status from English Heritage, so they cannot be demolished or even altered. There is a list at the end of Gray's book detailing all the existing cinema buildings in Britain, whether or not they are still working cinemas. Some are now office blocks, factories, showrooms, casinos, bingo halls etc, but, as long as they are still standing, they are included.

You can still visit some of them and imagine what they were like in their heyday. If you care

Audiences were agog during 3D's first flush of popularity in the 1950s.

Above: The fabulous Granada Tooting – cinema or Gothic cathedral of the silver screen?

Right: William Wellman's *Wings*, the first film to win an Oscar for Best Picture in 1929.

to play bingo, then visit the Granada Tooting in all its Gothic glory, albeit without its former atmospheric lighting which now has to be bright enough for members to read their bingo cards. Still, the ornate decorations are the same as they ever were, as you pass through the splendid baronial foyer with its plate glass and gold columns, and gaze at the infinite reflections in the magnificent hall of mirrors while en route to the auditorium with its murals of medieval troubadours. All that alone is worth the price of admission, with or without the bingo.

Would that we could say that the average multiplex offers as rewarding an experience. Most of the multi-screen monolith monsters (which can have 20 or more screens in one building) seem geared entirely to the selling of refreshments before you enter the auditorium and the advertising of consumer goods when you get there. Scant attention is given over to presentation, showmanship or the comfort of and service to patrons. Some of the smaller, independent cinemas, however, such as the Curzon, the Picturehouse, the Screens and Everyman groups, do try to offer an attractive ambience unhindered by the aroma of hot dogs, popcorn and nachos. But they, like the superbly renovated Rex cinema at Berkhamsted in Hertfordshire, or the Phoenix in East Finchley (the oldest surviving single-screen cinema in the country, dating from 1910), are definitely in the minority. It is no wonder, then, that most film fans over 35 will not go near a multiplex today, preferring instead to watch their films at home on DVD via Blockbuster or through loan schemes such as Lovefilm or the home-streaming facilities now offered by Netflix, with their unlimited choice of films and television series. Can you blame them? I can't.

If the cinemas themselves are not user-friendly because audiences eat, drink, chat and use their mobile phones while they are there, it is not surprising that serious filmgoers boycott them. Extraneous sounds from an audience are bad enough, but a current cavil is that the sound on the film itself is poor. If you look at an old black-and-white movie, say *Casablanca* from 1942, you can hear every pristine word. But try and figure out what they are saying in some of the current films and you will have your ears straining to catch the most important utterances. Complaints have recently been made about such films as *The Girl with the Dragon Tattoo*, *Pirates of the Caribbean* and the remake of *True Grit* in which many cinemagoers couldn't understand a word. The usual suspects are the mixing of music and special effects with dialogue and, of course, the loudest of the three is bound to win. In the live theatre, if you are hard of hearing, you can borrow an induction loop – perhaps this idea should be introduced more widely to the cinema as well.

Another way of avoiding missing any film dialogue would be to make more films like *The Artist*. Nobody could have possibly predicted that this allegedly 'silent' film would reap the universal success it has enjoyed. And who would have thought that a silent film could win multiple Oscars in 2011? Well, it did, and it was the first silent film to win a statuette since the initial Academy Awards ceremony in 1929 (which awarded Oscars to films of 1927-28) when William A Wellman's *Wings* was the first to receive the Best Picture Award. *The Artist* is, like any other 'silent' film, not actually silent as there never was any such animal. Silent films were always accompanied by either music from a piano player or an orchestra, band or other music group. *The Artist* uses inter-titles for its dialogue just as the earlier silent films did until around 1930, by which time studios had changed over to talkies. These titles could be translated into any language in the world, thus making the cinema a truly international visual medium. Of course, you cannot please everybody and there have been reports of complaints from Cineworld patrons refusing to pay to see *The Artist*, a film without spoken dialogue, and demanding their money back.

Several years back Thames Television sponsored a marvellous series called Thames Silents in which film historian Kevin Brownlow and his associate David Gill re-released full-length silent films often for cinema distribution. Such titles as Abel Gance's *Napoléon*, D W Griffith's *Birth of a Nation*, Lon Chaney in *The Phantom of the Opera* and other classics from Chaplin, Keaton, Fairbanks, Valentino and von Stroheim were brought to the attention of a generation of film fans who had probably never ever seen a silent film. Often Carl Davis wrote new music to accompany the films and there were live concert orchestras playing at the screenings. I remember seeing the silent version of *Ben-Hur* with Carl Davis conducting the London Symphony Orchestra in a screening at the London Palladium. It was truly magnificent.

Last year I enjoyed a similar experience at a screening of Stanley Kubrick's classic *2001: A Space Odyssey*, arguably the best science fiction film ever made, with all the effects achieved within the camera long before CGI was invented. This time the original music was played live over the screening of the film at the Royal Festival Hall and it was as good as seeing the original Cinerama presentation. The original film score by Alex North was not used because, after it had been written, Kubrick decided to substitute existing music instead. It seemed to work well and was an integral part of the movie. André de Ridder conducted the Philharmonia Orchestra and the Philharmonia Voices in music by Khachaturian, Ligeti, Richard Strauss and, best of all, Johann Strauss II, his *Blue Danube* waltz, which has become identified with spaceships gliding through the cosmos ever since.

This is the kind of simple excitement that needs to return to the cinema: so forget 3D, just screen a well-made film, with the best possible picture projection and sound system, without all the attendant flogging of food, drink and other goods and get back to basics. We need a little showmanship in the cinema, otherwise the customers will stay away in droves. If the Rex in Berkhamsted can do it, without trailers or ads or popcorn, and turn a once derelict site into a super cinema again, others must surely be able to do the same. It just takes a little thought, some care and a flair for showmanship.

Talking of showmanship, the Lumière brothers, Auguste and Louis, put on the first public cinematograph show at the Marlborough Hall in London's Regent Street Polytechnic in 1896 and they included their famous film *Arrival of a Train at a Country Station* (great title!), plus *Fall of a Wall* and *Bathing in the Mediterranean* among many other shorts. The programme caused a minor sensation as the audience ducked for cover when the train got nearer… and nearer… Such was the innocence of those early days of the movies. However, news is coming in that the Marlborough Hall, now part of the University of Westminster, is to become a cinema again. What goes around comes around…

And finally… Apart from letting 3D films go the way of all celluloid cans, can we now have a moratorium on vampire and zombie films – because enough is too much already. Just let them rest in peace for a decade or so… And let's also move on after the eight Harry Potter films and leave all that fantasy and magic and witchcraft and special effects alone, and instead make films about real people in real situations… And do you think that Hollywood could possibly stop sending us all their feeble rom-coms unless they are a) truly romantic or b) really funny… And to see what will be arriving on a cinema screen near you in 2012, turn to the end of this volume for Mansel Stimpson's round-up of films we hope to cover fully in our next edition.

Fred Niblo's 1925 version of *Ben-Hur*, a silent film but always with a musical accompaniment. Carl Davis conducted his score once again at the Southbank Centre in June 2012.

Top 20 UK *Box-Office Hits*

1

1 January – 31 December 2011

1. *Harry Potter and the Deathly Hallows Part 2*
2. *The King's Speech*
3. *The Inbetweeners Movie*
4. *Pirates of the Caribbean: On Stranger Tides*
5. *The Hangover Part II*
6. *The Twilight Saga: Breaking Dawn Part 1*
7. *The Transformers: Dark of the Moon*
8. *Sherlock Holmes: A Game of Shadows*
9. *Bridesmaids*
10. *Arthur Christmas*

2

3

11. *Johnny English Reborn*
12. *Tangled*
13. *Rise of the Planet of the Apes*
14. *Fast Five*
15. *Mission: Impossible – Ghost Protocol*
16. *The Smurfs*
17. *Kung Fu Panda 2*
18. *Black Swan*
19. *The Adventures of Tintin: The Secret of the Unicorn*
20. *Gnomeo and Juliet*

4

5

Top 10 **Box-Office Stars**

Star of the Year: *Daniel Radcliffe*

2. **Johnny Depp**
3. **Robert Downey Jr**
4. **Rowan Atkinson**
5. **Vin Diesel**
6. **Tom Cruise**
7. **Colin Firth**
8. **James McAvoy**
9. **Simon Pegg**
10. **Daniel Craig**

E ven as the echo faded from the tills commemorating the final segment of the Harry Potter franchise, Daniel Radcliffe – the highest-earning star in the world – was headlining another box-office hit. Bereft of his signature spectacles and even sporting some facial growth, Radcliffe played a father and widower in the genuinely unnerving *The Woman in Black*.

One might argue that the piece had already confirmed its commercial mettle in the theatre – the stage adaptation of Susan Hill's novel is, after all, the second longest-running play in the history of the West End, second only to *The Mousetrap*. Even so, one really can't ignore the appeal that Radcliffe wields. He's a household name, eminently likable (as demonstrated in his numerous TV appearances) and a good-looking lad, er, man. Anyway, by April of this year (2012) *The Woman in Black* was the top-grossing film of the year in the UK.

Most of the other hits of 2011 confirmed the escalating popularity of animation and computer graphics, leaving bona-fide movie stars in the shade. In fact, a chart like this has almost become redundant. Still, tradition dictates... Based on their respective track records, such familiar faces as Johnny Depp, Rowan Atkinson and Vin Diesel continue to dominate this table. Colin Firth, in the right role, still has enduring pulling power, as his Oscar-winning turn in *The King's Speech* affirmed. Another dominant star in the chart is James McAvoy, whose voice enriched the appeal of *Arthur Christmas* and *Gnomeo and Juliet*, while his star turn as Charles Xavier in *X-Men: First Class* added much to that smart and winning epic.

James Cameron-Wilson

Faces of the Year

by **James Cameron-Wilson**

Riz Ahmed in *Trishna*.

RIZ AHMED

Born: 1 December 1982 in Wembley, London, England.

Most Indian actors in Britain have found themselves typecast as British Indians. And there are few Indian hits to go round: *East is East* one year, *Slumdog Millionaire* nine years later. Riz Ahmed, the son of Pakistani immigrants, is bucking the trend. For a start, he went to Merchant Taylors' (the top-end public school) and then Oxford (where he read politics, philosophy and economics). With that background you'd expect him to be mixing with the British intellectual elite by now. However, while at Oxford (Christ Church) he founded a theatre group and helped launch a drum & bass club which now has venues in Manchester, York and Preston. A stint at the Central School of Speech and Drama seemed the obvious next step, and before he'd even graduated he was given the lead role in Michael Winterbottom's highly acclaimed *The Road to Guantanamo*.

While nurturing his film career, Ahmed has pursued a parallel – and successful – vocation as a rapper, going under the appellation of Riz MC. His track 'Post 9/11 Blues' was banned on the radio (for being politically ill-advised), while the video for 'Sour Times' featured Jim Sturgess and Plan B (aka Ben Drew). Ahmed has certainly spread his net wide and both Winterbottom and Plan B have helped boost his mushrooming career as a movie star. For his starring role as *Shifty* – in which he played a non-stereotypical Essex drug dealer – he was nominated as Best Actor in the British Independent Film Awards. He then played a New York delivery boy in Sally Potter's *Rage* (with Jude Law), was a none-too-successful suicide bomber in Chris Morris' original and daring *Four Lions*, and was a Roman cook in the exceedingly bloody *Centurion*.

However, it was 2012 that saw Ahmed's ubiquity assured. He re-teamed with Winterbottom to play a modern re-imagining of both Angel Clare and Alec d'Urberville in *Trishna*, in which Thomas Hardy's *Tess of the d'Urbervilles* is transplanted to India – with Freida Pinto as his Tess. He then played an Arab prince in Jean-Jacques Annaud's desert-and-oil epic *Black Gold*, was re-teamed with Ben Drew (aka Plan B) for the latter's directorial debut, the oddly titled *iLL Manors*, and then landed the starring role in his first Hollywood movie, Mira Nair's *The Reluctant Fundamentalist*. In the last-named he plays a Pakistani working on Wall Street during the fall-out of the September 11 attacks. And his co-stars are none other than Kate Hudson and Kiefer Sutherland.

Whisper it softly, but as a cosmopolitan chameleon Riz Ahmed could be becoming our very own Anthony Quinn.

JESSICA CHASTAIN

Born: 29 March 1981 in Northern California, USA.

Seldom does a complete unknown burst from anonymity to virtual ubiquity in the blink of a calendar eye. Within the space of months, due to the vicissitudes of distribution, Jessica Chastain had clocked up six movies. And no ordinary movies.

Playing the central character in a Terrence Malick supposed masterpiece – opposite none other than

Brad Pitt – is not a bad start. In fact, the beautiful and luminous Chastain had leading roles in two films nominated for Best Picture Oscars, while clocking up a nomination for herself in *The Help*, one of the surprise box-office hits of the year. In the latter she competed against a raft of more experienced screen actresses and stole virtually every scene she was in. As a piece of white trash with a heart of gold, her Celia Foote was at once credible, heartbreaking and hilarious – and a far cry from the role of Virgilia in Ralph Fiennes' *Coriolanus*. In Malick's deliriously acclaimed *The Tree of Life*, she provided a humane centre of gravity in the face of Brad Pitt's brutish authoritarian, not to mention some romping dinosaurs. She was a strong wife, too, in the critically revered *Take Shelter* – and was one of the film's finest assets – and was a gun-wielding Mossad agent in John Madden's *The Debt*. She had a gun licence, too, as a detective in Ami Canaan Mann's *Texas Killing Fields*, from the offspring of Michael Mann. And, perhaps predictably by now, Ms Chastain got better reviews than her director.

The sheer volume and calibre of her work perhaps played against her at the Oscars but there are plenty more movies coming up. She landed the title role in *Wilde Salome* opposite Al Pacino, joined Gary Oldman and Tom Hardy in John Hillcoat's *Lawless* and then appeared alongside James Franco in *Tar*, a biog of the American poet C K Williams. But the film most people are excited about is the next project from Mr Malick, *To the Wonder*. In spite of a cast boasting Rachel McAdams, Rachel Weisz, Ben Affleck and Javier Bardem, the wise money is on Ms Chastain securing a second Oscar nomination. Amazing, then, to think that in January 2011 she was a total unknown. Yet by the end of the year she had amassed more than 35 critics' awards. And the staggering thing is that she deserved every one of them.

Jessica Chastain in *The Help*.

Jean Dujardin in *The Artist*.

JEAN DUJARDIN
Born: 19 June 1972 in Rueil-Malmaison, Hauts-de-Seine, Île-de-France, France.

Jean Dujardin has the distinction of being the first French actor ever to win an Oscar. And for his role in *The Artist* he only uttered two words: "Wiz pleasure." You have to hand it to the Academy: in recent years they have doled out trophies to such foreign-speakers as Marion Cotillard, Christoph Waltz, Penélope Cruz and Javier Bardem. The surprise about Dujardin's win, though, is that few people outside France had even heard of him. Although he made his first film in 2002 and had clocked up 21 films in the meantime, he was not as recognisable a face as, say, Romain Duris, Vincent Cassel or Mathieu Amalric, let alone Daniel Auteuil.

But what a face: with his disarming smile and matinée idol looks, he was the perfect choice to play Hubert Bonisseur de La Bath – aka OSS 117 – in Michel Hazanavicius's James Bond spoof *OSS 117: Cairo, Nest of Spies*. Complete with rear projection and outmoded art direction, the film was a painstaking parody of 1960s spy films. It was successful enough to produce a sequel – *OSS 117: Lost in Rio*, also directed by Hazanavicius – and introduced Dujardin to an international, if limited, audience. Hazanavicius took the reins again on *The Artist*, another – and deeper – dip into movie nostalgia that harnessed all the charisma and sex appeal that Dujardin could deliver.

Physically far removed from the likes of Cassel and Auteuil (or Gérard Depardieu), Dujardin is the real deal, a George Clooney with a French accent. And unlike the John Gilberts of the silent era, he has a very charming voice. He is also a wonderful mover, although he was confined to a bed for most of Guillaume Canet's hugely enjoyable *Little White Lies* – co-starring fellow French Oscar winner Marion Cotillard. Next, he teamed up with Hazanavicius again – for *The Players* – but this time as the director and star of his own short contribution to a portmanteau comedy about male infidelity. In it he gets to exhibit his true versatility by playing five different characters. After that he was cast as an FSB officer in love with an American agent in the Éric Rochant thriller *Möbius*.

And, as soon as he improves his English, he is bound to be snapped up by Hollywood.

CHRIS HEMSWORTH
Born: 11 August 1983 in Melbourne, Australia.

He certainly looks like a movie star. With his piercing blue eyes, blond locks and angular jawline, Chris Hemsworth has more than his fair share of celestial attributes. Throw in a body hewn from granite and it just seems unjust. Like fellow Aussies Eric Bana, Cate Blanchett, Kylie Minogue and Rupert Murdoch, he was born in Melbourne; and like Heath Ledger, Naomi Watts and Guy Pearce, he began his acting career in the soapy ranks of the enduring *Home and Away* TV serial. For those who follow such things, he played the unbelievably handsome Kim Hyde and clocked up 171 episodes.

On film he appeared in the American thrillers *Ca$h* and *The Perfect Getaway* and then played the father of James T Kirk in J J Abrams' massively and unexpectedly successful *Star Trek*. His next movie was the one that cemented his fame, when he was cast in the title role of Kenneth Branagh's *Thor*, a role he narrowly nabbed from his younger brother Liam, another Melbourne-born hunk. *Thor* went on to gross $450 million worldwide and has, natch, prompted a sequel, *Thor 2* (great title). As the Norse god with the hammer, Hemsworth looked like, er, a god, and in spite of all the hair and muscles conveyed a disarming sense of humour.

Since then he's gone on to land starring roles in the Joss Whedon-produced *The Cabin in the Woods*, starred opposite Kristen Stewart and Charlize Theron in *Snow White and the Huntsman*, secured top billing in the $75m remake of *Red Dawn* and, of course, reprised his role as Thor in *Avengers Assemble*. Next, he'll be portraying the Surrey-born Formula One champ James Hunt in the Ron Howard bio *Rush*.

Oh, and with his brother Liam's on-off-on relationship with Miley Cyrus, he could end up being Hanna Montana's brother-in-law.

JEREMY IRVINE
Born: 1990 in Gamlingay, Cambridgeshire, England.

Before he'd turned 20, Jeremy Irvine had starred in a Spielberg blockbuster and had been cast as one of the most recognisable characters in the Dickensian canon. Not bad for a teenager whose only previous experience on screen was in the TV sketch show *Life Bites*.

Born Jeremy Smith, the actor took his grandfather's surname and trained for a year at the London Academy of Music and Dramatic Art. Initially the roles were slow in coming, although on stage he did land the part of a tree. And he wasn't even getting commercials off his auditions when he was called back to read for the lead in *War Horse*. It wasn't *Equus* but it did make a lot of money and was nominated for six Oscars, including a nod for Best Picture. And with his face on the poster – nestled beside that of the noble horse – he won himself an immediate (predominantly female) fan following.

He was then snapped up for Ol Parker's weepie *Now is Good*, playing the romantic lead opposite Dakota Fanning, and followed this with the role of Pip in Mike Newell's all-star *Great Expectations*. Next, he'll play the younger version of Colin Firth in the true-life drama *The Railway Man*, with Nicole Kidman.

Chris Hemsworth in *Snow White and the Huntsman*.

Jeremy Irvine in *War Horse*.

Felicity Jones in *Like Crazy*.

Rooney Mara in *The Girl with the Dragon Tattoo*.

FELICITY JONES

Born: 19 January 1984 in Birmingham, England.

For many, Felicity Jones will forever be associated with the voice of Emma, the promiscuous partner of Ed Grundy in *The Archers* (the enduring Radio 4 soap set in Ambridge). Indeed, having started her acting career at the age of 14 (playing the lead sorceress in the children's TV series *The Worst Witch*), Felicity had been doing very well for herself.

Then she got into the shower one day, convinced a friend to film her therein and posted the resultant video to the American film director Drake Doremus. He was duly impressed and cast her in *Like Crazy* – before she had even met her co-star Anton Yelchin, with whom she was to share a truly intense relationship on screen. The part won her the Special Jury Prize for Breakout Performance at Sundance, prompting the presenter America Ferrera to announce that "The 2011 Sundance Film Festival will go down as the year of the actress." A year later she turned down the lead in the $70 million action-fantasy epic *Snow White and the Huntsman* and was replaced by none other than Kristen Stewart.

In addition Miss Jones played Catherine Morland in the 2007 TV adaptation of *Northanger Abbey* (supported by Carey Mulligan), was a vivid Cordelia Flyte in the film version of *Brideshead Revisited* and played Miranda to Helen Mirren's Prospera in Julie Taymor's *The Tempest*. These were seriously classical roles, worthy of an actress who had read English at Oxford (Wadham College), but the media at large didn't really cotton on to her until she played the female lead in Ricky Gervais and Stephen Merchant's acidic and moving *Cemetery Junction* (2010), landed the title role in the Anglo-Austrian rom-com *Chalet Girl* and hit America as a lovelorn Brit in the critically revered *Like Crazy*.

Exceedingly pretty in an English Rose sort of way, Felicity Jones is smart and talented with it, with her screen career shaping up nicely. After the success of *Like Crazy* she teamed up with Maggie Gyllenhaal and Hugh Dancy for *Hysteria*, a period comedy about the invention of the vibrator; starred as a conflicted bride in the British comedy *Cheerful Weather for the Wedding*; and was then selected to play Charles Dickens' secret mistress in Ralph Fiennes' adaptation of the award-winning Claire Tomalin tome *The Invisible Woman*.

ROONEY MARA

Born: 17 April 1985 in Bedford, New York, USA.

In the Oscar sweepstakes of 2012, the wise money was on Tilda Swinton and Charlize Theron to snare Oscar nods alongside Meryl Streep. When neither was shortlisted but Rooney Mara was, the world took note. Who was this actress with the odd name, if actress she really was?

The actress was actually christened Patricia Mara, adopting her middle name Rooney for her stage moniker, which just happens to be the surname of her great-grandfather Art Rooney Sr, founder of the Pittsburgh Steelers football team. In fact, football is in her DNA. Her other great-grandfather, Tim Mara, founded the New York Giants, while her father, Tim Jr, is the 'vice president of player evaluation' for the Giants. But it was her mother's love of old movies and her older sister's success as an actress that veered Rooney towards a thespian path. Kate Mara had already starred in *Transsiberian* opposite Woody Harrelson and had the female lead in the Anglo-Canadian *Stone of Destiny* when Rooney was cast as Mark Zuckerberg's girlfriend in the opening five minutes and 22 seconds of David Fincher's *The Social Network*. It was she, as Erica Albright, who said to Zuckerberg (Jesse Eisenberg): "You're going to go through life thinking that girls don't like you because you're a nerd. And I want you to know, from the bottom of my heart, that that won't be true. It'll be because you're an asshole."

In Fincher's *The Girl with the Dragon Tattoo*, Mara's transformation into the Gothic, anorexic, lesbian, aloof and brilliant computer hacker Lisbeth Salander was extraordinary. She had a hard act to follow as the Swedish actress Noomi Rapace had already made the part her own in the original film. Yet Mara gave a fearless, intelligent take on the character, complete with Swedish accent. She certainly deserved her Oscar nomination.

Having displayed her remarkable versatility in two high-profile David Fincher films, Rooney is now on the fast-track to major stardom. Recalling a young Demi Moore – with a dash of Sean Young – she will next star in Steven Soderbergh's psychological thriller *The Bitter Pill*, with Jude Law, Channing Tatum and Catherine Zeta-Jones in support, and then teams up with Christian Bale, Ryan Gosling, Natalie Portman and Cate Blanchett for Terrence Malick's sexual drama *Lawless*. She was also signed up to star in *Brooklyn*, from a script by Nick Hornby, and joined Joaquin Phoenix and Amy Adams in an (as yet untitled) offbeat romance directed by Spike Jonze. Quite a kick-start.

EDDIE REDMAYNE

Born: 6 January 1982 in London, England.

In 2011 Eddie Redmayne made quite an impression on stage, on television and on the big screen. He was playing the title role in *Richard II* at the Donmar Warehouse, had the lead in the much-anticipated TV adaptation of Sebastian Faulk's *Birdsong* and was the

Eddie Redmayne in *Birdsong*.

central figure in the multi-Oscar-nominated *My Week with Marilyn*. He is not a conventionally good-looking pin-up but has a legion of followers, those who follow his every move and call themselves Redmaniacs. What is most striking about Redmayne, besides his soulful eyes, sensual lips and knife-edged jawline, is the sincerity he brings to every part.

An alumnus of Eton and Cambridge (Trinity College), Redmayne made his professional debut in *Twelfth Night* and in the next few years garnered a number of newcomer trophies. In 2006 he made his film debut playing the male lead in the Australian thriller *Like Minds* and in the same year was the son of Angelina Jolie in *The Good Shepherd*, directed by Robert De Niro. Immediately after that he signed up for some steamy sex with the considerably older Julianne Moore in Tom Kalin's *Savage Grace*, the true story of Barbara Daly Baekeland and her incestuous relationship with her son. He donned tights for the historical dramas *Elizabeth: The Golden Age* and *The Other Boleyn Girl*, was paired with Kristen Stewart in the American indie *The Yellow Handkerchief* and then, on TV, played Angel Clare to Gemma Arterton's *Tess of the d'Urbervilles*. There was more historical drama (or, rather, horror) in *Black Death*, with Sean Bean, and he had a supporting role in Stephen Poliakoff's wildly mannered and misjudged *Glorious 39*.

And then came 2011. His performance as Richard II at the Donmar won him the Critics' Circle Award for Best Shakespearean Performance, a trinket to join the Tony Award he won for Best Featured Actor in John Logan's *Red*. On stage he was mesmerising audiences, but he had yet to find a meaty role on film to call his own. But fear not, Redmaniacs. In his next movie he plays the love-struck rebel Marius Pontmercy in Tom Hooper's big-screen adaptation of *Les Misérables*. He not only gets to romance Amanda Seyfried but also has to sing. Now, there's a string to his bow that is sure to stir the hearts of his fans.

ANDREA RISEBOROUGH

Born: 20 November 1981 in Newcastle-upon-Tyne, England.

There aren't many actresses like Andrea Riseborough. She is fashionably slender but her elfin dimensions are in direct contrast to her enormous conviction and intelligence. On screen, she has a knack for drawing the camera to her; in person, she is physically striking and meticulously articulate, a sharp mind working miracles around her northern vowels. Sir Peter Hall, who directed her at the Theatre Royal Bath, has called her "one of the bravest and most impressive actresses I've come across in recent years."

RADA-trained, Riseborough has approached each new part with a prodigious resolve. First off she threw herself into the theatre – her roles in *Miss Julie* (as Miss Julie) and *Measure for Measure* (Isabella) earned her the Ian Charleson award – and then television. For the latter medium she played Angelica Fanshawe in *The Devil's Whore* and was a young Margaret Thatcher in *The Long Walk to Finchley*, for which

Andrea Riseborough in *The Devil's Whore*.

Emma Stone in *The Help*.

she was nominated for a BAFTA. She'd had brief bits in films (*Venus*, *Magicians*, Mike Leigh's *Happy-Go-Lucky*) but came into her own in *Never Let Me Go* (as an organ donor) and *Made in Dagenham* (as a sexy, dissident machinist), before landing the female lead in *Brighton Rock*. In the latter she provided a heart-breaking turn as the gullible, masochistic Rose, and then segued into two performances that established her as a leading lady of uncommon mettle. She was outstanding as both Wallis Simpson in Madonna's *W.E.* and as a farmer's wife thrown into the arms of a Nazi commander in Amit Gupta's haunting, elegiac and pared-back *Resistance*.

Next, she starred opposite Clive Owen in James Marsh's *Shadow Dancer* (as a former IRA terrorist), played a disillusioned newscaster in the American thriller *Disconnect*, and was teamed with James McAvoy in the British thriller *Welcome to the Punch*. She then found herself in Baton Rouge with Tom Cruise and Morgan Freeman in the sci-fi epic *Oblivion*, directed by Joseph Kosinski from his own graphic novel. Well, nobody saw that coming.

EMMA STONE
Born: 6 November 1988 in Scottsdale, Arizona, USA.

Emma Stone is successful, pretty and very, very funny. And, at the time of writing, she is just 23. She was a hit in *Easy A* as a high school student (who unwittingly lands a reputation as a scarlet woman) and was nominated for a Golden Globe. However, 2011 was the year that cemented her fame.

She grew up very fast, playing a lawyer who seduces the implacable Ryan Gosling in the hilarious, all-star *Crazy, Stupid, Love*. John Requa, co-director of the comedy, has nothing but praise for her "God-given timing. Somewhere living inside her is a 90-year-old vaudeville comedian," he says. "She's got a whip-smart brain." Indeed, when she coaxes Gosling to remove his shirt, her reaction is comic gold. "*Really*?" she marvels at the actor's torso. It was not a funny line on paper but she made it the funniest in the film.

A natural blonde christened Emily, the actress got her break as Laurie Partridge in the TV pilot of *The New Partridge Show* and then landed a regular slot on the Fox actioner *Drive*, which was cancelled after four episodes. She fared better on film, playing Jonah Hill's dream babe in *Superbad*, a derisory guitarist in *The Rocker*, a virginal sorority president in *The House Bunny* (in which she also sang), and a con artist in *Zombieland*. Already she was gaining a reputation as a scene-stealer. After *Easy A* – a part she fought for and made her own – she moved into drama with *The Help*, landing the central role of Skeeter Phelan. It's Skeeter who is the film's conscience – she is the journalist who pens the eponymous roman-à-clef – and Stone held her own in a cast of major heavyweights. She was even nominated as Outstanding Actress by the NAACP, an organisation dedicated to recognising those who further the cause of people of colour in film.

And the future looks bright. She has the female lead (Gwen Stacy) in the $220 million *The Amazing Spider-Man*, teams up with Gosling again (and Sean Penn) in the crime epic *The Gangster Squad* and features in the portmanteau comedy *Movie 43* alongside Hugh Jackman, Richard Gere, Kate Winslet, Gerard Butler and Halle Berry.

Releases *of the* *Year*

This section contains details of all the films released in the UK between 1 January and 31 December 2011.

Each film review is followed by the main credits for the film, beginning with names of the leading actors, then the Director, Producer(s), Screenplay Writer, Cinematographer, Production Designer or Art Director, Editor, Soundtrack Composer and Costume Designer.

For technical credits the normal abbreviations operate and are as follows:

Dir – for Director; Pro – for Producer; Ph – for Cinematographer; Pro Des – for Production Designer; Art Dir – for Art Director; M – for Composer; and Cos – for Costume Designer.

The production companies involved are listed, with the final name in the list being the distributor. The credits end with the film's running time, the country or countries of origin, the year of production, the UK release date and the British Board of Film Classification certificate.

Reviewers: Charles Bacon (CB), James Cameron-Wilson (JC-W), Jeremy Clarke (JC), Michael Darvell (MHD), Marshall Julius (MJ), Penny Lucas (PL), Jonathan Rigby (JR), George Savvides (GS), Mansel Stimpson (MS) and Derek Winnert (DW).

Star ratings

★★★★★ **Exceptional**
★★★★ **Very Good**
★★★ **Good**
★★ **Mediocre**
★ **Poor**

3D Sex & Zen: Extreme Ecstasy ★½

Do not be misled by the title. First off, this is not an Oriental sex manual in the manner of this year's *The Lovers' Guide 3D*. Nor is there much Zen around. It's a period romp from Hong Kong that attempts to exploit the new fashion for stereoscopic cinema – with a lot of t&a. Inspired by an ancient Chinese text called *The Carnal Prayer Mat*, the film is set during the Ming dynasty and concerns a newlywed scholar with considerable shortcomings in the bedroom… Still, while the standard of acting may be risible, the costumes are lovely. JC-W

❧ Hiro Hayama, Leni Lan, Saori Hara.
❧ *Dir* Christopher Suen, *Pro* Stephen Shiu, Stephen Shiu Jr and Ng Kin-hung, *Screenplay* Stephen Shiu, Stephen Shiu, Jr and Mark Wu, *Ph* Jimmy Wong, *Art Dir* Tony Yu, *M* Raymond Wong, *Cos* Cindy Cheng.

Local Production/One Dollar Productions-Metrodome. 109 mins. Hong Kong. 2011. Rel: 2 Sep 2011. Cert. 18.

7 Lives ★★★

Danny Dyer stars as a troubled father contemplating leaving his family for an exciting life with a seductive office client (Kate Ashfield). One night, three hoodies chase and mug him. Half dead, he experiences the lives of seven different people, including a hoodie, a homeless guy, a rock star, a boxer and his doctor (Julien Ball). As the seven lives intertwine, whose life would Dyer choose? With a solid, unusual idea for his feature debut, writer-director Paul Wilkins keeps the story entertaining and involving. Dyer gives a likable performance, making you care about his character's fate, so it's hard not to like this subtle, understated fantasy thriller. DW

❧ Kate Ashfield, Danny Dyer, Julien Ball, Nic Brimble, Martin Compston, Craig Conway, Theo Barklem-Biggs.

Opposite: Succour punch. Oscar nominee Viola Davis and Oscar winner Octavia Spencer in Tate Taylor's unexpectedly popular *The Help.*

❱ *Dir* and *Screenplay* Paul Wilkins, *Pro* Wilkins and Mike Parker, *Ph* James Friend and Nick Gordon Smith, *Ed* Nigel Galt, *M* Michael Price, *Cos* Heidi Miller.

Starfish Films-Black and Blue Films.
100 mins. UK. 2011. Rel: 7 Oct 2011. Cert. 15.

13 Assassins ★★★★½

This brilliantly staged action piece set in Feudal Japan may be more violent than the samurai classics it evokes but Miike Takashi honours their spirit in a way that Kitano's *Zatoichi* (2003) did not. The climactic battle lasts about 45 minutes, but if it's rather too long it is always breathtaking. Nevertheless, it's the film's respect for its predecessors and what they stood for artistically (it is actually a remake of a 1960s movie) that makes this great cinema. (Original title: *Jûsan-nin no shikaku*) MS

❱ Yakusho Kôji, Yamada Takayuki, Iseya Yusuke, Inagaki Goro, Ichimura Masachika.
❱ *Dir* Miike Takashi, *Pro* Umezawa Michihiko and others, *Screenplay* Tengan Daisuke from a story by Ikemiya Shoichiro, *Ph* Kita Nobuyasu, *Ed* Yamashita Kenji, *M* Endô Kôji, *Cos* Sawataishi Kazuhiro.

Sedic International (Japan)/Sedic Deux (Japan)/Rakueisha (Japan)-Artificial Eye.
125 mins. Japan/UK. 2010. Rel: 6 May 2011. Cert. 15.

30 Minutes or Less ★

Nick (Jesse Eisenberg) is a small-town pizza delivery guy who becomes the target of two criminal 'masterminds' (Danny McBride and Nick Swardson). The naïve duo believe they have the perfect plan to get rich. So, after they kidnap Nick, they strap a bomb to his chest and force him to rob a bank. It's a disappointing comedy from Ruben Fleischer, director of the hilarious *Zombieland*. The preposterous premise lacks credibility and the script is virtually laugh-free. GS

❱ Jesse Eisenberg, Danny McBride, Nick Swardson, Aziz Ansari, Michael Peña, Fred Ward, Bianca Kajlich.
❱ *Dir* Ruben Fleischer, *Pro* Ben Stiller, Stuart Cornfeld and Jeremy Kramer, *Screenplay* Michael Diliberti, from a story by Diliberti and Matthew Sullivan, *Ph* Jess Hall, *Pro Des* Maher Ahmad, *Ed* Alan Baumgarten, *M* Ludwig Göransson, *Cos* Christie Wittenborn.

Columbia Pictures/Red Hour Films/Media Rights Capital-Sony Pictures Releasing.
83 mins. Germany/Canada/USA. 2011. Rel: 16 Sep 2011. Cert. 15.

50/50 ★★½

Joseph Gordon-Levitt is superb as a 27-year-old who discovers that he has cancer and only a 50/50 chance of survival. However, his best friend is Seth Rogen on typically coarse comic form, while the female interest (Anna Kendrick, Bryce Dallas Howard) merely provides a standard rom-com storyline. Whether or not you can accept the mix probably depends on your response to the inclusion of a joke about Patrick Swayze dying of cancer. MS

❱ Joseph Gordon-Levitt, Seth Rogen, Anna Kendrick, Bryce Dallas Howard, Philip Baker Hall, Anjelica Huston.

Baker's dozen: Kôji Yakusho in Miike Takashi's breathtaking *13 Assassins*.

> *Dir* Jonathan Levine, *Pro* Evan Goldberg, Seth Rogen and Ben Karlin, *Screenplay* Will Reiser, *Ph* Terry Stacey, *Pro Des* Annie Spitz, *Ed* Zene Baker, *M* Michael Giacchino, *Cos* Carla Hetland..

Summit Entertainment/Mandate Pictures/Point Grey etc-Lionsgate.
100 mins. Canada/USA. 2011. Rel: 25 Nov 2011. Cert. 15.

127 Hours ★★★½

The story of Aron Ralston's ordeal in the Utah desert doesn't lend itself to a movie format but Danny Boyle pumps it up into a cinematic frenzy. Mixing flashbacks, hallucinations and video rewinds, the director exhibits his usual visual flair, aided by a totally engaging performance from James Franco. This is gruelling stuff but it's so well made that one is absorbed by Aron's narcissism and his need to find himself – albeit at the bottom of an empty canyon. Of course, were this not a true story we probably wouldn't give it the time of day. JC-W

> James Franco, Amber Tamblyn, Kate Mara, Clémence Poésy, Kate Burton, Lizzy Caplan, Treat Williams.
> *Dir* Danny Boyle, *Pro* Boyle, Christian Colson and John Smithson, *Screenplay* Boyle and Simon Beaufoy, *Ph* Anthony Dod Mantle and Enrique Chediak, *Pro Des* and *Cos* Suttirat Larlarb, *Ed* Jon Harris, *M* A R Rahman.

Cloud Eight/Decibel Films/Dune Entertainment/Everest Entertainment/Pathé-Warner Bros.
94 mins. USA/UK. 2010. Rel: 7 Jan 2011. Cert. 15.

Abduction ★★

Nineteen years old and taking his first steps outside the tweeny *Twilight* franchise with a thriller from director John Singleton, Taylor Lautner plays it safe with a girl-friendly actioner: less an all-out blood-fest, more an on-the-run teen romance with occasional gunplay. Like a Disney hero, Lautner loses his folks early on. Only it turns out they weren't his parents, but his CIA handlers, and he's been in hiding his whole life… But from whom? And why? Mysterious adventure ensues in this blandly watchable time-waster. And just in case you were wondering, yes, Lautner goes shirtless within the first five minutes. MJ

> Taylor Lautner, Lily Collins, Alfred Molina, Maria Bello, Jason Isaacs, Sigourney Weaver.
> *Dir* John Singleton, *Pro* Dan Lautner, Doug Davison, Ellen Goldsmith-Vein, Lee Stollman and Roy Lee, *Screenplay* Shawn Christensen, *Ph* Peter Menzies Jr, *Pro Des* Keith Brian Burns, *Ed* Bruce Cannon, *M* Edward Shearmur, *Cos* Ruth E Carter.

Lionsgate/Gotham Group/Mango Farms/Vertigo Entertainment/Tailor Made/Quick Six Entertainment-Lionsgate.
106 mins. USA. 2011. Rel: 28 Sep 2011. Cert. 12A.

Abel ★★½

Actor Diego Luna turns director and, taking a story about two Mexican brothers, offers a deconstruction of family life that exposes its horrors. It is well acted, but those who gave it awards obviously don't share my worries about the clash between the allegorical and the naturalistic. It's more black comedy than drama when the eponymous child, all of nine years old, returns from a psychiatric ward and takes over the patriarchal role in his family. It's bizarre but not involving. MS

> Karina Gidi, José María Yazpik, Christopher Ruíz-Esparza, Carlos Aragón.
> *Dir* Diego Luna, *Pro* Pablo Cruz, *Screenplay* Augusto Mendoza and Luna, *Ph* Patrick Murguía, *Pro Des* Brigitte Broch, *Ed* Miguel Schverdfinger, *M* Alejandro Castaños, *Cos* Anna Terrazas.

Canana/Aguascalientes Gobierno del Estado/Mister Mudd etc-Network Releasing.
82 mins. Mexico/USA. 2010. Rel: 7 Jan 2011. Cert. 15.

Las Acacias ★★★½

At the behest of his boss a lorry driver takes a woman and her baby across the border from Paraguay to Buenos Aires. This is a minimalistic road movie about a gradually developing relationship perfectly played and much admired by many. I respect it, but to my mind it needs greater emotional impact if it is to justify the slow pace and sparse dialogue. Nevertheless, it's a work of total integrity. MS

> Germán de Silva, Hebe Duarte, Nayra Calle Mamani.
> *Dir* Pablo Giorgelli, *Pro* Ariel Rotter, Giorgelli and others, *Screenplay* Giorgelli and Salvador Roselli, *Ph* Diego Poleri, *Art Dir* Yamila Fontán, *Ed* María Astrauskas, *Cos* Violeta Gauvry and Laura Donari.

Airecine/Utópica Cine/Proyecto Experience etc-Verve Pictures.
86 mins. Argentina/Spain. 2011. Rel: 2 Dec 2011. Cert. 12A.

Cave dweller: James Franco in his Oscar-nominated performance in Danny Boyle's stylish, gruelling *127 Hours.*

Accursed Blood ★

With nothing like enough blood, guts, scares or style to please horror fans, this is just another ropey haunted house flick in which Julie (Marnette Patterson) and her student pals start filming in the abandoned hotel of remote Goldfield, Nevada. They plan to video the ghost of Elizabeth (Ashly Rae), murdered (with her baby) and cursed by hotel owner George Winfield (Chuck Zito) when she betrayed him. Since the story is uninvolving, it doesn't help that the film is murky and cheap-looking and that (apart from Marnette) a lot of the acting is amateurish. Roddy Piper and Kellan Lutz are wasted in this boring, unsatisfying timewaster. (Original title: *Ghosts of Goldfield*) DW

❯ Kellan Lutz, Roddy Piper, Marnette Patterson, Mandy Amano, Scott Whyte, Chuck Zito, Ashly Rae.
❯ *Dir* Ed Winfield, *Pro* Debra Isaacs, *Screenplay* Dominic Biondi and Brian McMahon, *Ph* Adrian M Pruett and Roland 'Ozzie' Smith, *Pro Des* Monica Tullar, *Ed* Bryan Todd, *M* Steve Yeaman.

18th Avenue Productions Company/Barnholtz Entertainment.
83 mins. USA. 2007. Rel: 28 Jan 2011. Cert. 18.

The Adjustment Bureau ★★★½

Congressman David Norris (Matt Damon) was not meant to meet Elise Sellas (Emily Blunt) on the bus. In fact, he was meant to have spilled his coffee in the park. Such deviations from the master plan send ripples through David and Elise's future as the intensity of their feelings for each other threatens the watertight structure of our grand design. A sort of *Love Story* reinvented by *The Matrix*, George Nolfi's film might have been stronger had the central relationship showered more romantic sparks. As it is, Philip K Dick's central premise is intriguing enough to keep the plates spinning to a satisfactory conclusion. And the pace never lets up. JC-W

❯ Matt Damon, Emily Blunt, Anthony Mackie, John Slattery, Terence Stamp.
❯ *Dir* and *Screenplay* George Nolfi, *Pro* Nolfi, Chris Moore, Michael Hackett, Bill Carraro, Isa Dick Hackett and Joel Viertel, *Ph* John Toll, *Pro Des* Kevin Thompson, *Ed* Jay Rabinowitz, *M* Thomas Newman, *Cos* Kasia Walicka-Maimone.

Universal/Media Rights Capital/Gambit Pictures/Electric Shepherd-Universal.
105 mins. USA. 2011. Rel: 4 Mar 2011. Cert. 12A.

The Adventures of Tintin: The Secret of the Unicorn ★★★★

When boy reporter Tintin buys a model ship, little does he know what adventures are in store for him. It's the beginning of a search for lost treasure, with his friend Captain Haddock and Snowy the terrier dog being pursued by villains out to get the prize. As Spielberg's directing it's a cross between *Indiana Jones* and *Back to the Future* in style. Using motion capture is apt as Tintin comes from a comic book source: its technique unlike either animation or photography but a cross between the two. The film is assembled with great panache, making a smart and likable romp. Snowy the terrier is a real dog star. (Original title: *The Adventures of Tintin*) MHD

❯ The voices of Jamie Bell, Andy Serkis, Daniel Craig, Nick Frost, Simon Pegg, Daniel Mays, Toby Jones, Mackenzie Crook.
❯ *Dir* Steven Spielberg, *Pro* Spielberg, Kathleen Kennedy and Peter Jackson, *Screenplay* Steven Moffat, Edgar Wright and Joe Cornish, based on the comic book series by Hergé, *Art Dir* Andrew L Jones, *Ed* Michael Kahn, *M* John Williams, *Cos* Lesley Burkes-Harding.

Columbia Pictures/Paramount Pictures/Amblin Entertainment/Kennedy-Marshall/Nickelodeon Movies/WingNut Films etc-Paramount Pictures.
107 mins. USA/New Zealand. 2011. Rel: 26 Oct 2011. Cert. PG.

After the Apocalypse ★★★★

Antony Butts' compelling documentary focuses on the long-suffering people of Semipalatinsk in Kazakhstan who, during the Soviet era, were used as human guinea pigs in the testing of nuclear weapons. It is an agonising existence for these poor people, especially for Bibigul who is desperate to give birth to her baby despite warnings from Dr Toleukhan Nurmagambetov that her child may be born disabled. This haunting and deeply upsetting film is essential viewing. GS

❯ *Dir* and *Ph* Antony Butts, *Pro* Butts, Natasha Dack and Sarah Tierney, *Ed* Hugh Williams, *M* Tom Player.

Dartmouth Films-Tiger Lily Films.
65 mins. UK. 2010. Rel: 13 May 2011. Cert. 12A.

Steven Spielberg (right) on the set of his animated behemoth *The Adventures of Tintin: The Secret of the Unicorn*.

Age of Heroes ★★½

This film is based on the real-life events of Ian Fleming's 30 Commando – an inspiration for the modern-day SAS. This Special Forces regiment, led by Captain Jones (Sean Bean), is assigned to parachute into occupied Norway and capture a new radar technology from the Germans. A strong premise for this World War II adventure, but the underdeveloped script is a let-down and, despite impressive production values and picturesque cinematography, it is certainly not in the league of *The Heroes of Telemark* and *The Guns of Navarone*. GS

‣ Sean Bean, James D'Arcy, Danny Dyer, Izabella Miko, Sebastian Street, Rosie Fellner.
‣ *Dir* Adrian Vitoria, *Pro* James Brown, Lex Lutzus, Nick O'Hagan and James Youngs, *Screenplay* Vitoria and Ed Scates, *Ph* Mark Hamilton, *Pro Des* Richard Campling, *Ed* Chris Gill and Joe Parsons, *M* Michael Richard Plowman, *Cos* Elvis Davis.

Cinema Five/Giant Films/Matador/Metrodome/ Neon Park/Atlantic Swiss Productions-Metrodome Distribution.
90 mins. UK. 2011. Rel: 20 May 2011. Cert. 15.

Age of the Dragons ★

The main premise of transporting Herman Melville's *Moby Dick* to medieval times sounds great fun but unfortunately this takes itself far too seriously. Captain Ahab (Danny Glover) wants to revenge the dragon that killed his family when he was young... The actors' energy and enthusiasm are let down by a poor script and unimaginative special effects. As for the title – we had to endure 91 minutes expecting to see more than one dragon but to no avail. GS

‣ Danny Glover, Vinnie Jones, Corey Sevier, Sofia Pernas, Larry Bagby.
‣ *Dir* and *Ph* Ryan Little, *Pro* McKay Daines and Steven A Lee, *Screenplay* Daines, based on a story by Gil Aglaure and Anne K Black, inspired by Herman Melville's novel *Moby Dick*, *Pro Des* Debbie Farrer, *Ed* John Lyde, *M* J Bateman, *Cos* Anne Rose.

Dragon Quest Productions/KOAN/Cinedome-Metrodome Distribution.
91 mins. USA. 2011. Rel: 4 Mar 2011. Cert. 12A.

Albatross ★★½

Niall MacCormick's first cinema feature has been called a comedy drama. Not altogether unexpectedly, the writer, Tamzin Rafn, fails to make this mix work and her script is full of loose ends. It's a pity because there's potential in a tale contrasting two teenagers, well played by Jessica Brown Findlay and Felicity Jones (the former is too wild, the latter too repressed). Rafn was influenced by 1987's *Wish You Were*

Here, but that film was more persuasive in every way. MS

Cold comfort: Sean Bean in Adrian Vitoria's real-life B-movie, *Age of Heroes*.

‣ Sebastian Koch, Julia Ormond, Felicity Jones, Peter Vaughan, Jessica Brown Findlay.
‣ *Dir* Niall MacCormick, *Pro* Adrian Sturges, *Screenplay* Tamzin Rafn, *Ph* Jan Jonaeus, *Pro Des* Paul Cripps, *Ed* Mark Eckersley, *M* Jack Arnold, *Cos* Charlotte Holdich.

CinemaNX/Isle of Man Film-CinemaNX.
90 mins. UK. 2010. Rel: 14 Oct 2011. Cert. 15.

All American Orgy ★★★

There are crazy, offbeat laughs in this oddball comedy in which three neurotic couples set off for an orgy to try out the virtues of group sex. The silly bunch of swingers hope it will all lead to enlightenment or, if not, at least a fulfilling sexual encounter. The endless, low-key bickering and sex talk that ensues is highly chucklesome, making the film seem unusually original. Obviously ad-libbing much of the dialogue, the cast make their characters seem real and appealing as well as funny. Ted Beck, the screenwriter, is a standout, playing moustachioed weirdo Todd ('like a jaguar with AIDS'). A hit if you don't expect nudity and gross-out. (Original title: *Cummings Farm*) DW

‣ Laura Silverman, Ted Beck, Edrick Browne, Adam Busch, Brent Caballero, Aime-Lynn Chadwick.
‣ *Dir* and *Ed* Andrew Drazek, *Pro* Brent Caballero, Jordan Kessler and James T Bruce IV, *Screenplay* Ted Beck, *Ph* Dave McFarland, *Pro Des* Robert W Savina, *Cos* Katherine Wade.

Finish Films/Louisiana Media Productions-Phase 4 Films.
98 mins. USA. 2009. Rel: 11 Mar 2011. Cert. 18.

Alvin and the Chipmunks: Chipwrecked ★

The third Alvin movie is the weakest, a story aimed at under-sevens but with little to please their parents. Mixing live-action and computer animation at vast cost ($75million), it is at least crisply professional and efficient – and a nice little earner for its studio ($130million in America). Jason Lee again provides the appealingly quirky live character of Dave. He here joins forces with his old enemy and manager (David Cross) to rescue the Chipmunks and Chipettes when they go on a cruise, are swept off the ship and marooned. The funky pop tunes, fast pace, short running time and a few amusing lines help a little. DW

‣ Jason Lee, David Cross, Jenny Slate, and the voices of Justin Long, Matthew Gray Gubler, Jesse McCarthey, Anna Faris, Christina Applegate, Amy Poehler.
‣ *Dir* Mike Mitchell, *Pro* Ross Badasarian Jr and Janice Karman, *Screenplay* Jonathan Aibel and Glenn Berger, based on characters by Ross Bagdasarian and Janice Karman, *Ph* Thomas E Ackerman, *Pro Des* Richard Holland, *Ed* Peter Amundson, *M* Mark Mothersbaugh, *Cos* Alexandra Welker.

Fox 2000 Pictures/Regency Enterprises/TCF Vancouver Productions/ Bagdasarians-20th Century Fox. 87 mins. USA. 2011. Rel: 16 Dec 2011. Cert. U.

Amer ★★★

Is this an arthouse horror or a film of great pretensions? Well, actually a bit of both. It's the story of Ana from childhood through adolescence and finally to womanhood. Always independent and free-spirited, she grows up with a strong sense of danger and fear of impending violence. Is this a dream? The film hardly has any dialogue and relies heavily on strong visuals, sharp editing and clever use of sound. But the repetitive nature of the story and the thunderous score unfortunately become tiresome by the end. GS

‣ Cassandra Forêt, Charlotte Eugène Guibbaud, Marie Bos, Bianca Maria D'Amato, Jean-Pierre Vovk.
‣ *Dir* and *Screenplay* Hélène Cattet and Bruno Forzani, *Pro* François Cognard and Eve Commenge, *Ph* Manu Dacosse, *Pro Des* Alina Santos, *Ed* Bernard Beets, *Cos* Jackye Fauconnier.

Anonymes Films/Tobina Film/Canal + etc-Zootrope Films. 90 mins. France/Belgium. 2009. Rel: 7 Jan 2011. Cert. 15.

Amreeka ★★★

Culture crash: Nisreen Faour in Cherien Dabbis's powerful, autobiographical Amreeka.

Palestinian single mother Muna (Nisreen Faour) leaves the West Bank with her teenage son Fadi (Melkar Muallem) for a better life in America. But the time is 2003 and America is about to invade Iraq... This is a powerful story (based on director Cherien Dabis' own experiences) with strong performances, especially from Faour. The scenes between mother and son are very persuasive but the school sequences and those at the hamburger place where Muna eventually finds work lack subtlety and depth. GS

‣ Nisreen Faour, Melkar Muallem, Hiam Abbass, Alia Shawkat, Miriam Smith.
‣ *Dir* and *Screenplay* Cherien Dabis, *Pro* Christina Piovesan and Paul Barkin, *Ph* Tobias Datum, *Pro Des* Adrian Leroux, *Ed* Keith Reamer, *M* Kareem Roustom and Malik Williams, *Cos* Patricia J Henderson.

First Generation Films/Alcina Pictures/Buffalo Gal Pictures/ Eagle Vision Media Group/Manitoba Film & Music/National Geographic Entertainment etc-Dogwoof Pictures. 96 mins. USA/Canada/Kuwait. 2009. Rel: 7 Jan 2011. Cert. 12A.

An African Election ★★

If the title is uninspiring, at least the film supplies everything that it says on the tin. The place is Ghana, the period November-December 2008. Ghana was the first black African country to gain its independence but with this historical fact came all the traditions of political engineering and apparent vote fixing. It's a slick, articulate documentary and a must for all those interested in Ghanaian electioneering. But who would have thought that politics could be so reprobate? JC-W

‣ *Dir* Jarreth Merz and Kevin Merz, *Pro* Brigitte Agustoni, Franco Agustoni and Tiziana Soudani, *Screenplay* Erika Tasini and Shari Yantra Marcacci, *Ph* Topher Osborn, *Ed* Samir Samperisi, *M* Patrick Kirst.

Urban Republic-Dogwoof. 90 mins. Switzerland/USA/Ghana. 2011. Rel: 25 Nov 2011. Cert. PG.

Angels of Evil ★★½

Much inferior to Michele Placido's earlier crime drama *Romanzo Criminale* (2005), this is the rushed story of a man (Kim Rossi Stuart) looking back on his life while in solitary confinement. He comes across as a born criminal but, despite some basis in fact, the tale offers the man's own take on events which is not always convincing and lacks insight. There are gangs, fights, robberies and jail-breaks all crammed in here, but nothing to make this Italian drama seem fresh and interesting. (Original title: *Vallanzasca Gli angeli del male*) MS

➤ Kim Rossi Stuart, Filippo Timi, Valeria Solarino, Moritz Bleibtreu, Paz Vega.
➤ *Dir* Michele Placido, *Pro* Elide Melli and Fabio Conversi, *Screenplay* Kim Rossi Stuart, Placido, Antonio Leotti and others, *Ph* Arnaldo Catinari, *Art Dir* Tonino Zera, *Ed* Consuelo Catucci, *M* Negramaro, *Cos* Roberto Chiocchi.
Cosmo Production/21st Century Fox Italia/Babe Films etc-Artificial Eye.
128 mins. Italy/France/USA. 2010. Rel: 27 May 2011. Cert. 15.

Animal Kingdom ★★★½

Melbourne in the 1980s. This is the story of a family of criminals that also covers issues of police corruption. However, the central focus is on a teenager, J (James Frecheville), who, after his mother has died of an overdose, looks set to be drawn into the criminal life-style of his relatives who are dominated by a powerful matriarchal figure. The latter provides a great role for Jacki Weaver and David Michôd's debut feature is directed with assurance. It's a pity that the last quarter is less persuasive as a narrative. MS

➤ Ben Mendelsohn, Joel Edgerton, Guy Pearce, Luke Ford, Jacki Weaver, James Frecheville.
➤ *Dir* and *Screenplay* David Michôd, *Pro* Liz Watts, *Ph* Adam Arkapaw, *Pro Des* Jo Ford, *Ed* Luke Doolan, *M* Antony Partos, *Cos* Cappi Ireland.
Screen Australia /a Porchlight Films production etc-Optimum Releasing.
113 mins. Australia. 2009. Rel: 3 Jan 2011. Cert. 15.

Anonymous ★★★½

Did Shakespeare write his plays? The question has been asked before, when some said it was Francis Bacon, but now it is Edward de Vere, Earl of Oxford, who flourishes the quill in Roland Emmerich's highly entertaining rewriting of literary history. Here it seems unlikely that actor Will Shakespeare (Rafe Spall) could have even written his own name, as he seems such an utter twit! Rhys Ifans is a brooding Earl of Oxford, Vanessa Redgrave the older Queen Elizabeth, with daughter Joely Richardson as her younger self enjoying an affair with the youthful de Vere (Jamie Campbell Bower). It's all amusingly presented against a background of lovingly recreated Elizabethan England. MHD

➤ Rhys Ifans, Vanessa Redgrave, Rafe Spall, Sebastian Armesto, Edward Hogg, David Thewlis, Jamie Campbell Bower, Joely Richardson, Derek Jacobi, Mark Rylance.
➤ *Dir* Roland Emmerich, *Pro* Emmerich, Larry Franco and Robert Leger, *Screenplay* John Orloff, *Ph* Anna J Foerster, *Pro Des* Sebastian Krawinkel, *Ed* Peter R Adam, *M* Harald Kloser and Thomas Wander, *Cos* Lisy Christi.

Shakespeare in Doubt: Joely Richardson and Jamie Campbell Bower in Roland Emmerich's visually majestic *Anonymous*.

Columbia Pictures/Relativity Media/Centropolis Entertainment/Studio Babelsberg/Anonymous Pictures-Entertainment Film Distributors.
130 mins. UK/Germany. 2011. Rel: 28 Oct 2011. Cert. 12A.

Another Earth ★★½

On the night a duplicate Earth is discovered, a drunken student (Brit Marling) drives into a stranger's car, killing his son and pregnant wife. Four years later, her life and psyche in tatters, she attempts to make amends, while scientists and philosophers spout off in the background about alternate realities and such. Intriguing and authentically played with a grainy look and indie feel, this is not so much sci-fi as science-philosophy. Though a little too earnest in places, and rather too arty in others, it remains, nonetheless, a curious and interesting drama. MJ

▶ Brit Marling, William Mapother, Matthew-Lee Erlbach, D J Flava, Meggan Lennon, A J Diana.
▶ *Dir, Ph* and *Ed* Mike Cahill, *Pro* Cahill, Brit Marling, Hunter Gray and Nicholas Shumaker, *Screenplay* Cahill and Marling, *Pro Des* Darsi Monaco, *M* Fall On Your Sword, *Cos* Aileen Alvarez-Diana.

Artists Public Domain-20th Century Fox.
92 mins. USA. 2011. Rel: 9 Dec 2011. Cert. 12A.

Anuvahood ★

Not since the soft-core antics of Mary Millington in the mid-1970s has British cinema stooped so low. Terrible puns, exhausted cultural allusions and demented acting sum up the calibre of this urban swill. To get you in the mood: our protagonist 'K' (co-director/co-writer Adam Deacon) works at a supermarket called Laimsbury's (um, geddit?) and goes through the old De Niro routine of accosting himself

Minor planet: Brit Marling and William Mapother in Mike Cahill's curious and arty *Another Earth*.

in the mirror. He then befriends a new boy on the block, Enrique (Ollie Barbieri), whose every utterance is accompanied by a twang on a Spanish guitar – and it gets worse… JC-W

▶ Adam Deacon, Ollie Barbieri, Femi Oyeniran, Jazzie Zonzolo, Jaime Winstone, Paul Kaye, Linda Robson, Ashley Walters, Richard Blackwood, Perry Benson.
▶ *Dir* Adam Deacon and Daniel Toldand, *Pro* Deacon, Nick Taussig, Paul Van Carter, Daniel Toland and Terry Stone, *Screenplay* Deacon and Michael Vu, *Ph* Felix Wiedemann, *Pro Des* Matthew Button, *Ed* Seth Bergstrom, *M* Chad Hobson, *Cos* Rob Nicholls.

Gunslinger/Gateway Films/Cabin Fever Films/Creative Media-Revolver Entertainment.
88 mins. UK. 2011. Rel: 18 Mar 2011. Cert. 15.

Apollo 18 ★★

Think 'Paranormal Activity in Space' and you won't be far off. A so-so, sporadically scary sci-fi take on the found camera genre, *Apollo 18* tells the apparently true tale – and by true I mean totally made up – of a secret Moon mission menaced by alien ghost spiders. A slow-burning, outer-space spook-fest with better visuals than you'd expect from such a low-budget effort, it's no critic pleaser, certainly. But, if you're prepared to overlook the movie's many glaring leaps of logic and lose yourself in the jumpy foolishness of it all, it certainly has its moments. MJ

▶ Warren Christie, Lloyd Owen, Ryan Robbins, Mike Kopsa, Andrew Airlie.
▶ *Dir* Gonzalo López-Gallego, *Pro* Timur Bekmambetov and Michele Wolkoff, *Screenplay* Brian Miller, *Ph* José David Montero, *Pro Des* Andrew Neskoromny, *Ed* Patrick Lussier, *M* Harry Cohen, *Cos* Beverley Wowchuk, Cynthia Summers and Kate Main.

Dimension Films/Apollo 18 Productions/Bekmambetov Projects-Entertainment Film Distributors.
86 mins. USA/Canada. 2011. Rel: 2 Sep 2011. Cert. 15.

Archipelago ★★★½

As in Joanna Hogg's debut feature about tensions within a family, *Unrelated*, so too in *Archipelago* the irony is in the title. Another fractured family tries to cope, like a group of islands isolated from one another. The mother Patricia (Kate Fahy) organises a family holiday to the Scilly Isles with son Edward (Tom Hiddleston) and daughter Cynthia (Lydia Leonard) before Edward leaves for Africa. Tensions mount in an undercurrent of misgivings without really coming to fruition. Sadly the characters, in scenes of extended naturalistic improvisation, fail to wholly engage us, despite good work from all concerned. They really deserve what they get: each other. MHD

▶ Tom Hiddleston, Kate Fahy, Lydia Leonard, Amy Lloyd, Christopher Baker.
▶ *Dir* and *Screenplay* Joanna Hogg, *Pro* Gayle Griffiths, *Ph* Ed Rutherford, *Pro Des* and *Cos* Stéphane Collonge, *Ed* Helle le Fevre, *M* Viv Albertine.

Wild Horses Film Company-Artificial Eye.
109 mins. UK. 2010. Rel: 4 Mar 2011. Cert. 15.

Armadillo ★★★★

This prize-winning documentary by Janus Metz echoes the impressive *Restrepo* (2010) as it records the experiences of troops, this time Danish, in action in Afghanistan. Both films feature young soldiers but also look at the plight of locals and each offers a strong second half; here, that concerns medals for the killing of injured members of the Taliban in a ditch. The effect of experiencing war is differently felt by the Danes and by the Americans that we meet in these two films, but both are memorable and suitably disturbing documents. MS

▶ With Mads Mini, Daniel Ølby, Rasmus Munke, Kim Birkerød.
▶ *Dir* Janus Metz, *Pro* Ronnie Fridthjof and Sara Stockmann, *Ph* Lars Skree, *Ed* Per K Kirkegaard, *M* Uno Helmersson.

Fridthjof Film etc-Soda Pictures.
105 mins. Denmark/Norway/Sweden/Netherlands/UK/
Finland/Germany/Canada. 2010. Rel: 8 Apr 2011. Cert. 15.

Arrietty ★★★★

Based on the children's classic *The Borrowers*, this is a charming animated feature from Studio Ghibli. This time Hayao Miyazaki leaves the direction to Yonebayashi Hiromasa and the film is more traditional in tone – but that's suited to the tale of a boy who encounters the small creatures who live in empty spaces within the fabric of a house, Arrietty herself being one of them. There's menace to overcome, but the message is to embrace those different from ourselves. (Original title: *Karigurashi no Arrietty*) MS

▶ *Dir* Yonebayashi Hiromasa, *Pro* Suzuki Toshio (English language version Frank Marshall), *Screenplay* Miyazaki Hayao from the book *The Borrowers* by Mary Norton, *Art Dir* Takeshige Yoji and Yoshida Noboru, *Ed* Rie Matsubara, *M* Cécile Corbel, *Animation Supervisor* Yamashita Akihiko and Kagawa Megumi.

Studio Ghibli-Optimum Releasing.
94 mins. Japan. 2010. Rel: 29 July 2011. Cert. U.

The Art of Getting By ★★★

George (Freddie Highmore) is a lonely teenager who has managed to make it almost all the way through high school without doing any work. He has no friends at all but his life takes an

Plant life: a scene from Yonebayashi Hiromasa's charmingly traditional Arrietty.

unexpected turn when he is befriended by Sally (Emma Roberts) – the school's most popular girl. Highmore delivers a sensitive performance in this gentle comedy-drama. He has matured into a strong presence and his assured performance is complemented by the equally impressive Roberts. GS

▶ Freddie Highmore, Emma Roberts, Sasha Spielberg, Marcus Carl Franklin, Ann Dowd, Sam Robards.
▶ *Dir* and *Screenplay* Gavin Wiesen, *Pro* Gia Walsh, Darren Goldberg, Kara Baker and P Jennifer Dana, *Ph* Ben Kutchins, *Pro Des* Kelly McGehee, *Ed* Mollie Goldstein, *M* Alec Puro, *Cos* Erika Munro.

Goldcrest Films/Mint Pictures/Gigi Productions/Atlantic
Pictures/Island Sound Productions-20th Century Fox.
83 mins. USA. 2011. Rel: 2 Sep 2011. Cert. 12A.

Arthur ★½

In this feeble remake Russell Brand steps into Dudley Moore's shoes as the spoilt egotistical billionaire while Helen Mirren becomes his long-

Ready for her close-up: Bérénice Bejo in Michel Hazanavicius' magical and witty *The Artist*.

suffering nanny in the John Gielgud role. Brand's performance as the irresponsible drunkard is inconsistent to say the least. He certainly has presence but the film is overlong, the comedy not that funny and finally it is difficult to care much about this selfish brat, especially during this time of recession. GS

▶ Russell Brand, Helen Mirren, Jennifer Garner, Geraldine James, Nick Nolte.
▶ *Dir* Jason Winer, *Pro* Brand, Chris Bender, Larry Brezner, Michael Tadross, J C Spink and Kevin McCormick, *Screenplay* Peter Baynham from a story by Steve Gordon, *Ph* Uta Briesewitz, *Pro Des* Sarah Knowles, *Ed* Brent White, *M* Theodore Shapiro, *Cos* Juliet Polcsa.

Warner Bros Pictures/MBST Entertainment/Bender-Spink/Langley Park Productions-Warner Bros.
110 mins. USA. 2011. Rel: 22 Apr 2011. Cert. 12A.

Arthur Christmas ★★★★

It's good to have some British spin in a US animated feature and what could be more British than Aardman, here larding its super animation with in-jokes galore. The plot hinges on Gwen, a little girl who's had no visit from Santa Claus (voiced by Jim Broadbent). So, in a last-minute dash and ignoring his useless older brother Steve (Hugh Laurie), Arthur, Santa's younger offspring (James McAvoy), with the aid of his Grandsanta (Bill Nighy) and a batallion of elves, heads off with a special delivery. Packed with Aardman's

usual skilled and detailed animation, this is destined to enjoy seasonal revivals for years to come. MHD

▶ Voices of James McAvoy, Bill Nighy, Jim Broadbent, Hugh Laurie, Imelda Staunton, Ashley Jensen, Laura Linney, Eva Longoria, Michael Palin, Sanjeev Bhaskar, Robbie Coltrane, Dominic West, Tamsin Greig, Alistair McGowan.
▶ *Dir* Sarah Smith and Barry Cook, *Pro* Steve Pegram, *Screenplay* Smith and Peter Baynham, *Ph* Jericca Cleland, *Pro Des* Evgeni Tomov, *Ed* John Carnochan and James Cooper, *M* Harry Gregson-Williams, *Cos* Yves Barre.

Columbia Pictures/Aardman Animations/Sony Pictures Animation-Sony Pictures International.
97 mins. UK/USA. 2011. Rel: 11 Nov 2011. Cert. U.

The Artist ★★★★★

Just scraping into the list of film releases of 2011 – it opened in the UK on 30 December – Michel Hazanavicius' lovingly recreated take on the silent cinema when it turned to talkies is an absolute charmer. Whether it's because it was a refreshing change to see a black-and-white film with scarcely any spoken dialogue in its evocative reproduction of a bygone era, who knows, but it became a worldwide hit, scooped awards everywhere and swept the board at the Oscars. It may not happen again but, as it has, it's a brilliant tonic that restores one's faith in the cinema. And, of course, Uggie the dog helped too… MHD

▶ Jean Dujardin, Bérénice Bejo, John Goodman, James Cromwell, Penelope Anne Miller, Missi Pyle, Ed Lauter, Malcolm McDowell and Uggie the Dog.
▶ *Dir* and *Screenplay* Michel Hazanavicius, *Pro* Thomas Langmann and Emmanuel Montamat, *Ph* Guillaume Schiffman, *Pro Des* Laurence Bennett, *Ed* Hazanavicius and Anne-Sophie Bion, *M* Ludovic Bourse, *Cos* Mark Bridges.

Le Petite Reine/La Classe Américaine/Jouror Productions/uFilm/Canal+/France 3 Cinéma/JD Prod etc-Entertainment Film Distributors.
100 mins. France/Belgium. 2011. Rel: 30 Dec 2011. Cert. PG.

As Blood Runs Deep ★★★

Underrated Nick Stahl brings just the right gaunt-looking star presence to freshen up the clichés as a small-town detective who's called in to solve a boy's murder. It occurs when a house burglary by two young drifters (Kellan Lutz, Jonathan Tucker) goes wrong in fictional Meskada County. The dead boy's mother (Laura Benanti) exerts power in the rich town of Hilliard where the sheriff wants to be a law unto himself, and there's plenty of other tension too. Effectively dark and noir-ish, with a well fleshed-out script and powerful acting from a strong cast, this exceptional thriller is unusually haunting and involving. (Original title: *Meskada*) DW

▶ Nick Stahl, Rachel Nichols, Kellan Lutz, Jonathan Tucker, Laura Benanti.
▶ *Dir* and *Screenplay* Josh Sternfeld, *Pro* Ron Stein, Shawn Rice, Jen Gatien, Michael Goodin and Jay Kubassek, *Ph* Daniel D Sariano, *Pro Des* Jack Ryan, *Ed* Phyllis Housen, *M* Lee Curreri and Steve Weisberg, *Cos* Amy Kramer.

Aliquot Films/Four of a Kind Productions/Deerjen Films etc-Red Flag Releasing.
98 mins. USA. 2010. Rel: 26 Aug 2011. Cert. 15.

As If I Am Not There ★★★½

Based on actual incidents that occurred during the Bosnian war, this is a tale sincerely told. It's also a very grim narrative concerning a young teacher leaving Sarajevo for a village school and then being seized by soldiers along with all the local women and children. She is forced to offer sexual services to the men and later becomes pregnant. Should she abort? Generally convincing but not always so, the film is harsh but never exploitative. The filmmaker is Irish. MS

▶ Natasha Petrovic, Ferdja Stukan, Jelena Jovanova, Sanja Buric, Stellan Skarsgård.
▶ *Dir* and *Screenplay* (from the novel by Slavenka Drakulic) Juanita Wilson, *Pro* James Flynn, Nathalie Lichtenthaeler and Karen Richards, *Ph* Tim Fleming, *Pro Des* Bujar Mucha, *Ed* Nathan Nugent, *M* Kiril Dzajkovski, *Cos* Zaklina Krstevska.

A Wide Eye Films and Octagon Films production etc-Element Pictures Distribution.
110 mins. Ireland/Macedonia/Sweden/Germany. 2010. Rel: 1 July 2011. Cert. 18.

Atrocious ★

The Quintanilla family travel to their old rural farmhouse near Sitges for an Easter break. Teenage siblings Christian and July attempt to capture almost everything with a camera as well as unearth the mystery behind The Girl of Garraf Woods – she who disappeared some years earlier. This Spanish horror is yet another rip-off of the style of *The Blair Witch Project* and the use of the handheld camera is not exactly atrocious but still tiresome. GS

▶ Cristian Valencia, Clara Moraleda, Chus Pereiro, Sergi Martin, Xavi Doz, Jose Masegosa.
▶ *Dir, Screenplay* and *Ed* Fernando Barreda Luna, *Pro* David Sanz and Jessica Villegas Lattuada, *Ph* Ferrán Castera Mosquera, *Pro Des* Andrea Ancibar, *Cos* Abraham Romagosa.

Nabu Films/Silencio Rodamos Producciones-Celluloid Nightmares.
75 mins. Spain/Mexico. 2010. Rel: 16 Sep 2011. Cert. 15.

Attack the Block ★★★★

Far from being just another 'youf' film, *Attack the Block* offers a crafty spin on the 'close encounters with an alien' genre. On a Brixton housing estate something lands in the middle of a firework night celebration. A local gang on the prowl nick a mobile phone from a passing nurse (Jodie Whittaker) just as the alien hits a car roof. Finding a furry monster they capture and kill it. While wondering what to do with their trophy, more aliens hit the deck. Joe Cornish gives his young cast ample opportunity to shine and gets inspired performances, especially from John Boyega, Alex Esmail and Luke Treadaway. All in all it's an odd but really enjoyable movie. MHD

A very close encounter: the excellent John Boyega in Joe Cornish's entertaining and surprising *Attack the Block*.

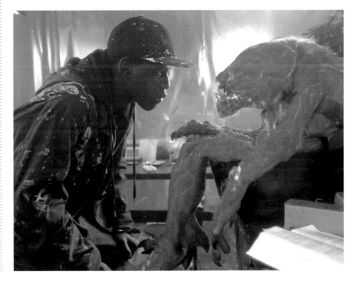

John Boyega, Jodie Whittaker, Alex Esmail, Leeon John, Franz Drameh, Simon Howard, Luke Treadaway, Jumayn Hunter, Nick Frost.
➤ *Dir* and *Screenplay* Joe Cornish, *Pro* Cornish, Nina Park and James Wilson, *Ph* Tom Townend *Pro Des* Marcus Rowland and Dick Lunn, *Ed* Jonathan Amos, *M* Steven Price, Felix Buxton and Simon Ratcliffe, *Cos* Rosa Dias.

StudioCanal Features/Film4/UK Film Council/Big Talk Pictures-StudioCanal.
88 mins. UK. 2011. Rel: 13 May 2011. Cert. 15.

Attenberg ★★★★

This underrated Greek drama offers a strange but engrossing experience. You may not be certain as to the exact aim of writer-director Athina Rachel Tsangari but her film, centred on a father-daughter relationship, echoes Ozu while also placing sexual issues to the fore in an unusually perceptive way. Ariane Labed as the 23-year-old who is both drawn to sex and frightened of it won an award, but this is a director's movie with its own vision. MS

➤ Ariane Labed, Vangelis Mourikis, Evangelia Randou, Yorgos Lanthimos.
➤ *Dir* and *Screenplay* Athina Rachel Tsangari, *Pro* Maria Hatzakou, Yorgos Lanthimos, Tsangari and others, *Ph* Thimios Bakatakis, *Pro Des* Dafni Kalogianni, *Ed* Sandrine Cheyrol and Matt Johnson, *Cos* Thanos Papastergiou and Vassilia Rozana.

Haos Films/Greek Film Centre/Faliro House Productions etc-Artificial Eye.
97 mins. Greece. 2010. Rel: 2 Sept 2011. Cert. 18.

The Awakening ★★★

Following the end of World War I, supernatural sceptic Florence Cathcart (Rebecca Hall) is invited by teacher Robert Mallory (Dominic West) to investigate a ghost at a Cumbrian boarding school. The ghost is allegedly that of a small boy who was murdered when the school was a family home. Florence's initial reaction is disbelief, but events take a turn in which she is forced to change her opinion while marooned with Mallory, the matron (Imelda Staunton) and one of the boys (Isaac Hempstead-Wright). Writer-director Nick Murphy endeavours to make these happenings plausible enough but, apart from a few moments of genuine frisson, the film mostly fails to convince. MHD

➤ Rebecca Hall, Dominic West, Imelda Staunton, Isaac Hempstead-Wright, Lucy Cohu, John Shrapnel, Shaun Dooley, Tilly Vosburgh.
➤ *Dir* Nick Murphy, *Pro* Sarah Curtis, Julia Stannard and David M Thompson, *Screenplay* Stephen Volk, Murphy, *Ph* Eduard Grau, *Pro Des* Jon Henson, *Ed* Victoria Boydell, *M* Daniel Pemberton, *Cos* Caroline Harris.

StudioCanal Features/BBC Films/Origin Pictures/Eagle Pictures/Scottish Screen/Creative Scotland/Lyp Sync Productions-Optimum Releasing.
107 mins. UK. 2011. Rel: 11 Nov 2011. Cert. 15.

Babies ★★★★

This charming documentary follows four babies across the globe from the day of their birth until their first birthday. The action effortlessly moves from Namibia to Mongolia, then from Japan to the USA. Director Thomas Balmès leaves his camera in front of his unaware protagonists as they begin to relate to their environment and nature. It is a simple idea and its humorous approach is both funny and touching, especially in the scene

Lickety-spit: Evangelia Randou and Ariane Labed in Athina Rachel Tsangari's strange and engrossing Attenberg.

where Ayarjargal, a Mongolian boy, plays with his parents' farm animals. (Original title: *Bébé(s)*) GS

▶ *Dir* Thomas Balmès, *Pro* Alain Chabat, Amandine Billot and Christine Rouxel, *Screenplay adaptation* by Balmes from an idea by Alain Chabat, *Ph* Jerome Almeras, Steeven Petitteville etc, *Pro Des* Jill Coulon, *Ed* Reynard Bertrand, *M* Bruno Coulais.

Canal+/Chez Wam/StudioCanal-StudioCanal. 79 mins. France. 2010. Rel: 4 Mar 2011. Cert. U.

Bad Teacher ★★★

For too long frat humour has been the province of the male comic. So it's good to see Cameron Diaz let her hair down – and push her tits out – as an educator consumed by lust, greed and self-interest. It's a one-note and somewhat predictable premise but it's crammed with funny moments and is never boring. It was Diaz who dared to slick her hair with Ben Stiller's semen in *There's Something About Mary* and now she wades in as champion of a new vanguard – hotly followed by Maya Rudolph and her *Bridesmaids*. JC-W

▶ Cameron Diaz, Justin Timberlake, Jason Segel, Lucy Punch, John Michael Higgins, Phyllis Smith, Paul Bates, Molly Shannon.
▶ *Dir* Jake Kasdan, *Pro* Jimmy Miller and David Householter, *Screenplay* Gene Stupnitsky and Lee Eisenberg, *Ph* Alar Kivlio, *Pro Des* Jefferson Sage, *Ed* Tara Timpone, *M* Michael Andrews, *Cos* Debra McGuire.

Columbia/Mosaic Media-Sony. 91 mins. USA. 2011. Rel: 17 June 2011. Cert. 15.

Bal – see Honey

Ballast ★★★½

Slow-moving but atmospheric, this example of American independent cinema is set in the Mississippi delta. There is luminous colour photography by Lol Crawley and a tale involving four central characters, three of whom are black. There's a young widow with a 12-year-old boy to bring up and the dead man's twin, despite being different in outlook, may be able to help. *Ballast* is a sensitive film that suggests possible redemption and then shows it slipping away. The regional accents are sometimes distancing but writer-director-editor-producer Lance Hammer emerges with credit. MS

▶ Michael J Smith, JimMyron Ross, Tarra Riggs, Johnny McPhail.
▶ *Dir, Ed* and *Screenplay* Lance Hammer, *Pro* Hammer and Nina Parikh, *Ph* Lol Crawley, *Pro Des* Jerel Levanway, *Cos* Caroline Eselin-Schaefer.

An Alluvial Film Company production-Axiom Films Limited 96 mins. USA. 2007. Rel: 18 Mar 2011. Cert. 15.

Dog days: JimMyron Ross in Lance Hammer's sensitive and atmospheric *Ballast*.

Barely Legal ★★

Attractive Melissa Johnston, Jeneta St Clair and Lisa Younger are bright, lively and sexy presences as college-bound best friends. Born on the same day, they decide to celebrate their 18th birthday by throwing a party and losing their virginity – like you do. This saucy teen-sex comedy was never intended to be subtle, but they have made it surprisingly amusing and appealing enough. It's nice that the script turns out to be old-fashioned and fairly innocent-seeming too, taking away any leering aspect from the nudity and raunchy storyline. Better than expected, it knows its target audience; it's just a shame it isn't actually funnier. DW

▶ Jeneta St Clair, Lisa Younger, Melissa Johnston, Morgan Benoit, Myko Olivier, Matt Miller.
▶ *Dir* Jose Montesinos, *Pro* David Michael Latt, *Screenplay* Naomi L Selfman, *Ph* Ben Demaree, *Pro Des* Elijah Flores, *Ed* Rob Pallatina, *Cos* Lauren Morelli.

The Global Asylum-The Asylum Home Entertainment. 86 mins. USA. 2011. Rel: 9 Dec 2011. Cert. 18.

Barney's Version ★★★★

Paul Giamatti finds an ideal role in this adaptation of Mordecai Richler's final novel. He plays Barney, who looks back on his life and on three marriages that didn't last. Rosamund Pike is enchanting as the one likable wife and this is an example of quintessentially Jewish tragi-comedy that I for one find far superior to *A Serious Man* (2009). However, there is a sense of the film playing down Barney's failings too much and that may alienate some. Nevertheless, it's a well-made film with exceptional supporting performances. MS

▶ Paul Giamatti, Rosamund Pike, Minnie Driver, Rachelle Lefevre, Scott Speedman, Dustin Hoffman, Bruce Greenwood, Mark Addy, Atom Egoyan.
▶ *Dir* Richard J Lewis, *Pro* Robert Lantos, *Screenplay*

Michael Konyves, based on the novel by Mordecai Richler, *Ph* Guy Dufaux, *Pro Des* Claude Paré, *Ed* Susan Shipton, *M* Pasquale Catalano, *Cos* Nicoletta Massone.

Serendipity Point Films/Fandango/Lyla Films etc-Universal Pictures International.
134 mins. Canada/Italy. 2010. Rel: 28 Jan 2011. Cert. 15.

Battle Los Angeles ★½

As Marine Staff Sergeant Michael Nantz (Aaron Eckhart) prepares to wind down his military career, Los Angeles is attacked by extraterrestrial forces… In a quest for documentary realism, director Jonathan Liebesman has delivered an incomprehensible alien attack movie with absolutely zero entertainment value. Without the gung-ho fun of *Independence Day* or even the cheesy spectacle of *2012*, this is a headache-inducing, incoherent and rather uninventive assault on the senses. Without a narrative to speak of (or any human dimension), it ends up being terribly dull – and absolutely pointless. JC-W

‣ Aaron Eckhart, Michelle Rodriguez, Ramon Rodriguez, Bridget Moynahan, Ne-Yo, Michael Peña.
‣ *Dir* Jonathan Liebesman, *Pro* Jeffrey Chernov, Neal H. Moritz and Ori Marmur, *Screenplay* Chris Bertolini, *Ph* Lukas Ettli, *Pro Des* Peter Wenham, *Ed* Christian Wagner, *M* Brian Tyler, *Cos* Sanja Milkovic Hays.

Columbia Pictures/Relativity Media/Original Film-Sony.
116 mins. USA. 2011. Rel: 11 Mar 2011. Cert. 12A.

Beastly ★★

Alex Pettyfer bares the body beautiful as rich,

The skin he lives in: Alex Pettyfer in Daniel Barnz's ill-formed *Beastly*.

sexy, popular, arrogant New York teen Kyle. He makes the mistake of playing a prank on a fellow high-schooler who turns out to be a witch. Mary-Kate Olsen co-stars as Kendra, who teaches Kyle a lesson by giving him a year to find someone who truly loves him or he's cursed to stay hideous. The underpowered script is, nevertheless, a slick, modern-day take on *Beauty and the Beast* targeted at girly teen audiences. Sadly, Vanessa Hudgens lacks spark as the bookish girl who gets under Kyle's lovely skin. It's ironic that Pettyfer even looks great as a skinhead with crazy tattoos and acne! DW

‣ Alex Pettyfer, Vanessa Hudgens, Mary-Kate Olsen. Peter Krause, Dakota Johnson.
‣ *Dir* and *Screenplay* Daniel Barnz, from the novel by Alex Flinn, *Pro* Susan Cartsonis, *Ph* Mandy Walker, *Pro Des* Rusty Smith, *Ed* Thomas J Nordberg, *M* Marcelo Zarvos, *Cos* Suttirat Larlarb.

CBS Films/Storefront Films-Paramount Pictures.
86 mins. USA. 2011. Rel: 22 Apr 2011. Cert. 12A.

Beautiful Lies ★★★★

If you are going to have a rom-com, it might as well be a Gallic one. Audrey Tautou (as kooky as ever) plays a hairdresser who receives an anonymous love letter from her adoring handyman (Sami Bouajila), whom she generally ignores. Because her jilted, singleton mother (Nathalie Baye) is depressed, she forwards the note to her, thereby instigating a series of awkward misunderstandings. A modern French farce, Pierre Salvadori's film, set on the coast, is all sunshine and brightness: just the right cheerful environment for this charming, romantic tosh garnished with funny and cherishable performances from Tautou, Baye and Bouajila. (Original title: *Des vrais mensonges*) MHD

‣ Audrey Tautou, Nathalie Baye, Sami Bouajila, Stéphanie Lagarde, Judith Chemla, Daniel Duval.
‣ *Dir* Pierre Salvadori, *Pro* Philippe Martin, *Screenplay* Salvadori and Benoît Graffin, *Ph* Gilles Henry, *Pro Des* Philippe Cord'homme, *Ed* Isabelle Devinck, *M* Philippe Eidel, *Cos* Virginie Montel.

Les Films Pelléas/TF1 Films Production/Tovo Films/ Canal+/Coficup/Wild Bunch/Cinémage 4-Trinity Film.
105 mins. France. 2010. Rel: 12 Aug 2011. Cert. 12A.

The Beaver ★★★★

It shouldn't work but it does. With fine unselfish support from Jodie Foster, who also directs, Mel Gibson gives what is arguably his best performance. He plays a businessman who, succumbing to depression, can only speak through a beaver glove puppet that he starts to wear on his hand. The film achieves a positive ending without being sentimental. Instead it attacks the big lie of the American Dream that we can all be heroes

by asking us to accept that everybody is to some extent flawed and imperfect. Not a masterpiece but seriously underestimated. MS

▶ Mel Gibson, Jodie Foster, Anton Yelchin, Jennifer Lawrence, Cherry Jones, Riley Thomas Stewart.
▶ *Dir* Jodie Foster, *Pro* Steve Golin, Keith Redmon and Ann Ruark, *Screenplay* Kyle Killen, *Ph* Hagen Bogdanski, *Pro Des* Mark Friedberg, *Ed* Lynzee Klingman, *M* Marcelo Zarvos, *Cos* Susan Lyall.

Summit Entertainment/Participant Media/Anonymous Content etc-Icon Film Distribution.
91 mins. USA/United Arab Emirates. 2011. Rel: 17 Jun 2011. Cert. 12A.

Beetle Queen Conquers Tokyo ★★★½

No, this is not the latest exploitation horror movie about an alien invasion but a cool documentary film that looks at the Japanese fascination with insects. Filmmaker Jessica Oreck of the American Museum of Natural History in New York endeavours to discover exactly why Japan is so besotted by all kinds of bugs, beetles and other creepy-crawlies, many of which are available to buy in Japanese shops and which some Japanese keep as house pets. To each his own, as they say. PL

▶ *Dir, Pro* and *Written by* Jessica Oreck, *Ph* Sean Price Williams, *Ed* Oreck and Theo Angell, *M* Paul Grimstad, Nate Shaw and J C Morrison.

Myriapod Productions-November Films
90 mins. USA/Japan. 2009. Rel: 1 July 2011. Cert. PG.

Beginners ★★★★★

This feature from Mike Mills is a remarkable work. Following his mother's death, Oliver (Ewan McGregor) has to adjust to his septuagenarian father (Christopher Plummer) coming out as gay. Without eschewing humour, the film provides a study of human loneliness which, showing both father and son in quest of a meaningful relationship, makes for a winning and moving experience. What's more it should appeal equally to gay and straight audiences and it is splendidly acted – not least by McGregor. MS

▶ Ewan McGregor, Christopher Plummer, Mélanie Laurent, Goran Visnjic.
▶ *Dir* and *Screenplay* Mike Mills, *Pro* Leslie Urdang, Dean Vanech, Miranda de Pencier and others, *Ph* Kasper Tuxen, *Pro Des* Shane Valentino, *Ed* Oliver Bugge Coutté, *M* Roger Neill, David Palmer and Brian Reitzell, *Cos* Jennifer Johnson.

Focus Features/Olympus Pictures/Parts & Labor-Universal Pictures International.
104 mins. USA. 2010. Rel: 22 July 2011. Cert. 15.

Benda Bilili! ★★★★½

The title means 'See Beyond' and Renaud Barret and Florent de la Tullaye's documentary

Late starter: An Oscar-winning Christopher Plummer with Ewan McGregor in Mike Mills' *Beginners*.

Street music: Ricky Likabu in Renaud Barret and Florent de la Tullaye's unsentimental and inspirational *Benda Bilili!*

Thieves to mind. Admittedly it's no masterpiece, but it's well acted and expertly photographed in colour by Javier Aguirresarobe. MS

❯ Demián Bichir, José Julián, Delores Heredia, Joaquin Cosió, Nancy Lenehan.
❯ *Dir* Chris Weitz, *Pro* Paul Junger Witt, Weitz and others, *Screenplay* Eric Eason from a story by Roger L. Simon, *Ph* Javier Aguirresarobe, *Pro Des* Missy Stewart, *Ed* Peter Lambert, *M* Alexandre Desplat, *Cos* Elaine Montalvo.
Summit Entertainment/Lime Orchard Productions/Witt-Thomas Productions/Depth of Field etc-E1 Films. 97 mins. USA. 2011. Rel: 29 July 2011. Cert. 12A.

Big Fat Gypsy Gangster ★★

Ricky Grover is a tour-de-force as Britain's hardest man, Bulla, the big fat gypsy gangster of the title who's released from prison after serving 16 years of a ten-year-sentence (don't ask!). Seeking to re-establish his criminal empire, Bulla is followed for a week by the crew of a Brit-loving American documentary filmmaker. This comedy mockumentary starts with a promisingly good idea but gradually lets the fun slip through its fingers. Still, with some hilarious scenes, ideas (underground bare-knuckle midget fighting!) and performances (notably from Peter Capaldi's probation officer and Rufus Hound's trainee psychic), it is a creditable effort from Grover, who co-writes, directs and stars. DW

❯ Ricky Grover, Steven Berkoff, Omid Djalili, Peter Capaldi, Rufus Hound, Dave Legeno, Geoff Bell, Leo Gregory.
❯ *Dir* Ricky Grover, *Pro* Grover, Paul Silver and Jonathan Sothcott, *Screenplay* Ricky and Maria Grover, *Ph* Gary Shaw, *Pro Des* Kasja Soderlund, *Ed* Jason de Vyea, *M* Tim Atack, *Cos* Heidi Miller.
Black and Blue Films/Bulla the Movie-4Digital Media. 91 mins. UK. 2011. Rel: 14 Sep 2011. Cert. 15.

Big Momma's: Like Father, Like Son ★

In this lame third outing of a series which ran out of steam long ago Martin Lawrence returns as FBI agent Malcolm Turner, always ready to wear his fat suit for another undercover case. After his teenage stepson Trent (Brandon T Jackson) witnesses a murder, they both dress up as women and hide in an all-girls' performing arts school, he as Big Momma and Trent as one of the students. It feebly attempts to parody *Fame* but it's dull and not remotely funny. GS

❯ Martin Lawrence, Brandon T Jackson, Jessica Lucas, Michelle Ang, Ana Ortiz, Brandon Gill.
❯ *Dir* John Whitesell, *Pro* David T Friendly and Michael Green, *Screenplay* Matthew Fogel, from a story by Fogel and Don Rhymer, based on characters

is a record of what can be done if you look beyond the here and now. A group of paraplegic musicians on the streets of Kinshasa try to earn enough to buy a mattress instead of their usual bed of cardboard. The band, called Staff Benda Bilili, playing from wheelchairs and improvised tricycles, join Roger Landu. He is a boy who made his own instrument out of a single guitar string, a tin can and a stick, and they eventually get to play a big concert together. All this is depicted in an inspirational, unsentimental way, proving that thinking positively can let you see beyond. MHD

❯ With Ricky Likabu, Roger Landu, Coco Ngambali, Cubbain Kabeya, Paulin Klara-Maigi.
❯ *Dir, Ph* and *Script* Renaud Barret and Florent de la Tullaye, *Pro* Barret, Tullaye, Nadim Cheikhrouha and Yves Chanvillard, *Ed* Jean-Christophe Hym, *M* Staff Benda Bilili.
Belle Kinoise/Screen Runner/Canal+/O L Production/Studio 37 etc-Trinity Filmed Entertainment. 85 mins. Democratic Republic of the Congo/France. 2010. Rel: 18 Mar 2011. Cert. PG.

A Better Life ★★★★

Set in LA, this film finds mainstream director Chris Weitz turning to something different. It may be less memorable than *Bread and Roses* (2000) or *The Visitor* (2007) but as a study of immigrants in America – Mexicans in this case – it is decidedly sympathetic. Indeed, with a father-son relationship at its heart it brings the classic *Bicycle*

by Darryl Quarles, *Ph* Anthony B Richmond, *Pro Des* Meghan C Rogers, *Ed* Priscilla Nedd-Friendly, *M* David Newman, *Cos* Leah Katznelson.

20th Century Fox Film Corporation/Regency Enterprises/New Regency/Friendly Films Productions/ Runteldat Entertainment etc-20th Century Fox. 107 mins. USA. 2011. Rel: 16 Feb 2011. Cert. PG.

The Big Picture ★★★

Aided by a striking lead performance from Romain Duris, this French drama gets by – but only just. He's a husband who without premeditation kills his wife's lover, but Chabrol's *La Femme infidèle* developed that situation far more compellingly. Similarly the film's second half, in which he improbably takes on the dead man's identity, carries echoes of *The Talented Mr Ripley*. Unfortunately it's far less memorable than the films it evokes. (Original title: *L'Homme qui voulait vivre sa vie*) MS

❯ Romain Duris, Marina Foïs, Niels Arestrup, Eric Ruf, Catherine Deneuve.
❯ *Dir* Eric Lartigau, *Pro* Pierre-Ange Le Pogam, *Screenplay* Lartigau, Laurent de Bartillat and others from the novel by Douglas Kennedy, *Ph* Laurent Dailland, *Art Dir* Olivier Radot, *Ed* Juliette Welfling, *M* Evgueni Galperine and Sacha Galperine, *Cos* Anne Schotte.

EuropaCorp/TF1 Films/CiBy 2000 etc-Artificial Eye. 115 mins. France. 2010. Rel: 22 July 2011. Cert. 15.

The Big Year ★★★

A tale of rival birdwatchers starring Steve Martin, Jack Black and Owen Wilson, *The Big Year* is a charming treat from David Frankel, director of *The Devil Wears Prada*. Less a laugh-out-loud gag-fest than it is a sweet, beguiling tale of competitive obsessives doing what comes naturally, it's a light drama with characters you'll quickly come to care about and much to make you smile. You don't even have to like birds to enjoy it, though it'll help if you're in a soppy mood. MJ

❯ Steve Martin, Jack Black, Owen Wilson, Rosamund Pike, JoBeth Williams, Kevin Pollak, John Cleese, Brian Dennehy, Anjelica Huston.
❯ *Dir* David Frankel, *Pro* Curtis Hanson, Stuart Cornfeld and Karen Rosenfelt, *Screenplay* Howard Franklin, inspired by the book by Mark Obmascik, *Ph* Lawrence Sher, *Pro Des* Brent Thomas, *Ed* Mark Livolsi, *M* Theodore Shapiro, *Cos* Monique Prudhomme.

Fox 2000 Pictures/Deuce Three/Red Hour Films/ Sunswept Entertainment/Dune Entertainment/ Ingenious Media-20th Century Fox. 100 mins. USA. 2011. Rel: 2 Dec 2011. Cert. PG.

Biutiful ★★★★½

Set in Barcelona, this film by Alejandro González Iñárritu tells the story of a man seeking redemption as he dies of cancer. His life has been played out in the criminal underside of the city but impending death makes him seek to do all he can to help his young children. There's an unexpectedly positive after-life element to this film, but it's a tough, unsentimental movie. In the key role Javier Bardem excels himself and, after an arguably over-obscure opening that's clarified only at the end, the film's power sustains its substantial length. MS

Ugly work: Alejandro González Iñárritu directs Javier Bardem in the absorbing and complex *Biutiful*.

➤ Javier Bardem, Maricel Álvarez, Eduard Fernández, Cheick Ndiaye, Diaryatou Daff, Li Lang Sofia Lin.
➤ *Dir* Alejandro González Iñárritu, *Pro* Iñárritu, Jon Kilik and Fernando Bovaira, *Screenplay* Iñárritu, Armando Bo and Nicolás Giacobone from Iñárritu's story, *Ph* Rodrigo Prieto, *Art Dir* Brigitte Broch, *Ed* Stephen Mirrione, *M* Gustavo Santaolalla, *Cos* Paco Delgado.

Menage Atroz, Mexico/MOD Producciones Spain/D Focus Features International etc-Optimum Releasing. 147 mins. Mexico/Spain/UK. 2009. Rel: 28 Jan 2011. Cert. 15.

Black Pond ★★★½

When Tom (Chris Langham) meets Blake (Colin Hurley) on a country walk while looking for Boy, his three-legged dog, he invites him home for a meal, regardless of the guy's apparent strangeness. Meanwhile, Tom's daughters Helen and Katie are sharing their London flat with Tim (Will Sharpe), who loves both of them. The dog is found dead. Could Blake have killed it? And, when Blake also dies, to whom does the finger of suspicion point? An odd plot is further complicated by an awkward appearance by Simon Amstell as a crazy psychotherapist with Tim as his patient. Comedy, is it? This jury is still out. MHD

➤ Chris Langham, Simon Amstell, Amanda Hadingue, Colin Hurley, Will Sharpe, Anna O'Grady, Helen Cripps.
➤ *Dir, Story* and *Ed* Will Sharpe and Tom Kingsley, *Screenplay* Will Sharpe, *Pro* Sarah Brocklehurst, *Ph* Simon Walton, *M* Will Sharpe and Arthur Sharpe, Raleigh Long and Will Sutcliffe.

Black Pond Film. 83 mins. UK. 2011. Rel: 11 Nov 2011. Cert. 15.

Black Power Mixtape 1967-1975 ★★★★

Documentary footage from Sweden (in admirable condition despite its age) is here assembled to

encourage reassessment of the American racial history of the period in which the Black Panthers came to the fore. However ready to endorse violence to bring about change, they were demonised by white capitalist America so their story emerges here from a less familiar angle. Recommended. MS

➤ With the voices of Angela Davis, Harry Belafonte, Sonia Sanchez, Robin Kelley.
➤ *Dir* and *Written by* Göran Hugo Olsson, *Pro* Annika Rogell, *Ed* Hanna Lejonqvist and Olsson, *M* Ahmir Questlove Thompson and Om'Mas Keith.

Story AB/Louverture Films/Sveriges Television etc-Soda Pictures. 100 mins. Sweden/USA/Norway/Germany/Switzerland/Finland/Greece. 2011. Rel: 21 Oct 2011. Cert. 12A.

Black Swan ★★★★½

Having shone a blinding light on the worlds of mathematics and wrestling, Darren Aronofsky now turns his attention to the universe of ballet. Securing a career-high performance from Natalie Portman, Aronofsky explores the emotional extremes of *Swan Lake* as the hard-working yet wilting violet Nina Sayers tackles the role of the tragic Swan Queen. It's a delirious slice of melodrama, exposing the all-consuming drama of a ballet production with the dazzling bravura of the silver screen – shored up by the giddy musical collaboration of Clint Mansell and Pyotr Tchaikovsky. Another turning point for the cinema of ballet. JC-W

➤ Natalie Portman, Vincent Cassel, Mila Kunis, Barbara Hershey, Winona Ryder.
➤ *Dir* Darren Aronofsky, *Pro* Ari Handel, Scott Franklin, Mike Medavoy, Arnold Messer and Brian Oliver, *Screenplay* Mark Heyman, Andrés Heinz and John McLaughlin, *Ph* Matthew Libatique, *Pro Des* Thérèse DePrez, *Ed* Andrew Weisblum, *M* Clint Mansell, *Cos* Amy Westcott.

Fox Searchlight/Protozoa Pictures/Phoenix Pictures/Cross Creek Pictures-20th Century Fox. 107 mins. USA. 2010. Rel: 21 Jan 2011. Cert. 15.

Blitz ★★

Tough cop Brant (Jason Statham) reluctantly pairs up with openly gay policeman Porter Nash (Paddy Considine) in order to catch a London police serial killer (Aidan Gillen). Their mission becomes more personal when Brant's mentor and boss Roberts (Mark Rylance) is murdered at his home by the psychotic killer, who calls himself Blitz... The story has potential but the script by Nathan Parker – the writer of *Moon* – disappoints, while Elliott Lester's uneven direction fails to deliver the goods, especially in the last act. GS

➤ Jason Statham, Paddy Considine, Aiden Gillen,

Civil light: Angela Davis in Göran Hugo Olsson's eye-opening Black Power Mixtape 1967-1975.

Zawe Ashton, David Morrissey, Ned Dennehy, Mark Rylance, Nicky Henson.
▸ *Dir* Elliott Lester, *Pro* Steve Chasman, Brad Wyman, Donald Kushner and Zygy Kamasa, *Screenplay* Nathan Parker, from the novel by Ken Bruen, *Ph* Rob Hardy, *Pro Des* Max Gottlieb, *Ed* John Gilbert, *M* Ilan Eshkeri, *Cos* Suzie Harman.

Lionsgate/Davis Films/Current Entertainment/Blitz Films/Junction Films/Kushner-Wyman Productions-Lionsgate.
97 mins. UK/France/USA. 2011. Rel: 20 May 2011. Cert. 18.

Blood in the Mobile ★★★★½

As easily happens with feature-length documentaries, this becomes a shade repetitive late on, but it's a gripping piece as compelling as any thriller. It traces the heroic endeavours of its Danish filmmaker, Frank Piasecki Poulsen, to make Nokia admit to the need for positive action to counter the use of criminally attained minerals in electronics generally and in mobile phones in particular. By way of evidence, he visits the Congo to reveal the exploitation in the mines and the way in which warlords control the mineral sales to attain the profits which fund their wars. Devastating. (Original title: *Blod i mobilen*) MS

▸ With Frank Piasecki Poulsen, Dr Frank Melcher, Pekka Isosomppi, Jim McDermott.
▸ *Dir* Frank Piasecki Poulsen, *Pro* Ole Tornbjerg,

Ph Adam Wallensten, Lars Skree and Poulsen, *Ed* Mikael K. Ebbesen, *M* Kristian Eidnes Andersen.

Koncern/Chili Film/Gebreuder Beetz Filmproduktion etc-Dogwoof Pictures.
85 mins. Denmark/Germany/Democratic Republic of Congo/Uganda/France/Finland /Norway/Greece/ Ireland/ Hungary/The Netherlands/Israel. 2010. Rel: 21 Oct 2011. No Cert.

Blooded ★★★★

First-time director Ed Boase impresses with this tight dramatic reconstruction of the extreme measures taken by the militant Real Animal League to punish a group of five hunters in the Highlands of Scotland. It is a controversial subject executed with sensitivity and care, and cleverly mixed with real-life footage. The result is a nail-biting adventure which is compelling and truly scary because it is all true. GS

▸ Nick Ashdon, Neil McDermott, Oliver Boot, Mark Dexter, Tracy Ifeachor.
▸ *Dir* Edward Boase, *Pro* Nick Ashdon, *Screenplay* James Walker, *Ph* Kate Reid, *Ed* Boase and Dan Susman, *M* Ilan Eshkeri, Jeff Toyne and Christoph Bauschinger, *Cos* Nell Knudsen.

Magma Pictures/Ptarmigan ACP-Revolver Entertainment.
80 mins. UK. 2011. Rel:·1 Apr 2011. Cert. 15.

Cygnet tune: Natalie Portman in her Oscar-winning performance in Darren Aronofsky's delirious *Black Swan.*

Blue Valentine ★★★★

Actors of the moment Ryan (*Drive*, *The Ides of March*, *Crazy, Stupid, Love.*) Gosling and Michelle (*Meek's Cutoff*, *My Week With Marilyn*) Williams collide as a happy/unhappy married couple who probably should never have got together. The film shows their relationship as it developed and as it is now falling apart. They go into it with their eyes or brains closed, with neither of them seeming able to understand what the other wants, a common factor in the breakdown of any relationship. Harrowing at times, the piece is all too believable and has magnificently perceptive performances by Gosling and Williams. Grim but good. MHD

❯ Ryan Gosling, Michelle Williams, John Doman, Mike Vogel, Marshall Johnson.
❯ *Dir* Derek Cianfrance, *Pro* Lynette Howell, Alex Orlovsky and Jamie Patricof, *Screenplay* Cianfrance, Joey Curtis and Cami Delavigne, *Ph* Andrij Parekh, *Pro Des* Inbal Weinberg, *Ed* Jim Helton and Ron Patane, *M* Grizzly Bear, *Cos* Erin Benach.
Incentive Filmed Entertainment/Silverwood Films/ Hunting Lane Films/Shade Pictures etc-StudioCanal. 112 mins. USA. 2010. Rel: 14 Jan 2011. Cert. 15.

Bobby Fischer Against the World ★★★★

A chess-playing child prodigy who grew to take on the might of the Russian masters and walked away, back in the 1970s, with the World Champion's crown, Bobby Fischer was also stone-cold crazy, a true eccentric who lived and breathed chess to the exclusion of all else. A revelatory, utterly captivating documentary by Liz Garbus, this reveals the ins and outs of Fischer's troubled childhood, his misery in the face of international fame, an unwilling icon with the weight of the Cold War on his shoulders, and finally his ignoble end as a fugitive enemy of the state. Remarkable and ghoulishly entertaining. MJ

❯ With Bobby Fischer, David Edmonds, Anthony Saidy, Susan Polgar, Henry Kissinger, Boris Spassky, Garry Kasparov.
❯ *Dir* Liz Garbus, *Pro* Garbus, Matthew Justus, Rory Kennedy and Stanley F Buchthal, *Ph* Robert Chappell, *Ed* Michael Levine and Karen Schmeer, *M* Philip Sheppard.
HBO Documentary Films/LM Media/Moxie Firecracker Films-Dogwoof Pictures. 93 mins. USA/UK/Iceland. 2011. Rel: 15 July 2011. Cert. 12A.

Born To Be Wild 3D + IMAX ★★★★

Director David Lickley splits the action between the lush rain forests of Borneo as he follows primatologist Dr Birute Mary Galdikas with her orang-utans, and the dry land of Kenya where Dr Daphne M Sheldrick provides a home for orphan baby elephants. This is an enchanting documentary film strikingly shot with IMAX cameras and in 3D, with some amazing sequences and authoritative narration from Morgan Freeman. Good family entertainment. GS

❯ Narrated by Morgan Freeman, with Doctors Daphne M Sheldrick and Birute Mary Galdikas.
❯ *Dir* David Lickley, *Pro* and *Screenplay* Drew Fellman, *Ph* David Douglas, *Ed* Beth Spiegel, *M* Mark Mothersbaugh.
IMAX Filmed Entertainment/Warner Bros Pictures. 40 mins. USA. 2011. Rel: 17 June 2011. Cert. U.

The Boy Mir: Ten Years in Afghanistan ★★★★

This remarkable documentary was made by Phil Grabsky, who returned to Afghanistan every year to follow the progress of eight-year-old Mir into a fully grown adult. It has taken ten years for Grabsky to complete this unique piece of work, his camera becoming a friend to this free-spirited boy as he matures in a dangerous and hostile environment. It is a brave piece of filmmaking and needs to be seen by every schoolchild in the country. GS

❯ *Dir* and *Ph* Phil Grabsky, *Pro* Cynthia Kane, Christi Collier and Amanda Wilkie, *Ed* Phil Reynolds.
Channel 4 Television/Independent Television Service/ Seventh Art Productions/NHK/Sveriges Television/ Télévision Suisse-Romande etc-NHK. 90 mins. UK/Austria/Sweden/Finland/Japan/France. 2011. Rel: 29 Sep 2011. No Cert.

Tough love: Ryan Gosling and Michelle Williams in Derek Cianfrance's harrowing *Blue Valentine*.

Anna Halprin with her husband, the acclaimed landscape architect Lawrence Halprin, in Ruedi Gerber's inspirational *Breath Made Visible: Anna Halprin.*

Break My Fall ★★½

The action follows the lives of four friends in East London. Liza (Kat Redstone) has relationship problems with her girlfriend Sally (Sophie Anderson), while rent boy Vin (Kai Brandon Ly) is secretly in love with Sally. Meanwhile Jamie (Collin Clay Chace) works in a gay cabaret bar but longs to settle down with a nice man. Curiously, it's difficult to care much about these characters but the energy of this low-budget film is admirable. GS

❯ Kat Redstone, Sophie Anderson, Kai Brandon Ly, Collin Clay Chace, Morgan Rhys, Rich Cline.
❯ *Dir* and *Screenplay* Kanchi Wichmann, *Pro* Wichmann, Billy Wiz and Matteo Rolleri, *Ph* Dawid Pietkiewicz, *Set Designer* Juliette Rodrigues, *Ed* Gaia Borretti, *Cos Supervisor* Ana Carolina Minozzo.
Break My Films-Peccadillo Pictures.
107 mins. UK. 2011. Rel: 22 July 2011. Cert. 18.

Breath Made Visible: Anna Halprin ★★★

Dance fans will be in heaven throughout Ruedi Gerber's documentary – a fabulous tribute to Anna Halprin, the pioneering American dance therapist and choreographer whose passionate belief that dance can transform anyone's life proves a breath of fresh air. Mixing new material (interviews with Merce Cunningham etc) with rare archive footage, Gerber stitches together a brilliantly edited and lovingly chosen toast to the lady, still dancing as she approaches her 90th birthday. He focuses on her setting-up of America's first multi-racial dance company, includes excerpts from her notorious nude *Parades and Changes* and movingly shows her belief in dance as healing, prompted by the AIDS pandemic. What a life force and inspiration! DW

❯ With Anna Halprin, Lawrence Halprin, Rana Halprin, Merce Cunningham, A A Leath, John Graham.
❯ *Dir* and *Pro* Ruedi Gerber, *Ph* Adam Teichman, *Ed* Françoise Dumoulin and C Peters, *M* Mario Grigorov.
ZAS Film-Argot Pictures.
82 mins. Switzerland/USA. 2009. Rel: 8 July 2011. No Cert.

Bridesmaids ★★★

There is a fundamental flaw at the heart of this funny, appealing rom-com. Kristen Wiig, the co-producer and co-writer, has cast herself as a loser in friendship, love and baking. Yet Wiig is so inherently attractive and bright that it's hard to take on board her character's failings. However, she is very funny and constantly rises above the stream of crass gags that punctuates the movie. The publicity suggests that women can be as crude as men, so it's sad to learn that co-producer Judd Apatow suggested the film's famous gross-out centrepiece. JC-W

❯ Kristen Wiig, Maya Rudolph, Rose Byrne, Chris O'Dowd, Wendi McLendon-Covey, Ellie Kemper, Melissa McCarthy, Jill Clayburgh, Matt Lucas, Terry Crews, Jon Hamm.
❯ *Dir* Paul Feig, *Pro* Judd Apatow, Barry Mendel and Clayton Townsend, *Screenplay* Annie Mumolo and

Rocking Brighton: Sam Riley gives Philip Davis a ride in Rowan Joffe's dated, charmless *Brighton Rock*.

Kristen Wiig, *Ph* Robert D Yeoman, *Pro Des* Jefferson Sage, *Ed* William Kerr and Michael L Sale, *M* Michael Andrews, *Cos* Leesa Evans and Christine Wada.

Universal/Relativity Media/Apatow Prods-Universal. 124 mins. USA. 2011. Rel: 24 June 2011. Cert. 15.

Brighton Rock ★★½

Can you remake a classic successfully? In the case of *Brighton Rock*, the Boulting Brothers' 1947 film set its own signature on Graham Greene's story of seaside sex and violence, tinged with a hint of religion. Rowan Joffe's new version is updated to 1964, the time of Mods and Rockers, but it creates such a dark, moody atmosphere that it leaves no room for enjoyment. Sam Riley's Pinkie is too charmless to have ever pulled Andrea Riseborough's naïve waitress Rose because there's just nothing to like. Helen Mirren, John Hurt and Philip Davis bring some relief but, generally speaking, this is an opportunity wasted. MHD

▶ Sam Riley, Andrea Riseborough, Helen Mirren, John Hurt, Philip Davis, Craig Parkinson, Nonso Anozie, Andy Serkis, Sean Harris, Maurice Roëves.
▶ *Dir* and *Screenplay* Rowan Joffe, from the novel by Graham Greene, *Pro* Paul Webster, *Ph* John Mathieson, *Pro Des* James Merifield, *Ed* Joe Walker, *M* Martin Phipps, *Cos* Julian Day.

BBC Films/Kudos Film and Television/Optimum Releasing-StudioCanal. 111 mins. UK. 2010. Rel: 4 Feb 2011. Cert. 15.

The British Guide to Showing Off ★★

In telling the story of gay entrepreneur Andrew Logan, filmed while he was preparing the 12th show of *The Alternative Miss World* in 2009 (he had started it in 1972), there was a chance both to be revealing about the man and informative about changing social attitudes to sexuality. Sadly, the opportunity was lost and what is on the screen may well appeal only to those who went to the shows and feel nostalgic about them. MS

▶ With Andrew Logan, Michael Davis, Grayson Perry, Ruby Wax.
▶ *Dir* Jes Benstock, *Pro* Dorigen Hammond, *Ph* Denzil Armour-Brown, Andrew David Clark and Johnny Cocking, *Ed* Stephen Boucher, *M* Mike 'Flowers' Roberts.

Film London/Living Cinema/Microwave etc-Verve Pictures. 97 mins. UK. 2011. Rel: 11 Nov 2011. Cert. 15.

Broken Lines ★★★

Set in Finsbury Park, London, this is a drama about two couples and the joint betrayal which links them. Sallie Aprahamian's direction shows an individual eye but by concentrating on the lovers (whose infidelity fails to arouse any sympathy) instead of on those they betray, she only engages us fitfully. On the plus side Paul

Bettany seizes his chances, but it's a criminal waste of Olivia Williams. MS

▶ Dan Fredenburgh, Doraly Rosa, Paul Bettany, Olivia Williams, Harriet Walter.
▶ *Dir* Sallie Aprahamian, *Pro* Douglas Cummins, *Screenplay* Dan Fredenburgh and Doraly Rosa, *Ph* Jean-Louis Bompoint, *Pro Des* Mike Kane, *Ed* Brand Thumim, *Cos* Caroline Harris.

Axiom Films/Aria Films/Matador Pictures-Axiom Films. 97 mins. UK. 2011. Rel: 30 Sep 2011. Cert. 15.

Brotherhood ★★★★

Fraternity president Frank (Jon Foster) bullies his fellow students to attempt a 'fake' robbery as part of an initiation ceremony, but Kevin (Lou Taylor Pucci) gets shot when things go wrong. Only Adam Buckley (Trevor Morgan) stands up against Frank's fraternity in a desperate attempt to save Kevin's life. This gripping film puts you in the middle of the action from the opening scene and doesn't let go until the final credits. Highly energetic with sharp editing and strong performances. GS

▶ Trevor Morgan, Lou Taylor Pucci, Arlen Escarpeta, Jon Foster, Jesse Steccato, Jenny Shakeshaft.
▶ *Dir* Will Canon, *Pro* Jason Croft, Steve Hein, Tim O'Hair and Chris Pollack, *Screenplay* Canon and Doug Simon, *Ph* Michael Fimognari, *Pro Des* Eric Whitney, *Ed* Josh Schaeffer, *M* Dan Marocco, *Cos* Leila Heise.

Hunting Lane Film/Instinctive Film/Roslyn Productions/ Three Folks Pictures-Sony Pictures. 76 mins. USA. 2010. Rel: 14 Jan 2011. Cert. 15.

Camp Hell ★

Although the publicity would have us believe it's a demonic horror, *Camp Hell* is, in reality, a peculiar psychological thriller suffocatingly packed with oddball religious dogma. Shot in 2007, the only reason it's been released now is because it contains a single short scene featuring a pre-fame Jesse Eisenberg, a fact that the film's publicists exploited beyond all reasonable bounds. Failing to resist the temptations of the flesh and awkwardly dry-humping a female inmate, a troubled lad in a fundamentalist Christian summer camp has the Devil to pay, possibly literally. Awful. MJ

▶ Dana Delaney, Andrew McCarthy, Caroline London, Will Denton, Bruce Davison, Jesse Eisenberg.
▶ *Dir* and *Screenplay* George Van Buskirk, *Pro* Buskirk, David Newman and Laylee Olfat, *Ph* Michael McDonough, *Pro Des* Carol Strober, *Ed* Misako Shimizu and Manya Williams, *M* Gary DeMichele, *Cos* Erika Munro.

Holedigger Films-New Films International. 99 mins. USA. 2010. Rel: 2 Dec 2011. Cert. 15.

Cane Toads: The Conquest 3D ★★★★

Following an hilarious original that came out in 1988, Mark Lewis revisits the titular amphibians, following them as they march across the Australian continent demanding supremacy. Initially the cane toads were brought to Queensland in 1935 from Hawaii in an attempt to control the greyback cane beetle, but these greedy pests began eating almost everything *but* the beetle. Lewis' documentary wittily presents this increasingly difficult national problem with a series of illuminating interviews and some amusing 3D effects. GS

▶ With Neil Young.
▶ *Dir, Pro* and *Screenplay* Mark Lewis, *Ph* Toby Oliver, Paul Nichola and Kathryn Milliss, *Pro Des* Daniel C Nyiri, *Ed* Robert DeMaio, *M* Martin Armiger.

Radio Pictures-Kaleidoscope Home Entertainment. 85 mins. USA/Australia. 2010. Rel: 30 Sep 2011. Cert. PG.

Captain America: The First Avenger ★★★

An asthmatic runt determined to fight for his country is given a biological makeover to become Captain America. But Hitler is the least of his problems… More than most superhero extravaganzas, *Captain America* suffers from CGI – computer-generated indigestion. This is due largely to the film's ambitious scope – fantastical armies and weaponry operating in a bygone era – but it does provide the odd fillip. V-Day celebrated in Trafalgar Square is a fleeting pleasure, while a car chase through 1940s Brooklyn is a more extended curio. The film's great weakness, though, is its paucity of thespian delights. JC-W

First edition: Chris Evans in the title role of Joe Johnston's ambitious, indigestible *Captain America: The First Avenger.*

Chris Evans, Tommy Lee Jones, Hugo Weaving, Hayley Atwell, Dominic Cooper, Toby Jones, Stanley Tucci, Neal McDonough, Derek Luke, J J Feild, Michael Brandon, Natalie Dormer, David Bradley, Samuel L. Jackson.

Dir Joe Johnston, *Pro* Kevin Feige, *Screenplay* Christopher Markus and Stephen McFeely, *Ph* Shelly Johnson, *Pro Des* Rick Heinrichs, *Ed* Robert Dalva and Jeffrey Ford, *M* Alan Silvestri, *Cos* Anna B Sheppard.

Marvel-Paramount Pictures.
124 mins. USA. 2011. Rel: 29 July 2011. Cert. 12A.

Carmen 3D ★★★★

Those who can't get to Covent Garden are here given the opportunity to view the Royal Opera's staging of Bizet's popular opera – and in 3D too. It's ably done and, although I do not regard that fine singer Christine Rice as a natural Carmen, she sings and acts well – as does Bryan Hymel as Don José. It remains a stage experience rather than a cinematic one, but it brings Francesca Zambello's production to a whole new public. MS

Christine Rice, Bryan Hymel, Aris Argiris, Maija Kovalevska.

Dir Julian Napier, *Pro* Phil Streather and Tim Wellspring, *Libretto* Henri Meilhac and Ludovic Halévy from Prosper Merimée's novel, *Ph* Sean MacLeod Phillips, *Pro Des* Tanya McCallin, *Ed* Napier and Stroo Oloffson, *M* Georges Bizet.

RealD/Royal Opera House-RealD Inc.
170 mins. UK 2011. Rel: 5 Mar 2011. Cert. PG.

Cavern can wait: Werner Herzog ponders his next move in his mesmerising *Cave of Forgotten Dreams*.

Cars 2 ★★½

The original *Cars* (2006) was such a one-off that a sequel would inevitably come with its set of problems. Inevitably the bar has been raised and, predictably, to diminishing returns. Thus the action is moved from Radiator Springs (in the American Southwest) to Tokyo, Italy and London. And the vehicles are not just anthropomorphised but are transmogrified into geishas, sumo wrestlers and even British royalty. However, bestowing the cars with lavatorial needs is another bladder entirely (we all know cars fart, but…). The sequel's worst error of judgment, though, is to give the original film's least appealing jalopy, Mater (Larry the Cable Guy), centre stage here. JC-W

Voices of Owen Wilson, Larry the Cable Guy, Michael Caine, Emily Mortimer, John Turturro, Eddie Izzard, Jason Isaacs, Thomas Kretschmann, Bonnie Hunt.

Dir John Lasseter and Brad Lewis, *Pro* Denise Ream, *Screenplay* Ben Queen, *Ph* Jeremy Lasky and Sharon Calahan, *Pro Des* Harley Jessup, *Ed* Stephen Schaffer, *M* Michael Giacchino.

Walt Disney/Pixar Animation-Walt Disney.
112 mins. USA. 2011. Rel: 22 July 2011. Cert. U.

Cave of Forgotten Dreams ★★★★

Werner Herzog's documentary embraces 3D to take us into the Chauvet cave in the south of France, containing Paleolithic paintings discovered only in 1994. Public access is severely limited in order to preserve these works created 35,000 years ago, so viewing them here is a rare privilege. It is accompanied by Herzog's own characteristically idiosyncratic commentary, but it's the use of 3D by an acclaimed director which got the film noticed. MS

With Jean Clottes, Julien Monney, Jean-Michel Geneste, Michel Philippe. Narrated by Werner Herzog.

Dir and *Screenplay* Werner Herzog, *Pro* Erik Nelson and Adrienne Ciuffo, *Ph* Peter Zeitlinger, *Ed* Joe Bini and Maya Hawke, *M* Ernst Reijseger.

Werner Herzog Filmproduktion/History Films/Creative Differences/Arte France/More4 etc-Picturehouse Entertainment.
90 mins. Canada/USA/France/UK. 2010. Rel: 25 Mar 2011. Cert U.

Cedar Rapids ★★★

A satire about competitive insurance salesmen attending a convention in Idaho, this finds Ed Helms moving from the mainstream world of *The Hangover* to the kind of comedy that features John C Reilly and aims at a more sophisticated audience. However, comparison with an earlier Fox Searchlight release, 2006's *Thank You For*

Smoking, underlines this script's uncertainties over where to go. The first half is far more effective than the second. MS

❧ Ed Helms, John C Reilly, Anne Heche, Isiah Whitlock Jr, Stephen Root.
❧ *Dir* Miguel Arteta, *Pro* Jim Burke, Alexander Payne and Jim Taylor, *Screenplay* Phil Johnston, *Ph* Chuy Chávez, *Pro Des* Doug Meerdink, *Ed* Eric Kissack, *M* Christophe Beck, *Cos* Hope Hanafin.

Fox Searchlight Pictures/Ad Hominem Enterprises etc-20th Century Fox.
87 mins. USA. 2011. Rel: 29 Apr 2011. Cert. 15.

Cell 211 ★★★★

A new prison guard, as yet unknown to the inmates, is making a preliminary visit and, when caught up in a riot, passes himself off as the inmate of cell 211 in order to survive. This very tough Spanish thriller, ably made by Daniel Monzón, is well acted by Luis Tosar and others. It's essentially a genre piece but does pose questions about prisons as a breeding ground for violence (as witness the film's neat concluding line). (Original title: *Celda 211*) MS

❧ Luis Tosar, Alberto Ammann, Antonio Resines, Marta Etura, Carlos Bardem.
❧ *Dir* Daniel Monzón, *Pro* Emma Lustres, Borja Peña and others, *Screenplay* Jorge Guerricaechevarriá and Monzón from the play *Celda 211* by Francisco Pérez Gandul, *Ph* Carles Gusi, *Art Dir* Antón Laguna, *Ed* Cristina Pastor, *M* Roque Baños, *Cos* Montse Sancho.

Vaca Films/Morena Films/Telecinco Cinema/La Fabrique 2 etc-Optimum Releasing.
113 mins. Spain/France. 2009. Rel: 15 July 2011. Cert. 18.

Chalet Girl ★★

Nineteen-year-old Kim Matthews (Felicity Jones) is thrilled when she gets a job as a chalet girl in a ski resort in the Alps. It's the luxury chalet of successful businessman Richard Masden (Bill Nighy) and it is not too long before Kim begins to fall for Masden's son Jonny (Ed Westwick). To say Phil Traill's mediocre film is predictable is a huge understatement. It's also rather uninspired in its execution, despite the likable performances. GS

❧ Felicity Jones, Ed Westwick, Bill Nighy, Brooke Shields, Bill Bailey, Tamsin Egerton, Sophia Bush.
❧ *Dir* Phil Traill, *Pro* Harriet Rees, Dietmar Güntsche, Wolfgang Behr and Pippa Cross, *Screenplay* Tom Williams, *Ph* Ed Wild, *Pro Des* Benedikt Herforth, *Ed* Robin Sales, *M* Christian Henson, *Cos* Leonie Hartard.

UK Film Council/Aegis Film Fund/Prescience/CrossDay/Kaleidoscope Films/Neue Bioskop Film etc-Momentum Pictures.
96 mins. UK/Germany/Austria. 2011. Rel: 16 Mar 2011. Cert. 12A.

The wrong number: Luis Tosar creates havoc in Daniel Monzón's heart-pounding *Cell 211.*

The Change-Up ★

An uptight lawyer, father and husband (Jason Bateman doing his usual Jason Bateman thing) switches places with his slacker, stoner, shagabout best mate (Ryan Reynolds doing his usual Ryan Reynolds thing) in this tacky body-swap comedy. A film as crass, unimaginative and predictable as this should at least have a bit of charm and a couple more jokes to paper over the cracks. Sure, there are a couple of guilty laughs, and a fair bit of nudity too, if that helps. But it's all so shabby and routine that it really outstays its welcome. MJ

❧ Ryan Reynolds, Jason Bateman, Leslie Mann, Olivia Wilde, Alan Arkin, Mircea Monroe.
❧ *Dir* David Dobkin, *Pro* Dobkin and Neal H Morris, *Screenplay* Jon Lucas and Scott Moore, *Ph* Eric Edwards, *Pro Des* Barry Robison, *Ed* Lee Haxall and Greg Hayden, *M* John Debney, *Cos* Betsy Heimann.

Original Film/Relativity Media/Big Kid Pictures-Universal Pictures International.
112 mins. USA. 2011. Rel: 16 Sep 2011. Cert. 15.

Children of the Revolution ★★★

Shane O'Sullivan's documentary about Ulrike Meinhof and Fusako Shigenobu – who emerged from the student revolutions of 1968 to become leading female revolutionaries of their time – is a deliberately uncomfortable but startling eye-opener. The two women set out to plot world revolution as leaders of the Baader Meinhof Group and the Japanese Red Army. Meanwhile, they found time to have children! The extraordinary thing is that Bettina Röhl and May Shigenobu, now authors and journalists, are the ones who explore the lives of their mothers. This is their candid, disturbingly thought-provoking take on their crazily difficult childhoods, lived on the run or being kidnapped. DW

❧ With May Shigenobu, Bettina Rohl, Astrid Prohl,

C change: Jean Dujardin (without the smile) in Bertrand Blier's provocative and enjoyable *The Clink of Ice*.

in the Room. Telling the story of a promising American politician who became Governor of New York, it records how sexual scandal brought him down while questioning the reliability of some of the evidence and just how the story broke. There's also the question of whether sexual peccadillos should end a politician's career and the film is absorbing for all of its 118 minutes. MS

▶ With Eliot Spitzer, Ken Langone, Peter Elkind, Zana Brazdek, Lloyd Constantine.
▶ *Dir* and *Written by* Alex Gibney, *Pro* Gibney, Jedd Wider and Todd Wider, *Ph* Maryse Alberti, *Ed* Plummy Tucker, *M* Peter Nashel.

Magnolia Pictures/A&E IndieFilms etc-Dogwoof Pictures. 118 mins. USA. 2010. Rel: 4 Mar 2011. Cert. 15.

The Clink of Ice ★★★★

Charles Faulque (Jean Dujardin) is a reclusive writer who spends most of his days endlessly drinking white wine in his remote country home. But his life takes an unexpected turn when he is visited by a stranger (Albert Dupontel), who claims that he is his cancer. Another provocative film from the always controversial and unpredictable Bertrand Blier, which despite its dark subject is an enjoyable and original comedy with a clever twist. (Original title: *Le Bruit des glaçons*) GS

▶ Jean Dujardin, Albert Dupontel, Anne Alvaro, Myriam Boyer, Christa Theret, Audrey Dana, Emile Berling.
▶ *Dir* and *Screenplay* Bertrand Blier, *Pro* David Poirot, *Ph* François Catonné, *Pro Des* Sylvie Salmon, *Ed* Marion Monestier, *Music Supervisor* Valérie Lindon.

Thelma Films/Manchester Films/France 2 Cinéma/ Uni Etoile/Canal+/France Télévision etc-Wild Bunch Distribution. 87 mins. France. 2010. Rel: 4 Feb 2011. Cert. 15.

Cold Fish ★★★

Japan's Sono Sion is a highly idiosyncratic writer-director. However, coming after the extraordinary *Love Exposure* this piece about a shop owner and his wife falling under the influence of a sadistic criminal is less interesting. Both the sex scenes and the horror element smack of exploitation cinema and, despite being well acted and technically accomplished, this is a deeply unpleasant movie. (Original title: *Tsumetai nettaigyo*) MS

▶ Fukikoshi Mitsuru, Denden, Kurosawa Asuka, Kajiwara Hikari, Kagurazaka Megumi.
▶ *Dir* Sono Sion, *Pro* Chiba Yoshinori and Kimura Toshiki, *Screenplay* Sono and Takahashi Yoshiki, *Ph* Kimura Shinya, *Pro Des* Matsuzaka Takashi, *Ed* Ito Junichi, *M* Harada Tomohide, *Cos* Araki Satoe.

Nikkatsu/Sushi Typhoon/Stair Way-Third Window Films. 146 mins. Japan. 2011. Rel: 8 Apr 2011. Cert. 18.

Erika Runge and archive footage of Ulrike Meinhof and Fusako Shigenobu.
▶ *Dir* and *Pro* Shane O'Sullivan, *Ph* Axel Schneppat, Robin Probyn and Bassem Fayad, *Ed* O'Sullivan, Fergal McGrath and Ben Yeates, *M* Giles Packham.

Irish Film Board/Transmission Films/Westdeutscher Rundfunk-Electric Sky Production Company/Film Group/ Entertainment/Films-Distributor. 92 mins. Ireland/UK/Germany. 2010. Rel: 26 Aug 2011. No Cert.

A Christmas Princess ★

When Jules (Katie McGrath) receives an unexpected Christmas invitation from an estranged relative, she travels with her niece and nephew to a European castle. This Cinderella-type fairy tale attempts to be another *Princess Diaries* but lacks its wit, style and production values, while an uncomfortable Roger Moore is a poor substitute for Julie Andrews. The predictable plot is not offensive in any way but is strictly for undemanding little girls. A Christmas turkey! (Original title: *A Princess for Christmas*) GS

▶ Katie McGrath, Roger Moore, Charlotte Salt, Sam Heughan, Travis Turner, Miles Richardson.
▶ *Dir* Michael Damian, *Pro* and *Screenplay* Michael and Janeen Damian, *Ph* Viorel Sergovici Jr, *Pro Des* John Welbanks, *Ed* Seth Flaum, *M* Mark Thomas, *Cos* Oana Draghici.

Riviera Films/Media Pro Studios-Motion Picture Corporation of America. USA. 2011. Rel: 21 Nov 2011. Cert. U.

Client 9 ★★★★

Sub-titled 'The Rise and Fall of Eliot Spitzer', this is an intriguing documentary feature by Alex Gibney, best known for *Enron: The Smartest Guys*

Cold Weather ★★★½

Aaron Katz's third feature finds him back in Portland, Oregon. Even so, it's a whole new world because this new story concerning a missing girl has echoes of Raymond Chandler and references to Conan Doyle. It's amiable and original, but as a thriller it is slight and as a humorous take on amateur sleuths it's less engaging than Ealing's *Hue and Cry* (1947). MS

➤ Cris Lankenau, Trieste Kelly Dunn, Raúl Castillo, Robyn Rikoon, Katy Rothert, Paul Rothert.
➤ *Dir* Aaron Katz, *Pro* Lars Knudsen, Brendan McFadden and others, *Screenplay* Katz, from a story by Katz, McFadden and Ben Stambler, *Ph* Andrew Reed, *Pro Des* Elliott Glick, *Ed* Katz and others, *M* Keegan DeWitt.

Parts and Labor/White Buffalo-Axiom Films.
97 mins. USA. 2009. Rel: 15 Apr 2011. Cert. 15.

Colombiana ★★½

What started out as a sequel to Luc Besson's sublime assassin thriller *Léon* has evolved over the years into something completely different. Well, not that different. If Jean Reno's supernaturally adroit hit man were a leggy, incredibly hot female assassin, then the result may have been Cataleya (Zoe Saldana). A Colombian orphan trained to kill by her uncle in Chicago, Cataleya has only one thing on her mind: to avenge the murder of her parents when she was just nine years old… *Colombiana* delivers pretty routine big bangs for your bucks, but the comely form of Saldana does take up much of the slack. JC-W

➤ Zoe Saldana, Jordi Mollà, Lennie James, Amandla Stenberg, Cliff Curtis, Michael Vartan, Jesse Borrego.
➤ *Dir* Olivier Megaton, *Pro* Luc Besson and Pierre-Ange Le Pogam, *Screenplay* Besson and Robert Mark Kamen, *Ph* Romain Lacourbas, *Pro Des* Patrick Durand, *Ed* Camille Delamarre, *M* Nathaniel Mechaly, *Cos* Olivier Bériot.

Europa Corp./TF1 Films/Grive Prods/Canal +/ CinéCinéma-Entertainment.
107 mins. USA/France. 2011. Rel: 9 Sep 2011. Cert. 15.

The Company Men ★★★

Being a film about redundancy in big business circles, this sounds like the kind of Hollywood movie that will be socially significant and intelligent. But in following the fate of three people who face dismissal the film fails to cohere and to find the right dramatic weight. It boasts a good cast but seems uncertain as to just what it wants to say, missing out on illuminating the heartbreak of unemployment. MS

➤ Ben Affleck, Chris Cooper, Kevin Costner, Tommy Lee Jones, Maria Bello, Suzanne Rico.
➤ *Dir* and *Screenplay* John Wells, *Pro* Claire Rudnick Polstein, Paula Weinstein and Wells, *Ph* Roger Deakins, *Pro Des* David J. Bomba, *Ed* Robert Frazen, *M* Aaron Zigman, *Cos* Lyn Paolo.

The Weinstein Company/Battle Mountain Films/Company Men Productions etc-Universal Pictures International.
104 mins. USA. 2010. Rel: 11 Mar 2011. Cert. 15.

Dead set: Zoe Saldana adds traction to Olivier Megaton's routine *Colombiana.*

Lincoln lawyers: James McAvoy and Tom Wilkinson in Robert Redford's rather traditional *The Conspirator*.

Conan the Barbarian ★½

Thirty years on from Arnold Schwarzenegger's action movie milestone comes a pretender to the throne, a bog standard bashing together of sword-and-sorcery clichés and lacklustre characters starring Hawaiian-born muscle man Jason Momoa. As dull and unsatisfying a remake as 2010's *Clash of the Titans*, only with more boobs and fewer monsters, this puny *Conan* sports sub-standard dialogue, murky 3D visuals, dreary production design, uninspired action choreography and stifling camerawork that lurks so close to the bloodletting, it's hard to see what's going on. By Crom, even *Conan the Destroyer* was better than this. Hell, even *Red Sonja* was better than this. MJ

❯ Jason Momoa, Stephen Lang, Rachel Nichols, Ron Perlman, Rose McGowan, Raad Rawi, and narrator Morgan Freeman.
❯ *Dir* Marcus Nispel, *Pro* Avi and Danny Lerner, Boaz Davidson, John Baldecchi, Joe Gatta, Henry Winterstern etc, *Screenplay* Sean Hood, Thomas Dean Donnelly and Joshua Oppenheimer, based on the character created by Robert E Howard, *Ph* Thomas Kloss, *Pro Des* Chris August, *Ed* Ken Blackwell, *M* Tyler Bates, *Cos* Wendy Partridge.
Millennium Films/Nu Image Films/Paradox Entertainment-Lionsgate.
113 mins. USA. 2011. Rel: 24 Aug 2011. Cert. 15.

Confessions ★★★★

Tetsuya Nakashima's stylish film tells the story of teacher Moriguchi (Takako Matsu), who one day declares to an indifferent seventh grade classroom that she will be resigning following the death of her four-year-old daughter. Then she accuses two of the students of her daughter's death and claims that she has infected the milk which they have just drunk with the HIV virus... This is an excellent film – always unpredictable and with a terrific soundtrack. (Original title: *Kokuhaku*) GS

❯ Takako Matsu, Yoshino Kimura, Masaki Okada, Yukito Nishii, Kaoru Fujiwara.
❯ *Dir* and *Screenplay* Tetsuya Nakashima, based on the novel by Kanae Minato, *Pro* Yûji Ishida, Genki Kawamura, Yoshihiro Kubota and Yukata Suzuki, *Ph* Masakazu Ato and Atsushi Ozawa, *Pro Des* Towako Kuwashima, *Ed* Yoshiyuki Koike, *M* Toyohiko Kanahashi.
DesperaDo/Hakuhodo DY Media Partners/Licri/Toho Company/Sony Music Entertainment etc-Third Window Films.
106 mins. Japan. 2010. Rel: 18 Feb 2011. Cert. 15.

The Conspirator ★★★★

Much better than you may have been led to believe, this is a historical drama convincingly staged and factual. Its subject is the little-known story of what happened to a woman, Mary Surratt, whose son was involved in the plot to assassinate Abraham Lincoln. She herself was put on trial and in questioning the justice of these events the film also invites us to draw parallels with what happened following 9/11. Robert Redford's direction is strictly traditional (why not?) and with a fine cast he gives us an engrossing story. MS

James McAvoy, Robin Wright, Kevin Kline, Evan Rachel Wood, Danny Huston, Colm Meaney, Tom Wilkinson, Johnny Simmons.

Dir Robert Redford, Pro Redford, Greg Shapiro, Bill Holderman and others, Screenplay James Solomon, Ph Newton Thomas Segal, Pro Des Kalina Ivanov, Ed Craig McKay, M Mark Isham, Cos Louise Frogley.

The American Film Company/Wildwood Enterprises-Universal Pictures International.
123 mins. USA. 2011. Rel: 1 July 2011. Cert. 12A.

Contagion ★★★★

Despite having a strong cast in which Matt Damon, Kate Winslet and Jennifer Ehle stand out, Steven Soderbergh's film takes the emphasis away from personal dramas. Instead this ensemble piece adopts a quasi-documentary tone which renders credible this study of attempts to counter a deadly virus of epidemic proportions. This is a thoroughly professional piece of work, but not perhaps one for those who favour escapist entertainment. MS

Matt Damon, Laurence Fishburne, Kate Winslet, Marion Cotillard, Jude Law, Jennifer Ehle, Bryan Cranston, Gwyneth Paltrow, Sanaa Lathan.

Dir Steven Soderbergh, Pro Michael Shamberg, Stacey Sher and Gregory Jacobs, Screenplay Scott Z Burns, Ph Peter Andrews (ie, Steven Soderbergh), Pro Des Howard Cummings, Ed Stephen Mirrione, M Cliff Martinez, Cos Louise Frogley.

Warner Bros Pictures/Participant Media/Double Feature Films/Regency Enterprises etc-Warner Bros.
106 mins. USA/UAE. 011. Rel: 21 Oct 2011. Cert. 12A.

Conviction ★★½

Like the classic Call Northside 777 (1948), this drama based on fact tells of a desperate attempt to prove that a condemned man is innocent of the killing for which he was sentenced to life imprisonment. In Conviction it's a sister (Hilary Swank) concerned over the fate of her brother (Sam Rockwell). But as told here many of the details seem unlikely and a grossly sentimental music score is no help at all. MS

Hilary Swank, Sam Rockwell, Minnie Driver, Melissa Leo, Peter Gallagher, Juliette Lewis.

Dir Tony Goldwyn, Pro Andrew Sugarman, Andrew S Karsch and Goldwyn, Screenplay Pamela Gray, Ph Adriano Goldman, Pro Des Mark Ricker, Ed Jay Cassidy, M Paul Cantelon, Cos Wendy Chuck.

Fox Searchlight Pictures/Omega Entertainment/Longfellow Pictures etc-20th Century Fox.
107 mins. USA/UK. 2010. Rel: 14 Jan 2011. Cert. 15.

Cooking with Stella ★★★½

In spite of the title, this is not another Nina's Heavenly Delights or even The Mistress of Spices. Stella is actually a housekeeper, a local New Delhi girl who works (and cooks) for a Canadian diplomat (Don McKellar) who fancies himself as a chef. The film is more about the clash of

Going viral: Marion Cotillard (centre) in Steven Soderbergh's cerebral thriller Contagion.

Gunfight at the E.T. Corral: Harrison Ford and Daniel Craig in Jon Favreau's daft, genre-jumping *Cowboys & Aliens*.

cultures (Canada vs India) than food, and about the ties that bind people who find themselves out of their respective elements. As Stella, Seema Biswas provides the lion's share of the laughs, although the film never loses its grip on reality. CB

▶ Seema Biswas, Don McKellar, Lisa Ray, Shriya Saran, Maury Chaykin.
▶ *Dir* Dilip Mehta, *Pro* David Hamilton, *Screenplay* Dilip Mehta and Deepa Mehta, *Ph* Giles Nuttgens, *Pro Des* Tamara Deverell, *Ed* Gareth C Scales, *M* Mychael Danna and Amritha Fernandes Bakshi, *Cos* Rashmi Varma.

Mongrel Media/Hamilton-Mehta Productions/BR Films/ Noble Nomad Pictures etc-Mara Pictures. 104 mins. Canada/India. 2009. Rel: 15 Apr 2011. No Cert.

Countdown to Zero ★★★★

Lucy Walker's documentary rightly sends shivers down our spines. The risk of the world ending through a nuclear catastrophe was strongly felt in the 1960s but has now largely slipped to the back of our consciousness. However, this well-assembled film reminds us that the danger is one that we cannot afford to ignore. The message is unrelentingly bleak but that's exactly what makes this essential viewing. MS

▶ With Valerie Plame Wilson, Mikhail Gorbachev, Jimmy Carter, Tony Blair, F W de Klerk.
▶ *Dir* and *Written by* Lucy Walker, *Pro* Lawrence Bender, *Ph* Robert Chappell, Gary Clarke and others, *Ed* Brad Fuller and Brian Johnson, *M* Peter Golub.

Magnolia Pictures/Participant Media/The History Channel etc-Dogwoof Pictures. 89 mins. USA. 2010. Rel: 24 June 2011. Cert. PG.

Country Strong ★★★

This pale echo of the recent *Crazy Heart* is another tale about the country music scene in America. Gwyneth Paltrow is good as a one-

time superstar hoping to get on stage again following a time in rehab and the tale involves four figures in professional and emotional rivalry. Unfortunately the screenplay fails to make convincing sense of the contradictory aspects within the characters. The best scene evokes Judy Garland and occurs in Dallas when a comeback concert goes disastrously wrong. MS

▶ Gwyneth Paltrow, Tim McGraw, Garrett Hedlund, Leighton Meester.
▶ *Dir* and *Screenplay* Shana Feste, *Pro* Jenno Topping and Tobey Maguire, *Ph* John Bailey, *Pro Des* David J Bomba, *Ed* Carol Littleton and Conor O'Neill, *M* Michael Brook, *Cos* Stacey Battat.

Screen Gems/Material Pictures-Sony Pictures Releasing. 117 mins. USA. 2010. Rel: 25 Mar 2011. Cert.12A.

Cowboys & Aliens ★★★

If you thought it was adventurous to cast him as James Bond, how about Daniel Craig as a cowboy? It is a little odd. As a grizzled cattle baron, Harrison Ford seems a bit more at home in the saddle and for the most part this is a standard, rather old-fashioned Western (complete with Keith Carradine as sheriff) – with aliens. It's actually based on the graphic novel of the same name and is a genre-crossing romp that has the good sense not to wink at its audience – and is so daft that you can't help but warm to it. JC-W

▶ Daniel Craig, Harrison Ford, Olivia Wilde, Sam Rockwell, Paul Dano, Clancy Brown, Keith Carradine, Adam Beach, David O'Hara.
▶ *Dir* Jon Favreau, *Pro* Brian Grazer, Ron Howard, Alex Kurtzman, Damon Lindelof, Roberto Orci and Scott Mitchell Rosenberg, *Screenplay* Lindelof, Kurtzman, Orci, Mark Fergus and Hawk Ostby, *Ph* Matthew Libatique, *Pro Des* Scott Chambliss, *Ed* Dan Lebental and Jim May, *M* Harry Gregson-Williams, *Cos* Mary Zophres.

Universal/DreamWorks/Reliance Entertainment/ Relativity Media/Imagine-Paramount Pictures. 118 mins. USA. 2011. Rel: 17 Aug 2011. Cert. 12A.

Crazy, Stupid, Love. ★★★½

Steve Carell commands top billing over a fabulous cast but hands most of the laughs to his co-stars. However, it's not Julianne Moore, Ryan Gosling, Kevin Bacon or even Marisa Tomei who earn the loudest guffaws. Working from a smart, hip screenplay by Dan Fogelman, Emma Stone once again proves that she's the funniest actress of her generation. But there is an enormous cast, a host of issues and themes, jokes, plot strands and side attractions – so much so that one sits in terror of the whole thing collapsing. Thanks to the adroit direction it doesn't, although the film's almost conventional ending may seem a little pat for some. JC-W

Steve Carell, Ryan Gosling, Julianne Moore, Emma Stone, Marisa Tomei, Kevin Bacon, Jonah Bobo, John Carroll Lynch, Analeigh Tipton, Liza Lapira.
Dir Glenn Ficarra and John Requa, Pro Steve Carell and Denise Di Novi, Screenplay Dan Fogelman, Ph Andrew Dunn, Pro Des William Arnold, Ed Lee Haxall, M Christophe Beck and Nick Urata, Cos Dayna Pink.
Carousel Productions-Warner Bros.
117 mins. USA. 2011. Rel: 23 Sep 2011. Cert. 12A.

Dancing Dreams ★★★★½

This is a rare opportunity to see the great choreographer Pina Bausch at work. She selected 40 German teenagers to be part of her dance piece *Contact Zone* and the film follows them through ten months of tough rehearsals. It is a huge challenge for the teenagers as they learn to use movement in order to express themselves and prepare for the nerve-racking opening night. This is a great documentary testament to the amazing talent of Bausch, who sadly died soon after the film was completed. (Original title: *Tanzträume*) GS

With Pina Bausch, Bénédicte Billet, Josephine Ann Endicott.
Dir Rainer Hoffmann and Anne Linsel from a concept by Linsel, Pro Anahita Nazemi and Gerd Haag, Ph Hoffmann, Ed Mike Schlömer, M Juan Llossas.
Real Fiction/Westdeutscher Rundfunk/Arte etc-Soda Pictures.
92 mins. Germany. 2010. Rel: 27 May 2011. No Cert.

The Dead ★★

Not to be confused with John Huston's final film, this is a low-budget British shocker set in Africa in the aftermath of a zombie apocalypse. Once again, the world is coming to an end and the final few survivors are struggling to keep their heads and humanity. As expected, frequent moments of dread are punctuated by lumbering, hungry zombies attacking from all angles. The one distinction this movie has over most other walking dead flicks is its wasteland setting, which is certainly exploited to great effect. Other than that, it is utterly bog standard. MJ

Rob Freeman, Prince David Oseia, David Dontoh, Elizabeth Akinbade, Benjamin C Akpa, Edward Bruce, Stephen Asare Amaning, Kwesi Asmah.
Dir, Screenplay and Ph Howard J Ford and Jon Ford, Pro Howard J Ford and Amir S Moallemi, Pro Des Daniel Gomme, Ed Howard J Ford, M Imran Ahmad.
Indelible Productions/Latitude Films-Anchor Bay Entertainment.
105 mins. UK. 2010. Rel: 2 Sep 2011. Cert. 18.

The Debt ★★

This unpersuasive thriller looks back from the 1990s to Berlin when it was a divided city in the 1960s. We learn of a kidnapping that went awry, but it is later events that lack conviction. However, what makes the film not just bad but offensive is that it

High-Schule Musical: a scene from Rainer Hoffmann and Anne Linsel's documentary *Dancing Dreams*.

An affair to
remember: Tom
Hiddleston and
Rachel Weisz in
Terence Davies'
nostalgic *The
Deep Blue Sea.*

bases an unconvincing story on the real-life horror
of surgeons who committed atrocities in the Nazi
concentration camps. Helen Mirren and Jessica
Chastain do what they can, while in contrast Sam
Worthington, involved in a romantic triangle with
Chastain and Marton Csokas, is wooden. But it's a
tasteless enterprise that does credit to no one. MS

▷ Helen Mirren, Sam Worthington, Jessica Chastain,
Tom Wilkinson, Marton Csokas.
▷ *Dir* John Madden, *Pro* Matthew Vaughn, Kris
Thykeir and others, *Screenplay* Vaughn, Jane Gold
and Peter Straughan, based on the film *Havov*,
Ph Ben Davis, *Pro Des* Jim Clay, *Ed* Alexander Berner,
M Thomas Newman, *Cos* Natalie Ward.

Miramax Films/MARV Films-Buena Vista International.
113 mins. USA/UK/Hungary/Israel. 2010. Rel: 30 Sep
2011. Cert. 15.

The Deep Blue Sea ★★★★

This sympathetic treatment of one of Terence
Rattigan's best plays, set in London around
1950, finds Terence Davies at last working with
actors again and what a great performance he
obtains from Rachel Weisz. She plays a judge's
wife overwhelmed by her passion for a former
war-time pilot whose feelings are genuine but less
intense than hers. Some touches smack more of
Davies than of Rattigan and Tom Hiddleston as
the lover cannot eclipse memories of Kenneth
More on stage, but this is far superior to the
Anatole Litvak film of 1955. MS

▷ Rachel Weisz, Tom Hiddleston, Simon Russell
Beale, Ann Mitchell, Barbara Jefford, Karl Johnson.
▷ *Dir* and *Screenplay* (adapted from the play
by Terence Rattigan) Terence Davies, *Pro* Sean
O'Connor and Kate Ogborn, *Ph* Florian Hoffmeister,
Pro Des James Merifield, *Ed* David Charap, *M* Samuel
Barber, *Cos* Ruth Myers.

UK Film Council/Film4/Camberwell-Fly Films etc-
Artificial Eye.
98 mins. UK. 2011. Rel: 25 Nov 2011. Cert. 12A.

Delhi Belly ★★★

Imran Khan stars as Tashi, a debt-ridden bachelor
planning to dump his scummy flatmates
(Kunaal Roy Kapur and Vir Das) for life with
his fiancée Sonia (Shenaz Treasury). Thanks to
some amazingly complex script contrivances,
they become the prey of a ruthless gangster
and a ring of vicious jewel smugglers. This
ambitious, raunchy, sometimes plain crude
Bollywood comedy-thriller is mostly in English,
aiming effectively at the international audience,
and adroitly orchestrated by director Abhinay
Deo. With plenty of laughs, thrills, likable
performances and some catchy tunes by Ram
Sampath, it's a lot of fun, keeping up a breathless
pace and rarely running out of steam. DW

▷ Imran Khan, Vir Das, Kunaal Roy Kapur, Shenaz
Treasury, Poorna Jaganathan, Kim Bodnia.
▷ *Dir* Abhinay Deo, *Pro* Aamir Khan, Ronnie
Screwvala, Kiran Rao and Jim Furgele, *Screenplay*

Akshat Verma, *Ph* Jason West, *Pro Des* Shashank Tere, *Ed* Huzefa Lokhandwala, *M* Ram Sampath, *Cos Supervisor* Malavika Kashikar.

Aamir Khan Productions/UTV Motion Pictures/Ferocious Attack Cow-UTV Motion Pictures.
103 mins. India. 2011. Rel: 1 July 2011. Cert. 15.

Demons Never Die ★½

Eight London students make a pact to end their lives but then a mysterious masked killer is out to get them before they can fulfil their wishes. This tries to be a British take on *Scream*, but it is all very basic with no real surprises and lacks tension. The acting is OK but ultimately these unlikable and self-pitying characters deserve what they get. GS

‣ Robert Sheehan, Ashley Walters, Tulisa Contostavlos, Jason Maza, Reggie Yates, Jacob Anderson.
‣ *Dir* and *Screenplay* Arjun Rose, *Pro* Rose, Maza, Rhian Williams and Joanne Podmore, *Ph* Toby Moore, *Pro Des* Paul Burns, *Ed* Tim Murrell, *M* The Angel, *Cos* Robert Lever.

S Kids-Exile Media Group.
93 mins. UK. 2011. Rel: 28 Oct 2011. Cert. 15.

The Devil's Double ★★★★

Because he resembled Uday Hussein, son of Saddam, Latif Yahia was forced to act as the tyrant's double for security reasons. Uday was a hideous creature who would pick up girls then drug, rape and kill them for his own pleasure. Latif, however, was quite the opposite, a kind, gentle and religious soul thrust into playing a role he loathed. In the film, based on Latif Yahia's own writings, Dominic Cooper plays both parts to the hilt: portraying the monstrous Uday and the sympathetic Latif with equal credibility. If the result is a tad suspect, the two performances by Cooper make up for any exploitative crudity in the film itself. MHD

‣ Dominic Cooper, Ludivine Sagnier, Raad Rawi, Philip Quast, Mimoun Oaïssa, Khalid Laith, Oona Chaplin, Latif Yahia.
‣ *Dir* Lee Tamahori, *Pro* Paul Breuls, Catherine Vandeleene, Emjay Rechsteiner and Michael John Fedun, *Screenplay* Michael Thomas, from the books by Latif Yahia, *Ph* Sam McCurdy, *Pro Des* Paul Kirby, *Ed* Luis Carballer, *M* Christian Henson, *Cos* Anna B Sheppard.

Staccato Films/Corsan/Corrino Media Corporation-Icon Film Distribution.
109 mins. Belgium/Netherlands. 2011. Rel: 12 Aug 2011. Cert. 18.

The Devil's Rock ★½

This horror film from New Zealand takes place in Guernsey on the eve of D-Day. Two commandos are sent to destroy a German base on the island but they soon discover that it is full of German dead bodies. They can hear piercing screams echoing around the corridors, which, like a magnet, draw them in closer. The story is very similar to *The Bunker* and *Outpost* where crazy Nazis are spooking the place, but here this familiar premise fails to either scare or thrill. GS

‣ Craig Hall, Matthew Sunderland, Gina Varela, Karlos Drinkwater, Luke Hawker, Jessica Grace Smith.
‣ *Dir* Paul Campion, *Pro* Leanne Saunders, *Screenplay* Campion, Paul Finch and Brett Ihaka, from a story by Campion, *Ph* Rob Marsh, *Pro Des* Mary Pike, *Ed* Jeff Hurrell, *M* Andrea Possee, *Cos* Tristan McCallum.

New Zealand Film Commission/Chameleon Pictures/ Devils Rock/Severe Features-Metrodome Distribution.
83 mins. New Zealand. 2011. Rel: 8 July 2011. Cert. 18.

Diary of a Wimpy Kid 2: Rodrick Rules ★★★

It's time for new friends for Greg Heffley (Zachary Gordon) and Rowley (Robert Capron) as they are about to begin seventh grade at school. In the meantime Greg's brother and chief tormentor Rodrick (Devon Bostick) has other plans in store for him despite their parents' feeble attempts to have them bond... An improvement on the original with spot-on casting. Gordon's wimpy kid is more sympathetic this time around while Capron's Rowley steals the show again. GS

‣ Zachary Gordon, Devon Bostick, Rachael Harris, Robert Capron, Steve Zahn, Peyton List.
‣ *Dir* David Bowers, *Pro* Bradford Simpson and Nina Jacobson, *Screenplay* Gabe Sachs and Jeff Judah, based on the book by Jeff Kinney, *Ph* Jack Green, *Pro Des* Brent Thomas, *Ed* Troy Takaki, *M* Edward Shearmur, *Cos* Tish Monaghan.

Fox 2000 Pictures/Color Force-20th Century Fox.
99 mins. USA. 2011. Rel: 27 May 2011. Cert. U.

The Dilemma ★★

Two friends since college are now partners in their own engine design company – bachelor

Double vision: Dominic Cooper as the Son of Saddam (or is he Latif Yahia?) in Lee Tamahori's shocking and fascinating *The Devil's Double*.

Ronny (Vince Vaughn) and the seemingly happily married Nick (Kevin James). Their peaceful and laidback attitude changes when Ronny finds out that Nick's wife Geneva (Winona Ryder) is cheating on him – should he tell him or not? The early, supposedly funny scenes fail miserably but curiously, when the film strikes a more serious tone, it becomes mildly interesting. GS

▶ Vince Vaughn, Kevin James, Winona Ryder, Jennifer Connelly, Channing Tatum, Queen Latifah.
▶ *Dir* Ron Howard, *Pro* Howard, Vaughn and Brian Grazer, *Screenplay* Allan Loeb, *Ph* Salvatore Totino, *Pro Des* Daniel B Clancy, *Ed* Daniel P Hanley and Mike Hill, *M* Lorne Balfe and Hans Zimmer, *Cos* Daniel Orlandi.

Universal Pictures/Imagine Entertainment/Spyglass Entertainment/Wild West Picture Show Productions-Universal Pictures International.
111 mins. USA. 2011. Rel: 21 Jan 2011. Cert. 12A.

Dolphin Tale ★★★

Whatever the original story was that 'inspired' this film, the result is truly moving. *Dolphin Tale* works so well because its narrative embraces three troubled characters, all of whom are redeemed by the willingness of others to fight an impossible cause. And dolphins make good cinema. Throw in the grizzled likes of Morgan Freeman and Kris Kristofferson to pour on the homilies and one has a family film designed to make us all a better person. It's a shame, then, that the production values are so mediocre and the music a little too pervasive. JC-W

▶ Harry Connick Jr, Ashley Judd, Kris Kristofferson, Morgan Freeman, Nathan Gamble, Cozi Zuehlsdorff, Ray McKinnon, Austin Stowell and Winter as herself.

▶ *Dir* Charles Martin Smith, *Pro* Richard Ingber, Broderick Johnson and Andrew A. Kosove, *Screenplay* Karen Janszen and Noam Dromi, *Ph* Karl Walter Lindenlaub, *Pro Des* Michael Corenblith, *Ed* Harvey Rosenstock, *M* Mark Isham, *Cos* Hope Hanafin.

Alcorn Entertainment/Arc Prods-Warner Bros.
112 mins. USA. 2011. Rel: 14 Oct 2011. Cert. U.

Donor Unknown ★★★★½

Jerry Rothwell's remarkable documentary follows 20-year-old JoEllen as she begins a quest to find her sperm donor father and her many half-siblings around the country. Donor 150 is Jeffrey Harrison, a lovable eccentric who lives alone with his four dogs and a pigeon in a trailer parked on Venice Beach, California. This gripping film is an honest and touching account of the children's burning desire to know more about their anonymous donor father and is the perfect companion piece to *The Kids Are All Right*. (Subtitle: 'Adventures in the Sperm Trade') GS

▶ *Dir* and *Ph* Jerry Rothwell, *Pro* Hilary Durman and Al Morrow, *Ed* Alan Mackay, *M* Max de Wardener.

Met Film Production/Redbird-Naked Edge Films.
78 mins. UK/USA. 2010. Rel: 3 June 2011. Cert. 12.

Don't Be Afraid of the Dark ★★

A remake, of sorts, of an obscure but well-regarded TV movie from 1973, *Don't Be Afraid of the Dark* takes place in a creepy, remote Gothic mansion from which normal folk would immediately flee. Not Alex (gaunt Guy Pearce) or his girlfriend Kim (Katie Holmes), though. Nor Alex's emotionally disturbed daughter Sally (Bailee Madison), whose careless explorations immediately unleash scores of tiny, evil, chattering monsters. More terrifying than these malicious mini-demons, however, is the blind stupidity and crass insensitivity of the leading adult characters in this largely scare-free, illogical, ho-hum yarn from producer Guillermo del Toro. MJ

▶ Guy Pearce, Katie Holmes, Bailee Madison, Jack Thompson, Garry McDonald, Julia Blake.
▶ *Dir* Troy Nixey, *Pro* Guillermo del Toro and Mark Johnson, *Screenplay* del Toro and Matthew Robbins, based on Nigel McKeand's 1973 teleplay, *Ph* Oliver Stapleton, *Pro Des* Roger Ford, *Ed* Jill Bilcock, *M* Marco Beltrami and Buck Sanders, *Cos* Wendy Chuck.

Miramax Films/FilmDistrict/Gran Via/Tequila Gang/Necropia-Optimum Releasing.
99 mins. USA/Australia/Mexico. 2010. Rel: 7 Oct 2011. Cert. 15.

Dream House ★★

A capable psychological thriller with a handful of spooky movie stylings, *Dream House* is less notable as art or entertainment than as

The dark night: Katie Holmes feels the chill in Troy Nixey's scare-free *Don't Be Afraid of the Dark*.

the film that witnessed the real-life romantic entanglement of co-stars Daniel Craig and Rachel Weisz. The tale is of a family that moves into a new home with old secrets. Although there are a few decent surprises in store, this Jim Sheridan mystery ultimately mines more familiar territory. "The movie didn't turn out great," said a candid Craig. "But I met my wife. Fair trade." MJ

▶ Daniel Craig, Naomi Watts, Rachel Weisz, Elias Koteas, Marton Csokas, Jane Alexander.
▶ *Dir* Jim Sheridan, *Pro* Daniel Bobker, Ehren Kruger, David C and James G Robinson, *Screenplay* David Loucka, *Ph* Caleb Deschanel, *Pro Des* Carol Spier, *Ed* Glen Scantlebury and Barbara Tulliver, *M* John Debney, *Cos* Delphine White.

Morgan Creek Productions/Cliffjack Motion Pictures-Universal Pictures.
92 mins. USA. 2011. Rel: 25 Nov 2011. Cert. 15.

Dreams of a Life ★★★

Carol Morley's documentary is genuinely concerned about the lonely death of Joyce Carol Vincent in 2003. She died in her London flat but her remains were only found three years later: how could anyone be so cut off from friends, family and society? Interviewees give conflicting views of the Joyce they knew but there are lots of distracting self-conscious re-enactments and loose ends. It's as daring as Andrea Dunbar's *The Arbor* (2010) but not half as successful. MS

▶ Zawe Ashton, Alix Luka-Cain, Neelam Bakshi, Cornell S John.
▶ *Dir* Carol Morley, *Pro* Cairo Cannon and James Mitchell, *Ph* Mary Farbrother and Lynda Hall, *Pro Des* Chris Richmond, *Ed* Chris Wyatt, *M* Barry Adamson, *Cos* Leonie Prendergast.

Film4/UK Film Council/Cannon and Morley Productions/Irish Film Board etc-Dogwoof Pictures.
95 mins. UK/Ireland. 2011. Rel: 16 Dec 2011. Cert. 12A.

Drive ★★★½

The Danish director Nicolas Winding Refn, who gave us *Bronson* (2008), is a filmmaker at the top of his game. Moving to LA, he shows just why the star, Ryan Gosling, chose him. The ever-excellent Carey Mulligan provides the love interest but essentially this is a tough thriller about a man for hire, one who drives for criminals but then gets in out of his depth. Sadly Refn overdoes the violence to the point of getting unintended laughs, but technically this is superb. MS

▶ Ryan Gosling, Carey Mulligan, Bryan Cranston, Ron Perlman, Oscar Isaac, Albert Brooks.
▶ *Dir* Nicolas Winding Refn, *Pro* Marc Platt, Adam Siegel and others, *Screenplay* Hossein Amini, from the novel by James Sallis, *Ph* Newton Thomas Sigel, *Pro Des* Beth Mickle, *Ed* Matthew Newman,

M Cliff Martinez, *Cos* Erin Benach.
FilmDistrict/Marc Platt/Motel Movies etc-Icon Film Distribution.
100 mins. USA. 2011. Rel: 23 Sept 2011. Cert. 18.

Drive Angry 3D ★★★½

The plot is very silly in the best graphic novel tradition and follows the adventures of Milton (Nicolas Cage), who breaks out from Hell in order to stop a vicious cult that murdered his daughter. He has three days before they sacrifice her baby and in his long journey for redemption he is joined by Piper (Amber Heard), a young, sexy waitress. The action is fast and furious, the 3D effects are spectacular and, surprisingly, Cage's humourless performance works. GS

▶ Nicolas Cage, Amber Heard, William Fichtner, Billy Burke, David Morse, Todd Farmer, Charlotte Ross.
▶ *Dir* Patrick Lussier, *Pro* Michael De Luca, René Besson and Adam Fields, *Screenplay* Lussier and Todd Farmer, *Ph* Brian Pearson, *Pro Des* Nathan Amondson, *Ed* Devon C Lussier and Patrick Lussier, *M* Michael Wandmacher, *Cos* Mary E McLeod.

Summit Entertainment/Millennium Films/Michael De Luca Productions/Nu Image/Saturn Films-Lionsgate.
104 mins. USA. 2011. Rel: 25 Feb 2011. Cert. 18.

Driving force: Ryan Gosling models that iconic jacket in Nicolas Winding Refn's elegiac and extraordinarily gripping *Drive*.

The Eagle ★★½

Roman soldier Marcus Aquila (Channing Tatum) begins a dangerous mission in order to solve the mystery behind his father's disappearance and that of his emblem – the Eagle of the Ninth. He goes north of Hadrian's Wall into the unknown land of Caledonia where he befriends Esca (Jamie Bell), a proud Briton who has been enslaved by the Romans. This is an ambitious epic, beautifully filmed, but the dialogue never convinces and it has homoerotic undertones which to its detriment are never explored. GS

▶ Channing Tatum, Jamie Bell, Donald Sutherland, Paul Ritter, Julian Lewis Jones, Douglas Henshall, Mark Strong.
▶ *Dir* Kevin MacDonald, *Pro* Duncan Kenworthy, *Screenplay* Jeremy Brock, based on the novel by Rosemary Sutcliff, *Ph* Anthony Dod Mantle, *Pro Des* Michael Carlin, *Ed* Justine Wright, *M* Atli Örvarsson, *Cos* Michael O'Connor.

Focus Features/Film4/Toledo Productions-Universal Pictures International.
114 mins. UK/USA. 2011. Rel: 25 Mar 2011. Cert. 12A.

Eleanor's Secret ★★★

An eccentric, book-loving aunt dies. She bequeaths her library to young Natanaël, who finds the characters in children's literature looking to him for protection. Nat is shrunk by the Wicked Fairy and, when his parents start selling the books, he has to set off on a quest to save his tiny friends, like Alice, Peter Pan, Sleeping Beauty, Red Riding Hood and Pinocchio. This involves learning to recite a magical phrase to save the books from a greedy antiques dealer. It's an enchanting fairytale and a gorgeous looking film – Rebecca Dautremer's drawings are wonderful, a picture book come alive, and the French animation will delight kids and adults alike. (Original title: *Kérity, la maison des contes*) DW

▶ The voices of Paul Bandey, Pascal Berger, Lorànt Deutsch, Joanne Farrel, Christine Flowers, Jeanne Moreau.

Before there was Kindle: a scene from Dominique Monféry's delightfully bookish *Eleanor's Secret*.

▶ *Dir* Dominique Monféry, *Pro* Jean-Pierre Quenet, Jean-Baptiste Lère and Anne-Sophie Vanhollebeke, *Screenplay* Anik Le Ray, Murielle Canta and Alexandre Révérand, based on a story by Le Ray, *Pro Des* Rebecca Dautremer and Richard Despres, *Ed* Cédric Chauveau, *M* Christophe Héral.

Gaumont-Alphanim/Lanterna Magica/Canal+/Cinéart/ Haut et Court/StudioCanal etc-Soda Pictures.
80 mins. France/Italy. 2009. Rel: 2 Mar 2011. Cert. U.

Elite Squad: The Enemy Within ★★★½

In the original *Elite Squad* (2007), José Padilha created a commercially successful drama about drug dealers in Rio de Janeiro. He portrayed corruption in the Special Police Operations Battalion too, but the film's attitudes seemed confused and the characters totally unsympathetic. This sequel is superior and, set ten years later, again deals with corruption. The action is well staged, but it lacks the stature of Padilha's documentary *Bus 174* (2002) and the subtitles come so thick and fast that it's difficult to keep up. (Original title: *Tropa de elite 2 – O inimigo agora è outro*) MS

▶ Wagner Moura, Irandhir Santos, André Ramiro, María Ribeiro, Seu Jorge, Milhem Cortaz.
▶ *Dir* José Padilha, *Pro* Marcos Prado and Padilha, *Screenplay* Bráulio Mantovani and Padilha from a story by Padilha and others, *Ph* Lula Carvalho, *Ed* Daniel Rezende, *M* Pedro Bromfman, *Cos* Cláudia Kopke.

Zazen Produções/Feijão Filmes/RioFilme/Globo Filmes etc-Revolver Entertainment.
115 mins. Brazil. 2010. Rel: 12 Aug 2011. Cert. 18.

Episode 50 ★

There's more paranormal activity as rival crews of psychic investigators team up for the first time for a special TV show, the season climax of Episode 50. Though one lot are secular sceptics seeking to expose the truth behind the myths about ghosts, the film is naturally on the side of the religious believers when they investigate a haunted institute and make contact with a deadly spirit. Some lamentable acting destroys any attempt to breathe life into such a threadbare idea. The lack of tension, feebly staged attempts at scares and annoyingly distracting score are the icing on a stale cake. DW

▶ Josh Folan, Chris Perry, Natalie Wetta, Keithen Hergott, Eleanor Wilson.
▶ *Dir* Joe Smalley and Tess Smalley, *Screenplay* Ian Holt from a story by Joe and Tess Smalley, *Ph* Oliver Cary, *Ed* Damian Drago, *M* Timothy Andrew Edwards.

Compound B/Impaler Entertainment-Metrodome Distribution.
78 mins. USA. 2011. Rel: 16 Sep 2011. Cert. 15.

Essential Killing ★★★★

This drama from the Polish director Jerzy Skolimowski is a visual tour-de-force. With Vincent Gallo as his lead actor, Skolimowski takes on the challenge of making the audience identify with a Muslim who had been forced to join the Taliban and is now a terrorist on the run in Europe, a fugitive who has escaped following capture and interrogation. Somewhat minimalist but undoubtedly intense, this film is within its limits something of a triumph. MS

▶ Vincent Gallo, Emmanuelle Seigner, Zach Cohen, Iftach Ofir.
▶ *Dir* Jerzy Skolimowski, *Pro* and *Screenplay* Ewa Piaskowska and Skolimowski, *Ph* Adam Sikora, *Pro Des* Joanna Kaczynska, *Ed* Réka Lemhényi and others, *M* Pawel Mykietyn, *Cos* Anne Hamre.

A Jeremy Thomas presentation/Skopia Film etc-Artificial Eye.
84 mins. Poland/Norway/Ireland/Hungary. 2010. Rel: 1 Apr 2011. Cert. 15.

Everything Must Go ★★★½

Starring Will Ferrell in an untypical role as an alcoholic deserted by his wife and struggling to stay on the wagon, this highly individual work from Dan Rush has its origins in a very short story by Raymond Carver. On film it seems overextended, more sentimental than true Carver, and prone to add the occasional joke for Ferrell's fans. Even so, it's far from ineffective and there's lovely work from Rebecca Hall (as a sympathetic neighbour) and Laura Dern (as an old flame). MS

▶ Will Ferrell, Rebecca Hall, Christopher C J Wallace, Michael Peña, Laura Dern.
▶ *Dir* and *Screenplay* (based on the short story *Why Don't You Dance?* by Raymond Carver) Dan Rush, *Pro* Marty Bowen and Wyck Godfrey, *Ph* Michael Barrett, *Pro Des* Kara Lindstrom, *Ed* Sandra Adair, *M* David Thom, *Cos* Mark Bridges.

Temple Hill Entertainment/Cowtown Cinema Ventures etc-G2 Pictures.
97 mins. USA. 2011. Rel: 14 Oct 2011. Cert. 15.

Everywhere and Nowhere ★★★

Young British Asian Ash (James Floyd) attempts to find his identity in modern-day London and is torn between his family's old-fashioned traditions and his passion for DJ'ing and clubbing. His friends are in a similar position – they want it all right now – while, according to them, their parents live on a different planet. Surprisingly, this familiar tale works, especially in the first half, but sadly, as the film reaches its climax, it becomes melodramatic and clichéd. GS

▶ James Floyd, Adam Deacon, Amber Rose Revah, Katia Winter, Alyy Khan, Shivani Ghai, Saeed Jaffrey, Art Malik, Sophie Berenice.
▶ *Dir* Menhaj Huda, *Pro* Sam Tromans, *Screenplay*

Hard sale: Will Ferrell in Dan Rush's overextended and sentimental *Everything Must Go.*

The great escapade: Louise Bourgoin in Luc Besson's *The Extraordinary Adventures of Adèle Blanc-Sec.*

Huda, Gurpreet Bhatti and Nazrin Choudhury, from a story by Huda, *Ph* Brian Tufano, *Pro Des* Murray McKeown, *Ed* Stuart Gazzard, *M* The Angel, *Cos* Matthew Price.

Arena Productions/Foton Films/Prime Focus-Mara Pictures.

96 mins. UK. 2011. Rel: 6 May 2011. Cert. 15.

The Extraordinary Adventures of Adèle Blanc-Sec ★★★★

The spirited Louise Bourgoin plays the intrepid Adèle in Luc Besson's fun movie derived from the comic books by Jacques Tardi. A comic policeman, a deadly pterodactyl and a mummified body brought to Paris from Egypt all play a part in these period adventures set in 1912. It's more pastiche than parody and comes with excellent production values, but fans of Mathieu Amalric may be disconcerted to find him unrecognisable when made up as the villain. (Original title: *Les Aventures extraordinaires d'Adèle Blanc-Sec*) MS

▶ Louise Bourgoin, Gilles Lellouche, Mathieu Amalric, Jacky Nercessian, Jean-Paul Rouve.
▶ *Dir* and *Screenplay* (from the comic books by Tardi) Luc Besson, *Pro* Virginie Besson-Silla, *Ph* Thierry Arbogast, *Art Dir* Hugues Tissandier, *Ed* Julien Rey, *M* Eric Serra, *Cos* Olivier Beriot.

EuropaCorp/TF1 Films Production/Canal+ etc-Optimum Releasing.

107 mins. France. 2010. Rel: 22 Apr 2011. Cert. 12A.

Fair Game ★★★★½

This under-rated film is built around Valerie Plame (the excellent Naomi Watts), who – and this is a true story – worked as an undercover officer for the CIA but was targeted as fair game by the authorities after her husband (Sean Penn) wrote an article that failed to support the American government's stance on Iraq's Weapons of Mass Destruction. The strains on their marriage are brilliantly conveyed and if you liked *In the Valley of Elah* (2007) you should like this. The camera movement is occasionally excessive but this is social/political comment at its most powerful. MS

▶ Naomi Watts, Sean Penn, Sam Shepard, Noah Emmerich, David Andrews, Michael Kelly.
▶ *Dir* and *Ph* Doug Liman, *Pro* Bill Pohlad, Jez Butterworth, Liman and others, *Screenplay* Jez and John-Henry Butterworth based on the books *The Politics of Truth* by Joseph Wilson and *Fair Game* by Valerie Plame Wilson, *Pro Des* Jess Gonchor, *Ed* Christopher Tellefsen, *M* John Powell, *Cos* Cindy Evans.

River Road Entertainment/Participant Media etc-E1 Entertainment UK.

108 mins. USA/United Arab Emirates. 2010. Rel: 11 Mar 2011. Cert. 12A.

Farewell ★★★½

A factual spy story with a difference, this film tells of a KGB Colonel who in 1981 decided that the right action for a true Russian patriot was to pass secret information to the Americans. As presented here, however, there's often a fictional feel to events and that makes it inferior to Christian Carion's previous film *Merry Christmas* (2005). Fellow director Emir Kusturica proves to be a rather stilted actor in the central role, but the events depicted are fascinating and Guillaume Canet gives valuable support. (Original title: *L'Affaire Farewell*) MS

▶ Emir Kusturica, Guillaume Canet, Alexandra Maria Lara, Ingeborga Dapkunaite, Willem Dafoe.
▶ *Dir* Christian Carion, *Pro* Christophe Rossignon and others, *Screenplay* Eric Raynaud with Carion based on Serguei Kostine's book *Bonjour Farewell*, *Ph* Walther Vanden Ende, *Art Dir* Jean-Michel Simonet, *Ed* Andréa Sedlacková, *M* Clint Mansell, *Cos* Corinne Jorry.
Nord-Ouest Films/Pathé/France 2 Cinéma etc-The Works. 113 mins. France. 2009. Rel: 29 Apr 2011. Cert. 12A.

Fast Five ★★★

In a spectacular ambush, former FBI agent Brian O'Conner (Paul Walker) springs Dom Toretto (Vin Diesel) from a prison bus. Hiding out in Rio de Janeiro, they set about planning a $100,000,000 heist – while being hunted by a formidable DSS agent (Dwayne Johnson)… There are a lot of 'how comes?' and 'what the hecks?' in this testosteronic joyride, but it sure does kick ass. As a muscular cartoon, *Fast Five* boasts some extraordinarily beautiful women, some very big biceps and a lot of very hot cars. Just don't go expecting rationale. (Alternative title: *Fast & Furious 5*) JC-W

▶ Vin Diesel, Paul Walker, Dwayne Johnson, Jordana Brewster, Tyrese Gibson, Chris 'Ludacris' Bridges, Joaquim de Almeida, Gal Gadot, Elsa Pataky, Eva Mendes.
▶ *Dir* Justin Lin, *Pro* Neal H. Moritz, Vin Diesel and Michael Fottrell, *Screenplay* Chris Morgan, *Ph* Stephen F. Windon, *Pro Des* Peter Wenham, *Ed* Kelly Matsumoto, Fred Raskin and Christian Wagner, *M* Brian Tyler, *Cos* Sanja Milkovic Hays.
Universal/Original Film/One Race Films-Universal. 130 mins. USA. 2011. Rel: 21 Apr 2011. Cert. 12A.

Fast Romance ★★★

Romantic stories interweave appealingly against a vital soundtrack in the unlikely, but beautifully shot, setting of Glasgow, where seven very different friends try to find love by trying something new. One night of speed dating will change their lives forever! William Ruane is excellent as lonely postman and videogame addict Gordo who's in love with café girl Nadine (Jo Freer), while Lesley Hart's dithering Lorna and Sarah McCardie's man-eating Susan are also striking creations. There's lively acting, a nice pace and a good heart in this fresh and amusing low-budgeter. It makes a welcome change, showing a nicer, softer side of Scotland than we usually get in movies. DW

▶ William Ruane, Jo Freer, Derek Munn, Lesley Hart, Sarah McCardie, Lawrence Crawford, Lynne McKelvey, Michael Howard.
▶ *Dir* Carter Ferguson, *Pro* Amanda Verlaque, *Screenplay* Debbie May and James McCreadie, *Ph* Ross Gerry, *Art Dir* Craig Reed, *Ed* Fiona Cairns, *M* Gordon Dougall, Nigel Dunn and Stephen Wright, *Cos* Sarah Michael.
Ickleflix Productions-Ickleflix Ltd. 97 mins. UK. 2011. Rel: 1 July 2011. Cert. 15.

Chest pains: Vin Diesel and The Rock, er Dwayne Johnson, swap shtick in Justin Lin's muscular *Fast Five*.

Faster ★★

In this revenge action thriller Dwayne Johnson plays Driver, a man on a mission to avenge the murder of his brother during a failed bank robbery that led to Driver's ten-year imprisonment. Nothing will stand in his way, not even bullets fired at his brain. This is not a superhero film, more like a Western in the style of *The Good, the Bad and the Ugly* but without any of its craft and sophistication. Fast but hollow. GS

‣ Dwayne Johnson, Billy Bob Thornton, Maggie Grace, Tom Berenger, Carla Gugino, Courtney Gains.
‣ *Dir* George Tillman Jr, *Pro* Tony Gayton, Robert Teitel, Martin Shafer and Liz Glotzer, *Screenplay* Joe Gayton and Tony Gayton, *Ph* Michael Grady, *Pro Des* David Lazan, *Ed* Dirk Westervelt, *M* Clint Mansell, *Cos* Salvador Pérez Jr.

TriStar Pictures/CBS Films/Castle Rock Entertainment/ State Street Pictures-TriStar Pictures.
98 mins. USA. 2010. Rel: 25 Mar 2011. Cert. 15.

Fight cub: Mark Wahlberg as Micky Ward in David O Russell's gritty if conventional *The Fighter.*

The Fighter ★★★½

Coming from director David O Russell, who once made such individual works as *Spanking the Monkey* (1994), this is a surprisingly conventional boxing saga taken from real life. However, since the boxer, Micky Ward (Mark Wahlberg), is dominated by his mother (Melissa Leo) and half-brother (Christian Bale), it's also a family drama about a man needing to assert himself. Wahlberg and Leo are excellent but I found Bale's Oscar-winning performance self-conscious and indulgent in a Methodic way. MS

‣ Mark Wahlberg, Christian Bale, Amy Adams, Melissa Leo, Mickey O'Keefe.
‣ *Dir* David O Russell, *Pro* David Hoberman, Mark Wahlberg and others, *Screenplay* Scott Silver, Paul Tamasy and Eric Johnson, from a story by Keith Dorrington and others, *Ph* Hoyte van Hoytema, *Pro Des* Judy Becker, *Ed* Pamela Martin, *M* Michael Brook, *Cos* Mark Bridges.

Paramount Pictures/Relativity Media/The Weinstein Company etc-Momentum Pictures.
116 mins. USA. 2010. Rel: 2 Feb 2011. Cert. 15.

Film Socialisme ★★½

Being an octogenarian now hasn't prevented Jean-Luc Godard from offering us a kind of essay film which finds him at his most extreme. On the plus side it's well photographed, with every shot perfectly composed, and it could be the work of no other filmmaker. Against that, it seems to express the impossibility of communicating ideas all too potently. Incomplete or absent subtitles (as requested by Godard) add to this and by the close only Godard fanatics will escape boredom. MS

‣ Jean-Marc Stehlé, Agatha Couture, Mathias Domahidy, Quentin Grosset, Patti Smith.
‣ *Dir* and *Screenplay* Jean-Luc Godard, *Pro* Ruth Waldburger and Alain Sarde, *Ph* Fabrice Arago and Paul Grivas.

Vega Film/Wild Bunch etc-New Wave Films.
102 mins. Switzerland/France. 2010. Rel: 8 July 2011. Cert. PG.

Final Destination 5 ★★★★

After a premonition Sam (Nicholas D'Agosto) warns his fellow bus passengers that the bridge they are approaching is about to collapse. He convinces most of his friends and some others to leave the bus just before the calamity but, having cheated death, this group of 'lucky ones' soon find themselves in more horrifying circumstances. Surprisingly the over-familiar premise works well here, with some decent 3D effects, while director Steven Quale delivers nail-biting set-pieces and concludes the series with a bang! GS

‣ Nicholas D'Agosto, Emma Bell, Miles Fisher, Arlen Escarpeta, David Koechner, Tony Todd.
‣ *Dir* Steven Quale, *Pro* Craig Perry and Warren Zide, *Screenplay* Eric Heisserer, based on characters created by Jeffrey Reddick, *Ph* Brian Pearson, *Pro Des* David Sandefur, *Ed* Eric Sears, *M* Bryan Tyler, *Cos* Jori Woodman.

New Line Cinema/Practical Pictures/Jellystone Films/
Zide-Warner Bros Pictures.
92 mins. USA/Canada. 2011. Rel: 26 Aug 2011. Cert. 15.

The Final Sacrifice ★★★

This film, allegedly seven years in the making,
was obviously a labour of love for director Ari
Taub. He wanted to tell a World War II story about
one of the few times when the Italians sided
with Germany in a final bid against the allies of
northern Italy, when local farmers and huntsmen
gave as good as they got, killing the Germans and
letting their fellow countrymen flee. Supposedly
based on letters found on the front line, the film
takes an ironic, if not always entirely satisfactory,
view of a long-forgotten part of the war. (Original
title: *Last Letters from Monte Rosa*) PL

▶ Daniel Asher, C J Barkus, Gianluca Bianco, Davidé
Borella, Achim Buchner.
▶ *Dir* Ari Taub, *Pro* Curtis Mattikow, *Screenplay* and
Ph Caio Ribeiro, *Pro Des* Joanna M Wright, *Ed* Taub
and Ribeiro, *M* Sergei Dreznin, *Cos* Cyrus Lee and
Charles Nohal.

Hit & Run Productions-Metrodome.
88 mins. USA. 2010. Rel: 14 Jan 2011. Cert. 15.

Fire in Babylon ★★★½

This film may or may not appeal solely to fans
of cricket, but Stevan Riley's documentary on
the West Indies team in the 1970s makes for
fascinating viewing either way. It gets across the
passion felt by the players particularly when
they were beaten by Australia, after which they
determined to improve their game. Under Viv
Richards' guidance they became one of the most
gifted teams in cricketing history and at the same
time struck a final blow against worldwide racial
prejudice. You may not share their passion for the
game, but their passion for life is undeniable. MHD

▶ With Colin Croft, Jeffrey Dujon, Joel Garner,
Lance Gibbs, Tony Greig, Clive Lloyd, Viv Richards
etc, commentary by Richie Benaud and Geoffrey
Boycott, and archive film of Ian Botham, Brian
Close, David Gower, David Frost etc.
▶ *Dir* and *Screenplay* Stevan Riley, *Pro* John Battsek
and Charles Steel, *Ph* Stuart Bentley and Balazs
Bolygo, *Ed* Ed Stevens.

Cowboy Films/Passion Pictures/ECN Motion Pictures/E
& G Productions etc-Revolver Entertainment.
87 mins. UK. 2010. Rel: 20 May 2011. Cert. 12.

First Night ★★★

Music, laughter and romance are on the lite-
bite menu again as industrialist and frustrated
amateur singer Richard E Grant decides to stage
opera at his country estate to help him woo
conductor Sarah Brightman. Thanks to an idea by
the late John Mortimer, Mozart's *Così fan tutte* is
the work in question, and it comes as no surprise
that the story involves life imitating art. The
film is thoroughly engaging and Grant is in his

Fatal attractions:
Emma Bell,
Nicholas D'Agosto
and Miles Fisher
in Ari Taub's
nail-biting *Final
Destination 5.*

Fancy free: Kenny Wormald and Julianne Hough in Craig Brewer's cheesy, slavishly loyal *Footloose*.

element in a highly amusing turn that's as suave and witty as it is hammy. All the sitcom-style performances are ideal and the actors come close to persuading you they're actually singing. DW

▶ Richard E Grant, Sarah Brightman, Jane How, Nigel Lindsay, Julian Ovenden, Susannah Fielding, Oliver Dimsdale, Tessa Peake-Jones.
▶ *Dir* Christopher Menaul, *Pro* Stephen Evans and Selwyn Roberts, *Screenplay* Menaul and Jeremy Sams, *Ph* Tim Palmer, *Pro Des* Stuart Walker, *Ed* St John O'Rorke, *M* Morgan Pochin, *Cos* Phoebe De Gaye.

Scorpio Films-SC Films International.
116 mins. UK. 2010. Rel: 14 Oct 2011. Cert. 15.

The First Grader ★

This African tale based on fact is about an octogenarian in Kenya claiming the right to participate in the government's offer of free education for all. It's intended to be heartwarming and it's competently made. Nevertheless, the film is deeply objectionable because the hero's past brings in his involvement with the Mau Mau and it totally falsifies history by playing down their violent actions. The film wilfully misleads and is to my mind a disgrace. MS

▶ Naomie Harris, Oliver Litondo, Tony Kgoroge, Vusumuzi Michael Kunene.
▶ *Dir* Justin Chadwick, *Pro* David M. Thompson, Sam Feuer and Richard Harding, *Screenplay* Ann Peacock, *Ph* Rob Hardy, *Pro Des* Vittoria Sogno, *Ed* Paul Knight, *M* Alex Heffes, *Cos* Sophie Oprisano.

BBC Films/UK Film Council/Sixth Sense Productions/ Blue Sky Films/Origin Pictures etc-Soda Pictures.
103 mins. UK/South Africa/France. 2010. Rel: 24 June 2011. Cert. 12A.

The Flaw ★★½

This is a documentary about the people who became victims after the financial crisis brought down banks in America. Unfortunately, this film by David Sington, who did such a good job on *In the Shadow of the Moon* (2006), is dry as dust with talking heads better suited to TV. It's also redundant since *Inside Job* [qv] tackled the subject in a far more rewarding way. MS

▶ With Robert Shiller, Robert Frank, Joseph Stiglitz, Dan Ariely, Robert Wade, Sarah Ludwig.
▶ *Dir* David Sington, *Ph* Clive North, *Ed* David Fairhead, *M* Philip Sheppard.

Studio Lambert/Dartmouth Films etc-Studio Lambert.
82 mins. UK. 2010. Rel: 3 June 2011. Cert. U.

Flying Monsters 3D ★★★★

This striking documentary is immaculately researched by David Attenborough, whose immense enthusiasm about his project is infectious. He is articulate in explaining that many millions of years ago serpents developed wings and became the fearsome pterosaurs, who ruled the skies before developing into pterodactyls and vanishing after a meteor crashed into the earth. This illuminating 3D experience is only 40 minutes long and is definitely worth the trip to IMAX. GS

▶ With David Attenborough and Douglas A Lawson.
▶ *Dir* Matthew Dyas, *Pro* Anthony Geffen, *Writer* David Attenborough, *Ph* Tim Cragg, *Art Dir* Humphrey Bangham, *Ed* Peter Miller, *M* Joel Douek.

Atlantic Productions-Sky Television.
40 mins. UK. 2011. Rel: 6 May 2011. Cert. PG.

Footloose ★★

Let us not forget that the first *Footloose* (1984) was pretty conventional. The remake, from the director of *Hustle & Flow*, no less, is slavishly loyal to the original, down to reproducing the steps and costumes. The language is a little rougher, Dennis Quaid more credible as the fire-and-brimstone preacher and Kenny Wormald less edgy than Kevin Bacon as the rebellious city kid Ren McCormack. But the cheese is still darn thick, including the cheddarest smooch of the year (against a setting sun). So, *Footloose* fans will love it. JC-W

▶ Kenny Wormald, Julianne Hough, Andie MacDowell, Dennis Quaid, Miles Teller, Ray McKinnon, Kim Dickens.
▶ *Dir* Craig Brewer, *Pro* Craig Zadan, Neil Meron, Dylan Sellers and Brad Weston, *Screenplay* Brewer and Dean Pitchford, *Ph* Amelia Vincent, *Pro Des* Jon Gary Steele, *Ed* Billy Fox, *M* Deborah Lurie, *Cos* Laura Jean Shannon, *Choreography* Jamal Sims.

Paramount/Spyglass Entertainment/Dylan Sellers Prods/

Zadan/Meron/Weston Pictures/MTV Films-Paramount Pictures.
113 mins. USA. 2011. Rel: 14 Oct 2011. Cert. 12A.

Forget Me Not ★★

When Will, a suicidal musician (Tobias Menzies), meets Eve, a free-spirited barmaid (Genevieve O'Reilly), they spend an evening together walking around London. They take a route that American filmmakers often follow, from Farringdon to the London Eye via Tower Bridge before crossing Westminster Bridge for Liberty's. The actors are fine in this feeble attempt to be another *Before Sunrise* but are let down by an underdeveloped script. The only highlight is Gemma Jones' excellent cameo as Eve's proud grandmother, determined to keep her dignity in a nursing home. GS

❧ Tobias Menzies, Genevieve O'Reilly, Gemma Jones, John Carlisle, Nigel Cooke, Ben Farrow.
❧ *Dir* Alexander Holt and Lance Roehrig, *Pro* Rebecca Long, *Screenplay* Mark Underwood, from a story by Underwood, Long and Steve Spence, *Ph* Shane Daly, *Pro Des* Anastasia Portas, *Ed* Kant Pan, *M* Michael J McEvoy, *Cos* Matthew Price.
Quicksilver Films-Kaleidoscope.
93 mins. UK. 2010. Rel: 6 May 2011. Cert. 15.

Four ★★★

This low-budget Brit thriller puts a slick, fresh gloss on a familiar plot: man hires detective to kidnap his wife's lover and to take him to a remote warehouse to scare and hurt him. Despite being made for £500,000 on one location in 17 days, this is a thoroughly professional, well-shot movie. There's plenty of tension, effectively laced with sly humour, as the anxiety factor mounts high on the twisty road to a satisfying conclusion. Heading the good cast, Martin Compston makes a strong impact as the lover and Sean Pertwee, as the sinister detective, slices the menacing ham as only he can. Well done, debut filmmaker John Langridge. DW

❧ Martin Compston, Craig Conway, Sean Pertwee, Kierston Wareing, George Morris.
❧ *Dir* John Langridge, *Pro* and *M* Raiomond Mirza, *Screenplay* Paul Chronnell, *Ph* Adrian Brown, *Pro Des* James Corker, *Ed* Langridge and Ben King, *Cos* Juliette Digonnet.
Oh My! Productions-High Fliers Films plc.
85 mins. UK. 2011. Rel: 21 Oct 2011. Cert. 15.

Four Days Inside Guantanamo ★★★★

The four days occurred in 2003 when Omar Ahmed Khadr was questioned at length. Despite having an Afghan father, he was himself Canadian, as were his interrogators, so he was misguidedly expecting some degree of understanding. Earlier he had been questioned and tortured at Bagram Air Force base regarding his involvement in fighting at the age of 15 in circumstances which had led the Americans to accuse him of being a war criminal. The footage from Guantanamo and the comments upon it are certainly not cinematic, but as an important, fair-minded record of events this is admirable. MS

❧ With Dr Raul Berdichevsky, Gar Pardy, Damien Corsetti.
❧ *Dir, Pro, written* and *filmed by* Luc Côté and Patricio Henriquez, *Ed* Andrea Henriquez.
Les Films Adobe Inc. etc-Dogwoof Pictures.
100 mins. Canada. 2010. Rel: 7 Oct 2011. Cert. 15.

Friends with Benefits ★★

As no-strings-attached bonking buddies, Justin Timberlake and Mila Kunis strain to jostle the parameters of the multiplex sex comedy. And while there's plenty of sex – the glossy, smutty, under-the-sheets kind of Hollywood sex – there's little comedy. The problem is that the high-flying, airbrushed types embodied by Justin and Mila have no grounding in reality. And while their characters criticise the cheesy excesses of the Hollywood rom-com, their own film indulges in the same superficial tropes. As a soft drink, it's the celluloid equivalent of a Red Bull: energetic, sweet, sticky and transitory. JC-W

❧ Justin Timberlake, Mila Kunis, Patricia Clarkson, Jenna Elfman, Bryan Greenberg, Richard Jenkins, Woody Harrelson, Emma Stone, Jason Segel, Rashida Jones.
❧ *Dir* Will Gluck, *Pro* Gluck, Liz Glotzer, Martin Shafer, Jerry Zucker and Janet Zucker, *Screenplay* Gluck, Keith Merryman and David A Newman, *Ph* Michael Grady, *Pro Des* Marcia Hinds, *Ed* Tia Nolan, *M* Halli Cauthery, *Cos* Renee Ehrlich Kalfus.
Screen Gems/Castle Rock/Zucker Prods/Olive Bridge Entertainment-Sony.
109 mins. USA. 2011. Rel: 9 Sep 2011. Cert. 15.

When Justin Slept with Mila: Ms Kunis and Mr Timberlake in Will Gluck's sweet and sticky *Friends with Benefits*.

Fright Night ★★★

It will be difficult for those who adored the 1985 *Fright Night* – which at the time seemed so fresh and ferociously funny – to view the remake in a kindly light. However, the reality is that most people who see the new film will be unfamiliar with the original. On that basis, then, the 3D version is a reasonably engaging, if familiar, horror-comic with several nice touches of throwaway humour. There are also some choice one-liners and striking aerial shots of suburban New Mexico courtesy of the Spanish cinematographer Javier Aguirresarobe. JC-W

▶ Anton Yelchin, Colin Farrell, Christopher Mintz-Plasse, David Tennant, Imogen Poots, Toni Collette.
▶ *Dir* Craig Gillespie, *Pro* Michael De Luca and Alison R. Rosenzweig, *Screenplay* Marti Noxon, *Ph* Javier Aguirresarobe, *Pro Des* Richard Bridgland, *Ed* Tatiana S Riegel, *M* Ramin Djawadi, *Cos* Susan Matheson.
Albuquerque Studios/DreamWorks/Gaeta/Rosenzweig Films/Michael De Luca Productions-Walt Disney.
105 mins. USA. 2011. Rel: 2 Sep 2011. Cert. 15.

From the Ashes ★★★

This documentary begins in the summer of 1981 – a time of political unrest around the country when Margaret Thatcher was rapidly destroying everything within her grasp. Meanwhile, national hero and England captain Ian Botham wins against all odds the famous Ashes and brings glory back to the country... Botham's rise and fall from grace is well researched but, unlike James Erskine's previous *One Night in Turin*, this is strictly for cricket aficionados only. GS

▶ With Ian Botham, Rodney Marsh, Kim Hughes, Dickie Bird, Gideon Haigh, narrated by Tom Hardy.
▶ *Dir* and *Written by* James Erskine, with Barney Ronay, *Pro* Erskine and Victoria Gregory, *Ph* Lol Crawley, Joel Devlin and Richard Malins, *Ed* Robin

Peters, Steve Parkinson and Ian Davies, *M* Chaz Jankel.
New Black Films/Greenacres Films-Kaleidoscope.
92 mins. UK. 2011. Rel: 6 May 2011. No Cert.

The Future ★★½

No less idiosyncratic than her earlier *Me and You and Everyone We Know*, this film from Miranda July may well divide opinion. The story is told by a cat voiced by July who also appears as one of a couple whose up and down relationship is under the microscope. Hamish Linklater is well cast as her partner but I continue to find July herself anything but a beguiling presence and you need to care about this quirky couple if the piece is to work. MS

▶ Miranda July, Hamish Linklater, David Warshofsky, Isabella Acres, Joe Putterlik.
▶ *Dir* and *Screenplay* Miranda July, *Pro* Gina Kwon, Roman Paul and Gerard Meixner, *Ph* Nikolai von Graevenitz, *Pro Des* Elliott Hostetter, *Ed* Andrew Bird, *M* Jon Brion, *Cos* Christie Wittenborn.
Film4/The Match Factory/Razor Film Produktion/GNK etc-Picturehouse Entertainment.
91 mins. Germany/USA/France. 2010. Rel: 4 Nov 2011. Cert. 12A.

Gasland ★★★★

Josh Fox's documentary is about the relentless drive to utilise gas under American soil, with developers often taking advantage of landowners unscrupulously. The film could be tighter, but it's admirably wide-ranging and vital in its message. It's not just a statement about an environmental danger but also a warning of social greed overriding the rights of the individual. Strongly recommended. MS

▶ With Mike Markhan, Marsha Mendenhall, Jesse Ellsworth, Amee Ellsworth, Dr Theo Colborn.
▶ *Dir*, *Ph* and *Written by* Josh Fox, *Pro* Trish Adlesic, Fox and Molly Gandour, *Ed* Matthew Sanchez.
International Wow Company etc-Dogwoof Pictures.
108 mins. USA. 2010. Rel: 17 Jan 2011. Cert. PG.

Genius Within: The Inner Life of Glenn Gould ★★★★

Made with the co-operation of the late Glenn Gould's estate, this documentary about the distinguished but eccentric and sometimes controversial pianist tends to ignore his critics. However, it's an in-depth look at his life as well as his career, incorporating tributes from fellow musicians and revealing comments from Cornelia Foss, who left her husband for Gould. Petula Clark appears briefly – Gould, it appears, was a fan of hers. MS

▶ With Jaime Laredo, Vladimir Ashkenazy, Cornelia Foss, Christopher Foss, Eliza Foss, Petula Clark.

Colin Farrell plays down his looks in Craig Gillespie's familiar but visually striking *Fright Night*.

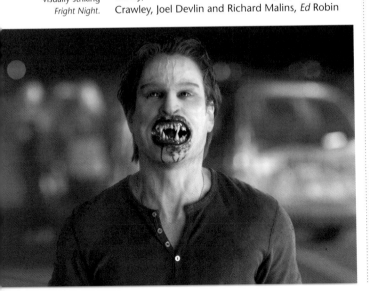

> *Dir* Michèle Hozer and Peter Raymont, *Pro* Raymont, *Ph* Walter Corbett and others, *Ed* Hozer.

White Pine Pictures etc-Verve Pictures.
111 mins. Canada/Sweden/The Netherlands/UK/ Germany/USA. 2009. Rel: 21 Jan 2011. Cert. U.

George Harrison: Living in the Material World ★★★★

Arguably but not necessarily overlong, this 3½ hour documentary by Martin Scorsese was a labour of love. The first half in particular intelligently places Harrison in context, deftly defining his role in The Beatles and capturing the feel of the times. The second half contrasts the wilder side of his nature with his essential and vital quest to find a value in life that comes from things spiritual. There's less about his contribution to cinema than you might expect. MS

> With Paul McCartney, Ringo Starr, George Martin, Astrid Kircherr, Terry Gilliam, Olivia Harrison.
> *Dir* Martin Scorsese, *Pro* Olivia Harrison, Scorsese, Nigel Sinclair and others, *Ph* Martin Kenzie and Robert Richardson, *Ed* David Tedeschi.

Grove Street Pictures/Spitfire Pictures/Sikelia Productions etc-BBC.
208 mins. USA. 2011. Rel: 4 Oct 2011. Cert. 12A.

Get Low ★★★★

Robert Duvall is at his best in this underrated and very individual film set in 1930s Tennessee. He plays an eccentric loner who requests a funeral party to take place ahead of his death. It's a touch sentimental at the close, but its blend of humour and drama (the loner is seeking to come to terms with his sense of guilt over past events) is adroit. In a fine cast Bill Cobbs offers magnificent support. MS

> Robert Duvall, Sissy Spacek, Bill Murray, Bill Cobbs, Lucas Black, Gerald McRaney.
> *Dir* and *Ed* Aaron Schneider, *Pro* Dean Zanuck and David Gundlach, *Screenplay* Chris Provenzano and C Gaby Mitchell, from a story by Provenzano and Scott Seeke, *Ph* David Boyd, *Pro Des* Geoffrey Kirkland, *M* Jan A P Kaczmarek, *Cos* Julie Weiss.

K5 International/Zanuck Independent/David Gundlach Productions etc-Sony Pictures Releasing.
103 mins. USA/Germany/Poland. 2009. Rel: 21 Jan 2011. Cert. PG.

Ghett'a Life ★★★★

Kingston ghetto teenager Derrick (Kevoy Burton) dreams of becoming a boxing champion and of representing his country at the Olympics. But his strict father categorically forbids him to join the gym, which is on the other side of his political divide... Chris Browne's eloquent film paints a clear picture of the violent world that tears Jamaica apart and elicits persuasive performances from his talented cast, particularly from the charismatic Burton as the young man determined to succeed against the odds. GS

> Winston Bell, Kevoy Burton, O'Daine Clarke, Carl Davis, Chris McFarlane.

All Things Must Pass: George and the Taj Mahal in Martin Scorsese's intelligent documentary, *George Harrison: Living in the Material World*.

▶ *Dir, Pro* and *Screenplay* Chris Browne, *Ph* Bobby Bukowski, *Pro Des* Simone Clarke, *Ed* Joel Burke and Wayne Jones, *M* Jon Williams, *Cos* Michelle Haynes.

Jamrock Films-Jinga Films.
104 mins. Jamaica. 2011. Rel: 2 Dec 2011. Cert. 15.

Ghosted ★★★

Jack (John Lynch), a vulnerable prisoner, gets a shock to the system when his wife ends their marriage on the anniversary of their son's death. But Jack's solitary existence takes an unexpected turn when Paul (Martin Compston) arrives to share his cell... The characters and performances are strong and there are some powerful scenes, especially towards the end. But the story, although interesting, adds nothing new to the overpopulated prison genre. GS

▶ John Lynch, David Schofield, Martin Compston, Art Malik, Craig Parkinson, Hugh Quarshie, Amanda Abbington.
▶ *Dir* and *Screenplay* Craig Viveiros, *Pro* Viveiros, James Friend and Rupert Bryan, *Ph* James Friend, *Pro Des* Danny Rogers, *Ed* Sam White and Kelvin Hutchins, *M* Amory Leader and Simon Williams, *Cos* Susan Gurley.

Motion Picture House/London Film and Media-Revolver Entertainment.
102 mins. UK. 2011. Rel: 24 June 2011. Cert. 18.

The Girl with the Dragon Tattoo ★★★½

Sensibly located in Sweden as before, this is David Fincher's able but somewhat impersonal remake of the first part of the best-selling Millenium trilogy by thriller writer Stieg Larsson. Familiarity draws attention to the plot contrivances, but Daniel Craig is on form and as his memorable co-investigator, Lisbeth Salander, Rooney Mara may be second best to Noomi Rapace but she's a good second best. MS

▶ Daniel Craig, Rooney Mara, Christopher Plummer, Stellan Skarsgård, Steven Berkoff, Robin Wright, Yorick van Wageningen, Joely Richardson, Geraldine James.
▶ *Dir* David Fincher, *Pro* Scott Rudin, Ole Søndberg and others, *Screenplay* Steven Zaillian from the novel by Stieg Larsson, *Ph* Jeff Cronenweth, *Pro Des* Donald Graham Burt, *Ed* Kirk Baxter and Angus Wall, *M* Trent Reznor and Atticus Ross, *Cos* Trish Summerville.

Columbia Pictures/Metro-Goldwyn-Mayer Pictures/Scott Rudin/Film Rites etc-Sony Pictures Releasing.
158 mins. USA/Sweden. 2011. Rel: 26 Dec 2011. Cert. 18.

Glee: The 3D Concert Movie ★★★

This concert documentary was shot during the 2011 'Glee Live! In Concert' summer tour featuring the *Glee* actors in character. A likeable film, it will certainly satisfy the many admirers of the hugely successful television series. The sheer energy and pure enjoyment of the participants is highly infectious. However, the 3D is a bit of a cheat as it is only used during the concert half of the film. GS

▶ Corey Monteith, Dianna Agron, Lea Michele, Chris Colfer, Ashley Fink, Mark Salling.
▶ *Dir* Kevin Tancharoen, *Pro* Dante Di Loreto, Ryan Murphy and Jeff Zachary, *Screenplay* Ian

Brennan, Brad Falchuk and Ryan Murphy, *Ph* Glen MacPherson, *Ed* Jane Moran, Tatiana S Riegel, Sonja Schenk and Myron Kerstein, *Music Supervisors* P J Bloom and Massimo Ruberto, *Cos Supervisor* Elizabeth Barrois.

Ryan Murphy Productions-20th Century Fox.
84 mins. USA. 2011. Rel: 19 Aug 2011. Cert. PG.

Gnomeo and Juliet 3D ★★★★

Two households in the gardens of Verona Drive – the Reds and the Blues – are at war until two young gnomes, Gnomeo (James McAvoy) and Juliet (Emily Blunt), fall for each other... There is plenty to enjoy in this funny, imaginative and unpredictable animated take on Shakespeare's play. The high-calibre cast lend their voices with great relish and gusto, particularly Ashley Jensen as the luscious frog Nanette, Juliet's confidante. GS

▶ The voices of James McAvoy, Emily Blunt, Ashley Jensen, Maggie Smith, Julie Walters, Michael Caine, Matt Lucas, Jason Statham, Ozzy Osbourne, Stephen Merchant, Patrick Stewart, Hulk Hogan, Richard Wilson, Dolly Parton.
▶ *Dir* Kelly Asbury, *Pro* Steve Hamilton Shaw, David Furnish and Baker Bloodworth, *Screenplay* Asbury, Shaw, Emily Cook, Mark Burton etc, based on an original screenplay by Rob Sprackling and John R Smith, from the Shakespeare play, *Pro Des* Karen deJong, *Ed* Catherine Apple, *M* Elton John, John Newton Howard and Chris Bacon.

Touchstone Pictures/Miramax Films/Rocket Pictures/Arc Productions/Starz Animation-Entertainment One.
84 mins. UK/USA. 2011. Rel: 11 Feb 2011. Cert. U.

Got to Run ★

Sexy lingerie travelling saleswoman Sara McGuire (Suzanne Kendall) relishes the opportunity to get away from her chauvinist car mechanic lover. She also takes advantage of her travels to go running in ten beautiful locations around Britain. The idea isn't bad for a short film but this feels like ten hours – as we have to watch Sara endlessly running around the country almost in real time. A real turkey. GS

▶ Suzanne Kendall, Jon-Paul Gates, Howard Corlett, Laura Michelle Cleary.
▶ *Dir, Pro* and *Screenplay* Robbie Moffat, *Ed* Simon Harris.

Palm Tree Productions-Palm Tree Distribution.
109 mins. UK. 2011. Rel: 14 June 2011. Cert. 12A.

Great Directors ★★★★

Film extracts (not always the more obvious ones) feature here alongside interview footage as filmmaker Angela Ismailos talks to ten directors of distinction. She can be idiosyncratic (not everyone would call Liliana Cavani one of the greats!) and she puts herself forward. Nevertheless her enthusiasm gets the interviewees talking, and it's good talk. Film buffs interested in serious cinema will not be bored. MS

▶ With Bernardo Bertolucci, Catherine Breillat, Liliana Cavani, Stephen Frears, Todd Haynes, Richard Linklater, Ken Loach, David Lynch, John Sayles, Agnès Varda, Angela Ismailos.
▶ *Dir* and *Screenplay* Angela Ismailos, *Ph* John Pirozzi, *Ed* Christina Burchard and Sabine Hoffmann, *M* Joel Douek.

Anisma Films-ICA
90 mins. USA. 2009. Rel: 1 Apr 2011. Cert. 15.

The Greatest Movie Ever Sold ★★★½

Morgan Spurlock's documentary finds him studying product placement in films even as he seeks sponsors to finance this film on that very basis. The movie charts his progress and it's both novel and amusing. Even so, one wonders if it offers enough to encourage the public to see it. Put it on television, however, and it would be welcomed as a fun programme, sometimes touching on serious issues. MS

▶ With Morgan Spurlock.
▶ *Dir* Morgan Spurlock, *Pro* Jeremy Chilnick, Spurlock and others, *Written by* Chulnick and Spurlock, *Ph* Daniel Marracino, *Ed* Thomas M Vogt, *M* Jon Spurney.

Snoot Entertainment/Warrior Poets-The Works.
87 mins. USA. 2011. Rel: 14 Oct 2011. Cert. 12A.

The Green Hornet ★★

Following the sudden death of his billionaire father, immature playboy Britt Reid (Seth Rogen) not only inherits his media empire but also his private chauffeur, car mechanic and

A gnome by any other name: a short version of Stephen Merchant as Paris in Kelly Asbury's imaginative *Gnomeo and Juliet*.

Bad company: Brendan Gleeson (centre) enjoys the attentions of Dominique McElligott and Sarah Greene in John Michael McDonagh's deliriously entertaining *The Guard*.

kung fu expert Kato (Jay Chou). This unlikely duo becomes a crime vigilante team by night, determined to clean up the city... It is a fun idea but sadly Rogen and Chou share zero chemistry while Christoph Waltz is simply wasted as Chodnofsky – the arch villain. GS

▶ Seth Rogen, Jay Chou, Christoph Waltz, Cameron Diaz, Tom Wilkinson, Edward James Olmos, David Harbour.
▶ *Dir* Michel Gondry, *Pro* Neal H Moritz, *Screenplay* Rogen and Evan Goldberg, based on the radio series by George W Trendle, *Ph* John Schwartzman, *Pro Des* Owen Paterson, *Ed* Michael Tronick, *M* James Newton Howard, *Cos* Kym Barrett.

Columbia Pictures/Original Film-Sony Pictures Releasing. 119 mins. USA. 2011. Rel: 14 Jan 2011. Cert. 12A.

Green Lantern ★½

A womaniser and cocky test pilot for the US Air Force is given a ring that turns him into a green superhero. But, in order to fulfil his potential, Hal Jordan (Ryan Reynolds) first needs to overcome his human fears... You have to pity the actors. They bring their egos, vulnerability and years of experience to the screen and are gobbled up by the special effects. *Green Lantern*, which squanders its impressive cast, is particularly silly and overblown, with nary a moment of true drama, humour or awesomeness. JC-W

▶ Ryan Reynolds, Blake Lively, Peter Sarsgaard, Mark Strong, Tim Robbins, Angela Bassett, Temuera Morrison, Taika Waititi, Jon Tenney, Geoffrey Rush.
▶ *Dir* Martin Campbell, *Pro* Donald De Line and Greg Berlanti, *Screenplay* Berlanti, Michael Green, Marc Guggenheim and Michael Goldenberg,

Ph Dion Beebe, *Pro Des* Grant Major, *Ed* Stuart Baird, *M* James Newton Howard, *Cos* Ngila Dickson.

Warner Bros/De Line Pictures/DC Entertainment-Warner Bros. 113 mins. USA. 2011. Rel: 17 June 2011. Cert. 12A.

The Green Wave ★★★★½

Despite a final section that is over-extended, this is a remarkable documentary which until then is perfectly paced. Using animation at intervals in the manner of *Waltz with Bashir*, it combines that with comments and with historical footage, some taken at the time of the 2009 election in Iran and some subsequently when those taking a stand against the regime of Mahmoud Ahmadinejad were ruthlessly put down. Told chronologically, the film makes the audience identify with events every step of the way. MS

▶ With Mohsen Kadivar, Mitra Khalatbari, Shadi Sadr and with the voices of Pegah Ferydoni and Navid Akhavan.
▶ *Dir* Ali Samadi Ahadi, *Pro* Oliver Stoltz and Jan Krüger, *Written by* Ahadi from an idea by Stoltz and Ahadi, *Art Dir* Ali Soozandeh, *Ed* Barbara Toennieshen and Andreas Menn, *M* Ali N Askin, *Animation* Sina Mostafawy and Soozandeh.

Dreamer Joint Venture Filmproduction etc-Dogwoof Pictures. 80 mins. Germany. 2010. Rel: 30 Sept 2011. Cert. 12A.

The Guard ★★★★

Brendan Gleeson, he of *In Bruges* and *Harry Potter*, here plays unconventional, unorthodox, unedifying and un-everything Sergeant Gerry Boyle, a member of the Irish Garda who prefers to do things his own way. When US FBI agent Wendell Everett (Don Cheadle) is seconded to him, he leads his new sidekick a merry old Irish jig as they set out on a drugs bust. John Michael McDonagh (brother of Martin McDonagh, who wrote and directed *In Bruges*) gives Gleeson another plum role to inhabit, full of wisecracks, black humour and a penchant for snorting with whores, in one of the funniest, most entertaining cop films of the year. MHD

▶ Brendan Gleeson, Don Cheadle, Liam Cunningham, David Wilmot, Mark Strong, Fionnula Flanagan.
▶ *Dir* and *Screenplay* John Michael McDonagh, *Pro* Chris Clark, Ed Guiney, Andrew Lowe and Flora Fernandez-Marengo, *Ph* Larry Smith, *Pro Des* John Paul Kelly, *Ed* Chris Gill, *M* Calexico, *Cos* Eimer Ni Mhaoldomhnaigh.

Crescendo Productions/Element Pictures/Reprisal Films/ Irish Film Board/UK Film Council-Optimum Releasing. 94 mins. Ireland. 2011. Rel: 19 Aug 2011. Cert. 15.

Guilty of Romance ★★★★

Sion Sono, the original talent behind *Love Exposure* and *Cold Fish*, directs another compelling film that cleverly combines heavy eroticism with murder. The story follows Izumi (Megumi Kagurazaka), the bored wife of a famous romantic novelist, who, as in *Belle de Jour*, enters a world of pornography and prostitution. Under Sono's masterful direction, Kagurazaka is simply magnificent in this sexually explicit thriller that builds up slowly to an explosive climax. (Original title: *Koi no tsumi*) GS

▶ Miki Mizuno, Makoto Togashi, Megumi Kagurazaka, Kazuya Kojima, Satoshi Nikaidô.
▶ *Dir* and *Screenplay* Sion Sono, *Pro* Yoshinori Chiba and Nobuhiro Iizuka, *Ph* Sôhei Tanikawa, *Ed* Jun'ichi Itô, *Music Director* Yasuhiro Morinaga, *Cos* Chiyoe Hakamada.

Django Film/Nikkatsu-Eureka Entertainment. 144 mins. Japan. 2011. Rel: 30 Sep 2011. Cert. 18.

Gunfighter's Pledge ★★★

Luke Perry is Sheriff Matt Austin as if to the brooding manner born in this welcome return to the old-fashioned Western formula with a vintage plot. Setting out to capture the escaped criminal (Kim Coates) who killed his wife and son, he tries to gun him down in a shootout but kills an innocent rancher instead. Perry then pledges to help the rancher's widowed sister (Jaclyn DeSantis) against a greedy villain (C Thomas Howell) who's trying to steal her land for its valuable water rights. A taut, satisfying plot is taken briskly to its properly inevitable conclusion in considerable style, with commanding performances by all four stars. DW

▶ Luke Perry, C Thomas Howell, Kim Coates, Jaclyn DeSantis, Francesco Quinn.
▶ *Dir* Armand Mastroianni, *Pro* Albert T Dickerson III, *Screenplay* Jim Byrnes, *Ph* James W Wrenn, *Pro Des* Yuda Acco, *Ed* Colleen Halsey, *M* Nathan Furst, *Cos* Heather Hershman.

Larry Levinson Productions/Grand Army Entertainment/ RHI Entertainment-Hallmark Channel. 84 mins. USA. 2008. Rel: 28 Oct 2011. Cert. PG.

Nom de porno: Megumi Kagurazaka in Sion Sono's masterful *Guilty of Romance.*

Armed and
ethereal: Saoirse
Ronan in Joe
Wright's stylish
but derivative
Hanna.

Hall Pass ★½

Rick and Fred (Owen Wilson and Jason Sudeikis) can't resist the temptation of looking at attractive women even in front of their wives (Jenna Fischer and Christina Applegate). They in turn, in an attempt to revitalise their marriages, allow their husbands to have a 'hall pass' – one week of total freedom with no questions asked. The disappointing script never takes any risks and it tries to have it both ways with a startlingly new message that the institution of marriage is ultimately the best. Bring on the sick bag! GS

❯ Owen Wilson, Jason Sudeikis, Jenna Fischer, Christina Applegate, Nicky Whelan, Richard Jenkins, Stephen Merchant, Bruce Thomas.
❯ *Dir* Bobby and Peter Farrelly, *Pro* Bobby and Peter Farrelly etc, *Screenplay* Bobby and Peter Farrelly, Pete Jones and Kevin Barnett, based on a story by Jones, *Ph* Matthew F Leonetti, *Pro Des* Arlan Jay Vetter, *Ed* Sam Seig, *Music Supervision* Tom Wolfe and Manish Raval, *Cos* Denise Wingate.
New Line Cinema/Conundrum Entertainment-Warner Bros.
105 mins. USA. 2011. Rel: 11 Mar 2011. Cert. 15.

The Hangover Part II ★½

It is now the turn of Stu (Ed Helms) to get married, and his three friends Phil (Bradley Cooper), Alan (Zack Galifianakis) and Doug (Justin Bartha) are eager to travel to Thailand for the wedding. And, like in Las Vegas, unsurprisingly the bachelor party goes disastrously wrong... The structure is exactly the same as the film feebly attempts to repeat the winning formula of the original, but this lazy comedy is devoid of any laughs until the closing credits. By then it is far too late to save the day. GS

❯ Bradley Cooper, Zack Galifianakis, Ed Helms, Justin Bartha, Paul Giamatti, Mike Tyson, Jeffrey Tambor.
❯ *Dir* Todd Phillips, *Pro* Phillips and Daniel Goldberg, *Screenplay* Phillips, Scot Armstrong and Craig Mazin, based on characters created by Jon Lucas and Scott Moore, *Ph* Lawrence Sher, *Pro Des* Bill Brzeski, *Ed* Debra Neil-Fisher and Mike Sale, *M* Christophe Beck, *Cos* Louise Mingenbach.
Warner Bros Pictures/Legendary Pictures/Living Films/
Green Hat Films-Warner Bros.
102 mins. USA. 2011. Rel: 26 May 2011. Cert. 15.

Hanna ★★½

A bizarre cross between *The Enigma of Kaspar Hauser* and *Nikita*, this is a stylish thriller bursting with interesting ideas, none of which are fully resolved. If it weren't for the central presence of Saoirse Ronan – whose ethereal beauty is perfect for the otherworldly Hanna – the film would be nothing more than a ragbag of recycled ideas. This is a shame as that old motif of something preternatural seeking its humanity is always an affecting one. Indeed, the most stirring moment among all the most improbable action sequences is when Hanna asks her father: "What does music feel like?" JC-W

Saoirse Ronan, Eric Bana, Cate Blanchett, Tom Hollander, Olivia Williams, Jason Flemyng, Jessica Barden.
Dir Joe Wright, Pro Leslie Holleran, Marty Adelstein and Scott Nemes, Screenplay Seth Lochhead and David Farr, Ph Alwin Küchler, Pro Des Sarah Greenwood, Ed Paul Tothill, M The Chemical Brothers, Cos Lucie Bates.

Focus Features/Holleran Company/Studio Babelsberg-Universal.
111 mins. USA/UK/Germany. 2011. Rel: 6 May 2011. Cert. 12A.

Happy Feet Two ★★★★★

The first *Happy Feet* was jaw-dropping, exhilarating entertainment, so it's quite an achievement to pull off a sequel that's every bit as good. A brand-new story sees the son of emperor penguin Mumble facing his own inadequacies – and trying to make his incongruity something special. Along the way he, Eric, encounters an ocker elephant seal, a flock of predatory skuas and a Scandinavian puffin. As in the first film there are some pretty suspenseful sequences and some invigorating musical set-pieces, while Brad Pitt and Matt Damon bring comic relief as a couple of bickering, wise-cracking krill, Will and Bill ("Goodbye krill world!"). JC-W

Voices of Elijah Wood, Robin Williams, Hank Azaria, Alecia Moore (Pink), Brad Pitt, Matt Damon, Sofia Vergara, Common, Ava Acres, Hugo Weaving, Anthony LaPaglia.
Dir George Miller, Pro George Miller, Bill Miller and Doug Mitchell, Screenplay Miller, Gary Eck, Warren Coleman and Paul Livingston, Ph David Dulac and David Peers, Pro Des David Nelson, M John Powell.

Warner Bros/Village Roadshow/Kennedy Miller Mitchell/ Dr D Studios-Warner Bros.
103 mins. USA/Australia. 2011. Rel: 2 Dec 2011. Cert. U.

Harry Potter and the Deathly Hallows Part 2 ★★★½

And now the end is near and so he takes his final curtain… Yes, after eight films and ten years in the making for this most successful franchise, with Daniel Radcliffe, man and boy, as the eponymous hero, it has all come to a halt. Having given up halfway through the series, this reviewer remains puzzled by the maze of plots, which here has Harry and friends looking for death-defying artefacts while polishing off the villainous Voldemort (Ralph Fiennes). It's all unbelievably spectacular in the special effects department but, by now, we have surely had enough of these fantasy projections. So it's goodbye from him… and hello Harry Potter Studio Tour. MHD

Daniel Radcliffe, Emma Watson, Rupert Grint, Ralph Fiennes, Michael Gambon, Alan Rickman, Warwick Davis, John Hurt, Helena Bonham Carter, Kelly Macdonald, Jason Isaacs, Ciarán Hinds, Maggie Smith, Robbie Coltrane, Gary Oldman, Timothy Spall, Emma Thompson, Miriam Margolyes, Julie Walters, Jim Broadbent, Gemma Jones, David Thewlis, Evanna Lynch, Mark Williams, Nick Moran.
Dir David Yates, Pro David Heyman, David Barron and J K Rowling, Screenplay Steve Kloves, from the book by J K Rowling, Ph Eduardo Serra, Pro Des Stuart Craig, Ed Mark Day, M Alexandre Desplat, Cos Jany Temime.

Warner Bros Pictures/Heyday Films/Moving Picture Company-Warner Bros Pictures.
130 mins. USA/UK. 2011. Rel: 15 July 2011. Cert. 12A.

Hatchet II ★★

Having escaped the bayou-butcher Victor Crowley, Danielle Harris' Marybeth returns to the Louisiana swamps with armed hunters to recover her family's bodies and take revenge. Starting where 2007's *Hatchet* ends, this old-school slasher sequel sees the return of Kane Hodder as the hatchet-wielding madman, shaping up as a scary, iconic killer. Pretty much standard quality for its low-budget genre, this still delivers sick thrills effectively enough as buckets of blood are delivered with a ripe supply of vile, slice-and-dice

The snow dance kid: Eric does his stuff in George Miller's invigorating *Happy Feet Two*.

deaths. Horror buffs must be thrilled that Tony Todd is back as the Rev Zombie but disappointed that Tamara Feldman doesn't return as Marybeth. *Hatchet III* is on its way. DW

▶ Danielle Harris, Kane Hodder, Tony Todd, Parry Shen, Tom Holland.
▶ *Dir* and *Screenplay* Adam Green, *Pro* Cory Neal, Derek Curl and Sarah Elbert, *Ph* Will Barratt, *Pro Des* Bryan A McBrien, *Ed* Ed Marx, *M* Andy Garfield, *Cos* Heather Allison.
ArieScope Pictures-Dark Sky Films.
85 mins. USA. 2011. Rel: 1 Apr 2011. Cert. 18.

Heartbeats ★★★½

Although echoing Godard's films of the sixties such as *Masculin Feminin,* this French Canadian work by 21-year-old Xavier Dolan, who also stars in it, is entirely of today: it will draw a young audience who recognise in it themselves and their friends. Sex here is largely about power and game-playing while ambiguous sexuality is an image that can be presented to the world. It rings true and could become a cult movie, but if you see the characters as superficial it outstays its welcome. (Original title: *Les Amours imaginaires*) MS

▶ Monia Chokri, Niels Schneider, Xavier Dolan, Anne Dorval, Anthony Huneault.
▶ *Dir, Screenplay, Ed* and *Cos* Xavier Dolan, *Pro* Dolan, Daniel Morin and Carole Mondello, *Ph* Stéphanie Weber-Biron, *Art Dir* Delphine Gélinas.
Mifilifilms Inc. etc-Network Releasing.
101 mins. Canada/France. 2010. Rel: 27 May 2011. Cert. 15.

Prickly issues: Garance Le Guillermic and Josiane Balasko in Mona Achache's poignant *The Hedgehog.*

The Hedgehog ★★★★½

Paloma (the endearing Garance Le Guillermic) is the 11-year-old daughter of a well-to-do Paris family whom she hates. Inspired by art and philosophy she plans to kill herself on her 12th birthday. However, she finds a soulmate in her apartment block, Renée (Josiane Balasko), the reclusive, widowed female janitor she calls a hedgehog – tough outside but soft inside. This delightful film details Paloma's relationship with Renée and that of Renée with Kakuro, her widowed neighbour, a Japanese man (Togo Igawa) who shows her great respect. The sadness of these small lives is beautifully captured in Mona Achache's poignant film, with heartbreaking performances from all concerned. (Original title: *Le Hérisson*) MHD

▶ Josiane Balasko, Garance Le Guillermic, Togo Igawa, Anne Brochet, Ariane Ascaride.
▶ *Dir* and *Screenplay* Mona Achache, from Muriel Barbery's novel *L'Elégance du hérisson, Pro* Mark Lombardo Anne-Dominique Toussaint, *Ph* Patrick Blossier, *Art Dir* Patrick Schmitt, *Ed* Julia Gregory, *M* Gabriel Yared, *Cos* Catherine Bouchard.
Les Films des Tournelles/Eagle Pictures/Topaze Bleue/ Pathé/France 2 Cinéma-CinéFile.
100 mins. France/Italy. 2009. Rel: 2 Sep 2011. Cert. 12A.

Hell and Back Again ★★★★★

Although we have seen many brilliant documentaries about the ghastly war in Afghanistan, Danfung Dennis' powerful film provides a fresh perspective and rates among the best. He follows the war through the eyes of 25-year-old Marine Sergeant Nathan Harris and subsequently his return home, after being severely injured by a bullet through his hip. It is a compelling film cleverly cutting back and forth between the war zone and the recovery process. GS

▶ With Nathan Harris, Ashley Harris and the Echo Company, 2nd Batallion, 8th Marines.
▶ *Dir* and *Ph* Danfung Dennis, *Pro* Dennis, Martin Herring and Mike Lerner, *Ed* Fiona Otway, *M* J Ralph.
Docurama Films-Independent Distribution.
88 mins. USA/UK/Afghanistan. 2011. Rel: 12 Oct 2011. No Cert.

The Help ★★★★½

Emma Stone plays Skeeter Phelan, a local journalist in 1960s America, investigating how white families treat their black maids – 'the help'. In fact, they are used as objects that merely clear up after the family. Skeeter organises the black women to rise up against the indifference shown towards them, even though the children adore their black minders and the servants are devoted to their charges. There's great acting here

with Stone as the spirited Skeeter, Viola Davis as the emotional Aibileen, Jessica Chastain as ditsy white mom Celia, and, perhaps best of all, Octavia Spencer as the rebellious Minny, who won't stand for any nonsense. MHD

▶ Emma Stone, Jessica Chastain, Viola Davis, Octavia Spencer, Bryce Dallas Howard, Sissy Spacek.
▶ *Dir* and *Screenplay* Tate Taylor, from the novel by Kathryn Stockett, *Pro* Chris Columbus, Mike Barnathan and Brunson Green, *Ph* Stephen Goldblatt, *Pro Des* Mark Ricker, *Ed* Hughes Winborne, *M* Thomas Newman, *Cos* Sharen Davis.

DreamWorks SKG/Reliance Entertainment/Harbinger Pictures/1492 Pictures/Participant Media/Imagenation Abu Dhabi-Touchstone Pictures.
146 mins. USA/India/United Arab Emirates. 2011. Rel: 26 Oct 2011. Cert. 12A

Henry's Crime ★★½

A likable caper comedy with an appealing cast and a whimsical sense of humour, this stars Keanu Reeves as an ex-con who, after being released from prison for a crime he didn't commit, decides he might as well commit the crime he did the time for. Namely, rob a bank,

with help from the fast-talking conman he befriended inside (James Caan) and a woman who knocks him down with her car (Vera Farmiga). A spirited and moderately smart, twisty-turny, jokey thriller, this is as easily watchable as it is utterly forgettable. MJ

▶ Keanu Reeves, Vera Farmiga, James Caan, Fisher Stevens, Danny Hoch, Bill Duke.
▶ *Dir* Malcolm Venville, *Pro* Stephen Hammel, Peter Graham, David Mimram, Lemore Syvan and Jordan Schur, *Screenplay* Sacha Gervasi and David White, from a story by Gervasi and Hammel, *Ph* Paul Cameron, *Pro Des* Chris Jones, *Ed* Curtiss Clayton, *M* Brendan Ryan and Fall On Your Sword, *Cos* Melisa Toth.

Firstar Films/Inspired Actions/Company Films-Entertainment Film Distributors.
108 mins. USA. 2010. Rel: 14 Jan 2011. Cert. 15.

Hereafter ★★★

Clint Eastwood's film begins stunningly as a tsunami suddenly hits Hawaii. However, although the writer is Peter Morgan (*The Queen*, *Frost/Nixon* etc), the plot clumsily blends three story lines. It involves American, French and

Book of revelation: Allison Janney and Emma Stone in Tate Taylor's brilliantly acted *The Help*.

Bourne again: Matt Damon explores the *Hereafter* in Clint Eastwood's sincere and sensitive drama.

English characters and offers a superficial, unconvincing take on the possibility of life after death. Worst of all, Clint borrows the Rachmaninov 2nd Piano Concerto from *Brief Encounter*. Prepare to cringe. MS

▶ Matt Damon, Cécile de France, George McLaren, Frankie McLaren, Bryce Dallas Howard, Marthe Keller, Derek Jacobi.
▶ *Dir* and *M* Clint Eastwood, *Pro* Eastwood, Kathleen Kennedy and Robert Lorenz, *Screenplay* Peter Morgan, *Ph* Tom Stern, *Pro Des* James J. Murakami, *Ed* Joel Cox and Gary D Roach, *Cos* Deborah Hopper.

Warner Bros. Pictures/Malpaso/Amblin Entertainment/Kennedy/Marshall-Warner Bros Distributors (UK).
129 mins. USA. 2010. Rel: 28 Jan 2011. Cert. 12A.

His & Hers ★★

Seemingly unscripted, women in the Irish Midlands, each speaking briefly, comment on life from birth to death. The concept would suit a radio programme, but it's not visual and we never see the husbands and sons who are mentioned. Neither charming nor cute but patronising and indiscreet, its focus is in any case incomplete (no divorcees, no lesbians) and the accompanying music score could not be more banal. MS

▶ With Leah Holohan, Grace McGee, Eimear Peters, Chloe O'Connor, Emily Rose McHugh.
▶ *Dir* and *Ed* Ken Wardrop, *Pro* Andrew Freedman, *Ph* Michael Lavelle and Kate McCullough, *M* Denis Clohessy.

Venom Films/Irish Film Board-Element Pictures Distribution.
83 mins. Ireland. 2009. Rel: 11 Mar 2011. Cert. U.

Hobo with a Shotgun ★

A Grindhouse-style exploitation flick with 1970s stylings, this tells a lurid, sadistic tale of bloody vengeance. An elderly Rutger Hauer takes the lead as a homeless nobody who confronts sinister, psychotic forces in a lawless, tumbledown town, trading his bindle for a shotgun and blowing gaping, bloody holes in every lunatic in sight. Wildly over-played with its head in the gutter and trashy dialogue, this is as depraved as the degenerates it depicts. Evidently it's meant to be a comedy, but it's a freak show so grotesque it's more evil than amusing. Please don't take this as a recommendation. MJ

▶ Rutger Hauer, Rob Wells, Brian Downey, Gregory Smith, Nick Bateman, Drew O'Hara.
▶ *Dir* Jason Eisener, *Pro* Frank Siracusa, Paul Gross, Niv Fichman and Rob Cotterill, *Screenplay* John Davies, from a story by Davies, Eisener and Cotterill, *Ph* Karim Hussain, *Pro Des* Ewen Dickson, *Ed* Jason Eisener, *M* Adam Burke, Russ Howard III and Darius Holbert, *Cos* Sarah Dunsworth.

Whizbang Films/Yer Dead Productions/Rhombus Media-Momentum Pictures.
86 mins. Canada. 2011. Rel: 15 July 2011. Cert. 18.

Holy Rollers ★★★½

Made in 2009 and set in Brooklyn, this is a film about a Hassidic Jew (Jesse Eisenberg) who becomes involved in the drugs trade. Often vivid but occasionally less persuasive, this drama gains from Eisenberg's sympathetic personality; his character is essentially that of a youth rebelling against his father and the set expectations of what his life will be. However, it lacks a real climax and pales by comparison with *Maria Full of Grace* (2004), which it sometimes recalls. MS

▷ Jesse Eisenberg, Justin Bartha, Ari Graynor, Danny A Abeckaser.
▷ *Dir* Kevin Asch, *Pro* Danny A Abeckaser, Tory Tunnel and others, *Screenplay* Antonio Macia, *Ph* Ben Kutchins, *Pro Des* Tommaso Ortino, *Ed* Suzanne Spangler, *M* MJ Mynarski, *Cos* Jacki Roach.

Deerjen Films/Lookbook Films/Safehouse Pictures/Gulfstream Films-Crabtree Films.
89 mins. USA. 2009. Rel: 8 Jul 2011. Cert. 15.

Honey ★★★

This Turkish film tells of the childhood of a boy whose later life has already been traced in two earlier films not released here. It's set on the Black Sea coast and the director brings in autobiographical elements. However, despite the atmospheric treatment of this rural setting, newcomers unfamiliar with the other parts of the trilogy may find it difficult to get really involved. It's easier to respect the film than to enjoy it. (Original title: *Bal*) MS

▷ Bora Altas, Erdal Besikçioglu, Tülin Özen.
▷ *Dir* and *Pro* Semih Kaplanoglu, *Screenplay* Kaplanoglu and Orçun Köksal, *Ph* Baris Özbiçer, *Art Dir* Naz Erayda, *Ed* Ayhan Ergürsel, Kaplanoglu and S Hande Güneri.

Kaplan Film Production/Heimatfilm/ZDF/Arte etc-Verve Pictures.
105 mins. Turkey/Germany. 2010. Rel: 15 July 2011. Cert. PG.

Honey 2 ★★

When talented dancer Maria Ramirez (Katerina Graham) gets released from a detention centre she joins a new dance group with life-changing results. *Honey 2* is lively and energetic, with impressive dance routines and slick choreography, but the clichéd script of this film is often laughable and is a huge let-down. However, Graham is a strong presence and manages to keep her dignity despite Bille Woodruff's pedestrian direction. GS

▷ Katerina Graham, Randy Wayne, Aaron Benjamin, Lonette McKee, Melissa Smith.
▷ *Dir* Bille Woodruff, *Pro* Paul Hellerman, *Screenplay* Alyson Fouse and Blayne Weaver, *Ph* David Klein, *Pro Des* Jerry Fleming, *Ed* Paul Millspaugh, *M* Tim Boland and Sam Retzer, *Cos* Cynthia Ann Summers.

Universal Films/Mark Platt Productions-Universal Pictures International.
110 mins. USA. 2011. Rel: 10 June 2011. Cert. PG.

Honeymooner ★½

Kentish Town, today. Just four weeks prior to his wedding day, Fran Goldman finds himself abandoned by his wife-to-be. A fairly gormless 29-year-old, Fran hangs around with his two best mates and discusses love, dating and precious little else... Running at a trim 73 minutes, *Honeymooner* hardly feels like a fully formed film. It has a certain appealing nonchalance but little in the way of wit, credibility or narrative. There are a couple of laughs in the entire thing but it's hard to know who to recommend this to besides twentysomething movie buffs living in Camden. JC-W

▷ Gerard Kearns, Chris Coghill, Al Weaver, Daisy Haggard.
▷ *Dir* and *Screenplay* Col Spector, *Pro* Alicia Brown and Radha Chakraborty, *Ph* Gerry Floyd, *Pro Des* and *Cos* Saffron Hunt, *Ed* Maria T Valente.

Honeymooner Ltd-Soda Pictures.
73 mins. UK. 2010. Rel: 21 Jan 2011. Cert. 15.

Hop ★★★

EB (voiced by Russell Brand) wants to be a drummer in a rock 'n' roll band rather than take over from his Easter Bunny father. But when he runs away to Los Angeles he is accidentally hit by Fred's car... This is probably Brand's best performance to date and Marsden is excellent as the unemployed Fred, who finds his match in this enjoyable but undemanding family film which blends animation with live action to good effect. GS

▷ James Marsden, Elizabeth Perkins, Kaley Cuoco, Gary Cole, David Hasselhoff, and the voices of Russell Brand, Hank Azaria, Hugh Laurie.
▷ *Dir* Tim Hill, *Pro* Christopher Meledandri and Michele Imperato, *Screenplay* Cinco Paul, Ken Daurio and Brian Lynch, based on a story by Paul and Daurio, *Ph* Peter Lyons Collister, *Pro Des* Richard Holland, *Ed* Peter S Elliot and Gregory Perler, *M* Christopher Lennertz, *Cos* Alexandre Welker.

Universal Pictures/Relativity Media/Illumination Entertainment-Universal Studios.
95 mins. USA. 2011. Rel: 1 Apr 2011. Cert. U.

Bunny games: Kaley Cuoco in Tim Hill's enjoyable but undemanding *Hop*.

Horrible Bosses

Career development: Reese Witherspoon and Paul Rudd in James L Brooks' cute romcom *How Do You Know.*

contest. Nick Moore encourages his actors to overact mercilessly and even the classy presence of Anjelica Huston as Henry's unfortunate teacher can't rescue this one. GS

▶ Theo Stevenson, Anjelica Huston, Richard E Grant, Parminder Nagra, Noel Fielding, Rebecca Front, Tyger Drew-Honey, Prunella Scales, Matthew Horne, Jo Brand.
▶ *Dir* Nick Moore, *Pro* Lucinda Whiteley and Rupert Preston, *Screenplay* Lucinda Whiteley, from the book by Francesca Simon, *Ph* Sam McCurdy, *Pro Des* Richard Bullock, *Ed* Simon Cozens, *M* Lester Barnes and Michael Price, *Cos* Colleen Kelsall.
Novel Entertainment Productions/Vertigo Films/ Prescience/Aegis Film Fund-Vertigo Films.
93 mins. UK. 2011. Rel: 29 July 2011. Cert. U.

How Do You Know ★★★★

Writer-director James L Brooks can be adept at rom-coms and is so here, although the film was absurdly undervalued. Conventional but skilled, the film offers two integrated plot lines. One features a romantic triangle (will Reese Witherspoon choose Paul Rudd or Owen Wilson?) and the other a father-son relationship (Rudd and Jack Nicholson) in which the father is a conniver. Brooks and his cast are entirely at home here. MS

▶ Reese Witherspoon, Owen Wilson, Paul Rudd, Jack Nicholson, Kathryn Hahn.
▶ *Dir* and *Screenplay* James L. Brooks, *Pro* Paula Weinstein, Laurence Mark, Brooks and Julie Ansell, *Ph* Janusz Kaminski, *Pro Des* Jeannine Oppewall, *Ed* Richard Marks and Tracey Wadmore-Smith, *M* Hans Zimmer, *Cos* Shay Cunliffe.
Columbia Pictures/Gracie Films/Road Rebel-Sony Pictures Releasing.
121 mins. USA. 2010. Rel: 28 Jan 2011. Cert. 12A.

How I Ended This Summer ★★½

This award-winning Russian film has a splendidly novel location, being set on an Arctic island. Here a college graduate arrives to assist the man in charge of the meteorological station. The relationship between the two men changes, but it happens so slowly that this minimalistic film with no supporting players is an endurance test. It's well played but not always convincing and the ambiguous ending is unhelpful. (Original title: *Kak ya provel etim letom*) MS

▶ Grigory Dobrygin, Sergei Puskepalis.
▶ *Dir* and *Screenplay* Alexei Popogrebsky, *Pro* Roman Borisevich and Alexander Kushaev, *Ph* Pavel Kostomarov, *Pro Des* Gennady Popov, *Ed* Ivan Lebedev, *M* Dmitry Katkhanov, *Cos* Svetlana Mikhailova.
TV Channel RUSSIA/Koktebel Film Company etc-New Wave Films.
130 mins. Russia. 2010. Rel: 22 Apr 2011. Cert. 12A.

Horrible Bosses ★★½

Jennifer Aniston plays an abusive, sexually predatory dentist, Colin Farrell is a balding, pot-bellied brat, and Kevin Spacey is a paranoid, sadistic taskmaster. They're all horrible bosses and it's the stars' relish for subverting their personas that makes up much of the enjoyment of this film from the director of *Four Christmases*. Oppressed by their working conditions, three best friends – the moronic, self-pitying types that you only find in American sitcoms – decide to become proactive and terminate their superiors. It's formulaic, ludicrous stuff, but there are surprising pockets of humour – much of it generated by accomplished actors letting their hair down. JC-W

▶ Jason Bateman, Charlie Day, Jason Sudeikis, Jennifer Aniston, Colin Farrell, Kevin Spacey, Jamie Foxx, Donald Sutherland, Julie Bowen, Ioan Gruffudd.
▶ *Dir* Seth Gordon, *Pro* Brett Ratner and Jay Stern, *Screenplay* Michaerl Markowitz, John Francis Daley and Jonathan Goldstein, *Ph* David Hennings, *Pro Des* Shepherd Frankel, *Ed* Peter Teschner, *M* Christopher Lennertz, *Cos* Carol Ramsey.
New Line Cinema/Rat Entertainment-Warner Bros.
97 mins. USA. 2011. Rel: 22 July 2011. Cert. 15.

Horrid Henry: The Movie ★

It is almost impossible to find anything positive to say about this misconceived project based on the popular children's books and television series, apart from some decent 3D effects. Henry (Theo Stevenson) has problems with spelling, and fails yet again to hand in his homework, but is determined to win the Ashton Primary talent

How Much Does Your Building Weigh, Mr Foster? ★★★★

The title is cumbersome but this is an admirable documentary about the life and work of the architect Norman Foster. It's informative for those not well-versed in architecture and the man himself, initially dubious about being filmed, comes across as a remarkable individual. There are worldwide locations to show off the buildings, an effective use of music and an aptly judged length (little more than 75 minutes). For older viewers it invites comparison with the BBC TV series *Monitor*. MS

❥ With Norman Foster, Richard Rogers, Bono, Alain De Botton. Narrated by Deyan Sudjic.
❥ *Dir* Norberto López Amado and Carlos Carcas, *Pro* Elena Ochoa, *Written by* Deyan Sudjic, *Ph* Valentín Álvarez, *Ed* Paco Cózar, *M* Joan Valent.

Art Commissioners/Aiete-Ariane Films/Mandarin Film-Dogwoof Pictures.
78 mins. UK/Spain/France. 2009. Rel: 28 Jan2011. No Cert.

How to Stop Being a Loser ★

James (Simon Phillips) is a 'dateless wonder' in search of a date. In his desperation he recruits the apparent expert in seduction, Ampersand (Craig Conway), who promises to give him a few tips. This unfunny comedy is not only misogynistic but also utterly misanthropic, and Richard E Grant – as another dateless wonder – wisely commits suicide before the opening credits. Nobody vaguely resembles a human being apart from the lovely Stephanie Leonidas, who manages to keep her dignity despite the mediocrity. GS

❥ Simon Phillips, Craig Conway, Richard E Grant, Billy Murray, Martin Kemp, Jill Halfpenny, Colin Salmon, Martin Compston, Stephanie Leonidas, Gemma Atkinson.
❥ *Dir* Dominic Burns, *Pro* Burns, Simon Phillips, Billy Murray, Jonathan Sothcott and Patricia Rybarczyk, *Screenplay* Chris Grezo, Alexander Williams and Rupert Knowles, *Ph* Alessio Valori, *Pro Des* Luis San Martin, *Ed* Richard Colton, *M* Matthew Williams, *Cos* Natalie Egleton.

Hawthorn Productions/Black and Blue Films/Press On Features/Templeheart Films-Crabtree Films.
109 mins. UK. 2011. Rel: 18 Nov 2011. Cert. 15.

Howl ★★★★

This highly individual and successful portrayal of the Beat poet Allen Ginsberg, with special reference to his famous (and notorious) poem 'Howl', is not a documentary. Instead it uses actors, incorporates animation and involves both readings from the poem and scenes of the 1957 obscenity trial concerning it. It's a film about the arts and censorship as well as one touching on gay issues. James Franco is splendid as Ginsberg and there is an exceptionally strong supporting cast. MS

❥ James Franco, David Strathairn, Jon Hamm, Bob Balaban, Mary-Louise Parker, Jeff Daniels, Alessandro Nivola, Treat Williams.
❥ *Dir* and *Screenplay* Rob Epstein and Jeffrey Friedman, *Pro* Elizabeth Redleaf, Christine Kunewa Walker, Epstein and Friedman, *Ph* Edward Lachman, *Pro Des* Thérèse DePrez, *Ed* Jake Pushinsky, *M* Carter Burwell, *Cos* Kurt and Bart, *Animation Design* Eric Drooker.

Werc Werk Works/Telling Pictures/Rabbit Bandini Productions etc-Soda Pictures.
84 mins. USA. 2010. Rel: 25 Feb 2011. Cert. 15.

Huge ★

This laugh-free comedy about stand-up comedians fails to even raise a smile. Talentless Warren (Johnny Harris) and the equally amateurish Clarke (Noel Clarke) join forces in order to make it huge as a double act. Ben Miller's dull film is based on a play which he wrote with Simon Godley and Jez Butterworth and performed at the Edinburgh Festival. It may have worked on stage but it certainly doesn't on celluloid. GS

❥ Noel Clarke, Johnny Harris, Thandie Newton, Ralph Brown, Tamsin Egerton, Michelle Ryan.
❥ *Dir* Ben Miller, *Pro* Colin Hall and Rebecca Farhall, *Screenplay* Miller, Simon Godley and Jez Butterworth, *Ph* Trevor Forrest, *Pro Des* Kristian Milsted, *Ed* Richard Graham, *M* Christian Henson, *Cos* Fiona Chilcott.

Fortuitous Films/Matador Pictures/Toff Media/Cinema Three/Regent Capital-Independent Distribution.
78 mins. UK. 2010. Rel: 8 July 2011. Cert. 15.

Poet's corner: Aaron Tveit and James Franco in Rob Epstein and Jeffrey Friedman's highly distinctive *Howl*.

Hugo ★★★★

Martin Scorsese's adaptation of a children's book introduces Hugo (Asa Butterfield), a young boy living in the 1930s in a Paris station, looking after the clocks as his father (Jude Law in flashback) once did. Hugo, trying to find the key to fit his father's automaton, meets Isabelle (Chloë Grace Moretz), goddaughter of the local toymaker (Ben Kingsley), who turns out to be Georges Méliès, the famous silent filmmaker. Scorsese then treats us to a history of early cinema including Méliès' most famous film *Le Voyage dans la lune*. It works surprisingly well as children's story and as film history, beautifully shot by Robert Richardson and designed by Dante Ferretti. MHD

▶ Ben Kingsley, Asa Butterfield, Sasha Baron Cohen, Chloë Grace Moretz, Ray Winstone, Emily Mortimer, Christopher Lee, Jude Law.
▶ *Dir* Martin Scorsese, *Pro* Scorsese, Johnny Depp, Graham King and Tim Headington, *Screenplay* John Logan, from the book *The Invention of Hugo Cabret* by Brian Selznick, *Ph* Robert Richardson, *Pro Des* Dante Ferretti, *Ed* Thelma Schoonmaker, *M* Howard Shore, *Cos* Sandy Powell.

Paramount Pictures/GK Films/Infinitum Nihil-Entertainment Film Distributors.
126 mins. USA. 2011. Rel: 2 Dec 2011. Cert. U.

The Human Centipede II (Full Sequence) ★★½

The action of Tom Six's sequel moves to London where Martin (Laurence R Harvey), a mentally disturbed car park attendant, spends most of his time watching *The Human Centipede* over and over again. There is only one solution for his fantasies – to recreate Dr Heiter's experiment but on a larger scale... Six's monochrome horror fantasy brings to mind David Lynch's *Eraserhead* and here Six mixes the chilling menace of the original with dark humour and extreme unpleasantness. GS

▶ Laurence R Harvey, Ashlynn Yennie, Maddie Black, Candace Caine, Dominic Borelli.
▶ *Dir* and *Screenplay* Tom Six, *Pro* Tom and Ilona Six, *Ph* David Meadows, *Pro Des* Thomas Stefan, *Ed* Nigel de Hond, *M* James Edward Barker.

Six Entertainment Company-Bounty Films.
84 mins. UK/Netherlands/USA. 2011. Rel: 4 Nov 2011.
Cert. 18.

I Am Number Four ★★★

John (Alex Pettyfer) is no ordinary teenager – he is on the run from ruthless enemies determined to destroy him, while his guardian Henri (Timothy Olyphant) keeps on moving him from town to town and changing his identity. But when they reach a small Ohio town John falls in love for the first time... D J Caruso keeps the action flowing with some impressive set-pieces but is let down by a plot which attempts to cash in on the *Twilight Saga* series. GS

▶ Alex Pettyfer, Timothy Olyphant, Teresa Palmer, Dianna Agron, Brian Howe, Patrick Sebes.
▶ *Dir* D J Caruso, *Pro* Michael Bay, *Screenplay* Alfred

Gough, Marti Noxon and Miles Millar, based on the novel *Pittacus Lore* by Jobias Hughes and James Frey, *Ph* Guillermo Navarro, *Pro Des* Tom Southwell, *Ed* Vince Filippone and Jim Page, *M* Trevor Rabin, *Cos* Marie-Sylvie Deveau.

DreamWorks SKG/Bay Films/Reliance Big Entertainment-Walt Disney Studios Motion Pictures. 109 mins. USA. 2011. Rel: 23 Feb 2011. Cert. 12A.

I Don't Know How She Does It ★★

In a slick but unendearing film of Allison Pearson's bestseller, Sarah Jessica Parker strains her lovable appeal as family breadwinner Kate Reddy, a Boston-based finance executive who, in this feeble comedy, has great difficulty juggling a career in hedge-fund managing, a husband (Greg Kinnear) and two young kids. Artificial and contrived, the lame script by Aline Brosh McKenna (*The Devil Wears Prada*, *Morning Glory*) just doesn't cut it and the heroine's constantly droning voice-over soon grates. Pierce Brosnan enlivens things in a stylish turn as SJP's New York work partner, and there are lively contributions from Christina Hendricks as her lawyer pal and Olivia Munn as her assistant. DW

▶ Sarah Jessica Parker, Pierce Brosnan, Greg Kinnear, Olivia Munn, Christina Hendricks, Kelsey Grammer.
▶ *Dir* Doug McGrath, *Pro* Donna Gigliotti, *Screenplay* Aline Brosh McKenna, from the novel by Allison Pearson, *Ph* Stuart Dryburgh, *Pro Des* Santo Loquasto, *Ed* Kevin Tent and Camilla Toniolo, *M* Aaron Zigman, *Cos* Renee Ehrlich Kalfus.

The Weinstein Company-Entertainment Film Distributors. 89 mins. USA. 2011. Rel: 16 Sep 2011. Cert. 12A.

I Saw the Devil ★★★★

Soo-hyun (Lee Byung-hun) swears vengeance when his fiancée is brutally murdered by a serial killer. She is the daughter of a retired police chief who provides Soo-hyun with information about the four suspects – so the hunt begins... Kim Jee-woon's striking revenge thriller demands attention from the opening shot and doesn't let go until the final credits. This gripping but very violent film is worth discovering before Hollywood grabs it and ruins it like Jee-woon's earlier *A Tale of Two Sisters*. (Original title: *Akmareul boatda*) GS

▶ Lee Byung-hun, Choi Min-sik, Jeon Gook-hwan, Jeon Ho-jin, Oh San-ha, Kim Yoon-seo.
▶ *Dir* Kim Jee-woon, *Pro* Kim Hyun-woo, *Screenplay* Park Hoon-jung, *Ph* Mogae Lee, *Pro Des* Cho Hwa-sung, *Ed* Nam Na-young, *M* Mowg, *Cos* Kwon Yoon-jin.

Softbank Ventures/Showbox-Mediaplex/Peppermint & Company/Siz Entertainment-Optimum Releasing. 141 mins. South Korea. 2010. Rel: 29 Apr 2011. Cert. 18.

I Spit On Your Grave ★★★

In this remake of the 1978 exploitation thriller, novelist Jennifer Hills' (Sarah Butler) idyllic retreat in a remote cabin in the woods turns into a living nightmare when a group of local thugs break in. But she manages to survive after acts of extreme cruelty and torture and returns to punish her tormentors... It is a routine revenge story with a gutsy and resourceful heroine, with each killing becoming more violent as the film goes on. GS

▶ Sarah Butler, Jeff Branson, Andrew Howard, Daniel Franzese, Rodney Eastman, Chad Lindberg, Mollie Milligan.
▶ *Dir* Steven R Monroe, *Pro* Lisa Hansen and Paul Hertzberg, *Screenplay* Stuart Morse, based on the 1978 screenplay by Meir Zarchi, *Ph* Neil Lisk, *Pro Des* Dins Danielsen, *Ed* Daniel Duncan, *M* Corey Allen Jackson, *Cos* Bonnie Stauch.

Family of the Year Productions-Cintel Films. 108 mins. USA. 2010. Rel: 21 Jan 2011. Cert. 18.

The Ides of March ★★★★

Set in Iowa, this is a drama showing how idealism all too often loses out in the rat race for political power. George Clooney's film hides its stage source adeptly and is very well played by a strong cast. Nevertheless, the writing falls short of that in such classics as *The Best Man* (1964) and *Advise and Consent* (1962) – or, indeed, Clooney's own *Good Night and Good Luck* (2005). It's pleasing enough but less memorable than one might have hoped. MS

▶ Ryan Gosling, George Clooney, Philip Seymour Hoffman, Paul Giamatti, Marisa Tomei, Jefffrey Wright, Evan Rachel Wood, Max Minghella, Jennifer Ehle.
▶ *Dir* George Clooney, *Pro* Clooney, Grant Heslov

Revenge is sweet-and-sour: Choi Min-sik, the star of *Old Boy*, makes a killing in Kim Jee-woon's very violent *I Saw the Devil*.

and Brian Oliver, *Screenplay* Clooney, Heslov and Beau Willimon based on the play *Farragut North* by Willimon, *Ph* Phedon Papamichael, *Pro Des* Sharon Seymour, *Ed* Stephen Mirrione, *M* Alexandre Desplat, *Cos* Louise Frogley.

Exclusive Media Group/Cross Creek Pictures/ Smokehouse/Appian Way etc-E1 Films. 101 mins. USA. 2011. Rel: 28 Oct 2011. Cert. 15.

Immortals ★★

For those who adored the digitalised heroism of *300*, the same producer's *Immortals* should flavour all the same parts. Visually it's a more imposing epic and there's plenty of computer-generated gore. This time it's Theseus (played by Henry Cavill, the upcoming *Man of Steel*) pitting his pecs against the taurine Hyperion (Mickey Rourke as a truly legendary bad-ass), with the gods chipping in from Olympus. Luke Evans makes a rather petulant and underwhelming Zeus – and is no match for Mickey's machismo – but then this really isn't a sermon for atheists. JC-W

❥ Henry Cavill, Freida Pinto, Mickey Rourke, John Hurt, Stephen Dorff, Luke Evans, Isabel Lucas, Stephen McHattie.
❥ *Dir* Tarsem Singh, *Pro* Mark Canton, Ryan Kavanaugh and Gianni Nunnari, *Screenplay* Charley Parlapanides and Vlas Parlapanides, *Ph* Brendan Galvin, *Pro Des* Tom Foden, *Ed* Wyatt Jones, Stuart Levy and David Rosenbloom, *M* Trevor Morris, *Cos* Eiko Ishioka.

Relativity Media/Virgin/Mark Canton Productions/ Atmosphere Entertainment/Hollywood Gang-Universal. 110 mins. USA. 2011. Rel: 11 Nov 2011. Cert. 15.

In a Better World ★★

This piece from the Danish filmmaker Susanne Bier won the 2011 Oscar for Best Foreign Language Film but did not deserve it. Set in both Denmark and Kenya, it offers a contrived and improbable story line. Evil erupts in both locations and two fathers and two sons play out a drama which by implication investigates the lawlessness below the surface of civilisation. That was done compellingly in Michael Haneke's *The White Ribbon* (2009) but here credibility fights a losing battle. (Original title: *Haevnen*) MS

❥ Mikael Persbrandt, Ulrich Thomsen, Markus Rygaard, William Jøhnk Juel Nielsen, Trine Dyrholm.
❥ *Dir* Susanne Bier, *Pro* Sisse Graum Jørgensen, *Screenplay* Bier and Anders Thomas Jensen, *Ph* Morten Søborg, *Pro Des* Peter Grant, *Ed* Pernille Bech Christensen and Morten Egholm, *M* Johan Söderqvist, *Cos* Manon Rasmussen.

Zentropa Entertainments16/Memfis Film International etc-Axiom Films. 118 mins. Denmark/Sweden/Norway. 2010. Rel: 19 Aug 2011. Cert. 15.

In Time ★★★

In this futuristic thriller time has replaced money – the rich can live forever by buying time, whereas poor people like Will (Justin Timberlake) have a daily struggle in order to live over 25. But Will is determined to stay alive and destroy the corrupt system... Andrew Niccol is a unique talent, as he demonstrated in his impressive debut *Gattaca*, and here he creates another dark world. Though

John Hurt gives some acting tips to Henry Cavill in Tarsem Singh's rather silly *Immortals*.

exceptionally well photographed by Roger Deakins, it's let down by one-dimensional performances from Timberlake and Amanda Seyfried as the rich heiress who joins forces with him. GS

➤ Justin Timberlake, Amanda Seyfried, Cillian Murphy, Shyloh Oostwald, Olivia Wilde.
➤ *Dir* and *Screenplay* Andrew Niccol, *Pro* Niccol, Marc Abraham and Eric Newman, *Ph* Roger Deakins, *Pro Des* Alex McDowell, *Ed* Zach Staenberg, *M* Craig Armstrong, *Cos* Colleen Atwood.

Regency Enterprises/New Regency/Strike Entertainment-20th Century Fox. 109 mins. USA. 2011. Rel: 1 Nov 2011. Cert. 12.

The Inbetweeners Movie ★★★★★

Far from ripping off the TV sitcom, this big-screen journey is as hilarious as ever. Yes, well, the boys do have to leave their regular environs and head for foreign parts, as is usual for TV spin-off movies, but, with the same writers and director from Channel 4, they can still do no wrong. Expanding their horizons to Crete allows the fun-seeking foursome to be even funnier and coarser than usual in their search for booze, birds and bunk-ups. Not only was the TV series the funniest comedy of the year, but the movie also wins hands down in its efforts to be ruder than a barrel-load of clunge. MHD

➤ Simon Bird, James Buckley, Blake Harrison, Joe Thomas, Emily Head, Lydia Rose Bewley, Anthony

Head, Greg Davies, David Schaal.
➤ *Dir* Ben Palmer, *Pro* Christopher Young, *Screenplay* Damon Beesley and Iain Morris, *Ph* Ben Wheeler, *Pro Des* Dick Lunn, *Ed* Charlie Fawcett and William Webb, *M* Mike Skinner and Michael Price, *Cos* Emma Bevan.

Film4/Bwark Productions/Young Films-Entertainment. 97 mins. UK. 2011. Rel: 19 Aug 2011. Cert. 15.

Incendies ★★★★★

Riveting story-telling and brilliantly intense performances from an unfamiliar cast make this French Canadian film memorable. On their mother's death two siblings are encouraged to trace the father they had never known and discover, too, that they have a brother in the Middle East. The mother's story told in flashbacks is intercut with their own discoveries. The folly of war and its tragic ironies become central to a tale true to the Middle East generally rather than specifically (it's better not to distract yourself by trying to pinpoint the unnamed setting). That point aside, this is a masterpiece and you would never guess that Denis Villeneuve's film is based on a stage play. MS

➤ Lubna Azabal, Mélissa Désormeaux-Poulin, Maxim Gaudette, Rémy Girard, Abdelghafour Elaaziz.
➤ *Dir* Denis Villeneuve, *Pro* Luc Déry and Kim McCraw, *Screenplay* Villeneuve with Valérie Beaugrand-Champagne from the play by Wajdi

Over-sexed and overseas: Simon Bird, Joe Thomas, James Buckley and Blake Harrison in the phenomenally successful The Inbetweeners Movie.

Mouawad, *Ph* André Turpin, *Pro Des* André-Line Beauparlant, *Ed* Monique Dartonne, *M* Grégoire Hetzel, *Cos* Sophie Lefebvre.

Christal Films/micro_scope/TS Productions etc-Trinity Filmed Entertainment.
131 mins. Canada/France. 2010. Rel: 24 June 2011. Cert. 15.

The Insatiable Moon ★½

A New Zealand home for the homeless is threatened with closure while one of its residents, the charismatic Arthur (Rawiri Paratene), a self-proclaimed Maori second son of God, sets out to save the world... The story of this worthy debut project is interesting but District Court Judge Rosemary Riddell's heavy-handed and sentimental direction fails to make it work. From the evidence of this she shouldn't give up her day job. GS

▶ Rawiri Paratene, Sara Wiseman, Ian Mune, Greg Johnson, Mick Innes, Jason Hoyte.
▶ *Dir* Rosemary Riddell, *Pro* Mike Riddell, Pip Piper and Rob Taylor, *Screenplay* Mike Riddell, *Ph* Thomas Burstyn, *Pro Des* Brent Hargreaves, *Ed* Paul Maxwell, *M* Neville Copland, *Cos* Chantelle Gerrard.

The Insatiable Moon-Blue Dolphin Film Distribution.
101 mins. New Zealand. 2010. Rel: 4 Mar 2011. Cert. 15.

Whisper it loudly: Ty Simpkins in James Wan's genuinely unnerving Insidious.

Inside Job ★★★★

Here's that rarity: a documentary feature shot in the widescreen format. Charles Ferguson's engrossing film takes a chronological look at developments leading to the banking crisis until it reaches a final section headed 'Accountability'. Often disturbing and occasionally hilarious (economists do not always emerge well!), this is an intelligent, informative work. Music used, including pop songs, can seem out of place but the photography is superb and Matt Dillon delivers the commentary sensibly without frills. MS

▶ With William Ackman, Daniel Alpert, Eliot Spitzer, Eric Halperin, Kristin Davis.
▶ *Dir* and *Written by* Charles Ferguson, *Pro* Ferguson and Audrey Marrs, *Ph* Kalyanee Mam, Svetlana Cvetko and Gray Mitchell, *Ed* Chad Beck and Adam Bolt, *M* Alex Heffes.

Sony Pictures Classics/Representational Pictures/Screen Pass Pictures-Sony Pictures Releasing.
109 mins. USA. 2010. Rel: 18 Feb 2011. Cert. 12A.

Insidious ★★★

As an attractive young couple and their two kids move into a new house, the wife starts to imagine strange noises and apparitions... When, in 2004, James Wan directed the original *Saw*, he set a new benchmark for the horror film. Here, he returns to more traditional territory, orchestrating a genuinely unnerving symphony of creaking doors, demented whispers and sudden loud noises. Let's say that this time around Wan is a little more insidious. The first half is an object lesson in producing genuine unease and heartbeat acceleration. But the later scenes are, perhaps inevitably, a little over-baked. JC-W

▶ Patrick Wilson, Rose Byrne, Barbara Hershey, Lin Shaye.
▶ *Dir* James Wan, *Pro* Jason Blum, Oren Peli and Steven Schneider, *Screenplay* Leigh Whannell, *Ph* David M. Brewer and John R. Leonetti, *Pro Des* Aaron Sims, *Ed* Kirk Morri and James Wan, *M* Joseph Bishara, *Cos* Kristin M Burke.

FilmDistrict/Stage 6 Films/Alliance Films/IM Global/Haunted Movies-Momentum Pictures.
102 mins. USA. 2010. 29 Apr 2011. Cert. 15.

The Interrupters ★★★★½

Back in 1995 Steve James made one of the great American documentaries, *Hoop Dreams*. This new work of his is almost as remarkable. Set in Chicago, it's about an organisation known as Cease Fire which, employing reformed criminals and others related to gangsters, uses their ability to make people in that world listen. They intervene to prevent yet more violence in the form of equally violent retaliation. The shaping

of the film may not be perfect, but James is a born filmmaker and this tribute to Cease Fire is a heartwarming experience. MS

▶ *Dir* and *Ph* Steve James, *Pro* Alex Kotlowitz and James, *Ed* Aaron Wickenden and James, *M* Joshua Abrams.

Kartemquin Films/WGBH/Frontline/BBC Storyville etc-Dogwoof Pictures.

128 mins. USA/UK/Canada/Norway/Sweden/Denmark. 2011. Rel: 12 Aug 2011. Cert. 15.

Ironclad ★★

In 13th century England King John (Paul Giamatti) signs the Magna Carta against his wishes but soon after begins a war across the country in order to regain his power. However, his vicious and ruthless plans are challenged when he reaches the castle of Rochester as Baron Albany (Brian Cox) leads a group of rebel warriors and Templar Knights against him... The first half is strong and gritty, but the endlessly repetitive battle sequences lose their impact well before the end. GS

▶ James Purefoy, Brian Cox, Kate Mara, Derek Jacobi, Paul Giamatti, Charles Dance, Jason Flemyng, Jamie Foreman, Mackenzie Crook, Aneurin Barnard, Annabelle Apsion.
▶ *Dir* Jonathan English, *Pro* English, Rick Benattar and Andrew J Curtis, *Screenplay* English, Erick Kastel and Stephen McDool, from a story by English, *Ph* David Eggby, *Pro Des* Joseph C Nemec III, *Ed* Peter Amundson and Gavin Buckley, *M* Lorne Balfe, *Cos* Beatrix Aruna Pastor.

VIP Medienfonds 4/Rising Star/Silver Reel/Premiere Picture/ContentFilm International/Mythic International

Entertainment etc-Warner Bros.
121 mins. UK/USA/Germany. 2011. Rel: 4 Mar 2011. Cert. 15.

Island ★★½

The island of the title is the Isle of Mull and the images of it are striking and atmospheric. However, it's unfortunate that the tale told seems increasingly unconvincing, and the first sentence (it comes in voice over) tells us too much too soon: it's a woman revealing that she has tracked down her birth mother and plans to kill her. There is good playing from Natalie Press as the protagonist and from Colin Morgan as the son of the intended victim, but neither can overcome the implausible elements which are only increased when melodrama is added to the mother's story too. MS

▶ Natalie Press, Colin Morgan, Janet McTeer, Tanya Franks, Denise Orita.
▶ *Dir* Brek Taylor and Elizabeth Mitchell, *Pro* Amy Gardner, Clare Tinsley and Charlotte Wontner, *Screenplay* Mitchell from the novel by Jane Rogers, *Ph* Rain Li, *Pro Des* Damien Creagh, *Ed* Sam Sneade, *M* Michael Price, *Cos* Tamar Zaig.

Soda Pictures/Nikki Black Films/Finite Films etc-Soda Pictures.
90 mins. UK. 2010. Rel: 22 Apr 2011. Cert. 12A.

It's Kind of a Funny Story ★★★★

Troubled 16-year-old Craig (Keir Gilchrist) wants to end his life by jumping off Brooklyn Bridge. Instead he checks himself into a psychiatric ward in which he has to remain for at least five days.

Any old iron: Jason Flemyng (centre) in Jonathan English's gritty but repetitive *Ironclad*.

A not-so-plain
Jane: Michael
Fassbender,
as Rochester,
embraces Mia
Wasikowska in
Cary Fukunaga's
Jane Eyre, the
19th film version.

Initially he regrets his decision, but soon learns more about life than ever before in this strange environment thanks to his friendship with Bobby (Zack Galifianakis). This dark comedy is sensitively directed and well acted, particularly by Galifianakis as the free-spirited mental patient. GS

▷ Keir Gilchrist, Zach Galifianakis, Emma Roberts, Lauren Graham, Jim Gaffigan, Viola Davis.
▷ *Dir* and *Screenplay* Anna Boden and Ryan Fleck, from the novel by Ned Vizzini, *Pro* Kevin Misher and Ben Browning, *Ph* Andrij Parekh, *Pro Des* Beth Mickle, *Ed* Anna Boden, *M* Broken Social Scene, *Cos* Kurt and Bart.

Focus Features/Wayfare Entertainment/Misher Films/ Gowanus Projections/Journeyman Pictures-Universal Pictures.
101 mins. USA. 2010. Rel: 7 Jan 2011. Cert. 12A.

Jack Goes Boating ★

This New York tale about two contrasted couples is based on a stage play and sounds like it. One couple have a disintegrating marriage, but the main focus is on Jack (Philip Seymour Hoffman also making his directorial debut) and his hesitant yet persistent wooing of Connie (Amy Ryan). Hoffman lacks the warmth that Ernest Borgnine brought to *Marty* (1955) and as director misjudges the balance between comedy and drama. This is a major disappointment. MS

▷ Philip Seymour Hoffman, Amy Ryan, John Ortiz, Daphne Rubin-Vega.

▷ *Dir* Philip Seymour Hoffman, *Pro* Marc Turtletaub, Peter Saraf and others, *Screenplay* Bob Glaudini, based on his play, *Ph* Mott Hupfel, *Pro Des* Thérèse DePrez, *Ed* Brian A Kates, *M* Grizzly Bear, *Cos* Mimi O'Donnell.

Overture Films/Big Beach/Cooper's Town etc-Trinity Filmed Entertainment.
91 mins. USA. 2010. Rel: 4 Nov 2011. Cert. 15.

Jane Eyre ★★★★½

It may take a few minutes to settle, and it ends a shade inconclusively, but this is nevertheless a splendidly realised account of Charlotte Brontë's novel. Michael Fassbender is a fine Rochester, while Judi Dench as the housekeeper is pitch-perfect in support. However, it is Mia Wasikowska in her best performance yet who makes this special: you can forget the plot contrivances when you identify with her courageous, determined Jane seeking to find fulfilment in life as her own person. MS

▷ Mia Wasikowska, Michael Fassbender, Jamie Bell, Judi Dench, Su Elliott.
▷ *Dir* Cary Joji Fukunaga, *Pro* Alison Owen and Paul Trijbits, *Screenplay* Moira Buffini, based on the novel by Charlotte Brontë, *Ph* Adriano Goldman, *Pro Des* Will Hughes-Jones, *Ed* Melanie Ann Oliver, *M* Dario Marianelli, *Cos* Michael O'Connor.

Focus Features/BBC Films/Ruby Films etc-Universal Pictures.
121 mins. UK/USA. 2011. Rel: 9 Sep 2011. Cert. PG.

Jig ★★★★

An engaging documentary about the 40th annual Irish Dancing World Championships may sound like a contradiction in terms but Sue Bourne's film defies expectations. She follows the gruelling training of young hopefuls from around the globe – from Northern Ireland to Russia, then England via Holland to America. They only have one thing in common – they are desperate to fulfil their dream and win the prestigious world contest in Glasgow. Highly watchable and very touching, with a nail-biting climax. GS

❯ *Dir* and *Pro* Sue Bourne, *Ph* Ed Clarke, Dan Etheridge and Jason Weidner, *Ed* Colin Monie, *M* Patrick Doyle.

BBC Scotland/Creative Scotland/Headgear Films-Screen Media Films.

99 mins. UK. 2011. Rel: 6 May 2011. Cert PG.

John Carpenter's The Ward ★★★½

A group of attractive young women, including Kirsten (Amber Heard), are patients in a mental hospital where something dark and mysterious is lurking. Kirsten is being kept there against her will and is desperate to get out before it is too late... After a series of stinkers, this is the first film from Carpenter for seven years and he delivers the goods with a suitably atmospheric thriller boasting a clever twist. GS

❯ Amber Heard, Mamie Gummer, Danielle Panabaker, Laura-Leigh, Lyndsy Fonseca, Jared Harris.
❯ *Dir* John Carpenter, *Pro* Andrew Spaulding, Mike Marcus, Doug Manoff and Peter Block, *Screenplay* Michael Rasmussen and Shawn Rasmussen, *Ph* Yaron Orbach, *Pro Des* Paul Peters, *Ed* Patrick McMahon, *M* Mark Kilian, *Cos* Lisa Caryl.

FilmNation Entertainment/Premiere Picture/Echo Lake Entertainment/North by Northwest Entertainment/ Modern VideoFilm/A Bigger Boat-Warner Bros.

88 mins. USA. 2010. Rel: 21 Jan 2011. Cert. 15.

Johnny English Reborn ★★

Rowan Atkinson's fumbling MI7 operative is an intriguing creation. While hopelessly accident-prone, he is not without a certain canny intuition, being a haphazard alloy of Mr Bean, Inspector Clouseau and James Bond. In this sequel he is appointed to track down a terrorist organisation and is assigned a sidekick in the form of an eager, awestruck black teenager. The problem with the franchise is that the Bond spoof is so late 1960s. Even the gadgets that English has at his disposal are not that exciting by today's standards: and so we are left with just a smidgen of old-fashioned charm. JC-W

❯ Rowan Atkinson, Gillian Anderson, Dominic West, Rosamund Pike, Daniel Kaluuya, Richard Schiff, Stephen Campbell Moore, Tim McInnerny.
❯ *Dir* Oliver Parker, *Pro* Tim Bevan, Eric Fellner and Chris Clark, *Screenplay* William Davies and Hamish McColl, *Ph* Danny Cohen, *Pro Des* Jim Clay, *Ed* Guy Bensley, *M* Ilan Eshkeri, *Cos* Beatrix Aruna Pasztor.

Universal/Relativity Media/StudioCanal/Working Title-Universal.

101 mins. USA/UK/France. 2011. Rel: 7 Oct 2011. Cert. PG.

Judy Moody and the Not Bummer Summer ★★

Jordana Beatty (14) kicks up sparks in a sweet and energetic turn as third-grader Judy Moody who plans her most exciting summer ever. Based on Megan McDonald's books, with the script co-written by her, this is an unsurprising small kids' comedy, targeting its audience without quite enough charm or gusto. Showing nice rapport with Beatty, Heather Graham is another bright spot as free-spirited artist Aunt Opal, who's spending the summer looking after Judy and her kid brother Stink (Parris Mosteller). With catchy music it's pleasurable fun for young girls, although parents would be less patient with its lack of good laughs and story dynamism. DW

❯ Jordana Beatty, Heather Graham, Preston Bailey, Parris Mosteller, Kristoffer Winters, Janet Varney.
❯ *Dir* John Schultz, *Pro* Gary Magness and Sarah Siegel-Magness, *Screenplay* Megan McDonald and Kathy Waugh, from the *Judy Moody* book series by McDonald, *Ph* Shawn Maurer, *Pro Des* Cynthia Kaye Charette, *Ed* John Pace III, *M* Richard Gibbs, *Cos* Mary Jane Fort.

Smokewood Entertainment Group/Reel FX Creative Studios-Universal Pictures International.

91 mins. USA. 2011. Rel: 21 Oct 2011. Cert. PG.

Knife move: Rowan Atkinson adopts a few more tics in Oliver Parker's old-fashioned *Johnny English Reborn*.

Julia's Eyes ★★★½

Julia (Belén Rueda) begins a race against time in order to find what led to her blind twin sister's suicide – because Julia, like her sister, suffers from a degenerative disease that will soon leave her blind too. This is a gripping film with stunning cinematography and excellent production values. Guillem Morales' vision and confident direction make it a compelling experience, although the dark, dreamlike world that Julia enters occasionally feels less persuasive. (Original title: *Los ojos de Julia*) GS

❯ Belén Rueda, Lluis Homar, Pablo Derqui, Joan Dalmau, Boris Ruiz, Dani Codina, Francesc Orella.
❯ *Dir* Guillem Morales, *Pro* Guillermo del Toro, Juan Carlos Caro, Joaquin Padro and José Torrescusa, *Screenplay* Morales and Oriol Paulo, *Ph* Oscar Faura, *Pro Des* Balter Gallart, *Ed* Joan Manel Vilaseca, *M* Fernando Velázquez, *Cos* Maria Reyes.

Universal Pictures International/Antena 3 Films/Canal+ España/Catalan Film & Television/Mes Films etc-Optimum Releasing.
112 mins. Spain. 2010. Rel: 20 May 2011. Cert. 15.

Good to go: Jennifer Aniston supplies some calibre to Dennis Dugan's Just Go With It.

Junkhearts ★★★

Eddie Marsan is deeply impressive here as an ex-soldier traumatised by his experiences in Belfast and the awarded newcomer Candese Reid does well as the homeless girl he befriends in London's Brick Lane. But unfortunately plot developments are less persuasive and a separate story line leading to a foreseeable plot twist interrupts the main narrative tiresomely. MS

❯ Eddie Marsan, Tom Sturridge, Romola Garai, Candese Reid, John Boyega.
❯ *Dir* Tinge Krishnan, *Pro* Karen Katz, *Screenplay* Simon Frank, *Ph* Catherine Derry, *Pro Des* Kristian Milsted, *Ed* Alistair Reid, *M* Christopher N Bangs, *Cos* Camille Benda.

Hustle Productions/Coded Pictures/Disruptive Element Films-Soda Pictures.
92 mins. UK. 2011. Rel: 4 Nov 2011. Cert. 18.

Just Do It: A Tale of Modern Outlaws ★

This well-intentioned but heavily one-sided documentary follows UK direct action groups campaigning for various green causes. They occupy a power station and mobilise protests on massed bicycles at the 2009 G20 Summit in Copenhagen; they make tea in tents and talk to coppers. Would that there were some debate about all this rather than just gung-ho enthusiasm for their methods and the causes on offer. JC

❯ *Dir* and *Ph* Emily James, *Pro* Lauren Simpson, *Art Dir* Doctor Dee, *Ed* Julian Rodd, James Leadbitter and Kurt Engfehr, *M* DJ Rubbish.

Left Field Films-Dogwoof Pictures.
90 mins. UK. 2011. Rel: 15 July 2011. Cert. 12A.

Just Go With It ★★½

A successful plastic surgeon is forced to invent a wife in order to ensnare a beautiful blonde half his age… As Adam Sandler packages go, this one works better than most. The man himself goes through the usual motions – laidback, amiable, funny – but is blessed by a three-dimensional co-star in Jennifer Aniston at the top of her game. The piece also accumulates a certain sweetness and there are some genuinely funny moments (a lot at the expense of the cosmetically altered). Based on the 1969 comedy *Cactus Flower*, which won Goldie Hawn an Oscar. JC-W

❯ Adam Sandler, Jennifer Aniston, Nick Swardson, Brooklyn Decker, Dave Matthews, Nicole Kidman.
❯ *Dir* Dennis Dugan, *Pro* Jack Giarraputo, Adam Sandler and Heather Parry, *Screenplay* Allan Loeb and Timothy Dowling, *Ph* Theo Van de Sande, *Pro Des* Perry Andelin Blake, *Ed* Tom Costain, *M* Rupert Gregson-Williams.

Columbia Pictures/Happy Madison-Sony.
116 mins. USA. 2011. Rel: 11 Feb 2011. Cert. 12A

Justice ★★★

What would you do if your wife was raped and
beaten to within an inch of her life? What would
you do if you knew who the rapist was and the
police could do nothing? Well, *Justice* wears a
number of moral hats but doffs them all to the
mother of genera. There is some excellent stunt
work – pedestrians on the freeway, a car pushed
off the roof of a multi-storey – and an intelligent
villain. And like most Donaldson thrillers (*No
Way Out*, *Dante's Peak*, *The Recruit*) the film makes
a good Saturday night out. Just don't expect to
remember it Monday morning. JC-W

▶ Nicolas Cage, January Jones, Guy Pearce, Harold
Perrineau, Jennifer Carpenter, Xander Berkeley,
Kathleen Wilhoite.
▶ *Dir* Roger Donaldson, *Pro* Tobey Maguire and
Ram Bergman, *Screenplay* Robert Tannen, *Ph* David
Tattersall, *Pro Des* J Dennis Washington, *Ed* Jay
Cassidy, *M* J Peter Robinson, *Cos* Caroline Eselin.

Endgame Entertainment/Aura Film/Fierce
Entertainment/Material Pictures/Ram Bergman
Productions/Maguire Entertainment-Momentum
Pictures.
104 mins. USA/UK/Italy. 2011. Rel: 18 Nov 2011. Cert. 15.

Justin Bieber: Never Say Never 3D ★★★

Justin Bieber's warm personality and innocence
are easily transported to the big screen in this
likable documentary. There are extracts from
family videos demonstrating his talent from a
very young age before he became a YouTube
phenomenon. But the core of the film follows
Justin and his plethora of fans as he tours from
Canada to New York's Madison Square Garden.
It is all very watchable but we never get to know
the real person, just the persona. GS

▶ Justin Bieber, Boys II Men, Miley Cyrus, Sean
Kingston, Ludacris, Jaden Smith, Snoop Dogg.
▶ *Dir* Jon M Chu, *Pro* Usher Raymond, Antonio
Reid, Jane Lipsitz, Scooter Braun and Dan Cutforth,
Ph Reed Smoot, *Pro Des* Devorah Herbert, *Ed* Jay
Cassidy, Jillian Twigger Moul and Avi Youabian,
M Deborah Lurie, *Cos* Kurt and Bart.

MTV Films/AEG Live/Island Def Jam Music Group/
Scooter Braun Films/Magical Elves Productions/Insurge
Pictures-Paramount Pictures.
105 mins. USA. 2011. Rel: 18 Feb 2011. Cert. U.

Kaboom ★★½

Seemingly seeking to emulate David Lynch as
well as his own wilder works, Gregg Araki here
captures contemporary teenage life but then
falls into absurdity. The second half features
mysterious sects, a witch and, ultimately, the end
of the world. An extraordinary mix of this kind
can work (think *Donnie Darko*) but Araki can't
bring it off. Long before the end what had looked
like a film of ideas – albeit ideas above its station
– becomes puerile. MS

▶ Thomas Dekker, Haley Bennett, Chris Zylka,
Roxane Mesquida, Juno Temple.

But not as we
know it: Thomas
Dekker in Gregg
Araki's absurd
Kaboom.

> *Dir, Screenplay* and *Ed* Gregg Araki, *Pro* Andrea Sperling and Araki, *Ph* Sandra Valde-Hansen, *Pro Des* Todd Fjelsted, *M* Ulrich Schnauss, Mark Peters and others, *Cos* Trayce Gigi Field.

Why Not US Productions/Desperate Pictures/Wild Bunch etc-Artificial Eye.
86 mins. USA/France. 2010. Rel: 10 June 2011. Cert. 15.

Kill List ★★★★½

The 'list' comprises the number of bodies to be taken out by Jay (Neil Maskell) and Gal (Michael Smiley), hit men who need to raise cash to pay their bills. The film is set in suburban Britain and the ordinariness of the setting clashes ironically with the crazy events taking place. This is a truly black horror-comic and writer-director Ben Wheatley displays an obvious relish for the absurdity of violence, as witness the list: a librarian, a priest, an MP and a hunchback. Terrifyingly authentic performances from Maskell and Smiley as well as MyAnna Buring as Jay's wife combine with, among other delights, an awful but hilarious dinner party scene. MHD

> Neil Maskell, MyAnna Buring, Harry Simpson, Michael Smiley, Emma Fryer, Struan Rodger.
> *Dir* Ben Wheatley, *Pro* Claire Jones and Andrew Starke, *Screenplay* Wheatley and Amy Jump, *Ph* Laurie Rose, *Pro Des* David Butterworth, *Ed* Robin Hill, *M* Jim Williams, *Cos* Lance Milligan.

Rook Films/Warp X-Optimum Releasing.
95 mins. UK. 2011. Rel: 2 Sep 2011. Cert. 18.

Kill the Irishman ★★★★

British actor Ray Stevenson is excellent as Danny Greene, an Irish thug and longshoreman working for mobsters in Cleveland during the 1970s, in this startling true story. He rises from rags to riches and falls again, infuriating the Mafia, surviving many attempts to kill him and becoming a bit of a folk hero. Defying what looks like a TV budget, this stylishly shot gangster movie is held back by script problems, with too many clichés and jarringly duff lines, but it still stays involving and gripping throughout. Christopher Walken, Val Kilmer, Paul Sorvino, Robert Davi, Tony Lo Bianco and Vinnie Jones form the finest character support line-up. DW

> Ray Stevenson, Vincent D'Onofrio, Val Kilmer, Christopher Walken, Linda Cardellini, Vinnie Jones, Tony Lo Bianco, Robert Davi, Paul Sorvino.
> *Dir* Jonathan Hensleigh, *Pro* Tommy Reid, Bart Rosenblatt, Al Corley and Eugene Musso, *Screenplay* Hensleigh and Jeremy Walters, from the book *To Kill the Irishman* by Rick Porrello, *Ph* Karl Walter Lindenlaub, *Pro Des* Patrizia von Brandenstein, *Ed* Douglas Crise, *M* Patrick Cassidy, *Cos* Melissa Bruning.

Anchor Bay Films/Code Entertainment/Sweet William Productions/Dundee Entertainment-Eagle Films.
106 mins. USA. 2011. Rel: 25 Aug 2011. Cert. 18.

Killing Bono ★★★

During the 1980s Dublin brothers Neil and Ivan McCormick (Ben Barnes and Robert Sheehan) struggle to hit the big time as rock 'n' roll musicians while their old school mates U2 have rocketed to the top. The first half of this engaging comedy based on true events has terrific energy, but as the film develops it loses some of its impact. Barnes is on good form as the obstinate musician prepared to sacrifice almost anything in order to reach his goal. GS

> Ben Barnes, Robert Sheehan, Ralph Brown, Pete Postlethwaite, Jason Byrne, Sam Cory, Seán Doyle, Mark Griffin, Luke Treadaway.
> *Dir* Nick Hamm, *Pro* Simon Maxwell, Ian Flooks,

Unavoidable contract: Neil Maskell in Ben Wheatley's stark, unsettling *Kill List*.

Mark Huffam and Piers Tempest, *Screenplay* Dick Clement, Ian La Frenais, Simon Maxwell and Ben Bond, based on Neil McCormick's book *Killing Bono: I Was Bono's Doppelganger, Ph* Kieran McGuigan, *Pro Des* Tom McCullagh, *Ed* Billy Sneddon, *Music Supervisor* Tarquin Gotch, *Cos* Lorna Marie Mugan.

Northern Ireland Screen/Cinema Three/Generator Entertainment/Greenroom Entertainment/Isotope Films/Matador Pictures/Molinaire Studio etc-Paramount Pictures.

114 mins. UK/Ireland. 2011. Rel: 1 Apr 2011. Cert. 15.

Killer Elite ★★★

Even though there may be a factual basis to it, this is a non-stop action thriller set in 1980 featuring a reluctant assassin. The scorn of many critics may be understandable (just contrast this with the imagination displayed in, say, *Source Code*) but, although overlong, *Killer Elite* will appeal to its target audience. Jason Statham does the heroics well, Clive Owen is strong and it is what it is. MS

❯ Jason Statham, Clive Owen, Robert De Niro, Ben Mendelsohn, Yvonne Strahovski, Aden Young.
❯ *Dir* Gary McKendry, *Pro* Sigurjon Sighvatsson, Steven Chasman and others, *Screenplay* Matt Sherring, from the book *The Feather Men* by Ranulph Fiennes, *Ph* Simon Duggan, *Pro Des* Michelle McGahey, *Ed* John Gilbert, *M* Johnny

Klimek and Reinhold Heil, *Cos* Katherine Milne.

Omnilab Media/Ambience Entertainment etc-Entertainment Film Distributors.
116 mins. Australia/USA/UK. 2011. Rel: 23 Sept 2011. Cert. 15.

The King's Speech ★★★★

This eminently British film turned over a minor page in Royal Family history and went straight to the public's heart, scooping every award going. David Seidler's artful screenplay details the public speaking difficulties of the reluctant King George VI following his brother's abdication. He was helped with his stammer by one Lionel Logue, an Australian therapist whose unorthodox methods provide the film with most of its delights. Lovingly filmed and with the classiest cast of the year, it garnered plaudits all round, particularly for Colin Firth, but some might say his role was eclipsed by the astonishing Geoffrey Rush as the King's eccentric aide. MHD

❯ Colin Firth, Geoffrey Rush, Helena Bonham Carter, Guy Pearce, Derek Jacobi, Michael Gambon, Claire Bloom, Timothy Spall, Anthony Andrews, Jennifer Ehle, Eve Best.
❯ *Dir* Tom Hooper, *Pro* Gareth Unwin, Iain Canning, Emile Sherman, *Screenplay* David Seidler, *Ph* Danny Cohen, *Pro Des* Eve Stewart, *Ed* Tariq Anwar, *M* Alexandre Desplat, *Cos* Jenny Beavan.

Royal pardon? Colin Firth in his Oscar-winning performance as George VI in Tom Hooper's award-laden *The King's Speech*.

— **Knuckle**

Martial artlessness: Crane, Tigress, Po, Monkey and Viper in Jennifer Yuh Nelson's "terminally painful" *Kung Fu Panda 2*.

The Weinstein Company/UK Film Council/Momentum Pictures/See Saw Films/Bedlam/FilmNation Entertainment etc-Momentum Pictures.
118 mins. UK. 2010. Rel: 7 Jan 2011. Cert. 12A.

Knuckle ★★

Billed as 'the hardest hitting documentary of the year', this ramshackle home movie focuses on two travelling clans bent on beating the excreta out of each other. The interesting part is that documentarian Ian Palmer filmed the feud over a 12-year period; consequently, we get to see the young protagonists lose their hair and gain their beer guts. But, with its rough-and-ready camerawork and pink-and-grey palette, *Knuckle* is a visually unappetising filmic experience. Guy Ritchie's take on the phenomenon of bare-knuckle fighting in *Snatch* (also featuring Irish gypsies) was an altogether more entertaining affair. JC-W

▶ *Dir*, *Screenplay* and *Ph* Ian Palmer, *Pro* Palmer, Teddy Leifer, Nick Fraser and Alan Maher, *Ed* Oliver Huddleston, *M* Jessica Dannheisser and Ilan Eshkeri.
Bord Scannan na hEireann/Irish Film Board/BBC Storyville/ Irish Film Board/Rise Films-Revolver Entertainment.
96 mins. Ireland/UK. 2011. Rel: 5 Aug 2011. Cert. 15.

Kung Fu Panda 2 ★★

Po, the kung fu fighting panda, is back following his first multi-million dollar success at the box-office. That said, if you enjoyed *Panda 1*, you'll love its sequel. This time Po (voiced by Jack Black) has to save China (where else?) from a once-exiled royal peacock called Lord Shen (Gary Oldman) and his new-found weapon of destruction. With the aid of Po's Furious Five, Tigress (Angelina Jolie), Monkey (Jackie Chan), Mantis (Seth Rogen), Viper (Lucy Liu) and Crane (David Cross), plus advice from mentor Shifu (Dustin Hoffman), Po wins the day. You may like

this sort of thing but this seasoned old viewer found it terminally painful. MHD

▶ Voices of Jack Black, Angelina Jolie, Jackie Chan, Dustin Hoffman, Michelle Yeoh, Lucy Liu, Gary Oldman, Seth Rogen, David Cross, Jean-Claude Van Damme.
▶ *Dir* Jennifer Yuh Nelson, *Pro* Melissa Cobb, *Screenplay* Jonathan Aibel and Glenn Berger, *Pro Des* Raymond Zibach, *Ed* Maryann Brandon and Clare Knight, *M* John Powell and Hans Zimmer.
DreamWorks Animation-Paramount Pictures.
91 mins. USA. 2011. Rel: 10 June 2011. Cert. PG.

The Lady ★★

Luc Besson directs a weighty drama detailing how Aung San Suu Kyi (Michelle Yeoh) became the leader of Burma's pro-democracy movement – and the toll this took on her English resident university lecturer husband Michael Aris (David Thewlis) and their kids. Trying earnestly to represent the historical facts, the proceedings rapidly become something of a plod. The two leads, though, are well cast. JC

▶ Michelle Yeoh, David Thewlis, Jonathan Raggett, Jonathan Woodhouse, Susan Wooldridge, Benedict Wong.
▶ *Dir* Luc Besson, *Pro* Besson, Andy Harries, Jean Todt and Virginie Silla, *Screenplay* Rebecca Frayn, *Ph* Thierry Arbogast, *Pro Des* Hugues Tissandier, *Ed* Julien Ray, *M* Eric Serra, *Cos* Olivier Bériot.
Europa Corp/Left Bank Pictures/Canal+/France 2 Cinéma/ France Télévision-Entertainment Film Distributors.
132 mins. France/UK. 2011. Rel: 30 Dec 2011. Cert. 12A.

Larry Crowne ★★

This is the familiar tale of a grown-up guy who goes back to school. Familiar, because it's already been milked by Rodney Dangerfield in *Back to School*, Adam Sandler in *Billy Madison* and Oliver

Litondo in *The First Grader*. Worse, it's the sort of film that Tom Hanks was unfairly accused of epitomising when, in fact, he was serving up the likes of *Saving Private Ryan* and *Road to Perdition*. Genial, coy and bland, it is the cinematic equivalent of polystyrene. And with Hanks credited as producer, director and co-writer, he has only himself to blame. JC-W

‣ Tom Hanks, Julia Roberts, Bryan Cranston, Cedric the Entertainer, Taraji P Henson, Gugu Mbatha-Raw, Pam Grier, Rita Wilson.
‣ *Dir* Tom Hanks, *Pro* Hanks and Gary Goetzman, *Screenplay* Hanks and Nia Vardalos, *Ph* Philippe Rousselot, *Pro Des* Victor Kempster, *Ed* Alan Vody, *M* James Newton Howard, *Cos* Albert Wolsky.

Universal/Vendome Pictures/Playtone-Optimum Releasing.
98 mins. USA. 2011. Rel: 1 July 2011. Cert. 12A.

Last Night ★★★

This is a woman's picture of a traditional kind. Set in Manhattan, it features Keira Knightley as a wife suspicious as to the fidelity of her husband (the dull Sam Worthington) and herself tempted by a former beau (Guillaume Canet). It's not memorable, but the right audience may enjoy it since it is ably mounted and Knightley is entirely at home in her role. MS

‣ Keira Knightley, Sam Worthington, Guillaume Canet, Eva Mendes, Griffin Dunne.
‣ *Dir* and *Screenplay* Massy Tadjedin, *Pro* Nick Wechsler, Tadjedin and Sidonie Dumas, *Ph* Peter

Deming, *Pro Des* Tim Grimes, *Ed* Susan E. Morse, *M* Clint Mansell, *Cos* Ann Roth.

Miramax Films/Nick Wechsler Productions/Westbourne/
Gaumont etc-Optimum Releasing.
93 mins. USA/France. 2009. Rel: 3 June 2011. Cert. 12A.

Legacy: Black Ops ★★★

Idris Elba gives a riveting central performance as psychologically wounded Black Ops operative Malcolm Gray in this gripping and thoughtful thriller that twists and turns satisfyingly. A member of a botched covert operation in Eastern Europe, he killed the family of a terrorist who then captured and tortured him. Escaping from an army medical facility, he's now going crazy in a shabby Brooklyn room, pondering who betrayed him. Spoiler hint: his brother (Eamonn Walker) is an ambitious Republican senator. Not always believable maybe, but consistently fascinating, this is an unusual, extremely well-paced, carefully crafted movie that works through intelligence, tension, atmosphere and strong acting. (Original title: *Legacy*) DW

‣ Idris Elba, William Hope, Monique Gabriela Curnan, Scott O'Keefe, Clarke Peters, Julian Wadham, Eamonn Walker.
‣ *Dir* and *Screenplay* Thomas Ikimi, *Pro* Ikimi, Arabella Page Croft and Kieran Parker, *Ph* Jonathan Harvey, *Pro Des* Gordon Rogers, *Ed* Ikimi and Richard Graham, *M* Mark Kilian, *Cos* Harriet Edmonds.

Black Camel Pictures-Kaleidoscope.
93 mins. Nigeria/UK. 2010. Rel: 11 Mar 2011. Cert. 15.

Double Infidelity: Keira Knightley in Massy Tadjedin's dull and rarefied *Last Night*.

Life Goes On ★★½

It's good to see Satyajit Ray's Sharmila Tagore again but sad that it should be in this London-based tale of an Indian family, The director Sangeeta Datta dares to speak of wanting to promote meaningful cinema yet this is no more than soap opera. Each member of the family has his or her own drama but the writing is banal and the attempts to find parallels with Shakespeare's *King Lear* are risible. Pity the players. MS

❧ Girish Karnad, Om Puri, Sharmila Tagore, Soha Ali Khan, Mukulika Banerjee, Neerja Naik.
❧ *Dir* and *Screenplay* Sangeeta Datta, *Ph* Robert Shacklady, *Pro Des* Vipul Sangoi, *Ed* Arghyakamal Mitra, *M* Soumik Datta.

Stormglass Productions/SD Films LLP-Crabtree Films. 120 mins. UK. 2009. Rel: 11 Mar 2011. Cert. 12A.

Life, Above All ★★★★

The Boy in the Striped Pyjamas (2008) showed how serious a film can be even when young teenagers are part of the target audience. This film set in South Africa has a 12-year-old heroine and might well appeal to that audience as well as to adults. It's a thoughtful, dramatic tale of village life, but it's best to approach it without advance knowledge of which serious issues are going to become crucial to the story. MS

❧ Khtomotso Manyake, Keaobaka Makanyane, Harriet Manemela, Lerato Mvelase.
❧ *Dir* Oliver Schmitz, *Pro* Oliver Stoltz, *Screenplay* Dennis Foon, based on Allan Stratton's novel *Chandra's Secrets*, *Ph* Bernhard Jasper, *Pro Des* Christiane Rothe, *Ed* Dirk Grau, *M* Ali N Askin, *Cos* Nadia Kruger.

Dreamer Joint Venture/Enigma Pictures etc-Peccadillo Pictures.

Village of the damned: Keaobaka Makanyane and Khomotso Manyaka in Oliver Schmitz's compelling, even reviving *Life, Above All.*

106 mins. Germany/South Africa/Canada/France. 2010. Rel: 27 May 2011. Cert. 12A.

Life in a Day ★★★½

This film finds Kevin Macdonald putting together footage taken during one day, 24 July 2010, in response to an invitation for such material put out on YouTube. In effect 4,500 hours of film were cut down to 95 minutes, going through the day hour by hour. Some of it is striking, but it's less meaningful than one would have hoped. Although decidedly uneven, YouTube users especially may welcome it. MS

❧ *Dir* Kevin Macdonald, *Pro* Liza Marshall, *Ed* Joe Walker, *M* Harry Gregson-Williams and Matthew Herbert.

YouTube/Scott Free Films etc-Scott Free. 95 mins. UK/USA/Republic of Korea. 2011. Rel: 17 June 2011. Cert. 12A.

The Light Thief ★★★★

It's an engaging novelty to see a film from Kyrgyzstan. This piece by Aktan Arym Kubat concerns a villager who as an electrician has ways to help his neighbours pay less for their supply. But what starts as a relatively gentle Tati-like comedy darkens and the second half suggests a political allegory. There's enough despair here to bring out the irony in the dedication, which reads 'To my grandchildren with wishes of happiness and luck.' (Original title: *Svet-ake*) MS

❧ Aktan Arym Kubat, Taalaikan Abazova, Askat Sulaimanov, Aran Amanov.
❧ *Dir* Aktan Arym Kubat, *Pro* Altynai Koichumanova, Cedomir Kolar and others, *Screenplay* Kubat and Talip Ibrimov, *Ph* Hasan Kydyraliyev, *Pro Des* Talgat Asyrankulov, *Ed* Peter Markovic, *M* André Matthias, *Cos* Inara Abdieva.

Pallas Film/A.S.A.P. Films/Volya Films/Oy Art/ZDF/Arte etc-Soda Pictures. 80 mins. Germany/France/The Netherlands/Kyrgyzstan. 2010. Rel: 29 July 2011. Cert. 15.

Limitless ★★★½

Edward Morra (Bradley Cooper) is a washed-up novelist with chronic writer's block. Then he takes a drug that enables him to complete his book in a week – and to learn Italian and the piano, to boot. In one week…? *Limitless* is a great ride and is directed with considerable visual flair. In fact, the film is so good that one hopes for something a little more profound than what is on offer. And there's a fatal flaw in Morra's modus operandi. If the guy is so intelligent, how come he doesn't stash away his miracle drug in more than one place? JC-W

Bradley Cooper, Abbie Cornish, Robert De Niro, Andrew Howard, Anna Friel, Johnny Whitworth, Robert John Burke.
▶ *Dir* Neil Burger, *Pro* Leslie Dixon, Ryan Kavanaugh and Scott Kroopf, *Screenplay* Leslie Dixon, from the novel *The Dark Fields* by Alan Glynn, *Ph* Jo Willems, *Pro Des* Patrizia von Brandenstein, *Ed* Tracy Adams and Naomi Geraghty, *M* Paul Leonard-Morgan, *Cos* Jenny Gering.

Relativity Media/Virgin/Rogue/Many Rivers Productions/Boy of the Year/Intermedia Film-Momentum Pictures.
104 mins. USA. 2011. Rel: 23 Mar 2011. Cert. 15.

The Lincoln Lawyer ★★½

What happens when a criminal defence attorney – who is not known for losing his cases – discovers that his latest client is a monster as guilty as hell? This is the third lawyer Matthew McConaughey has played on film, but would you trust him as a legal practitioner? Maybe that's why McConaughey is such good casting in this tale of a crisis of conscience – in what is otherwise a conventional and straightforward courtroom drama. Only near the climax is a feed of tension introduced, while for the rest of the time the true mystery lies in piecing together McConaughey's professional and domestic past. JC-W

▶ Matthew McConaughey, Marisa Tomei, Ryan Phillippe, William H Macy, Josh Lucas, John Leguizamo, Frances Fisher, Michael Peña, Bob Gunton, Pell James, Michael Paré.
▶ *Dir* Brad Furman, *Pro* Sidney Kimmel, Tom Rosenberg, Gary Lucchesi, Richard Wright and Scott Steindorff, *Screenplay* John Romano, from the novel by Michael Connelly, *Ph* Lukas Ettlin, *Pro Des* Charisse Cardenas, *Ed* Jeff McEvoy, *M* Cliff Martinez, *Cos* Erin Benach.

Lionsgate/Lakeshore Entertainment/Sidney Kimmel Entertainment/Stone Village Pictures-Entertainment.
118 mins. USA. 2011. Rel: 18 Mar 2011. Cert. 15.

The Lion King [re-release in 3D] ★★★★★

Disney's most financially successful animated feature gets converted into 3D. The tale of the young lion prince betrayed by his uncle, who must come to terms with his history to fulfil his destiny, hasn't dated; the whole thing still looks and sounds impressive. The 3D conversion is peerless, yet adds surprisingly little – even in the superlative wildebeest stampede sequence. JC

▶ Voices of Matthew Broderick, James Earl Jones, Jeremy Irons, Jonathan Taylor Thomas, Nathan Lane, Robert Guillaume, Rowan Atkinson, Whoopi Goldberg, Cheech Marin.
▶ *Dir* Roger Allers and Rob Minkoff, *Pro* Don Hahn, *Screenplay* Irene Mecchi, Jonathan Roberts, Linda Woolverton etc, *Pro Des* Chris Sanders, *Ed* Ivan Bilancio, *M* Hans Zimmer, *Songs by* Elton John and Tim Rice.

Walt Disney Pictures-Walt Disney Studios Motion Pictures.
89 mins. USA. 2011. Rel: 7 Oct 2011. Cert. U.

Brainspotting: Bradley Cooper checks Abbie Cornish's sternum in Neil Burger's stylish and entertaining *Limitless*.

Beach bums: Marion Cotillard admires Jean Dujardin's winter attire in her boyfriend's vivid if overlong *Big Chill* redux *Little White Lies.*

A Little Bit of Heaven ★

This is a disappointing film from Nicole Kassell following her hugely impressive debut with *The Woodsman*. The fiercely independent Marley Corbett (Kate Hudson) is afraid of commitment but falls for her doctor Julian Goldstein (Gael Garcia Bernal) when she is diagnosed with cancer... Hudson is typically annoying while Bernal is seriously miscast and the talents of Kathy Bates and Peter Dinklage are simply wasted in this preposterous and over-sentimental film. GS

▶ Kate Hudson, Lucy Punch, Gael Garcia Bernal, Kathy Bates, Peter Dinklage, Whoopi Goldberg, Treat Williams.
▶ *Dir* Nicole Kassell, *Pro* Robert Katz, Mark Gill, John Davis, Adam Schroeder and Neil Sacker, *Screenplay* Gren Wells, *Ph* Russell Carpenter, *Pro Des* Stuart Wurtzel, *Ed* Stephen A Rotter, *M* Heitor Pereira, *Cos* Ann Roth.

The Film Department/Davis Entertainment-Entertainment Film Distributors.
106 mins. USA. 2011. Rel: 4 Feb 2011. Cert. 12A.

Little White Lies ★★★½

French actor turned director Guillaume Canet follows up his successful thriller *Tell No One* with this ensemble piece about a group of friends from Paris on a trip to the coast. In that context a series of plot lines are played out and at 154 minutes there is plenty of time for that. Basically it's soap opera for audiences in their thirties who can identify with the characters. If something deeper was intended it's not realised, but the talented cast carry it. (Original title: *Les petits mouchoirs*) MS

▶ François Cluzet, Marion Cotillard, Benoît Magimel, Gilles Lellouche, Jean Dujardin.
▶ *Dir* and *Screenplay* Guillaume Canet, *Pro* Alan Attal, *Ph* Christophe Offenstein, *Art Dir* Philippe Chiffre, *Ed* Hervé de Luze, *Cos* Carine Sarfati.

Les Productions du Trésor/Caneo Films/EuropaCorp / M6 Films etc-Lionsgate.
154 mins. France/Belgium. 2010 Rel: 15 Apr 2011. Cert. 15.

Living in Emergency: Stories of Doctors Without Borders ★★★★½

An honest, unauthorised examination of the humanitarian organisation Médecins Sans Frontières, this is a documentary that shows it as it is. Focusing on four different doctors, the Anglo-American filmmaker Mark N Hopkins takes no sides as his camera follows the action in war-torn Congo and post-war Liberia. There are no heroes and the ethics are messy, which is undoubtedly how humanitarian aid really is. It's a complex, gripping document and the protagonists every bit as engrossing as those served up by a fictitious screenplay. Fascinating stuff, proficiently executed. CB

▶ With Christopher Brasher, Davinder Gil, Tom Krueger, Chiara Lepora.

> *Dir* Mark N Hopkins, *Pro* Naisola Grimwood, Mark N Hopkins, Daniel Holton-Roth, *Ph* Sebastian Ischer, *Ed* Ischer, Doug Rossini and Bob Eisenhardt, *M* Bruno Coulais.

Red Floor Pictures-Arts Alliance Media.
93 mins. USA. 2008. Rel: 11 Mar 2011. Cert. 15.

Living on Love Alone ★★★★

Julie (Anaïs Demoustier) is an attractive young woman in search of a suitable job. After a series of disastrous temp jobs she meets a young actor (Pio Marmaï) who sweeps her off her feet and takes her on a mysterious trip to Spain... Demoustier is outstanding as the vulnerable heroine who believes she has found her soulmate in the charismatic Marmaï. The two actors share a strong chemistry in Isabelle Czajka's well-plotted and unpredictable drama. (Original title: *D'Amour et d'eau fraîche*) GS

> Anaïs Demoustier, Pio Marmaï, Laurent Poitrenaux, Jean-Louis Coullo'ch, Christine Brücher.
> *Dir* and *Screenplay* Isabelle Czajka, *Pro* Patrick Sobelman, *Ph* Crystel Fournier, *Art Dir* Nathaly Dubois, *Ed* Isabelle Manquillet, *M* Éric Neveux, *Cos* Judith de Luze.

Agat Films & Cie/France 3/Pickpocket Productions/ France Télévision/Canal+/CinéCinéma etc-Ciné Lumière. 90 mins. France. 2010. Rel: 21 Jan 2011. Cert. 12A.

A Lonely Place to Die ★★★½

The Scottish Highlands, today. Climbers find a kidnapped girl in the mountains and become the target of the criminals responsible. The finale is over the top but until then this is a gripping, suspenseful thriller that is well characterised, not least the female roles played by Melissa George and Kate Magowan. MS

> Melissa George, Ed Speleers, Sean Harris, Kate Magowan, Alec Newman, Stephen McCole.
> *Dir* Julian Gilbey, *Pro* Michael Loveday, *Screenplay* and *Ed* Julian and William Gilbey, *Ph* Ali Asad, *Pro Des* Matthew Button, *M* Michael Richard Plowman, *Cos* Hayley Nebauer.

Carnaby International Films/Eigerwand Media/Molinare London-Kaleidoscope Home Entertainment. 99 mins. UK. 2011. Rel: 7 Sept 2011. Cert. 15.

Louise-Michel ★

This is from Benoît Delépine and Gustave Kervern who gave us *Aaltra* (2004). This film is just as individual and just as likely to divide audiences. Here there's a neat idea (a factory is closed down and employees agree to find a hit man to kill their former boss). But the development is painfully inept, silly rather than comic, with a propensity for pointless bad taste (there's a joke centred on the destruction of New

York's Twin Towers). You may disagree, of course: but, then again, you might not. MS

> Yolande Moreau, Bouli Lanners, Benoît Poelvoorde, Albert Dupontel.
> *Dir* and *Screenplay* Benoît Delépine and Gustave Kervern, *Pro* Mathieu Kassovitz and Benoît Jaubert, *Ph* Hugues Poulain, *Art Dir* Paul Chapelle, *Ed* Stéphane Elmadjian, *M* Gaëtan Roussel, *Cos* Cécile Roullier.

MNP Entreprise/No Money Productions/Arte France Cinéma etc-Axiom Films. 95 mins. France. 2008. Rel: 1 Apr 2011. Cert. 12A.

Love's Kitchen ★

After his wife's tragic death, London chef Rob Haley (Dougray Scott) attempts to rebuild his life and career by opening a restaurant in a remote pub in the middle of the English countryside. Coincidentally, the celebrated American food critic Kate Templeton (Claire Forlani) happens to live just round the corner... This dull confection lacks the most important ingredients of all, a good script and direction, while the blending of real-life husband and wife (Scott and Forlani) curiously lacks chemistry. GS

> Claire Forlani, Dougray Scott, Lee Boardman, Gordon Ramsay, Cherie Lunghi, Simon Callow, Peter Bowles, Caroline Langrishe.
> *Dir* and *Screenplay* James Hacking, *Pro* Hacking, Simone Ling, J Alan Davis, Duncan and Nicholas Napier-Bell, *Ph* Jordan Cushing, *Pro Des* Will Randall, *Ed* Rupert Hall and Kant Pan, *M* Tom Howe, *Cos* Lisa Mitton.

Trifle Films/Just Nuts Films-Eagle Films. 93 mins. UK. 2011. Rel: 24 June 2011. Cert. 15.

Love Like Poison ★★★½

Take note: the young actress Clara Augarde is astoundingly good in this study of a 14-year-old in Brittany. It's a film about burgeoning sexual

Remote control: Holly Boyd and Melissa George in Julian Gilbey's exciting wilderness thriller *A Lonely Place to Die.*

yearnings and about possible conflicts with religious views on sex. This is an interesting debut by director Katell Quillévéré but, despite her involvement in the writing, it's not really clear what the film wants to say. MS

▶ Clara Augarde, Lio, Michel Galabru, Stefano Cassetti, Thierry Neuvic, Youen Leboulanger-Gourvil.
▶ *Dir* Katell Quillévéré, *Pro* Justin Taurand, *Screenplay* Quillévéré with Mariette Désert, *Ph* Tom Harari, *Art Dir* Anna Falguerès, *Ed* Thomas Marchand, *M* Olivier Mellano, *Cos* Mahemiti Deregnaucourt.
Les Films du Bélier/Arte France Cinéma/Canal+/ CinéCinéma etc-Artificial Eye.
85 mins. France. 2010. Rel: 13 May 2011. Cert. 15.

Machine Gun Preacher ★★★½

This is the true story of builder Sam Childers, former drug addict and dealer who, after leaving jail, eventually starts up his own business, finds religion through his wife and takes up voluntary work in Southern Sudan. Rescuing homeless children, he sets out to build his own orphanage while fighting the Lord's Resistance Army, terrorists who kidnap young kids and turn them into soldiers. It's a moving story, well told if a little too much like an action adventure, and Gerard Butler is strong casting as Childers (who is still working in the Sudan now). At least Marc Forster's film gives the tragedy a profile it might not otherwise have had. MHD

▶ Gerard Butler, Michelle Monaghan, Kathy Baker, Michael Shannon, Madeline Carroll.
▶ *Dir* Marc Forster, *Pro* Butler, Robbie Brenner, Craig

Chapman, Gary Safady and Deborah Giarratana, *Screenplay* Jason Keller, *Ph* Roberto Schaefer, *Pro Des* Philip Messina, *Ed* Matt Chesse, *M* Asche & Spencer and Thad Spencer, *Cos* Frank L Fleming.
Relativity Media/Apparatus Productions/Virgin Produced/GG Filmz/Mpower Pictures/Merlina Entertainment etc-Lionsgate.
129 mins. USA. 2011. Rel: 2 Nov 2011. Cert. 15.

Mademoiselle Chambon ★★★★

This is a fine, quiet French film about the pain caused by love. This is shown through the story of a working class husband (excellent Vincent Lindon) falling for his young daughter's teacher, the eponymous Mademoiselle (played by Sandrine Kiberlain, Lindon's ex in real life). Comparisons with *Brief Encounter* mislead because this is not grandly romantic, but in its own way it is as authentic as Lean's masterpiece. MS

▶ Vincent Lindon, Sandrine Kiberlain, Aure Atika, Arthur Le Houérou, Michèle Goddet.
▶ *Dir* Stéphane Brizé, *Pro* Miléna Poylo and Gilles Sacuto, *Screenplay* Brizé and Florence Vignon from the novel by Éric Holder, *Ph* Antoine Héberlé, *Art Dir* Valérie Saradjian, *Ed* Anne Klotz, *M* Ange Ghinozzi, *Cos* Ann Dunsford.
TS Productions/F comme Film/Arte France Cinéma etc-Axiom Films.
101 mins. France. 2009. Rel: 23 Sep 2011. Cert. 12A.

Magic to Win ★★★

This likable if lightweight Hong Kong special effects romp from *Ip Man* director Wilson Yip has a college professor lose his magical powers to a girl student volleyball player after physically colliding with her. Since he's a good magician involved in a war against evil counterparts, this threatens dire consequences for humankind and mayhem ensues (on a budget). Pretty silly, rapidly churned out stuff, yet its modicum of charm saves it. (Alternative title: *Happy Magic*) (Original title: *Hoi sam mo fa*) JC

‣ Tonny Jan, Raymond Wong, Louis Koo, Wu Chun, Karena Ng, Wu Jing, Yan Ni, Bak-Ming Wong.
‣ *Dir* Wilson Yip, *Pro* Bak-Ming Wong, *Screenplay* Edmond Wong, *Ph* Man Po Cheung, *Pro Des* Wai Yan Wong, *Ed* Ka-Fei Chung, *M* Andy Cheung and Tsang-Hei Chiu.
Pegasus Motion Pictures/Huayi Brothers-Pegasus Motion Pictures Distribution.
100 mins. Hong Kong/China. 2011. Rel: 16 Dec 2011. Cert. PG.

Magic Trip ★★★★

Alison Ellwood and Alex Gibney's eccentric documentary tells the story of Ken Kesey, the celebrated writer of *One Flew Over the Cuckoo's Nest*, at the time when he travelled across America with a psychedelic Magic Bus. That time was 1964 and this pre-hippie hallucinatory trip was inspired by Jack Kerouac's *On the Road*, including passengers such as Neal Cassady, also immortalised in the book. This enjoyable film includes footage never seen before and the fun is infectious. (Subtitle: 'Ken Kesey's Search for a Kool Place') GS

‣ Narrated by Stanley Tucci, with archive film of Kesey, Timothy Leary, Jack Kerouac, Neal Cassady, Allen Ginsberg, Jerry Garcia, The Grateful Dead.
‣ *Dir* and *Screenplay* Alex Gibney and Allison Ellwood, based on the words and recordings of Ken Kesey, *Pro* Gibney, Will Clarke and Alexandra Johnes, *Ed* Elwood.
A&E Indie Films/Phoenix Wiley-Magnolia Pictures.
107 mins. USA. 2011. Rel: 18 Nov 2011. Cert. 15.

Mammuth ★★½

This has the highly watchable Gérard Depardieu on board but it's in keeping with the previous work of Benoît Delépine and Gustave Kervern (see, for example, *Louise-Michel*). Consequently it's likely to divide opinion. Plot-wise it has Depardieu taking to the road to trace his former employers to prove entitlement to his pension. The actor captures the sadness of this, but this very episodic piece seeks to be comic too and for me there's not a single laugh to be had. MS

‣ Gérard Depardieu, Yolande Moreau, Isabelle Adjani, Miss Ming, Benoît Poelvoorde, Bouli Lanners.
‣ *Dir* and *Screenplay* Benoît Delépine and Gustave

Kervern, *Pro* Jean-Pierre Guérin, *Ph* Hugues Poulain, *Art Dir* Paul Chapelle, *Ed* Stéphane Elmadjian, *M* Gaëtan Roussel, *Cos* Florence Laforge.
GMT Productions/No Money Productions production/ Arte France Cinéma etc-Axiom Films.
91 mins. France. 2010. Rel: 3 June 2011. Cert. 15.

Margaret ★★★★

Several outstanding performances are to be found here, including that of Anna Paquin as a strong-minded but naïve teenager who, after contributing to a fatal accident, discovers that idealism and justice do not necessarily win the day. She is intensely real and individual – a few have found her insufferable – in what is a fascinating but occasionally contrived drama from Kenneth Lonergan of *You Can Count On Me* (2000). Disputes over the final cut may claim some of the blame but, if flawed, this is nonetheless intelligent and absorbing film-making. MS

‣ Anna Paquin, J Smith-Cameron, Jean Reno, Jeannie Berlin, Alison Janney, Matthew Broderick, Kieran Culkin, Mark Ruffalo, Matt Damon, Sarah Steele.

Mushrooming talent: Ken Kesey in Alex Gibney and Allison Ellwood's eccentric and enjoyable *Magic Trip*.

> *Dir* and *Screenplay* Kenneth Lonergan, *Pro* Sydney Pollack, Gary Gilbert and Scott Rudin, *Ph* Ryszard Lenczewski, *Pro Des* Dan Leigh, *M* Nico Muhly, *Cos* Melissa Toth.

Fox Searchlight Pictures/Camelot Pictures/Gilbert Films/Mirage Enterprises/Scott Rudin Productions-20th Century Fox.
150 mins. USA. 2008. Rel: 2 Dec 2011. Cert. 15.

Mars Needs Moms ★

This is a disappointing performance-capture animation from Disney with unimaginative set-pieces. The only exciting thing about this dull film is the title. Milo (Seth Green), a nine-year-old boy, is determined to get his mom (Joan Cusack) back after she has been kidnapped by Martians. The script is witless and the repetitive message about family values that they keep hammering out is extremely tiresome. GS

> Seth Green, Dan Fogler, Joan Cusack, Elisabeth Harnois, Tom Everett Scott.
> *Dir* Simon Wells, *Pro* Robert Zemeckis, Steve Starkey, Jack Rapke and Stephen J Boyd, *Screenplay* Simon and Wendy Wells, from the book by Berkeley Breathed, *Ph* Robert Presley, *Pro Des* Doug Chiang, *Ed* Wayne Wahrman, *M* John Powell, *Cos* Erich A Muller etc.

Walt Disney Pictures/ImageMovers Digital-Walt Disney Studios Motion Pictures.
88 mins. USA. 2011. Rel: 8 Apr 2011. Cert. PG.

The Mechanic ★★½

High-elite assassin Arthur Bishop (Jason Statham) wants one last job before he retires. But things take an unexpected turn when he is asked to kill his mentor and friend Harry (Donald Sutherland). The Charles Bronson 1972 original made an impression with its extreme violence but now this remake feels more or less like any other contemporary action blockbuster. Statham is effective and gets strong support from Ben Foster as Harry's son. GS

> Jason Statham, Ben Foster, Donald Sutherland, Tony Goldwyn, Mini Anden, James Logan.
> *Dir* Simon West, *Pro* René Besson and David Winkler, *Screenplay* Lewis John Carlino and Richard Wenk, from a story by Carlino, *Ph* Eric Schmidt, *Pro Des* Richard Lassalle, *Ed* Todd E Miller and T G Herrington, *M* Mark Isham, *Cos* Christopher Lawrence.

Millennium Films/Nu Image/Chartoff-Winkler Productions-Lionsgate.
93 mins. USA. 2011. Rel: 28 Jan 2011. Cert. 15.

Meek's Cutoff ★★½

I am an admirer of Kelly Reichardt's minimalistic movies (*Old Joy, Wendy and Lucy*) but I'm out of step with those who endorse this particular one. Oregon in 1845 provides the setting for this slow-paced portrait of travellers and their everyday life in the Wild West. But, since they are reduced to figures in a landscape (long shots predominate), it is hard to identify with them, and that's essential in this kind of film-making. For me it's a misfire. MS

> Michelle Williams, Bruce Greenwood, Will Patton, Zoe Kazan, Paul Dano, Shirley Henderson.
> *Dir* and *Ed* Kelly Reichardt, *Pro* Neil Kopp, Anish Savjani and others, *Screenplay* Jon Raymond, *Ph* Christopher Blauvelt, *Pro Des* David Doernberg, *M* Jeff Grace, *Cos* Vicki Farrell.

Evenstar Films/filmscience/Harmony/Primitive Nerd-Soda Pictures.
102 mins. USA. 2010. Rel: 15 Apr 2011. Cert. PG.

One car *The Mechanic* couldn't fix: Jason Statham staying cool in Simon West's humdrum remake.

Melancholia ★★★½

The melancholia of the title refers not only to the general mood of the film's characters but also to an imaginary planet that is about to collide with Earth and destroy it. The setting is a wedding at a grand hotel where bride Justine (Kirsten Dunst) is finding it less than a happy occasion. Her sister Claire (Charlotte Gainsbourg) tries to carry on leading a normal life in the face of their impending doom. Lars von Trier's wilfully wayward camerawork is irritating and, even if the situation is intriguing enough, seldom does the vision allow one to care anything very much for these gloom-ridden puppets. MHD

❯ Kirsten Dunst, Charlotte Gainsbourg, Alexander Skarsgård, Charlotte Rampling, John Hurt, Stellan Skarsgård, Kiefer Sutherland, Udo Kier.
❯ *Dir* and *Screenplay* Lars von Trier, *Pro* Louise Vesth and Meta Louise Foldager, *Ph* Manuel Alberto Claro, *Pro Des* Jette Lehmann, *Ed* Molly M Stensgaard and Morten Hojbjerg, *Music Supervisor* Mikkel Maltha, *Cos* Manon Rasmussen.

Zentropa Entertainments/Memfis Film/Liberator Productions/Arte France Cinéma/Sveriges Television/ Canal+/CinéCinéma/Nordisk Film Distribution/Danish Film Institute/Swedish Film Institute etc-Artificial Eye.
136 mins. France/Denmark/Sweden/Germany. 2011. Rel: 30 Sep 2011. Cert. 15.

Men on the Bridge ★★★

The bridge in question is the Bosphorus Bridge in Istanbul and filmmaker Asli Özge, blending together the stories of three men linked to

this location, successfully blurs the boundaries between fiction and documentary. The tales are intercut and they convince, but there's not enough depth and detail to make this honest work resonate. Compare this depiction of everyday problems with the classic *Bicycle Thieves* and you see what's lacking. (Original title: *Igne Deligi*) MS

❯ Fikret Portakal, Murat Tokgöz, Umut Ilker, Cemile Ilker, Ibrahim Çayirci.
❯ *Dir* and *Screenplay* Asli Özge, *Pro* Fabian Massah and Özge, *Ph* Emre Erkmen, *Ed* Vessela Martschewski, Aylin Zoi Tinel and Christof Schertenleib.

Endorphine Production/Yeni Sinemacilik/Kaliber Film etc-Verve Pictures.
90 mins. Germany/Turkey/The Netherlands/Finland. 2009. Rel: 28 Jan 2011. Cert. 15.

The Messenger ★★★½

There's originality here in the focus on Casualty Notification Officers who, as military personnel in America, have to break news of death in action to relatives. The device of showing an experienced hand and a newcomer working together is added, but the film segues into a love story between the newcomer (Ben Foster) and the newly widowed Olivia (Samantha Morton). Sadly this is then largely sidelined to concentrate on the older officer (Woody Harrelson). This becomes exasperating because Morton is brilliant and it's Olivia's story that we want to follow. MS

❯ Ben Foster, Woody Harrelson, Samantha Morton, Jena Malone, Steve Buscemi, Eamonn Walker.

Woebegone days: Kirsten Dunst in the part that won her the Best Actress trophy at Cannes, in Lars von Trier's baffling and challenging *Melancholia*.

Past midnight: Owen Wilson and Marion Cotillard in Woody Allen's delightful *Midnight in Paris*.

▶ *Dir* Oren Moverman, *Pro* Mark Gordon, Lawrence Inglee and Zach Miller, *Screenplay* Alessandro Camon and Moverman, *Ph* Bobby Bukowski, *Pro Des* Stephen Beatrice, *Ed* Alex Hall, *M* Nathan Larson, *Cos* Catherine George.

Omnilab Media Group/Mark Gordon Company/GOOD Worldwide etc-The Works.
113 mins. USA/Australia/British Virgin Islands. 2009. Rel: 17 June 2011. Cert. 15.

Midgets vs Mascots ★★★

It's *Borat* plus *Jackass* as two teams of five compete to win $10 million at a dodgy tournament set up in the will of ex-mascot dwarf Big Red. With shockingly crude and sexual content, graphic nudity and swearing throughout, there's plenty of offensive material in this ultra-wacky comic mockumentary – foul challenges, big laughs, raunchy moments, wild stunts and even good performances. The 4'10" Gary Coleman floors 6'8" former NBA star Scottie Pippen and there's alligator wrestling plus vomiting and diarrhoea in a milk-drinking contest before the film bottles out and shows its heart of gold. Not for everybody but this guilty pleasure is arguably very funny. DW

▶ Richard Howland, Mark Hapka, Akie Kotabe, Brittney Powell, Paul Rae. Gary Coleman, Scottie Pippen.
▶ *Dir* Ron Carlson, *Pro* Brad Keller and Joey Stewart, *Screenplay* Kevin Andounian, *Ph* Marc Carter, *Pro Des* Jason Hammond, *Ed* Christian Hoffman, *Music Supervisor* Michael Lloyd, *Cos* Lisa Albertson.

RCMVM-Kaleidoscope.
85 mins. USA. 2009. Rel: 10 Jan 2011. Cert. 18.

Midnight in Paris ★★★★★

Not one but two Woody Allen movies this year and both see him back on form. *You Will Meet a Tall Dark Stranger* [qv] is the lesser of the two, for *Midnight in Paris* is a total delight. Owen Wilson as Hollywood screenwriter Gil visits Paris with his fiancée and some friends. While they check out the obvious tourist routes, Gil finds himself magically transported to the Paris of the 1920s, where he meets the likes of Hemingway, Dalí, Gertrude Stein and Cole Porter as well as the captivating Adriana (Marion Cotillard). It's a beautifully handled conceit full of witty observations, a believable journey into nostalgia that is totally winning. MHD

▶ Owen Wilson, Rachel McAdams, Kurt Fuller, Mimi Kennedy, Marion Cotillard, Carla Bruni, Adrian Brody, Kathy Bates, Michael Sheen, Tom Hiddleston, Corey Stoll.
▶ *Dir* and *Screenplay* Woody Allen, *Pro* Jaume Roures, Stephen Tenenbaum and Letty Aronson, *Ph* Darius Khondji and Johane Debas, *Pro Des* Anne Seibel, *Ed* Alisa Lepselter, *M* Stephane Wrembel, *Cos* Sonia Grande.

Gravier Productions/Pontchartrain Productions/ Mediapro/Versatil Cinema/Televisio de Catalunya-Sony Pictures Classics.
94 mins. Spain/USA. 2011. Rel: 7 Oct 2011. Cert. 12A.

Miss Bala ★★★½

This is more straightforward and less uneven than Gerardo Naranjo's earlier feature *I'm Gonna Explode* but the very high praise bestowed by

some on this drama surprises me. It's about a Mexican woman (the excellent Stephanie Sigman) drawn into assisting criminals by acting as a mule. Ultimately it may emerge as a metaphorical comment on the state of Mexico but as a personal tale it is far less involving than *Maria Full of Grace* (2003), of which we are reminded. MS

‣ Stephanie Sigman, Noe Hernández, Lakshmi Picazo, Leonor Victorica, Irene Azuela, James Russo.
‣ *Dir* and *Ed* Gerardo Naranjo, *Pro* Pablo Cruz, *Screenplay* Naranjo and Mauricio Katz, *Ph* Mátyás Erdély, *Art Dir* Ivonne Fuentes, *M* Emilio Kauderer, *Cos* Anna Terrazas.

Canana/Fox International Productions etc-Metrodome Distribution.
113 mins. Mexico/USA. 2011. Rel: 28 Oct 2011. Cert. 15.

Mission: Impossible – Ghost Protocol ★★★½

As long as they continue to construct feats of engineering like the Burj Khalifa in Dubai, the team that is M:I will find ways of exploiting them. And as Tom Cruise approaches 50 – but still looks phenomenal – a new director takes over the franchise, injecting fresh juice into a scenario involving the old 'global destruction' chestnut. Brad Bird previously brought us the CGI cartoon *The Incredibles* and his first foray into live-action is no less incredible. As Tom Cruise and Simon Pegg join forces, scores are settled, friendships formed and passports worn thin as the circus rattles across Belgrade, Moscow, Dubai, Mumbai and Seattle. JC-W

‣ Tom Cruise, Jeremy Renner, Simon Pegg, Paula Patton, Michael Nyqvist, Tom Wilkinson, Ving Rhames, Michelle Monaghan.
‣ *Dir* Brad Bird, *Pro* Tom Cruise, J J Abrams and Bryan Burk, *Screenplay* André Nemec and Josh Appelbaum, *Ph* Robert Elswit, *Pro Des* James D Bissell, *Ed* Paul Hirsch, *M* Michael Giacchino, *Cos* Michael Kaplan.

Paramount/Skydance Productions/Bad Robot/FilmWorks/Stillking Films/TC Productions- Paramount Pictures.
133 mins. USA/United Arab Emirates. 2011. Release: 26 Dec 2011. Cert. 12A.

Moneyball ★★★½

This is an American variant on *The Damned United* (2009), being a tale of sport which focuses on a manager and on the dramas off the pitch. Brad Pitt plays the real-life Billy Beane, who in 2002 brought a new approach to baseball, but fictional elements are added and it makes for a surprisingly conventional undertaking given that it was written by Steven Zaillian and Aaron Sorkin and directed by *Capote*'s Bennett Miller. There is excellent work from Pitt and his co-star Jonah Hill. MS

‣ Brad Pitt, Jonah Hill, Philip Seymour Hoffman, Robin Wright, Chris Pratt, Stephen Bishop.
‣ *Dir* Bennett Miller, *Pro* Michael De Luca, Rachael Horovitz and Brad Pitt, *Screenplay* Steven Zaillian and Aaron Sorkin from a story by Stan Chervin based on the book by Michael Lewis, *Ph* Wally Pfister, *Pro Des* Jess Gonchor, *Ed* Christopher Tellefsen, *M* Mychael Danna, *Cos* Kasia Walicka Maimone.

Columbia Pictures/Scott Rudin/Michael de Luca/Film Rites-Sony Pictures Releasing.
133 mins. USA. 2011. Rel: 25 Nov 2011. Cert. 12A.

Monte Carlo ★½

This frothy but overlong tale follows the adventures of three friends from Texas on a highly anticipated trip to Paris. Their holiday is a huge disappointment but when Grace (Selena Gomez) is mistaken for a spoiled British heiress they find themselves in Monte Carlo. The leads inject enough energy to make it mildly watchable but Thomas Bezucha's direction by numbers almost sinks the ship. GS

‣ Selena Gomez, Leighton Mester, Kate Cassidy, Corey Monteith, Andie MacDowell, Brett Cullen.
‣ *Dir* Thomas Bezucha, *Pro* Nicole Kidman, Alison Greenspan, Per Saari, Rick Schwartz and Denise Di Novi, *Screenplay* Bezucha, April Blair and Maria Maggenti, from a screen story by Kelly Bowe based on the book *Headhunters* by Jules Bass, *Ph* Jonathan Brown, *Pro Des* Hugo Luczyc-Wyhowski, *Ed* Jeffrey Ford, *M* Michael Giacchino, *Cos* Shay Cunliffe.

Fox 2000 Pictures/Walden Media/Regency Enterprises/New Regency Pictures/Mid Atlantic Films/Blossom Films-20th Century Fox.
109 mins. USA/Hungary. 2011. Rel: 21 Oct 2011. Cert. PG.

Simon Pegg gives Tom Cruise a hand (well, two, actually) in Brad Bird's awesome *Mission: Impossible – Ghost Protocol*, the most popular in the series.

Talk back: Diane Keaton and Harrison Ford swap digs in Roger Michell's occasionally comical *Morning Glory*.

Morning Glory ★★★

It's hard to reconcile the polished tropes of *Morning Glory* with the director of *The Mother* and *Enduring Love* – even if the film does exhibit some of the feel-good bonhomie of Roger Michell's *Notting Hill*. Even so, considering the lack of intellectual fibre in contemporary morning TV that Harrison Ford's acerbic Mike Pomeroy so laments, it would have been nice to see more of it here. The script does throw up several genuinely funny moments and Jeff Goldblum steals the show as a plumb-straight executive delivering some deliciously arid retorts. If only Rachel McAdams' desperate-to-please TV producer hadn't been quite so exasperating. JC-W

▶ Rachel McAdams, Harrison Ford, Diane Keaton, Patrick Wilson, Jeff Goldblum, Ty Burrell, John Pankow, Matt Malloy.
▶ *Dir* Roger Michell, *Pro* J J Abrams and Bryan Burk, *Screenplay* Aline Brosh McKenna, *Ph* Alwin Kuchler, *Pro Des* Mark Friedberg, *Ed* Daniel Farrell, Nick Moore and Steven Weisberg, *M* David Arnold, *Cos* Frank L Fleming.

Bad Robot/Goldcrest Pictures-Paramount Pictures.
107 mins. USA. 2010. Rel: 21 Jan 2011. Cert. 12A.

Mother's Day ★½

After a failed bank robbery three sadistic brothers return to their childhood home and begin to terrorise the present owners and their guests. Then their fierce mother arrives with a plan. Darren Lynn Bousman's disappointing film fails to introduce the characters properly, thus making it difficult to care. The story has potential but doesn't really work thanks to a miscast and unconvincing Rebecca De Mornay as the Mother from Hell. GS

▶ Rebecca De Mornay, Jaime King, Patrick Flueger, Deborah Ann Woll.
▶ *Dir* Darren Lynn Bousman, *Pro* Brett Ratner, Brian Witten, Jay Stern and Richard Saperstein, *Screenplay* Scott Milam, based on the 1980 screenplay by Charles Kaufman and Warren Leight, *Ph* Joseph White, *Pro Des* Anthony A Ianni, *Ed* Hunter M Via, *M* Bobby Johnston, *Cos* Leslie Kavanagh.

LightTower Entertainment/Rat Entertainment/Troma Entertainment/Genre Co/Widget Films/Sierra Pictures III-Optimum Releasing.
112 mins. USA. 2010. Rel: 10 June 2011. Cert. 18.

Mr Popper's Penguins ★

High-flying businessman Jim Carrey inherits a crateload of penguins that turns his life upside down. A terrific turn from Ophelia Lovibond as his alliteration-spouting personal assistant and an amazing sequence where the birds slide belly-first down the interior spiral walkways of New York's Guggenheim can't save the rest of this from being unwatchable, manufactured Hollywood family fodder. JC

▶ Jim Carrey, Carla Gugino, Angela Lansbury, Ophelia Lovibond, Madeline Carroll, Jeffrey Tambor.
▶ *Dir* Mark Waters, *Pro* John Davis, *Screenplay* John Morris, Jared Stern and Sean Anders, from the novel by Richard and Florence Atwater, *Ph* Florian Ballhaus, *Pro Des* Stuart Wurtzel, *Ed* Bruce Green, *M* Rolfe Kent, *Cos* Ann Roth.

20th Century Fox/Centro Digital Pictures/Davis Entertainment-20th Century Fox.
94 mins. USA. 2011. Rel: 5 Aug 2011. Cert. PG.

My Dog Tulip ★★★★★

Unable to connect with a human life-partner, writer Joe Ackerley acquired a German shepherd dog and to his delight she turned out to be his perfect best friend. He enjoyed training her, walking her and trying to get her to mate. Husband and wife team Paul and Sandra Fierlinger have adapted Ackerley's tribute to Tulip into one of the most imaginatively drawn animated features you will ever encounter. No sentimental Disney fluff here, but all the nastier sides of owning a dog are covered including an emphasis on excretion. It's all a total delight and grumpy old Ackerley (judiciously voiced by Christopher Plummer) and his bitch will amuse you immeasurably. MHD

‣ Voices of Christopher Plummer, Lynn Redgrave, Isabella Rossellini, Peter Gerety, Brian Murray, Paul Hecht, Euan Morton.
‣ *Dir, Screenplay* and *Animation* Paul and Sandra Fierlinger, from the book by J R Ackerley, *Pro* Howard Kaminsky, Norman Twain and Frank Pellegrino, *Ed* Paul Fierlinger, *M* John Avarese.
Norman Twain Productions-Axiom Films.
83 mins. USA. 2009. Rel: 6 May 2011. Cert. 12.

My Kidnapper ★★½

Confused story-telling and insistent music seriously mar what should have been a striking documentary about filmmaker Mark Henderson coming face to face with the man who previously kidnapped Mark and seven others in Colombia. That had been part of an attempt to publicise through hostage-taking human rights issues in that country. The simple, direct approach of a film like *Enemies of the People* (2009) was required, but that's exactly what is missing here. MS

‣ With Mark Henderson, Reinhilt Weigel, Ido Guy, Erez Eltawil.
‣ *Dir* and *Pro* Mark Henderson and Kate Horne, *Ph* Guillermo Galdos and Tom Swindell, *Ed* Tom Herrington and Rupert Houseman, *M* Richard Spiller.
Renegade Pictures/ZDF/ARTE etc-Renegade Pictures.
83 mins. UK/Colombia/Germany. 2010. Rel: 11 Feb 2011. No Cert.

My Week with Marilyn ★★★½

Like Garbo, Miss Monroe needed only a single name to identify her. Michelle Williams captures Marilyn's little-girl vulnerability and the film demonstrates well the frustrations of colleagues waiting for her to work. In the event, Marilyn's performance was the best part of *The Prince and the Showgirl*, Olivier's doomed 1956 film, in which he overacted and she appeared gloriously to be doing nothing. Colin Clark's memoirs of an assistant director who had to take care of the unreliable star make for an entertaining screenplay by Adrian Hodges. Eddie Redmayne as Clark remains enigmatic, but Williams conveys enough of Marilyn's charisma and Kenneth Branagh, hilariously, has Olivier off to a T. MHD

‣ Michelle Williams, Eddie Redmayne, Kenneth Branagh, Judi Dench, Toby Jones, Emma Watson, Julia Ormond, Dominic Cooper, Zoë Wanamaker, Derek Jacobi.
‣ *Dir* Simon Curtis, *Pro* Harvey Weinstein and David Parfitt, *Screenplay* Adrian Hodges, based on Colin Clark's books *My Week with Marilyn* and *The Prince, the Showgirl and Me*, *Ph* Ben Smithard, *Pro Des* Donal Woods, *Ed* Adam Recht, *M* Conrad Pope, *Cos* Jill Taylor.
The Weinstein Company/BBC Films/UK Film Council/ Lipsync Productions/ Trademark Films-Entertainment Film Distributors.
99 mins. UK/USA. 2011. Rel: 25 Nov 2011. Cert. 15.

Mysteries of Lisbon ★★★★

The last film from the late Raúl Ruiz, strikingly individual but far more approachable than you might expect, is a long (almost four and a half hours) adaptation of a Portuguese novel with echoes of Balzac, set in the 19th century. The main plot thread concerns a boy brought up as an orphan who comes to learn about his

Hello Norma Jean: Michelle Williams as Monroe in Simon Curtis' entertaining, hilarious *My Week with Marilyn*.

parentage, but his tale is filled out by subsidiary ones interconnected with it. Stylishly done, this is in essence a work about the human need for stories and a celebration of them. (Original title: *Misterios de Lisboa*) MS

▷ Adriano Luz, Maria João Bastos, Ricardo Pereira, Clotilde Hesme, Afonso Pimentel, João Luís Arrías, Rui Morisson, Léa Seydoux.
▷ *Dir* Raúl Ruiz, *Pro* Paulo Branco, *Screenplay* Carlos Saboga from the novel by Camilo Castelo Branco, *Ph* André Szankowski, *Art Dir* Isabel Branco, *Ed* Valeria Sarmiento and Carlos Madaleno, *M* Jorge Arriagada and Luis de Freitas Branco.
Clap Filmes/Alfama Films/Radio Televisão Portugal etc-New Wave Films.
266 mins. Portugal/France/Brazil. 2010. Rel: 9 Dec 2011. Cert. PG.

NEDS ★★½

Glasgow in the 1970s. Peter Mullan's third work as director is centred on a youth who in his early teens finds himself drawn into a group of Non Educated Delinquents (NEDS). The first half is for the most part persuasively real (which extends to Scottish accents that don't aid understanding) and Conor McCarron is fine in the central role. However, surreal elements are incongruously added, leading to a bizarre final scene. The film seems to fall apart. MS

▷ Conor McCarron, Gregg Forrest, Peter Mullan, Gary Milligan, Joe Szula, John Joe Hay.
▷ *Dir* and *Screenplay* Peter Mullan, *Pro* Alain de la Mata, Marc Massonnier and Olivier Delbosc,

Ph Roman Osin, *Pro Des* Mark Leese, *Ed* Colin Monie, *M* Craig Armstrong, *Cos* Rhona Russell.
Film4/UK Film Council/blue light/Fidélité Films/Studio Urania etc-E1 Films.
124 mins. UK/France/Italy. 2010. Rel: 21 Jan 2011. Cert. 18.

Nénette ★★★★★

Nicolas Philibert, who made the much admired *Être et Avoir* in 2002, gives us in the overlooked *Nénette* one of the most original films I have ever seen. Nénette is a 40-year-old orang-utan, a prize specimen in the Paris menagerie in the Jardin des Plantes. We hear comments by the public, by keepers and others but the camera is exclusively on her. We are invited to meditate – about animals, about zoos, about God and whatever else comes to mind – so the audience creates the film by what they bring to it. Extraordinary if not for everybody. MS

▷ With the voices of Abel Morin, Lucie Morin, Agnès Laurent, Georges Peltier.
▷ *Dir* and *Ed* Nicolas Philibert, *Pro* Serge Lalou and Alain Esmery, *Ph* Katell Djian and Philibert, *M* Philippe Hersant.
Les Films d'ici/Forum des Images/CinéCinéma etc-Artificial Eye.
70 mins. France. 2010. Rel: 4 Feb 2011. Cert. PG.

Never Let Me Go ★★★

This adaptation of Kazuo Ishiguro's novel offers an imaginary version of present-day life in which scientific discoveries have led to people becoming organ donors and thus destined to have short

Every which way: *Nénette* takes centre stage in Nicolas Philibert's original and extraordinary documentary.

lives themselves. A love triangle emerges in this context but some aspects of the tale seriously lack conviction. The unforgettable consolation is that the fine young actress Carey Mulligan is at her best: she radiates screen presence. MS

▶ Carey Mulligan, Andrew Garfield, Keira Knightley, Charlotte Rampling, Sally Hawkins.
▶ *Dir* Mark Romanek, *Pro* Andrew Macdonald and Allon Reich, *Screenplay* Alex Garland from the novel by Kazuo Ishiguro, *Ph* Adam Kimmel, *Pro Des* Mark Digby, *Ed* Barney Pilling, *M* Rachel Portman, *Cos* Rachael Fleming and Steven Noble.

**Fox Searchlight Pictures/DNA Films/Film4 etc-20th Century Fox.
104 mins. USA/UK. 2010. Rel: 11 Feb 2011. Cert. 12A.**

New Year's Eve ★

Garry Marshall's lazy, sentimental film tells several intertwining New York stories. Robert De Niro is dying in hospital while his attractive nurse (Halle Berry) needs to talk on Skype with her husband who is serving in Iraq. Meanwhile Michelle Pfeiffer quits her boring PA job and seeks adventure in the arms of delivery boy Zac Efron. There is no reality whatsoever in any segment and the less said about Sarah Jessica Parker's self-conscious performance the better, while the irritating, syrupy soundtrack makes things even worse. GS

▶ Michelle Pfeiffer, Zac Efron, Robert De Niro, Sarah Jessica Parker, Halle Berry, Jessica Biel, Josh Duhamel, Hilary Swank, Abigail Breslin, Katherine Heigl, Ashton Kutcher.
▶ *Dir* Garry Marshall, *Pro* Mike Karz, Josie Rosen,

Wayne Allan Rice, Toby Emmerich and Richard Brener, *Screenplay* Katherine Fugate, *Ph* Charles Minsky, *Pro Des* Mark Friedberg, *Ed* Michael Tronick, *M* John Debney, *Cos* Gary Jones.

**New Line Cinema/Karz Entertainment/Wayne Rice/New York Streets Film Projects-Warner Bros Pictures.
118 mins. USA. 2011. Rel: 8 Dec 2011. Cert. 12A.**

New York, I Love You ★½

This disappointing portmanteau film follows *Paris, je t'aime* (2006), with Shanghai promised (or should that read threatened?) as the next city in line. With one exception each episode here has a different director and this time around two were cut from the release print. Even so, most of the pieces are slight and all of them are forgettable. The best direction comes from Allen Hughes and the best acting from veterans Eli Wallach and Cloris Leachman, but most of the material is feeble. MS

▶ Natalie Portman, Ethan Hawke, Chris Cooper, Robin Wright Penn, Julie Christie, John Hurt, Eli Wallach, Cloris Leachman, Andy Garcia, Irrfan Khan, James Caan, Anton Yelchin, Christina Ricci.
▶ *Dir* Jiang Wen, Mira Nair, Shunji Iwai, Yvan Attal, Brett Ratner, Allen Hughes, Shekhar Kapur, Natalie Portman, Fatih Akin, Joshua Marston and Randy Balsmeyer, *Pro* Emmanuel Benbihy and Marina Grasic, *Screenplays* Portman, Akin, Marston, Anthony Minghella and others, *Ph* Various, *Pro Des* Teresa Mastropierro, *Ed* Various, *M* Various, *Cos* Victoria Farrell.

**Vivendi Entertainments/Visitor Pictures/Plum Pictures/Grosvenor Park Media etc-The Works.
103 mins. USA. 2008. Rel: 4 Feb 2011. Cert. 15.**

Future tense: Domhnall Gleeson, Carey Mulligan, Keira Knightley and Andrea Riseborough in Mark Romanek's chilling, otherworldly *Never Let Me Go.*

Tokyo story: Rinko Kikuchi and Ken'ichi Matsuyama in Tran Anh Hung's very beautiful and very long *Norwegian Wood*.

The Next Three Days ★★½

The French film *Pour elle*, released here in 2009 as *Anything for Her*, was hardly outstanding. Nevertheless it gripped us as a husband went to extreme lengths to rescue his wife, unjustly convicted of murder, from jail. This Hollywood remake pushes the material to even greater extremes and ends up being ludicrous. Russell Crowe can't save it, but there's a memorable, almost silent cameo from Brian Dennehy. MS

❧ Russell Crowe, Elizabeth Banks, Brian Dennehy, Olivia Wilde, Liam Neeson, Lennie James.
❧ *Dir* and *Screenplay* Paul Haggis, based on the screenplay *Pour elle* by Fred Cavayé and Guillaume Lemans, *Pro* Michael Nozik, Haggis and others, *Ph* Stéphane Fontaine, *Pro Des* Laurence Bennett, *Ed* Jo Francis, *M* Danny Elfman, *Cos* Abigail Murray.

Lionsgate/Hwy61/Fidélité Films etc-Lionsgate.
133 mins. USA. 2010. Rel: 5 Jan 2011. Cert. 12A.

No Strings Attached ★★

When Adam meets Emma they embark on a relationship entirely based on nookie – no cuddles or dates allowed… The first problem is that *No Strings Attached* presents itself as a rom-com. More unfortunately, it looks like *When Harry Met Sally…* with sex (and shorter orgasms). But neither Ashton Kutcher nor Natalie Portman possesses the personality or funny bones of Billy Crystal and Meg Ryan, or the chemistry. Ms Portman herself is not a natural comic – nor does her director have the comic smarts of, say, Jason Reitman. JC-W

❧ Natalie Portman, Ashton Kutcher, Kevin Kline, Cary Elwes, Greta Gerwig, Lake Bell, Olivia Thirlby, Chris 'Ludacris' Bridges, Mindy Kaling.
❧ *Dir* Ivan Reitman, *Pro* Reitman, Jeffrey Clifford and Joe Medjuck, *Screenplay* Elizabeth Meriwether, *Ph* Rogier Stoffers, *Pro Des* Ida Random, *Ed* Dana E. Glauberman, *M* John Debney, *Cos* Julie Weiss.

Paramount/Cold Spring Pictures/Spyglass Entertainment/ Montecito Picture Company/Handsomecharlie Films/ Katalyst Films/PIC Agency-Paramount Pictures.
107 mins. USA. 2011. Rel: 25 Feb 2011. Cert. 15.

Norwegian Wood ★★½

Unexpectedly Tran Anh Hung, he of *The Scent of Green Papaya*, returns with this adaptation of Haruki Murakami's novel, filmed in Japan with a Japanese cast. It's very beautiful but very long and I found it difficult to become concerned with the young hero or with the two contrasted women in his life. The outward impassivity of the Japanese hinders appreciation of a love story in which audience identification with the characters is crucial, but lovers of the novel may be entranced. MS

❧ Matsuyama Ken'Ichi, Kikuchi Rinko, Mizuhara Kiko, Kora Kengo, Kirishima Reika.
❧ *Dir* and *Screenplay* (from the novel by Haruki Murakami) Tran Anh Hung, *Pro* Ogawa Shinji, *Ph* Mark Lee Ping Bin, *Pro Des* Yen Khe Lugurn and Ataka Norifumi, *Ed* Mario Battistel, *M* Jonny Greenwood, *Cos* Lugurn.

Asmik Ace Entertainment/Fuji Television Network/ Fortissimo Films-Soda Pictures.
134 mins. Japan/Hong Kong. 2010. Rel: 11 Mar 2011. Cert. 15.

Nothing to Declare ★★★

In a tiny border town Belgian customs officer Ruben (Benoît Poelvoorde) hates the idea of sharing his job with French officer Mathias (Dany Boon). And things get even worse when Mathias falls for Ruben's sister... A very likable comedy but not as funny as Boon's earlier and hugely successful *Bienvenue chez les Ch'tis*. The characters verge on the stereotypical despite the strong presence of Poelvoorde and Boon. (Original title: *Rien à déclarer*) GS

▶ Benoît Poelvoorde, Dany Boon, Julie Bernard, Karin Viard, Christel Pedrinelli, Joachim Ledeganck.
▶ *Dir* Dany Boon, *Pro* Eric Hubert and Jérôme Seydoux, *Screenplay* Dany and Yaël Boon, *Ph* Pierre Aïm, *Ed* Luc Barnier and Géraldine Rétif, *M* Phillippe Rombi, *Costume Supervisor* Nathalie Leborgne.
Pathé/Les Productions du Ch'timi/TFI Films Production/ CinéCinéma/ Canal+ etc-Pathé.
108 mins. France. 2010. Rel: 11 Feb 2011. Cert. 15.

One Day ★★★½

David Nicholls has adapted his own best-selling novel, the one which famously looks in on its two main characters at yearly intervals over some two decades, starting on 15 July 1988. Emma (Anne Hathaway) and Dexter (Jim Sturgess) soon become best friends but might become more, despite Dexter's obvious shortcomings. Unless you worry about Hathaway's Yorkshire accent, both leads play well with the strongest of support from Rafe Spall and Patricia Clarkson. Not expecting it to end as it does, I questioned aspects of the finale but for most of its length this is sound mainstream entertainment. MS

▶ Anne Hathaway, Jim Sturgess, Patricia Clarkson, Rafe Spall, Ken Stott, Romola Garai, Tom Mison, Jodie Whittaker.
▶ *Dir* Lone Scherfig, *Pro* Nina Jacobson, *Screenplay* David Nicholls based on his book, *Ph* Benoît Delhomme, *Pro Des* Mark Tildesley, *Ed* Barney Pilling, *M* Rachel Portman, *Cos* Odile Dicks-Mireaux.
Focus Features/Random House Films/Color Force etc-Universal Pictures International.
108 mins. USA/UK. 2011. Rel: 24 Aug 2011. Cert. 12A.

One Life ★★★★

Four years in the making, this is a cinema feature from BBC Earth Films. It's less outstanding than *Earth* (2007) but in studying animals and other creatures to be found around the world it admirably fulfils its remit. Admittedly the narration sometimes seems too consciously aimed at children, but the youngsters present at the screening I attended were rapt throughout. MS

▶ With narration by Daniel Craig.

▶ *Dir* and *Written by* Michael Gunton and Martha Holmes, *Pro* Martin Pope and Michael Rose, *Ed* David Freeman, *M* George Fenton.
BBC Earth Films/IM Global/Magic Light Pictures etc-Kaleidoscope Home Entertainment.
85 mins. UK/USA 2011. Rel: 22 July 2011. Cert. U.

Oranges and Sunshine ★★★½

The debut of Jim Loach, son of Ken, is a heartfelt drama. Taken from real life, it tells of Margaret Humphreys (played with conviction by Emily Watson). While acting as a social worker in Nottingham, she uncovered facts about young children having been deported to Australia after the British authorities falsely told them their parents were dead. Some late scenes are unexpectedly unconvincing but the film is 'worthy' in a good way. MS

▶ Emily Watson, David Wenham, Hugo Weaving, Richard Dillane, Lorraine Ashbourne.
▶ *Dir* Jim Loach, *Pro* Emilie Sherman, Iain Canning and Camilla Bray, *Screenplay* Rona Munro from the book *Empty Cradles* by Margaret Humphreys, *Ph* Denson Baker, *Pro Des* Malinda Doring, *Ed* Dany Cooper, *M* Lisa Gerrard, *Cos* Cappi Ireland.
Screen Australia/Little Gaddesden Productions etc-Icon Film Distribution.
105 mins. UK/Australia. 2010. Rel: 1 Apr 2011. Cert. 15.

Oslo, August 31st ★★★★

Based on the same novel which yielded Louis Malle's masterpiece *Le Feu follet* in 1964, this Norwegian film seems valid in its contemporary setting. It shows 48 hours in the life of a man so disenchanted with existence that he is on the verge of suicide. Andreas Danielsen Lie is compelling in this role and Joachim Trier's film is sympathetic, even if it lacks the haunting quality that marked Malle's treatment. (Original title: *Oslo, 31. August*) MS

The Norwegian would: Anders Danielsen Lie in Joachim Trier's compelling *Oslo, August 31st*.

▶ Anders Danielsen Lie, Malin Crépin, Aksel M. Thanke, Hans Olav Brenner, Ingrid Olava.
▶ *Dir* Joachim Trier, *Pro* Yngve Sæther, Hans-Jørgen Osnes and Sigve Endresen, *Screenplay* Eskil Vogt and Trier from the novel *Le Feu follet* by Pierre Drieu La Rochelle, *Ph* Jakob Ihre, *Pro Des* Jørgen Stangebye Larsen, *Ed* Olivier Bugge Coutté, *M* Ola Fløttum, *Cos* Ellen Dæhli Ystehede.

Motlys/Don't Look Now etc-Soda Pictures.
96 mins. Norway/Sweden/Denmark/Germany. 2011. Rel: 4 Nov 2011. Cert. 15.

Our Day Will Come ★½

Romain Gavras' dreamlike experimental film follows the adventures of two unlikely friends, Patrick (Vincent Cassel) and Remy (Olivier Barthelemy) as they begin a long journey from France to Ireland and freedom... It's difficult to make much sense of the narrative as these two unsympathetic anti-heroes regularly explode into acts of extreme violence for no particular reason. Is this a dream or a nightmare? Ultimately, who cares? GS

▶ Vincent Cassel, Olivier Barthelemy, Justine Lerooy, Vanessa Decat, Rodolphe Blanchet.
▶ *Dir* Romain Gavras, *Pro* Cassel and Éric Névé, *Screenplay* Gavras and Karim Boukercha, *Ph* Andre Chemetoff, *Pro Des* Christian Vallat, *Ed* Benjamin Weill, *M* Sebastian, *Cos* Nathalie Benros.

120 Films/Les Chauves-Souris/TF1 Droits Audiovisuels/Cinémage 4/CinéCinéma etc-Optimum Releasing.
83 mins. France. 2010. Rel: 29 July 2011. Cert. 18.

Outside the Law ★★★

Technically adroit though it is, this film from Rachid Bouchareb is disappointing after the brilliance of the deeply humane *Days of Glory*. Mainly set between 1953 and 1962, it's the story of three Algerian brothers who, eventually coming together in Paris, take different attitudes over the fight for their country's independence.

Bouchareb's own views remain unclear. Is this humane man condoning violence or not? Has he sorted out his own possibly conflicted feelings on this issue? (Original title: *Hors la loi*) MS

▶ Jamel Debbouze, Roschdy Zem, Sami Bouajila, Chafia Boudraa, Bernard Blancan.
▶ *Dir* Rachid Bouchareb, *Pro* Jean Bréhat, *Screenplay* Olivier Lorelle and Bouchareb, *Ph* Christophe Beaucarne, *Art Dir* Yan Arlaud, *Ed* Yannick Kergoat, *M* Armand Amar, *Cos* Édith Vespérini.

AARC/Tassili Films/Tessalit Productions/StudioCanal etc-ICO/Optimum Releasing.
139 mins. France/Algeria/Belgium/Tunisia/Italy. 2010. Rel: 6 May 2011. Cert. 15.

Page One: Inside the New York Times ★★★★

This documentary serves a double purpose: it gives us a close and not wholly uncritical view of life in a major newspaper office and it offers a broader picture of the threat to traditional journalism stemming from modern technology, including the internet. It's able and accomplished. A central figure is the columnist David Carr, a striking figure who talks of his former drug addiction but is arguably given too much space. However, this is a good and informative film. MS

▶ With Tim Arango, David Carr, Bill Keller, Julian Assange, Carl Bernstein.
▶ *Dir* and *Ph* Andrew Rossi, *Pro* and *Written by* Rossi and Kate Novack, *Ed* Chad Beck, Christopher Branca and Sarah Devorkin, *M* Paul Brill.

Magnolia Pictures/Patrticipant Media and History-Dogwoof Pictures.
92 mins. USA. 2011. Rel: 23 Sep 2011. Cert. 15.

Paranormal Activity 3 ★★★

Young sisters Katie (Katie Featherston) and Kristi Ray (Sprague Grayden) befriend Tobi, an invisible demon that lives in their home. It's useful that the girls have a disbelieving mother (Lauren Bittner) whose live-in boyfriend Dennis (Chris Smith) is a video wiz. After an earthquake, Dennis is convinced an invisible figure is stalking the girls, so he sets up his cameras to find out. As the demon terrorises the house, there's plenty to scream about in this surprisingly effective prequel. There are well-staged shocks and scares en route to a cover-your-face finale. Tense and creepy, the film returns to a winning formula and makes it work once more. DW

▶ Katie Featherston, Sprague Grayden, Chris Smith, Lauren Bittner, Jessica Brown, Chloe Csengary, Dustin Ingram.
▶ *Dir* Henry Joost and Ariel Schulman, *Pro* Oren Peli, Steven Schneider and Jason Blum, *Screenplay*

Little demons: Chloe Csengery and Jessica Brown in Henry Joost and Ariel Schulman's tense and creepy *Paranormal Activity 3*.

SEP 24 1988
PM 3:06:18

Christopher Landon, based on Peli's film *Paranormal Activity*, *Ph* Magdalena Gorka, *Pro Des* Jennifer Spence, *Ed* Gregory Plotkin, *Cos* Leah Butler.

Paramount Pictures/Blumhouse Productions/Room 101-Paramount Pictures.

83 mins. USA. 2011. Rel: 21 Oct 2011. Cert. 15.

Parked ★★★

When Fred Daly (Colm Meany) returns to Ireland he has nowhere to live but his car. With no address he is unable to claim benefits, but he soon begins to challenge the system when he befriends Cathal (Colin Morgan), an easygoing, dope-smoking 21-year-old who 'parks' beside him. Darragh Byrne's touching film benefits tremendously from the honest performances and strong chemistry between its two lead characters, an unlikely friendship with a positive outlook on life despite the circumstances. GS

▶ Colm Meaney, Colin Morgan, Milka Ahlroth, Stuart Graham, Michael McElhatton.
▶ *Dir* Darragh Byrne, *Pro* Jacqueline Kerrin and Dominic Wright, *Screenplay* Ciaran Creagh, *Ph* John Conroy, *Pro Des* Owen Power, *Ed* Guy Montgomery and Gareth Young, *M* Niall Byrne, *Cos* Susan Scott.

Ripple World Pictures/Helsinki Film Oy-Element Pictures Distribution.

94 mins. Ireland/Finland. 2011. Rel: 25 Nov 2011. Cert. 15.

Passenger Side ★★★★★

Matthew Bissonnette's engaging film vividly portrays his adopted city, Los Angeles. It's a resident's view and a somewhat minimalist but atmospheric work. It centres on the complex relationship between two contrasted brothers. The banter, the rivalry, the hostility and the bond are most convincingly presented and the film ends by sidestepping potential melodrama in favour of a quietly persuasive gesture. It's a haunting film that grows even better on being viewed a second time. MS

▶ Adam Scott, Joel Bissonnette, Richard Medina, Mickey Cottrell, Robin Tunney.
▶ *Dir* and *Screenplay* Matthew Bissonnette, *Pro* Corey Marr, *Ph* Jonathon Cliff, *Ed* Matthew Hannam, *Cos* Melissa Clemens.

Corey Marr Productions and 105 Films etc-Axiom Films Limited.

85 mins. Canada. 2009. Rel: 1 Apr 2011. Cert. 15.

Patagonia ★★½

The concept here is promising: two intercut tales of travellers. In one a couple journey from Wales to Patagonia, while in the other an octogenarian of Welsh stock is accompanied by a teenage neighbour as she returns to her roots. In execution, however, the latter thread, with Marta Lubos as the old woman, is far more interesting than the former, but both tales end up by becoming unbelievable. Ultimately the cast can't save the film from disaster. MS

▶ Matthew Rhys, Marta Lubos, Nahuel Pérez Biscayart, Nia Roberts, Duffy.
▶ *Dir* Marc Evans, *Pro* Rebekah Gilbertson and Flora Fernandez-Marengo, *Screenplay* Laurence Coriat and Evans, *Ph* Robbie Ryan, *Pro Des* and *Cos* Marie

Sibling rivalry: Joel Bissonnette and Adam Scott in Matthew Bissonnette's engaging and atmospheric *Passenger Side*.

Lanna, *Ed* Mali Evans, *M* Joseph LoDuca and Angelo Badalamenti.

S4C/The Film Agency for Wales/Rainy Day/Boom Films etc-Verve Pictures.
119 mins. UK/USA/Switzerland. 2009. Rel: 4 Mar 2011. Cert. 15.

Paul ★★★

The title is funny. So is the idea of a Spielbergian extraterrestrial with a bad cigarette habit and a potty mouth. Cast Seth Rogen as the eponymous alien and throw in Simon Pegg and Nick Frost as a couple of sightseeing geeks from the Old Country and you have a promising package. There are some very funny moments, a lot of in-jokes (Paul ordering Reese's Pieces) and a slew of well-judged performances (Kristen Wiig is a delight and very funny as a devout creationist). Much of it is also over-egged, some of it madly derivative, but it's an enjoyable Saturday night ride. JC-W

▶ Simon Pegg, Nick Frost, Jason Bateman, Kristen Wiig, Sigourney Weaver, Blythe Danner, Bill Hader, Jane Lynch, John Carroll Lynch, Jeffrey Tambor, and the voice of Seth Rogen.
▶ *Dir* Greg Mottola, *Pro* Nira Park, Tim Bevan and Eric Fellner, *Screenplay* Simon Pegg and Nick Frost, *Ph* Lawrence Sher, *Pro Des* Jefferson Sage, *Ed* Chris

Swingin' in the rain: Wim Wenders' Oscar-nominated celebration of the dance of Pina Bausch.

Dickens, *M* David Arnold, *Cos* Nancy Steiner.

Universal/Relativity Media/Working Title/Big Talk Productions-Universal.
103 mins. USA/UK/Spain/France. 2011. Rel: 14 Feb 2011. Cert. 15.

Pearl Jam 20 ★★★

Cameron Crowe was a music journalist before he became an award-winning filmmaker (*Jerry Maguire, Almost Famous* etc). In this illuminating documentary he celebrates 20 years of Pearl Jam – the grunge band that made a brief appearance in Crowe's 1992 film *Singles*. With a series of interviews, including one with rival Kurt Cobain, Crowe draws a clear picture of the band's early formative years, their overnight success and final comeback following years of obscurity. GS

▶ With Cameron Crowe, Jeff Ament, Matt Cameron, Stone Gossard, Mike McCready, Eddie Vedder, Chris Cornell.
▶ *Dir* and *Screenplay* Cameron Crowe, *Pro* Crowe, Kelly Curtis, Andy Fischer, Morgan Neville and Barbara McDonough, *Ph* Nicola Marsh, *Ed* Kevin Klauber and Chris Perkel, *M* Pearl Jam.

Tremolo Productions/Vinyl Films-Echo Bridge Entertainment.
109 mins. USA. 2011. Rel: 20 Sep 2011. Cert. 15.

Perfect Sense ★★★½

First becoming unable to smell, people unexpectedly lose their senses one by one in this sci-fi drama which becomes a love story. If the plot echoes *Blindness* (2008), the finale recalls Don McKellar's superior *Last Night* (1998) in which the world ends. David Mackenzie directs like a master, but the writing, less than consistently convincing, makes it an uneven film. Interesting even so. MS

▶ Ewan McGregor, Eva Green, Ewen Bremner, Stephen Dillane, Denis Lawson.
▶ *Dir* David Mackenzie, *Pro* Gillian Berri and Malte Grunert, *Screenplay* Kim Fupz Aakeson, *Ph* Giles Nuttgens, *Pro Des* Tom Sayer, *Ed* Jake Roberts, *M* Max Richter, *Cos* Trisha Biggar.

BBC Films/Zentropa Entertainments5 /Scottish Screen/ Danish Film Institute etc-Arrow Film Distributors.
92 mins. UK/Denmark/Sweden/Ireland. 2010. Rel: 7 Oct 2011. Cert. 15.

Pina ★★★

Wim Wenders puts 3D to good use in this tribute to the late Pina Bausch. Admirers of her work as a choreographer may be entranced by these extracts from her creations and by the heartfelt appreciation expressed here by dancers and colleagues. However, for the uninitiated her aims go unexplained, the works are not always

identified and the intrusion of film techniques seems alien to dance designed for the stage. MS

▶ With Pina Bausch, Regina Advento, Lutz Forster. Narrated by Sandrine Pillon.
▶ *Dir* and *Written by* Wim Wenders, *Pro* Wenders and Gian-Piero Ringel, *Ph* Hélène Louvart and Jörg Widmer, *Art Dir* Peter Pabst, *Ed* Toni Froschhammer, *M* Thorn Hanreich, *Cos* Mariön Cito and Rolf Börzik.

HanWay Films/Neue Road Movies etc-Artificial Eye. 103 mins. Germany/France/UK. 2011. Rel: 22 Apr 2011. Cert. U.

Pirates of the Caribbean: On Stranger Tides ★★★★

At last Captain Jack Sparrow (Johnny Depp) has found his match in Angelica (Penélope Cruz) in this, the fourth and best of the series. Together Jack and Angelica embark on the Queen Anne's Revenge in search of the Fountain of Youth, but old enemies and the Spanish fleet are also on the quest. The opening sequences in London are simply spectacular, with a delicious cameo from Keith Richards. (Does this face look as if it's been to the Fountain of Youth?) The middle section loses some momentum but then the mermaids arrive... GS

▶ Johnny Depp, Penélope Cruz, Geoffrey Rush, Ian McShane, Kevin McNally, Keith Richards, Richard Griffiths, Judi Dench.
▶ *Dir* Rob Marshall, *Pro* Jerry Bruckheimer,

Screenplay Ted Elliott and Terry Rossio, based on characters created by them, Stuart Beattie and Jay Wolpert and suggested by the novel by Tim Powers, *Ph* Dariusz Wolski, *Pro Des* John Myhre, *Ed* Michael Kahn, Wyatt Smith and David Brenner, *M* Hans Zimmer, *Cos* Penny Rose.

Walt Disney Pictures/Jerry Bruckheimer Films/Moving Picture Company-Walt Disney Studios Motion Pictures. 136 mins. USA. 2011. Rel: 18 May 2011. Cert. 12A.

Planeat ★★★

This environmental documentary aims to turn everybody who watches it into a vegetarian. Three scientists spend their lives researching a diet which is good for our health, the environment and the future of the planet. They claim that protein and red meat are major causes of cancer and that farmers waste more produce than they actually get in return, in feeding the meat industry. Make sure you eat first before you see it – preferably red meat because it may be your last time. GS

▶ Documentary based on the research of T Colin Campbell, Gidon Eshel and Caldwell Esselstyn Jr, with Yvonne O'Grady, narrator.
▶ *Dir, Written, Filmed* and *Ed* Shelley Lee Davies and Or Shlomi, *Pro* Christo Hird, *Additional photography* Amiram Bukowski and Thomas M Campbell, *M* Ernie Wood, *Animation* Lilli English and Yaya Halawani.

Studio 58/Dartmouth Films/The Fledgling Fund/ SoundNode-Dartmouth Films. 72 mins. USA. 2010. Rel: 20 May 2011. Cert. U.

Jungle fever: Johnny Depp and Penélope Cruz in Rob Marshall's *Pirates of the Caribbean: On Stranger Tides*.

For better or verse: the veteran Korean actress Yoon Jung-Hee in Lee Chang-Dong's complex and visually striking *Poetry*.

Poetry ★★★★½

The fifth feature by Korea's Lee Chang-Dong but the first to be released here, this film contains one of the year's best performances. It's by veteran actress Yoon Jung-Hee. She plays a grandmother who responds differently from other materialistically minded parents on learning that her grandson was one of a group of students whose rape of a girl led to her suicide. The film may be slightly overlong but it encompasses much more than its overt plot line. It criticises inhumanity in societies and posits values that touch on art and religion. Remarkable. (Original title: *Shi*) MS

▶ Yoon Jung-Hee, David Lee, Kim Hira, Ahn Nae-Sang.
▶ *Dir*, *Pro* and *Screenplay* Lee Chang-Dong, *Ph* Kim Hyunseok, *Art Dir* Sihn Jeomhui, *Ed* Kim Hyun, *Cos* Lee Choongyeon.
UniKorea/Daiphana Distribution/Pinehouse Film etc-ICA and Arrow Film Distributors.
139 mins. Republic of Korea/France. 2010. Rel: 29 July 2011. Cert. 12A.

Point Blank ★★★★

This is a precision-tooled machine of a movie, a French thriller about a male nurse (Gilles Lellouche) whose pregnant wife (Elena Anaya) is kidnapped. Eventually we discover who the kidnappers are and learn their motives, but this is essentially a high-powered drama with twists. The climax may push things, but modern action thrillers tend to favour exaggeration: this film follows the pattern but does it with panache. (Original title: *À bout portant*) MS

▶ Gilles Lellouche, Roschdy Zem, Gérard Lanvin, Elena Anaya, Mireille Perrier, Claire Perot.
▶ *Dir* Fred Cavayé, *Pro* Cyril Colbeau-Justin and Jean-Baptiste Dupont, *Screenplay* Cavayé and Guillaume Lemans, *Ph* Alain Duplantier, *Art Dir* Philippe Chiffre, *Ed* Benjamin Weill, *M* Klaus Badelt, *Cos* Marie-Laure Lasson.
Gaumont/LGM Films/TF1 Films etc-Vertigo Films.
84 mins. France/Spain. 2010. Rel: 10 June 2011. Cert. 15.

The Portuguese Nun ★★★½

French director Eugène Green here offers a love letter to Lisbon. It's a slow-moving, deeply Catholic film influenced by Bresson and centres on the situation of a French actress involved in the filming of a Portuguese novel. That story features a nun, as does the work we are watching, and each involves a love story, but it's the question of what makes life meaningful that is the central issue. Non-Catholics may be at a disadvantage, but it's a strikingly individual film. MS

▶ Lenor Baldaque, Ana Moreira, Adrien Michaux, Beatriz Batarda.
▶ *Dir* and *Screenplay* Eugène Green, *Pro* Luís Urbano & Sandro Aguilar, *Ph* Raphaël O'Byrne, *Art Dir* Zé Branco, *Ed* Valerie Loiseleux.
O Som e a Fúria/MACT Productions etc-ICA Cinema.
127 mins. Portugal/France. 2009. Rel: 21 Jan 2011. No Cert.

Post Mortem ★★★½

Although not alive at the time, Chile's Pablo Larraín here looks back to 1973 to comment on the military coup that led to the death of President Allende. Taking a line that also makes his film relevant to other regimes such as Nazi Germany, Larrain hones in not on oppressors or revolutionaries but on non-political people caught up in events. His film is grim and slow but well acted and, despite some problematic moments, it makes its statement more clearly than did its predecessor, 2008's *Tony Manero*. MS

❯ Alfredo Castro, Antonia Zegers, Jaime Vadell, Amparo Noguera, Aldo Parodi, Marcelo Alonso.
❯ *Dir* Pablo Larraín, *Pro* Juan de Dios Larraín, *Screenplay* Pablo Larraín and Mateo Iribarren, *Ph* Sergio Armstrong, *Ed* Andrea Chignoli, *M* Alejandro Castaños and Juan Cristobel Meza, *Cos* Muriel Parra.
Hubert Bals Fund/World Cinema Fund etc-Network Releasing.
98 mins. Chile/Germany/Mexico. 2010. Rel: 9 Sept 2011. Cert. 15.

Potiche ★★★★

When Richard (Fabrice Luchini), husband of umbrella factory owner Suzanne (Catherine Deneuve), falls ill, his wife is forced to run the business herself and finds that the workers prefer her style of management, particularly when they're considering strike action. She is aided in no uncertain ways by ex-lover Maurice (Gérard Depardieu), who also wants to help in other ways too. This was once a boulevard comedy (it's based on a play) and only the French could get away with such an entertaining and good-humoured piece. Deneuve and Depardieu are delightful together in this ooh-la-la treat. MHD

❯ Catherine Deneuve, Gérard Depardieu, Fabrice Luchini, Karin Viard, Judith Godrèche.
❯ *Dir* and *Screenplay* François Ozon, based on the play by Pierre Barillet and Jean-Pierre Grédy, *Pro* Eric and Nicolas Altmeyer, *Ph* Yorick Le Saux, *Pro Des* Katia Wyszkop, *Ed* Laure Gardette, *M* Philippe Rombi, *Cos* Pascaline Chavanne.
Mandarin Cinéma/FOZ/France 2 Cinéma/Scope Pictures/ Wild Bunch/Canal+/ SCOPE Invest etc-StudioCanal.
103 mins. France. 2010. Rel: 17 June 2011. Cert. 15.

Powder ★★

Mark Elliott's charmless dark comedy tells the story of Liverpool band The Grams as they attempt to hit the big time. Their journey takes them first to London, then to Ibiza (where else?), and then to the V Festival for a big showdown. In the meantime they tear each other apart with petty jealousies and mindless drug excesses. It is difficult to care much about these egotistical characters in this over-familiar setting. GS

❯ Liam Boyle, Alfie Allen, Ralf Little, Jo Woodcock, Oliver Lee, Aneurin Barnard, Neil Bell, Sharon Byatt.
❯ *Dir* Mark Elliott, *Pro* and *M* David A Hughes, *Screenplay* adapted from his novel by Kevin Sampson, *Ph* Mark Waters, *Pro Des* Mally Smith, *Ed* Mark Elliott, *Cos* Nicky Barron.
Red Union Films-Soda Pictures.
105 mins. USA. 2010. Rel: 26 Aug 2011. Cert. 15.

Comédie Française: Judith Godrèche and Catherine Deneuve in François Ozon's all-star *Potiche*.

The vampires' vicar: Paul Bettany in Scott Stewart's humourless *Priest*.

Priest 3D ★★

Following years of brutal warfare with the vampires, the Church is now in control and the few remaining bloodsuckers have been moved to isolated reservations. However, after a recent attack by the vampires, a veteran priest of the wars (Paul Bettany) begins a quest to find his kidnapped niece against the Church's orders. The production values are good, with a spectacular climax, but Scott Stewart's humourless horror Western (adapted from a graphic novel) lacks danger and tension. GS

❧ Paul Bettany, Cam Giganet, Maggie Q, Karl Urban, Brad Dourif, Christopher Plummer, Mädchen Amick.
❧ *Dir* Scott Stewart, *Pro* Michael De Luca, Joshua Donen and Mitchell Peck, *Screenplay* Cory Goodman, based on Min-Woo Hyung's graphic novel series *Priest*, *Ph* Don Burgess, *Pro Des* Richard Bridgland, *Ed* Lisa Zeno Churgin, *M* Christopher Young, *Cos* Ha Nguyen.

Screen Gems/Michael De Luca Productions/Stars Road Entertainment/Buckaroo Entertainment etc-Sony Pictures Releasing.
87 mins. USA. 2011. Rel: 6 May 2011. Cert. 12A.

The Princess of Montpensier ★★★

Sad to say, this French period drama from Bertrand Tavernier set in the 1560s is lacklustre. An adaptation of a 17th century novel, it is more serious than Tavernier's *D'Artagnan's Daughter* (1994). However, its broad canvas, incorporating a tragic love story, never makes us feel truly involved. It's watchable enough, but compare it with Eric Rohmer's *The Lady and the Duke* and it's a matter of chalk and cheese. (Original title: *La Princesse de Montpensier*) MS

❧ Mélanie Thierry, Lambert Wilson, Gaspard Ulliel, Grégoire Leprince-Ringuet, Raphaël Personnaz.
❧ *Dir* Bertrand Tavernier, *Pro* Eric Heumann, *Screenplay* Jean Cosmos, François Olivier Rousseau and Tavernier from the story by Madame de Lafayette, *Ph* Bruno de Keyser, *Art Dir* Guy-Claude François, *Ed* Sophie Brunet, *M* Philippe Sarde, *Cos* Caroline de Vivaise.

Paradis Films/StudioCanal/France 2 Cinéma/France 3 Cinéma/Pandora Filmproduktion etc-Optimum Releasing.
140 mins. France/Germany. 2010. Rel: 8 July 2011. Cert. 15.

Prom ★★

Nova (Aimee Teegarden) is busy organising the prom but disaster strikes when the building where the decorations are stored accidentally burns down. So she has to pair with 'bad' boy Jesse Richter (Thomas McDonell) and make new decorations as time is running out... This is slow, predictable and old-fashioned, with a cast that doesn't entirely persuade as high school kids. Thankfully, Johnny Depp lookalike Thomas McDonell manages to be convincing despite his surroundings. GS

❧ Aimee Teegarden, Thomas McDonell, DeVaughn Nixon, Danielle Campbell.
❧ *Dir* Joe Nussbaum, *Pro* Ted Griffin and Justin Springer, *Screenplay* Katie Wech, *Ph* Byron Shah, *Pro Des* Mark White, *Ed* Jeffrey M Werner, *M* Deborah Lurie, *Cos* Shoshana Rubin.

Walt Disney Pictures/Rickshaw Productions-Buena Vista International.
104 mins. USA. 2011. Rel: 3 June 2011. Cert. U.

Project Nim ★★★

Although this doomed 1973 experiment – in which chimpanzee Nim was treated like a human being, dressed in clothes, given pizza and joints etc – has a certain fascination, the main interest is in the scientists who undertook it. There are no real answers as to why they did it; director James (*Man on Wire*) Marsh says it was inspired by language, and indeed Nim was 'taught' sign language. However, a chimp is still a chimp however much you monkey around with it, and Nim remained wild and ferocious until he was beyond handling. Moved to an animal home he became lonely and dejected: a sad way to treat any animal and an even sadder view of humanity. MHD

❧ With Herbert Terrace, Laura-Ann Petitto, Bob Ingersoll, Stephanie LaFarge and chimpanzee Nim

Chimpsky (after Noam Chomsky, get it?).

❯ *Dir* James Marsh, *Pro* Simon Chinn, *Ph* Michael Simmonds, *Pro Des* Markus Kirschner, *Ed* Jinx Godfrey, *M* Dickon Hinchliffe, *Cos* Kathryn Nixon.

Passion Pictures/BBC Films/Red Box Films-Icon Film Distribution.

93 mins. USA. 2011. Rel: 12 Aug 2011. Cert. 12A.

Puss in Boots ★★★★★

This spin-off from *Shrek 2* compares favourably with the first two *Shrek*s. Antonio Banderas voices the 'swordscat' and serial lover whose alliance with good egg gone bad Humpty Dumpty (voice: Zach Galifianakis) sours their relationship. Cat burglar Kitty Softpaws (voice: Salma Hayek) provides knockabout love interest. The animation is up to par while the well-choreographed action set-pieces look stunning in 3D. JC

❯ Voices of Antonio Banderas, Salma Hayek, Zach Galifianakis, Billy Bob Thornton, Amy Sedaris, Guillermo del Toro.

❯ *Dir* Chris Miller, *Pro* Latifa Ouaou, Joe M Aguilar, *Screenplay* Tom Wheeler, Jon Zack, David H Steinberg and Brian Lynch, from a story by Will Davies, based on characters by Charles Perrault, *Pro Des* Guillaume Aretos, *Ed* Eric Dapkiewicz, *M* Henry Jackman.

DreamWorks Animation-Paramount Pictures.

90 mins. USA. 2011. Rel: 9 Dec 2011. Cert. U.

Putty Hill ★★★½

A young man dies of a drug overdose in Baltimore. Shot in an almost documentary style and using non-professional actors, this atmospheric and sometimes poetic film studies his friends, acquaintances and family. As a non-judgmental look at modern youth, it's very effective, but the later sequences seem over-long and at times one is distracted by wondering where the border between fiction and reality lies. MS

❯ Sky Ferreira, Zoe Vance, Charles 'Spike' Sauers, James Siebor, Dustin Ray.

❯ *Dir* Matt Porterfield, *Pro* Jordan Mintzer, Steve Holmgren, Joyce Kim and Eric Bannat, *Story* Porterfield and Mintzer, *Ph* Jeremy Saulnier, *Art Dir* Sophie Toporkoff, *Ed* Marc Vives, *Cos* Sara Jane Gerrish.

Hamilton Film Group/Cloud Society etc-ICA Films.

85 mins. USA. 2011. Rel: 17 Jun 2011. Cert. 15.

Le Quattro Volte ★★★★

Shot in Calabria, this extraordinary work contains almost no dialogue and consequently has no subtitles. Visually it is magnificent and there are humorous moments worthy of Jacques Tati. However, the audience is left to fathom for itself the links that the film's

Top cat: the eponymous feline as voiced by Antonio Banderas in Chris Miller's marvellously inventive *Puss in Boots*.

creator, Michelangelo Frammartino, seeks to establish between four elements in nature: the mineral, the vegetable, the animal and the human. Much of this can be elusive, but those willing to take the plunge will recognise this study of life as a unique if demanding work of art. MS

▶ Giuseppe Fuda, Isidoro Chiera, Iolanda Manno, Cesare Ritorto.
▶ *Dir* and *Written by* Michelangelo Frammartino, *Pro* Marta Donzelli, Francesca Zanza and others, *Ph* Andrea Locatelli, *Ed* Benni Atria and Maurizio Grillo, *Cos* Gabriella Maiolo.
Vivo Film/Essential Filmproduktion/Invisibile Film/ Ventura Film etc-New Wave Films.
88 mins. Italy/Germany/Switzerland. 2010. Rel: 27 May 2011. Cert. U.

R: Hit First, Hit Hardest ★★★

As in *Cell 211*, *A Prophet* and *Hunger*, this multi-award-winning Danish drama shows the dehumanising effects of serving time. And Rune, the 'R' of the title, is reduced to nothing more than a number, or indeed a letter… For anybody who hasn't seen *A Prophet* (the best of the recent prison movies), this unrelenting drama may come as a revelation, although it tramples across very familiar territory. It is authentic, violent, non-judgmental and competent – everything you'd expect. It also swept the Danish Oscars (the Robert Awards), which does elevate a minor eyebrow. JC-W

Rough justice: Pilou Asbæk in Michael Noer and Tobias Lindholm's accomplished, violent and unrelenting *R: Hit First, Hit Hardest*.

▶ Pilou Asbæk, Dulfi Al-Jabouri, Roland Møller.
▶ *Dir* and *Screenplay* Michael Noer and Tobias Lindholm, *Pro* Rene Ezra and Tomas Radoor, *Ph* Magnus Nordenhof Jønck, *Pro Des* Holger Vig, *Ed* Adam Nielsen, *Cos* Lotte Stenlev.
Nordisk Film-Soda Pictures.
99 mins. Denmark. 2010. Rel: 26 Aug 2011. Cert. 18.

Rabbit Hole ★★

This originated as a play and it sounds like it every step of the way. It's about parents whose son has been killed in a road accident, and it deals with conflicting reactions and difficult adjustments. It's not the theme but the theatrical dialogue and the eventual sentimentality which sink this film and make it seem wholly superficial. Nevertheless, one sees talent in newcomer Miles Teller as a youth who has a crucial role in the story. MS

▶ Nicole Kidman. Aaron Eckhart, Dianne Wiest, Tammy Blanchard, Miles Teller.
▶ *Dir* John Cameron Mitchell, *Pro* Leslie Urdang, Kidman and others, *Screenplay* David Lindsay-Abaire, based on his play, *Ph* Frank G DeMarco, *Pro Des* Kalina Ivanov, *Ed* Joe Klotz, *M* Anton Sanko, *Cos* Ann Roth.
Olympus Pictures/Blossom Films/OddLot Entertainment-Metrodome Distribution.
91 mins. USA. 2010. Rel: 4 Feb 2011. Cert. 12A.

Rango ★★★★

Animated features, in Disney's heyday, used to be rare events. Now, a full-length cartoon appears almost every week and most seem not worth drawing breath for. *Rango* is an exception because it's aimed more at adults than kids. Rango (Johnny Depp) is a chameleon who's stranded when his cage falls off a truck. He ends up in Dirt, a desert town short of water. Becoming the local sheriff, Rango sets out to discover who's drained their vital fluid. Imaginatively composed and shot, with loads of in-jokes about other films, including a lookalike Clint, *Rango* is both amusing and informative. Leave the young'uns at home and go have a blast. MHD

▶ The voices of Johnny Depp, Isla Fisher, Abigail Breslin, Ned Beatty, Alfred Molina, Bill Nighy, Harry Dean Stanton, Ray Winstone.
▶ *Dir* Gore Verbinski, *Pro* Verbinski, Graham King and John B Carls, *Screenplay* John Logan, based on a story by Logan, Verbinski and James Ward Byrkit, *Pro Des* Mark 'Crash' McCreery, *Ed* Craig Wood, *M* Hans Zimmer.
Nickelodeon Movies/Blind Wink Productions/GK Films-Paramount Pictures.
107 mins. USA. 2011. Rel: 4 Mar 2011. Cert. PG.

Real Steel ★★★

Charlie (Hugh Jackman) compensates for his own failure as a fighter by providing gigantic robots for boxing. But he owes money to almost everybody and needs one last chance. Then his estranged 11-year-old son Max (Dakota Goyo) arrives on the scene and things take a miraculous turn… This is predictable to say the least, but

the special effects, particularly during the fight sequences, are mind-blowing, especially if seen on the giant IMAX screen. GS

▶ Hugh Jackman, Dakota Goyo, Evangeline Lily, Anthony Mackie, James Rebhorn, Hope Davis.
▶ *Dir* Shawn Levy, *Pro* Levy, Robert Zemeckis, Don Murphy and Susan Montford, *Screenplay* John Gatins, from a story by Dan Gilroy and Jeremy Leven, based on Richard Matheson's short story *Steel*, *Ph* Mauro Fiore, *Pro Des* Tom Meyer, *Ed* Dean Zimmerman, *M* Danny Elfman, *Cos* Marlene Stewart.

DreamWorks SKG/Touchstone Pictures/Reliance Entertainment/ImageMovers/ Angry Films/21 Laps Entertainment-Walt Disney Studios Motion Pictures.
127 mins. USA/India. 2011. Rel: 14 Oct 2011. Cert. 12A.

Red Hill ★★★★

Constable Shane Cooper (Ryan Kwanten) relocates from the big city to the small farming village of Red Hill with his very pregnant wife. But on his first day at work Shane finds himself in the middle of a bloody confrontation when a convicted murderer escapes from prison and arrives at Red Hill seeking revenge... This hugely atmospheric and well-constructed Australian action thriller has all the ingredients of a good Western and is blessed with a very sympathetic performance from Kwanten as the reluctant hero. GS

▶ Ryan Kwanten, Steve Bisley, Tom E Lewis, Claire van der Boom, Christopher Davis.

▶ *Dir, Screenplay* and *Ed* Patrick Hughes, *Pro* Hughes and Al Clark, *Ph* Tim Hudson, *Pro Des* Enzo Iacono, *M* Dmitri Golovko, *Cos* Nicola Dunn.

Hughes House Film/McMahon International Pictures/ Wildheart Films/Wolf Creek Pictures/Screen Australia-Eagle Films.
95 mins. Australia. 2010. Rel: 13 May 2011. Cert. 15.

Red Riding Hood ★★

In a remote village close to a forest, every full moon the villagers try to appease a wolf with animal offerings. Meanwhile Valerie (Amanda Seyfried) is torn between two men – the wealthy Henry (Max Irons) and her childhood friend Peter (Shiloh Fernandez). The set-up is not dissimilar to *The Village* and of course *Twilight* (also directed by Catherine Hardwicke). Most of the cast is wasted, particularly Lukas Haas as a villager whose sole purpose is to pose as a suspect. This fairy tale lacks direction and most of all bite. GS

▶ Amanda Seyfried, Lukas Haas, Gary Oldman, Shiloh Fernandez, Billy Burke, Julie Christie, Virginia Madsen, Max Irons.
▶ *Dir* Catherine Hardwicke, *Pro* Leonardo DiCaprio, Julie Yorn and Jennifer Davisson, *Screenplay* David Johnson, *Ph* Mandy Walker, *Pro Des* Tom Sanders, *Ed* Nancy Richardson and Julia Wong, *M* Alex Heffes and Brian Reitzell, *Cos* Cindy Evans.

Warner Bros Pictures/Random Films/Appian Way-Warner Bros.
100 mins. USA/Canada. 2011. Rel: 15 Apr 2011. Cert. 12A.

The Australian who went up a hill... Ryan Kwanten in Patrick Hughes' hugely atmospheric *Red Hill.*

Not a prayer:
Michael Parks
excels in Kevin
Smith's violent
satire *Red State.*

Red State ★★★★

When three horny teenagers respond to an online invitation for sex with an older woman (Melissa Leo), they find themselves at the mercy of a mad preacher (Michael Parks) who holds them captive. In the meantime Federal Agent Joseph Keenan (John Goodman) is preparing an attack. The acting is outstanding in Kevin Smith's violent satire on Middle America's Christian extremism, with another powerful performance from Leo. But it's Parks who steals the movie as the utterly insane preacher determined to exterminate anyone who resists his faith. GS

▶ Michael Parks, Melissa Leo, John Goodman, Haley Ramm, Michael Angarano, Kyle Gallner.
▶ *Dir, Screenplay* and *Ed* Kevin Smith, *Pro* Jonathan Gordon, *Ph* David Klein, *Pro Des* Cabot McMullen, *Cos* Beth Pasternak.
The Harvey Boys/NVSH Productions-Entertainment One.
88 mins. USA. 2011. Rel: 30 Sep 2011. Cert. 18.

Red, White and Blue ★★★½

Simon Rumley's erotically charged movie is refreshingly original. In Austin Texas, Erica (Amanda Fuller) is a free-spirited young woman who doesn't believe in love but enjoys one-night stands. However, when she meets the mysterious Nate (Noah Taylor) her life takes an unexpected turn. There is virtually no dialogue in the first ten minutes and it's a true cinematic experience before changing gear and becoming an extremely violent and shocking revenge drama. GS

▶ Amanda Fuller, Noah Taylor, Marc Senter, Jon Michael Davis, Nick Ashy Holden, Patrick Crovo.
▶ *Dir* and *Screenplay* Simon Rumley, *Pro* Rumley and Bob Portal, *Ph* Milton Kam, *Pro Des* Josh Crist, *Ed* Rob Hall, *M* Richard Chester, *Cos* Tessa Justman.
Rumleyvision/ScreenProjex/Fidelity Films-Trinity Filmed Entertainment.
104 mins. USA. 2010. Rel: 30 Sep 2011. Cert. 18.

The Referees ★★★½

This documentary follows a group of football referees during the 2008 European Championship and focuses entirely on them. Their concentration is admirable and the game is always seen from their point of view in this fascinating film. British referee Howard Webb is given the opportunity to explain his controversial decision to award a penalty to Austria, which resulted in death threats to his family and a statement from the Polish prime minister that he wanted to kill him. A surprisingly engaging documentary! (Original title: *Les Arbitres*) GS

▶ With Howard Webb, Roberto Rosetti, Michel Platini, Massimo Busacca.
▶ *Dir* Eric Cardot, Lehericey Delphine and Yves Hinant, *Executive Pro* Thibaut Potdevin, *Ph* Vincent Huffy, Antonio Capurso, Manolo D'Arthuis, Didier Hill-Derive and David Gladsteen, *Pro Des* Josh Norton, *Ed* Françoise Tourmen, *M* Erlin A Velberg.
Entre Chien et Loup-Soda Pictures.
77 mins. Belgium. 2009. Rel: 5 Aug 2011. Cert. 15.

The Resident ★★★

From Hammer's revived house of horror comes a creepy stalker thriller starring Hilary Swank as a newly single ER surgeon who's thrilled to find an affordable New York apartment. Moving straight in, she kicks off a flirtatious relationship with her landlord (Jeffrey Dean Morgan). But he turns out to be a right pervy psycho, going through her stuff, spying on her nightly, and that's just for starters... Disturbing, unnerving and gleefully twisted, this nerve-jangling, next-gen Hammer flick comes with a certified seal of approval in the form of a small supporting role for horror veteran Christopher Lee. MJ

▶ Hilary Swank, Jeffrey Dean Morgan, Lee Pace, Christopher Lee, Aunjanue Ellis, Sean Rosales.
▶ *Dir* Antti J Jokinen, *Pro* Simon Oakes and Guy East, *Screenplay* Jokinen and Robert Orr, *Ph* Guillermo Navarro, *Pro Des* J Dennis Washington, *Ed* Stuart Levy and Bob Murawski, *M* John Ottman, *Cos* Ann Roth.
Hammer Film Productions-Icon Film Distribution.
91 mins. UK/USA. 2010. Rel: 11 Mar 2011. Cert. 15.

Resistance ★★★½

Set in Wales and reimagining history to show Britain taken over by the Germans after Dunkirk, this film may not always work but it does suggest a genuine attempt at a work of art. Issues of collaboration and common humanity arise involving a local woman (Andrea Riseborough) and a sympathetic German officer (Tom Wlaschiha) and both play well. It's atmospheric too, but certain plot aspects are unpersuasive. A gallant effort at the very least. MS

▶ Andrea Riseborough, Tom Wlaschiha, Sharon Morgan, Alexander Doetsch, Michael Sheen.
▶ *Dir* Amit Gupta, *Pro* Richard Holmes and Amanda Faber, *Screenplay* Gupta and Owen Sheers from the latter's novel, *Ph* John Pardue, *Pro Des* Adrian Smith, *Ed* Chris Barwell, *M* Mark Bradshaw, *Cos* Nigel Egerton.
Big Rich Films/The Film Agency for Wales etc-Metrodome Distribution.
92 mins. UK. 2011. Rel: 25 Nov 2011. Cert. PG.

Restless ★★½

Here's further proof that the camera loves Mia Wasikowska. Even so, Jason Lew's sentimental screenplay about a traumatised orphan (Henry Hopper) falling for a girl dying of cancer (Mia) is a non-starter, and all the more so because the young hero is given a ghost as his best friend! The film is dedicated to the late Dennis Hopper and there's a real look of dad in Henry. MS

▶ Henry Hopper, Mia Wasikowska, Ryo Kase, Schuyler Fisk, Jane Adams, Chin Han.
▶ *Dir* Gus Van Sant, *Pro* Brian Grazer, Ron Howard,

Bryce Dallas Howard and Van Sant, *Screenplay* Jason Lew, *Ph* Harris Savides, *Pro Des* Anne Ross, *Ed* Elliot Graham, *M* Danny Elfman, *Cos* Danny Glicker.
Sony Pictures Classics/Imagine Entertainment etc-Sony Pictures Releasing.
91 mins. USA. 2011. Rel: 21 Oct 2011. Cert. PG.

Retreat ★★★

Trying to save their marriage after the still-birth of their first child, journalist Kate (Thandie Newton) and architect Martin (Cillian Murphy) escape to a remote island off Scotland where they once had a romantic holiday. Following a storm, Jack (Jamie Bell) is washed up on the shore, injured and in military fatigues, carrying a gun. When they take him in, he claims a deadly airborne virus is sweeping through Europe. The three fine actors really make this unusual idea work in this excellent peril thriller. The filming is very atmospheric and the handling satisfyingly intense but it's the powerful performances that give it class and credibility. DW

▶ Cillian Murphy, Jamie Bell, Thandie Newton, Jimmy Yuill, Marilyn Mantle.
▶ *Dir* Carl Tibbetts, *Pro* Gary Sinyor, *Screenplay* Tibbetts and Janice Hallett, *Ph* Chris Seager, *Ed* Jamie Trevill, *M* Ilan Eshkeri, *Cos* Louise Page.
Ripple World Pictures/Magnet Films-Sony Pictures Releasing.
90 mins. UK. 2011. Rel: 14 Oct 2011. Cert. 15.

Reuniting the Rubins ★★★

Timothy Spall stars as uptight lawyer Lenny Rubin, who puts his dream retirement on hold when his ailing mother (Honor Blackman) emotionally blackmails him into getting his estranged grown-up children back together for a Jewish holiday. She begs to see her warring dysfunctional grandkids reunited before she dies. "They hate each other," he says. "They love each

Peep-show: Jeffrey Dean Morgan and Hilary Swank get physical in Antti J Jokinen's unnerving and gleefully twisted *The Resident*.

other," she says. This funny, touching, heart-warming comedy-drama provides enjoyable, thought-provoking entertainment that will strike a strong chord for those with elderly relatives. Dear but difficult, Blackman's Jewish gran is a tour-de-force, while Spall and Rhona Mitra both impress too. Not obvious casting but it works. DW

▶ Rhona Mitra, Timothy Spall, Honor Blackman, James Callis, Blake Harrison, James Vaughan.
▶ *Dir* and Screenplay Yoav Factor, *Pro* Factor and Jonathan Weissler, *Ph* Miles Cook, *Pro Des* Byron Broadbent, *Ed* Anthony Stadler, *M* Tim Atack, *Cos* Alan Flyng.
Factor Films-Kaleidoscope.
97 mins. UK. 2010. Rel: 21 Oct 2011. Cert. PG.

Revenge: A Love Story ★★

This is an absolute must for sadists who don't care whether or not their pleasures make any sense. Here, a self-appointed midwife delights in cutting foetuses out of pregnant women and letting them haemorrhage to kingdom come. But that's nothing compared to the over-the-top climax featuring a church boys' choir. Technically, the film is top-hole, which makes the whole thing harder to stomach. And it's very stylish. (Original title: *Fuk sau che chi sei*) CB

▶ Juno Mak, Sola Aoi, Siu-hou Chin, Tony Ho, Tony Liu.
▶ *Dir* Ching-Po Wong, *Pro* Conroy Chan Chi-Chung, *Screenplay* Ching-Po Wong, Juno Mak and Lai-yin Leung, from a story by Mak, *Ph* Jimmy Wong, *Art Dir* Cinnie Fung, *Ed* Ching-Po Wong and Ka-Fai Chung, *M* Dan Findlay, *Cos* Wen Choi and Rennie Tse.
ETA Limited/852 Films-All Rights Entertainment.
90 mins. Hong Kong. 2010. Rel: 25 Nov 2011. Cert. 18.

Amorous vengeance: Ching-Po Wong's sadistic, brutal and very stylish Revenge: A Love Story.

Ride, Rise, Roar ★★★★

This terrific documentary follows David Byrne's concert during 'The Songs of David Byrne & Brian Eno Tour'. Apart from Byrne's excellent songs, there is a lot of exciting stuff to enjoy –

the dance auditions where three amazing dancers are finally selected, as well as the rehearsals. It's a truly ensemble show and by the end you get to know each member individually. Unique talents in a unique show! GS

▶ Documentary about musicians David Byrne and Brian Eno with Lily Baldwin, Layla Childs, Mark De Gli Antoni, Paul Frazier, Jenni Muldaur etc.
▶ *Dir* Hillman Curtis, *Pro* Will Schluter and Ben Wolf, *Ph* Ben Wolf, *Pro Des* Jon Pollak, *Ed* Curtis and Matt Boyd, *M* David Byrne and Brian Eno.
Hillmancurtis Films/Ravel Films/Topiary Productions-Kaleidoscope Home Entertainment.
87 mins. USA. 2010. Rel: 21 Jan 2011. Cert. 12A.

Rio ★★★½

The team behind *Ice Age* jump a number of degrees up the thermometer to present a slick, breezy tale of love and ecology in and around the vibrant metropolis of Rio de Janeiro. Here, an extremely rare blue macaw finds himself lost and alone in a world a million miles from the cosy Minnesota bookshop in which he grew up. This allows the filmmakers to draw upon the vivid extremes of both the real and urban jungles of Brazil, while introducing a wide variety of characters. It's no *Rango* or *Tangled* but is a sweet, funny and highly entertaining ride. JC-W

▶ Voices of Anne Hathaway, Jesse Eisenberg, Jemaine Clement, Leslie Mann, Tracy Morgan, George Lopez, will.i.am, Jane Lynch, Jamie Foxx, Wanda Sykes.
▶ *Dir* Carlos Saldanha, *Pro* Bruce Anderson and John C Donkin, *Screenplay* Don Rhymer, Joshua Sternin and Jeffrey Ventimilia, *Ph* Renato Falcão, *Ed* Harry Hitner, *M* John Powell, *Sound* Randy Thom.
Blue Sky Studios/20th Century Fox Animation-20th Century Fox.
95 mins. USA. 2011. Rel: 8 Apr 2011. Cert. U.

Rio Breaks ★★★★

More than a documentary about surfing (although that plays a part in it), this is a compelling look at youngsters from the favelas of Rio de Janeiro. Two of them are central here, both being boys who might escape the criminal milieu with its drug-dealing gang wars if they devote themselves to becoming sports professionals. The film may be over-long but it's gripping – not a sports documentary but a social one. MS

▶ With Fabio da Costa Saldanha, Naamã de Araújo, Martines Uzêda, Rogério Silva de Oliveira.
▶ *Dir* and *Ph* Justin Mitchell, *Pro* Vince Medeiros and Mitchell, *Written by* Medeiros and Mitchell with John Maier, *Ed* René Guerra and Mitchell, *M* Jeff Kite.
The Breadcrumb Trail/Forward Entertainment/Prodrigo Films etc-Mr Bongo Films.
85 mins. USA/Italy. 2009. Rel: 3 June 2011. Cert. 12A.

Rise of the Planet of the Apes
★★★★½

Who would have thought? The cause of the apes' dominion over our planet was due to the introduction of a drug designed to cure Alzheimer's. Decades after Roddy McDowall re-invented himself in a monkey suit, this prequel re-boots the franchise using all the legerdemain of computer graphics. But this thrilling adventure succeeds more through its human-ape interaction than through any excesses of animated Armageddon. With only his second feature, the Exeter-born Rupert Wyatt channels Rick Jaffa and Amanda Silver's imaginative script into a riveting escapade that combines the wonders of science, Charles Darwin and Desmond Morris. JC-W

▶ James Franco, Freida Pinto, John Lithgow, Brian Cox, Tom Felton, Andy Serkis, David Oyelowo, Jamie Harris.
▶ Dir Rupert Wyatt, Pro Peter Chernin, Dylan Clark, Rick Jaffa and Amanda Silver, Screenplay Jaffa and Silver, Ph Andrew Lesnie, Pro Des Claude Paré, Ed Conrad Buff and Mark Goldblatt, M Patrick Doyle, Cos Renée April.

20th Century Fox/Chernin Entertainment/Dune Entertainment-20th Century Fox.
104 mins. USA. 2011. Rel: 11 Aug 2011. Cert. 12A.

Risen ★★★

Stuart Brennan is punchy as Howard Winstone, who in 1968, aged 29, became Featherweight Champion of the World despite having lost the tips of three fingers in an industrial accident at home in Merthyr Tydfil, leaving him unable to make a fist with his right hand. Despite flaws in acting and scripting, this is a fine, realistic boxing film, with the accent on authenticity and power in the action in the ring. A good story well told within a tiny budget, this proves a remarkable and compelling experience, with much credit due to Joe Bone, who coached the actors and was stand-in for the boxing choreography. Brennan also co-wrote with director Neil Jones. DW

▶ Stuart Brennan, John Noble, Shane Richie, Erik Morales, Edward E White, Boyd Clack.
▶ Dir and Ed Neil Jones, Pro and Screenplay Brennan and Jones, Ph Louis Fonseca, Pro Des Felix Coles and Katrina Thomas, M Alan Deacon, Cos Leila Headon, Gemma Bedeau, Sophia Douglas and Dawn Thomas-Mondo.

Burn Hand Film Productions/Templeheart Films-Scanbox Entertainment.
121 mins. UK. 2010. Rel: 13 May 2011. Cert. 12A.

The Rite ★★

When Michael Kovak (Colin O'Donaghue), a doubting American seminary student, is sent to the Vatican to study exorcism, he is soon taken under the wing of Father Lucas (Anthony Hopkins), a legendary priest who has performed thousands of exorcisms throughout the years. A thin and one-dimensional script lets down not only the strong premise (inspired by true events) but also director Mikael Håfström's ability to create atmosphere. GS

▶ Anthony Hopkins, Colin O'Donoghue, Alice Braga, Ciarán Hinds, Rutger Hauer, Toby Jones.
▶ Dir Mikael Håfström, Pro Tripp Vinson and Beau

Chimps off the old block: Rupert Wyatt's thrilling blockbuster Rise of the Planet of the Apes was better than anybody could have hoped for.

Flynn, *Screenplay* Michael Petroni, suggested by the book by Matt Baglio, *Ph* Ben Davis, *Pro Des* Andrew Laws, *Ed* David Rosenbloom, *M* Alex Heffes, *Cos* Carlo Poggioli.

New Line Cinema/Contrafilm/Fletcher and Company/ Mid Atlantic Films-Warner Bros.
114 mins. USA/Hungary. 2011. Rel: 25 Feb 2011. Cert. 15.

Robotropolis ★★½

Sometime in the near future a press conference is called to inaugurate New Town, a city to be run entirely by robots. However, one of the robots breaks down and begins to slaughter its masters. The pressure is on for the reporters to get their story while trying to avoid being killed by robots. A standard plot gathers little in the way of originality and, apart from odd scenes (a robot playing in a football game starts to run riot, for example), this is fairly routine stuff. It's one for robot-horror nuts only. PL

▶ Zoe Naylor, Graham Sibley, Edward Foy, Lani Tupu, Jourdan Lee Khou, Karina Sindicich.
▶ *Dir* and *Screenplay* Christopher Hatton, *Pro* Hatton, Leon Tong and Ehud Bleiberg, *Ph* Byron Werner, *Ed* Eva Contis and Scott Markus, *M* Ramón Balcázar.
Boku Films/Compound B-Metrodome Distribution.
90 mins. Singapore/USA. 2011. Rel: 2 Sep 2011. Cert. 15.

Romantics Anonymous ★★★

Either charming or silly according to taste, this French-Belgian co-production tells of how the world's best but very shy chocolate maker (Isabelle Carré) saves Jean-René's business from bankruptcy while winning the even shyer Jean-René for herself. Benoît Poelvoorde is splendid in this role, but you need to have a sweet tooth to accept the complete lack of sophistication. (Original title: *Les Émotifs anonymes*) MS

▶ Benoît Poelvoorde, Isabelle Carré, Lorella Cravotta, Swann Arlaud, Lise Lamétrie.
▶ *Dir* Jean-Pierre Améris, *Pro* Philippe Godeau and Nathalie Gastaldo, *Screenplay* Améris and Philippe Blasband from an idea by Améris, *Ph* Gérard Simon, *Art Dir* Sylvie Olivé, *Ed* Philippe Bourgueil, *M* Pierre Adenot, *Cos* Nathalie du Roscoät.
Pan-Européenne/StudioCanal/France 3 Cinéma/Rhône-Alpes Cinéma/Climax Films/RTBF etc-Picturehouse Entertainment.
78 mins. France/Belgium. 2010. Rel: 2 Dec 2011. Cert. 12A.

The Roommate ★

Rebecca (Leighton Meester) is the roommate from Hell in this cheap rip-off of *Single White Female*. She becomes totally obsessive about her college roommate Sara (Minka Kelly) and turns her life upside down, leading to a predictable and violent denouement. The script never rings true while the actors struggle to make sense of their dialogue. In *Country Strong* Meester proved she has star quality but here it is almost impossible to tell. GS

▶ Minka Kelly, Leighton Meester, Cam Giganet, Billy Zane, Aly Michalka, Frances Fisher.
▶ *Dir* Christian E Christiansen, *Pro* Roy Lee, Doug Davison and Irene Yeung, *Screenplay* Sonny Mallhi, Richard Robertson and Chris and Nick Bylsma, *Ph* Phil Parmet, *Pro Des* Jon Gary Steele, *Ed* Randy Bricker and Richard Robertson, *M* John Frizzell, *Cos* Maya Lieberman.
Screen Gems/Vertigo Entertainment-Sony Pictures Releasing.
91 mins. USA. 2011. Rel: 8 Apr 2011. Cert. 15.

The Round Up ★★★½

The title of Rose Bosch's film refers to the round-up of Jews in Paris in the summer of 1942 and, like *Sarah's Key* [qv], indicts the French for their part in it. Towards the end the film succumbs to melodrama and sentimentality, but it's still a striking narrative and preferable to its rival. The great Sylvie Testud contributes a deeply felt cameo and the film deserves to be seen despite its flaws. (Original title: *La Rafle*) MS

▶ Jean Reno, Mélanie Laurent, Hugo Leverdez, Gad Elmaleh, Raphaëlle Agogué, Sylvie Testud.
▶ *Dir* and *Screenplay* Rose Bosch, *Pro* Ilan Goldman, *Ph* David Ungaro, *Art Dir* Olivier Raoux, *Ed* Yann Malcor, *M* Christian Henson, *Cos* Gilles Bodu-Lemoine.
Légende/Légende Films/Gaumont etc-Revolver Entertainment.
125 mins. France/Germany/Hungary. 2010. Rel: 17 June 2011. Cert. 12A.

Centre of detention: Jean Reno and Mélanie Laurent in Roselyne Bosch's sentimental and melodramatic *The Round-Up*.

Route Irish ★★★★

Underestimated in some quarters, this drama from Ken Loach involves a former soldier (Mark Womack) questioning the official version and seeking the truth about the death of a childhood friend in Iraq. What he discovers draws on real-life facts about profit-making companies that use and exploit mercenaries. An unexpectedly bleak denouement adds extra weight to the film's warning about greed and corruption. MS

▶ Mark Womack, Andrea Lowe, John Bishop, Trevor Williams, Geoff Bell, Talib Rasool.
▶ *Dir* Ken Loach, *Pro* Rebecca O'Brien, *Screenplay* Paul Laverty, *Ph* Chris Menges, *Pro Des* Fergus Clegg, *Ed* Jonathan Morris, *M* George Fenton, *Cos* Sarah Ryan.

Sixteen Films/Why Not Productions/Wild Bunch/Les Films de Fleuve etc-Artificial Eye.
109 mins. UK/France/Italy/Belgium/Spain. 2010. Rel: 18 Mar 2011. Cert. 15.

Rubber ★★★½

Robert is an abandoned tyre in the desert that suddenly comes to life and begins to kill everything in sight. A narrator tells the audience that this is a film entirely built around the 'no reason' theory, as in *Love Story* where the two lovers fell in love for no reason and *JFK* where the president was shot for no reason. This suitably eccentric film is very funny and is perfect for a 1970s-style late-night show. GS

▶ Stephen Spinella, Wings Hauser, Roxanne Mesquida, Ethan Cohn, Charley Koontz.
▶ *Dir, Screenplay, Ph* and *Ed* Quentin Dupieux, *Pro* Julien Berlan and Gregory Bernard, *Pro Des* Zack Bangma, *M* Dupieux and Gaspard Augé, *Cos* Jamie Bresnan.

Realitism Films/Elle Driver/Backup Films/Canal+/Arte France etc-Optimum Releasing.
82 mins. France/Angola. 2010. Rel: 8 Apr 2011. Cert. 15.

The Rum Diary ★★★½

The director of *Withnail & I* returns with this version of Hunter S Thompson's semi-autobiographical novel set in Puerto Rico in the early 1960s. Being about a writer (Johnny Depp) finding his voice and also about corrupt developers, it's less wild than *Fear and Loathing in Las Vegas* but it's not short on humour, often related to drink and drugs. The mix is a bit uneasy at times, but it's engaging, well acted and notable too for the potent glamour of Amber Heard. MS

▶ Johnny Depp, Aaron Eckhart, Michael Rispoli, Amber Heard, Richard Jenkins, Giovanni Ribisi.
▶ *Dir* and *Screenplay* (from the novel by Hunter S Thompson) Bruce Robinson, *Pro* Johnny Depp, Christi Dembrowski and others, *Ph* Dariusz Wolski, *Pro Des* Chris Seagers, *Ed* Carol Littleton, *M* Christopher Young, *Cos* Colleen Atwood.

GK Films/Infinitum Nihil/Film Engine-Entertainment Film Distributors.
120 mins. USA. 2010. Rel: 11 Nov 2011. Cert. 15.

Rum is the word: Johnny Depp as a thinly veiled doppelgänger of his old friend Hunter S Thompson in Bruce Robinson's *The Rum Diary*.

Dogsitting: Gianni
Di Gregorio
contemplates his
lot in *The Salt of
Life*, which he also
directed and
co-wrote.

The Salt of Life ★★★★★

After *Mid-August Lunch* writer-director Gianni
Di Gregorio is back in the lead role of… Gianni.
He no longer lives with Mama but has a wife, a
daughter with a problem boyfriend, and a noisy
neighbour. They all, like Mama, impose on him to
run errands or walk the dog. He's surrounded by
beautiful women but what he really wants is some
attention, a little love and perhaps excitement. Di
Gregorio produces another funny-sad slice of life,
not all sweetness and light, but with a little salt to
rub in Gianni's minor wounds. In its own quiet,
observant way, this film is a little masterpiece.
(Original title: *Gianni e le donne*) MHD

❧ Gianni Di Gregorio, Valeria de Franciscis Bendoni,
Alfonso Santagata, Elisabetta Piccolomini, Valeria
Cavalli, Aylin Prandi.
❧ *Dir* Gianni Di Gregorio, *Pro* Angelo Barbagallo,
Screenplay Di Gregorio and Valerio Attanasio, *Ph*
Gogò Bianchi, *Pro Des* Susanna Cascella, *Ed* Marco
Spoletini, *M* Ratchev and Caratello, *Cos* Silvia Polidori.
Isaria Productions/BiBi Film/Rai Cinema etc-Artificial Eye.
90 mins. Italy. 2011. Rel: 12 Aug 2011. Cert. 12A.

Sanctum 3D ★★★

A group of underwater divers are on a dangerous
expedition in a remote cave led by the Australian
Frank McGuire (Richard Roxburgh). His 17-year-
old son Josh (Rhys Wakefield) joins the group but
after a tropical storm they all get trapped deep
in the cave… Director Alister Grierson shoots the
underwater sequences magnificently but fails to
set up his characters properly. The dialogue and
acting are uneven, but once the adventure begins
most of the action is underwater and thankfully
there is hardly any time for dialogue. GS

❧ Richard Roxburgh, Ioan Gruffudd, Rhys Wakefield,
Alice Parkinson, Allison Cratchley, Christopher Baker.
❧ *Dir* Alister Grierson, *Pro* Andrew Wight,
Screenplay Wight and John Garvin, from a story
by Wight, *Ph* Jules O'Loughlin, *Pro Des* Nicholas
McCallum, *Ed* Mark Warner, *M* David Hirschfelder,
Cos Supervisor Michael Davies.
Universal Pictures/Relativity Media/Great Wight/Sanctum
Australia/Wayfarer Entertainment-Universal Pictures.
108 mins. USA/Australia. 2011. Rel: 4 Feb 2011. Cert. 15.

Sarah's Key ★★★

This French drama finds the admirable Kristin
Scott Thomas playing an American journalist
in Paris who becomes obsessed by the need to
discover the full story of Sarah Starzyoski. Its
roots are in the real-life seizure of Jews in 1942
as also dramatised in *The Round Up* [qv]. What
happens in the flashbacks is far more intense
than the journalist's investigations, but the film's
major weakness lies in the many improbabilities
in the story line taken from a popular novel.
(Original title: *Elle s'appelait Sarah*) MS

❧ Kristin Scott Thomas, Mélusine Mayance, Niels
Arestrup, Michel Duchaussoy, Dominique Frot,
Aidan Quinn.

▶ *Dir* Gilles Paquet-Brenner, *Pro* Stéphane Marsil, *Screenplay* Serge Joncour and Paquet-Brenner from the novel by Tatiana de Rosnay, *Ph* Pascal Ridao, *Art Dir* Françoise Dupertuis, *Ed* Hervé Schneid, *M* Max Richter, *Cos* Eric Perron.

Hugo Productions/Studio 37/TF1 Droits Audiovisuels/ France 2 Cinéma/Canal+ etc-Optimum Releasing. 110 mins. France. 2011. Rel: 5 Aug 2011. Cert. 12A.

Sawako Decides ★★★½

When her father gets seriously sick Sawako (Hikari Mitsushima) decides to leave her job and boyfriend in Tokyo and move back to her rural hometown. She begins to work at her father's struggling factory, packing freshwater clams, but soon finds opposition from the other women working there. Director Yûya Ishii elicits a terrific performance from Mitsushima as the confused young woman who is in practically every scene and who effortlessly carries this eccentric and enjoyable film. (Original title: *Kawa no soko kara konnichi wa*) GS

▶ Hikari Mitsushima, Kotaro Shiga, Ryô Iwamatsu, Kira Aihara, Masashi Endô.
▶ *Dir* and *Screenplay* Yûya Ishii, *Pro* Mayumi Amano, *Ph* Yukihiro Okimura, *Art Dir* Tatsuo Ozeki, *Ed* Koichi Takahashi, *M* Chiaki Nomura, *Cos* Kyoko Baba.

Avex Entertainment/USEN Corporation/Imagica/Tokyo Broadcasting System etc-Third Window Films. 112 mins. Japan. 2010. Rel: 8 July 2011. Cert. 12A.

Scream 4 ★★½

More than a decade after the curtains closed on the beloved *Scream* trilogy, director Wes Craven's self-referential rollercoaster returns, now a quadrilogy. Though it lacks the freshness and surprise factor of the original, this utterly unnecessary slasher remains rather a lot of fun. A tongue-in-cheek horror flick that throws franchise originals Neve Campbell, Courteney Cox and David Arquette in with young bloods Emma Roberts and Hayden Panettiere, *Scream 4* hurls us back to the slasher capital of the USA, Woodsboro, for additional bloody mayhem and a reasonably generous sprinkle of audience-pleasing moments. MJ

▶ Neve Campbell, Courteney Cox, Anna Paquin, Emma Roberts, Hayden Panettiere, Kristen Bell, David Arquette.
▶ *Dir* Wes Craven, *Pro* Craven, Kevin Williamson and Iya Labunka, *Screenplay* Kevin Williamson, *Ph* Peter Deming, *Pro Des* Adam Stockhausen, *Ed* Peter McNulty, *M* Marco Beltrami, *Cos* Debra McGuire.

The Weinstein Company/Dimension Films/Corvus Corax/Outerbanks Entertainment etc-Entertainment Film Distributors. 111 mins. USA. 2011. Rel: 15 Apr 2011. Cert. 15.

A Screaming Man ★★★★★

Again set in Chad and the finest film yet from Mahamat-Saleh Haroun, this prize-winning work looks at life today in that part of the world by concentrating on the relationship – a complex one – between a father and his son. The second half may be a shade predictable, but this is a brilliantly acted and deeply humane work. The ultimate tragedy is fully confronted but there's a touch of poetry in it too. A remarkable film. (Original title: *Un Homme qui crie*) MS

▶ Youssouf Djaoro, Diouc Koma, Emile Abossolo M'Bo, Hadjé Fatimé N'Goua, Djénéba Koné.

Not going swimmingly: Youssouf Djaoro in Mahamat-Saleh Haroun's pertinent and remarkable *A Screaming Man.*

> *Dir* and *Screenplay* Mahamat-Saleh Haroun, *Pro* Florence Stern, *Ph* Laurent Brunet, *Art Dir* Ledoux Madeona, *Ed* Marie-Hélène Dozo, *M* Wasis Diop and Djénéba Koné, *Cos* Celine Delaire.

Pili Films/Goï-Goï Productions/Entre Chien et Loup etc-Soda Pictures.
91 mins. France/Chad/Belgium/Cameroon/Burkina Faso/The Netherlands. 2010. Rel: 13 May 2011. Cert. PG.

Screwed ★½

Sam Norwood (James D'Arcy) is a traumatised Iraq soldier forced to take a job as a prison officer. But life in this brutal institution is as violent and desperate as that on the streets of Baghdad... Despite D'Arcy's energetic and credible hero, Reg Traviss' clichéd film about the corrupt world of the prison service is directed by numbers, with stereotypical characters, and adds nothing new to an overpopulated genre. GS

> James D'Arcy, Noel Clarke, Frank Harper, Kate Magowan, Jamie Foreman, David Hayman.
> *Dir* Reg Traviss, *Pro* James Harris and Ronnie Thompson, *Screenplay* Thompson and Colin Butts, based on a book by Thompson, *Ph* Bryan Loftus, *Pro Des* Kajsa Soderlund, *Ed* John Palmer, *M* George Kallis, *Cos* Rebecca Gore.

Screwed Film-Lionsgate.
110 mins. UK. 2011. Rel: 3 June 2011. Cert. 18.

Season of the Witch ★

When Behmen (Nicolas Cage) and Felson (Ron Perlman) return from the Crusades they find everything destroyed by the plague. The church then assigns them to escort a girl (Claire Foy), whom they believe to be a witch and thus responsible for the devastation, to a remote monastery. There monks will try and get rid of the curse... Dominic Sena's uninspired direction lacks tension and suspense in this ludicrous medieval drama. GS

Though hardly looking his best, the venerable Christopher Lee was one of the few bright spots in the plague-eaten horror-thriller *Season of the Witch*.

> Nicolas Cage, Ron Perlman, Claire Foy, Stephen Campbell Moore, Christopher Lee, Stephen Graham, Ulrich Thomsen.
> *Dir* Dominic Sena, *Pro* Alex Gartner and Charles Roven, *Screenplay* Bragi Schut, *Ph* Amir Mokri, *Pro Des* Uli Hanisch, *Ed* Bob Ducsay, Dan Zimmerman and Mark Helfrich, *M* Atli Örvarsson, *Cos* Carlo Poggioli.

Atlas Entertainment/Relativity Media-Momentum Pictures.
95 mins. USA. 2010. Rel: 7 Jan 2011. Cert. 15.

Self Made ★★

Following a newspaper advertisement, film director Gillian Wearing chose seven applicants to undergo acting lessons and develop a character. Lian plays Cordelia in *King Lear* and draws on her own experience with her father, while Asheq wants to play a violent scene in order to exorcise brutal memories of his childhood. Manic depressive 48-year-old Dave is determined to commit suicide when he reaches 55 but at the moment he is happy to play Mussolini. It is a sad, depressing film which gives Method acting a bad name. GS

> With actors Sam Rumbelow, Tim Woodward, Helen Coverdale, Andrew Husband and Lesley Robinson, Dave Austin, Asheq Akhtar, Lian Stewart as themselves.
> *Dir* Gillian Wearing, *Pro* Lisa Marie Ruso, *Screenplay* Wearing and Leo Butler, *Ph* Roger Chapman, *Pro Des* Jamie Leonard, *Ed* Luke Dunkley and Daniel Goddard, *M* Daniel Pemberton, *Cos* Mel O'Connor.

Fly Film Company/UK Film Council/Arts Council of England/Northern Film & Media/Channel 4 Britdoc Foundation-Cornerhouse (Manchester).
88 mins. UK. 2010. Rel: 2 Sep 2011. Cert. 15.

Senna ★★★★½

Asif Kapadia's best film since *The Warrior* (2001) is an absorbing documentary about the Formula One champion Ayrton Senna, who died in a crash in 1994 at the age of 34. Assembling existing footage and adding comments by way of voice-overs, Kapadia wholly succeeds in making us live this man's life with him. Consequently it will absorb even viewers uninterested in motor racing as such. The only flaw is the lightening of tone in the images behind the end credits – a move which may or may not have been foisted on the filmmaker. MS

> With Alain Prost, Neyde Senna, Viviane Senna, John Bisignano, Professor Sid Watkins.
> *Dir* Asif Kapadia, *Pro* James Gay-Rees, Tim Bevan and Eric Fellner, *Written by* Manish Pandey, *Ph* Interview Crew: Jake Polonsky, *Ed* Gregers Sall and Chris King, *M* Antonio Pinto.

Universal Pictures/StudioCanal/Working Title etc-Universal Pictures International.
106 mins. USA/UK/France. 2010. Rel: 3 June 2011. Cert. 12A.

A Separation ★★★★

If ever a film deserved all its awards, this is it. *A Separation* portrays life in Iran as it might occur anywhere. People have their problems, but not just the political ones we hear about. In an ordinary family in Tehran husband Nader (Payman Moaadi) is torn between a father with dementia and a wife, Simin (Leila Hatami), who wants a divorce so that she can go abroad with her family. They separate and Nader employs Razieh (Sareh Bayat) to look after his father, but the carer brings her own problems which escalate the situation to breaking point. Director-writer-producer Farhadi gets heartstopping performances from his brilliant cast, who will have you in tears. (Original title: *Jodaeiye Nader az Simin*) MHD

▷ Payman Moaadi, Leila Hatami, Sareh Bayat, Shahab Hosseini, Sarina Farhadi.
▷ *Dir, Pro* and *Screenplay* Asghar Farhadi, *Ph* Mahmoud Kalari, *Pro Des* Keyvan Moghaddam, *Ed* Hayedeh Safiyari, *M* Sattar Oraki.
Asghar Farhadi-Artificial Eye.
123 mins. Iran. 2011. Rel: 1 July 2011. Cert. PG.

Shadow ★★

Jake Muxworthy stars as David, a young soldier serving in Iraq, who leaves for a mountain-biking excursion in Europe and meets dreamgirl Angeline (Karina Testa), as well as a couple of troublemaker hunters and a psycho who lives in an isolated house with a torture room in the basement. There's a good cargo of escalating tension, scares and nasty shocks in this slick and gripping Italian horror-thriller that covers familiar *Hostel*-style ground while still offering a few surprises. The atmosphere veers from creepy to gruesome to deliver the required thrills, which it manages with considerable style, atmosphere and gore, if little originality. DW

▷ Jake Muxworthy, Karina Testa, Nuot Arquint, Chris Coppola, Ottaviano Blitch.
▷ *Dir* Federico Zampaglione, *Pro* Massimo Ferrero, *Screenplay* Federico and Dominico Zampaglione and Giacomo Gensini, *Ph* Marco Bassano, *Pro Des* Davide Bassan, *Ed* Eric Strand, *M* Andrea Moscianese, *Cos* Raffaella Fantasia.
Blu Cinematografica-Jinga Films.
77 mins. Italy. 2009. Rel: 28 Apr 2011. Cert. 18.

Shark Night 3D ★½

Stupid, horny teenagers are on the menu in this largely moronic monster movie about duplicitous rednecks, careless youths and the blandly computer-generated freshwater sharks that are driven to consume them. It's no *Deep Blue Sea*, or even *Jaws 3D*. But, as guilty entertainment goes, it's sure to go down well with beer and low expectations. Good-bad, late-night, cult-flavoured nonsense with a fair few unintentional laughs, it's for dedicated fans of schlock cinema and no one else. MJ

Father's day: Payman Moaadi with Ali-Asghar Shahbazi in Asghar Farhadi's *A Separation*, which won the Oscar for Best Foreign Language Film.

▷ Sara Paxton, Dustin Milligan, Chris Carmac, Katharine McFee, Joshua Leonard.
▷ *Dir* David R Ellis, *Pro* Mike Fleiss, Lynnette Howell and Chris Briggs, *Screenplay* Will Hayes and Jesse Studenberg, *Ph* Gary Capo, *Pro Des* Jaymes Hinkle, *Ed* Dennis Virkler, *M* Graeme Revell, *Cos* Amanda Steeley.

Incentive Filmed Entertainment/Silverwood Films/Next Films/Sierra/Affinity-Entertainment Film Distributors. 90 mins. USA. 2011. Rel: 30 Sep 2011. Cert. 15.

Sherlock Holmes: A Game of Shadows ★½

When chronicling the exploits of a figure as ingenious as Sherlock Holmes it would help if the storyteller had a commensurate IQ. While marginally more coherent than its predecessor, *A Game of Shadows* is still over-produced, over-edited, over-scored and over-long. Robert Downey Jr recycles his Sherlock as dishevelled superman and little lustre is added by the presence of Noomi Rapace in her first English-speaking role. As a film about brilliant minds, the sequel's most satisfying moment comes when Holmes and Moriarty play a game of chess without a chessboard – which really does make a mockery of the film's $140 million budget. JC-W

▷ Robert Downey Jr, Jude Law, Noomi Rapace, Jared Harris, Rachel McAdams, Stephen Fry, Eddie Marsan, Kelly Reilly, Geraldine James, Wolf Kahler.
▷ *Dir* Guy Ritchie, *Pro* Joel Silver, Lionel Wigram, Susan Downey and Dan Lin, *Screenplay* Kieran Mulroney and Michele Mulroney, *Ph* Philippe Rousselot, *Pro Des* Sarah Greenwood, *Ed* James Herbert, *M* Hans Zimmer, *Cos* Jenny Beavan.

Warner Bros/Village Roadshow/Silver Pictures/Wigram Prods/Lin Pictures-Warner Bros. 128 mins. USA/UK. 2011. Rel: 16 Dec 2011. Cert. 12A.

The Silence ★★½

In a German town a girl is raped and killed. Years later another girl disappears and it looks as though events are repeating themselves. Given the able cast here, this might have been a powerful thriller. But, using a nudging music score, newcomer Baran bo Odar, writer and director, has come up with a story riddled with improbable plot developments, including the most unlikely motive for a crime that I have ever encountered! (Original title: *Das letzte Schweigen*) MS

▷ Ulrich Thomsen, Wotan Wilke Möhring, Katrin Sass, Burghart Klaussner, Karoline Eichhorn.
▷ *Dir* and *Screenplay* (from the novel *Das Schweigen* by Jan Costin Wagner) Baran bo Odar, *Pro* Jantje Friese, Odar and others, *Ph* Nikolaus Summerer, *Pro Des* Yesim Zolan and Christian M Goldbeck, *Ed* Robert Rzesacz, *M* Pas de Deux, Michael Kamm and Kris Steininger, *Cos* Katharina Ost.

Cine Plus/Lüthje & Schneider Film/ARTE etc-Soda Pictures. 119 mins. Germany. 2010. Rel: 28 Oct 2011. Cert. 15.

The Silent House ★★

'Real fear in real time' claimed the publicity for this spectral Uruguayan offering, inevitably calling forth subjective quibbles about what constitutes 'real fear' but also some doubts regarding 'real time'. Apparently shot in a single uninterrupted take, there's nevertheless an editor credit and viewers will be tempted, like Eric Morecambe, to 'see the join[s]'. As a girl and her father go about renovating

Mobile Holmes. Jude Law, Noomi Rapace and Robert Downey Jr find themselves in Paris in Guy Ritchie's lamentable *Sherlock Holmes: A Game of Shadows*.

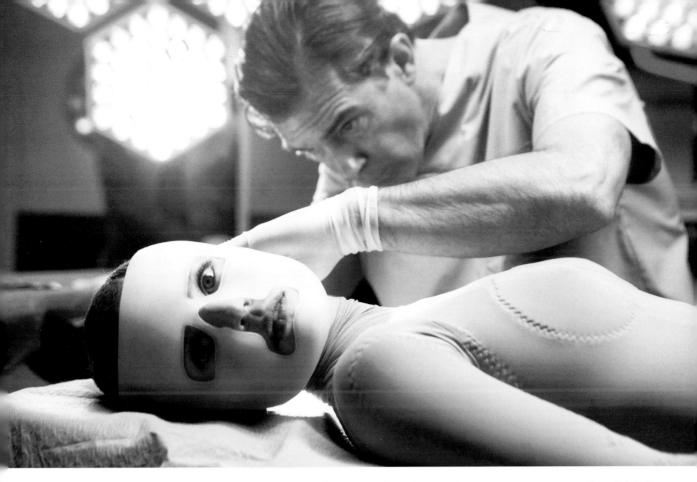

a rundown country cottage, carefully built tension alternates with tedium and is eventually undone by a credulity-busting twist. Florencia Colucci is impressive, however, and there's real technical skill on show, albeit in the service of a gimmick. (Original title: *La casa muda*) JR

▶ Florencia Colucci, Abel Tripaldi, Gustavo Alonso, Maria Salazar.
▶ *Dir* and *Ed* Gustavo Hernández, *Pro* Gustavo Rojo, *Screenplay* Oscar Estévez, from a story by Hernández and Gustavo Rojo, *Ph* Pedro Luque, *Pro Des* Federico Capra, *M* Hernán González, *Cos* Capra, Carolina Duré and Natalia Duré.

Tokio Films-Optimum Releasing.
86 mins. Uruguay. 2011. Rel: 8 Apr 2011. Cert. 15.

Sket ★★

'Sket' is a derogatory street term for a woman with little integrity or dignity. Well, *Sket* is full of skets. As it happens, girl gangs are becoming an increasing problem on the streets of Britain, although it's doubtful any will look like the prefabricated bunch here. Made up of a brunette, a blonde, a black and an Indian, the girls look more like All Skets or The Sket Girls. One would wish to embrace a low-budget film that attempts to shed fresh light on the troubled waters of contemporary Britain, but very little in Nirpal Bhogal's directorial debut rings true. JC-W

▶ Ashley Walters, Emma Hartley-Miller, Aimee Kelly, Riann Steele, Katie Foster-Barnes.
▶ *Dir* and *Screenplay* Nirpal Bhogal, *Pro* Nick Taussig, Paul Van Carter, Daniel Toland and Terry Stone, *Ph* Felix Wiedemann, *Pro Des* Melanie Light, *Ed* Richard Elson, *M* Chad Hobson, *Cos* Guy Speranza.

Gunslinger/Gateway Films/Creativity Media-Revolver Entertainment.
83 mins. UK. 2011. Rel: 28 Oct 2011. Cert. 15.

The Skin I Live In ★★★

If this is a triumph at all (some seem to think that it is), it is one of style over content. Pedro Almodóvar is a masterly filmmaker but his story, about a surgeon (Antonio Banderas) creating a new skin, sidesteps Hammer and obvious horror for an ill-structured and absurdly melodramatic tale with a startling conclusion. For anyone familiar with the director's themes and preoccupations, the secret twist is really no surprise at all. (Original title: *La piel que habito*) MS

▶ Antonio Banderas, Elena Anaya, Marisa Paredes, Jan Cornet, Roberto Álamo, Eduard Fernández.
▶ *Dir* Pedro Almodóvar, *Pro* Esther García, *Screenplay* Almodóvar with Augustin Almodóvar from the novel *Mygale* (*Tarantula*) by Thierry Jonquet, *Ph* José Luis Alcaine, *Art Dir* Antxón Gómez, *Ed* José Salcedo, *M* Alberto Iglesias, *Cos* Paco Delgado.

El Deseo/Blue Lake Entertainment/FilmNation Entertainment etc-Pathé Distribution.
120 mins. Spain/USA. 2011. Rel: 26 Aug 2011. Cert. 15.

Face off: Antonio Banderas attends to Elena Anaya's physiognomy in Pedro Almodóvar's ill-structured and melodramatic *The Skin I Live In.*

Spooning beauty:
Emily Browning
and Peter Carroll
in Julia Leigh's
fearless and
hypnotic *Sleeping
Beauty*.

Sleeping Beauty ★★★½

Emily Browning plays Lucy, a student who takes
odd jobs in a medical laboratory and as a semi-
nude waitress in order to make ends meet. She
finds an even odder job with even odder ends,
working as a drugged sex object for which old men,
losing their sexual stamina, are willing to play
and pay. At first Lucy is happy to be used in this
way until she discovers what is really happening.
Novelist Julia Leigh's first film is impressive enough
(she was mentored by Jane Campion) but the air
of coldness surrounding the piece hardly invites
warmth from an audience, although Browning's
performance has to be admired. MHD

▶ Emily Browning, Ewen Leslie, Rachael Blake, Peter
Carroll, Chris Haywod, Hugh Keays-Byrne.
▶ *Dir* and *Screenplay* Julia Leigh, *Pro* Jessica Brentnall,
Ph Geoffrey Simpson, *Pro Des* Annie Beauchamp, *Ed*
Nick Meyers, *M* Ben Frost, *Cos* Shareen Beringer.
**Screen Australia/Magic Films/Screen NSW/Big Ears
Productions/Spectrum Films etc-Revolver Entertainment.
101 mins. USA. 2011. Rel: 14 Oct 2011. Cert. 18.**

A Small Act ★★★★

This delightful documentary illustrates how
help offered to somebody less well-off can start
a chain encouraging similar acts down the
years. Very well constructed, the film features a
human rights lawyer born in poverty in a Kenyan
village but it tells too the story of his Jewish
benefactress. *A Small Act* is the best kind of feel-
good film: unsentimental and true. MS

▶ With Hilde Back, Chris Mburu, Patrick Kimani
Nyambura, Ruth Wairimu, Caroline Gaceri.
▶ *Dir* and *Written by* Jennifer Arnold, *Pro* Arnold,
Patti Lee and Jeffrey Soros, *Ph* Lee, *Ed* Carl Pfirman
and Tyler Hubby, *M* Joel Goodman.
**HBO Documentary Films/Harambee Media etc-
Dogwoof Pictures.
88 mins. USA/Australia. 2010. Rel: 15 Apr 2011.
Cert. 12A.**

The Smurfs in 3D ★

This silly, part live-action, part animated feature
follows the adventures of the tiny blue Smurfs
after they are thrown out of their village by the
evil wizard Gargamel (Hank Azaria). Ending up in
New York's Central Park they must find their way
back into their magical world before Gargamel
tracks them down... Director Raja Gosnell fails to
inject enough energy into this witless and bland
version of the popular television series. It's not
even mildly interesting and even the 3D effects
are unmemorable. GS

▶ Hank Azaria, Neil Patrick Harris, Jayma Mays, Sofia
Vergara, Tim Gunn.
▶ *Dir* Raja Gosnell, *Pro* Jordan Kerner, *Screenplay*
J David Stern, David N Weiss, Jay Scherick and
David Ronn, from a story by Stern and Weiss, based
on characters created by Peyo, *Ph* Phil Meheux,
Pro Des Bill Boes, *Ed* Sabrina Plisco, *M* Heitor Pereira,
Cos Rita Ryack.
**Columbia Pictures/Sony Pictures Animation/Kerner
Entertainment Company-Sony Pictures Releasing.
103 mins. USA. 2011. Rel: 12 Aug 2011. Cert. U.**

Snow Flower and the Secret Fan ★★★½

Wayne Wang's best film since *The Joy Luck Club* (1995) looks at women's lives both in 19th century China and today, when many from the Far East settle in America. Combining two tales to bring out the parallels as well as the contrasts (the two lead actresses play dual roles) sometimes makes for a bitty narrative. Nevertheless, this is well designed and ably played and should be enjoyed by the audience at which it is aimed. MS

❥ Gianna Jun, Li Bingbing, Vivian Wu, Hugh Jackman, Jiang Wu, Coco Chiang.
❥ *Dir* Wayne Wang, *Pro* Wendi Murdoch and Florence Sloan, *Screenplay* Angela Workman, Ron Bass, and Michael K Ray from the book by Lisa See, *Ph* Richard Wong, *Pro Des* and *Cos* Man Lim Chung, *Ed* Deirdre Slevin, *M* Rachel Portman.

Fox Searchlight Pictures/Big Feet etc-20th Century Fox.
104 mins. People's Republic of China/USA. 2011. Rel: 4 Nov 2011. Cert. 12A.

Snowtown ★★★

Horrendous real-life serial murders in the suburbs of Adelaide are the basis of this portrayal of how a teenager got sucked in by coming to regard the killer, John Bunting, as a surrogate father figure. This is more an art-house film than an exploitation movie, but the somewhat comparable *Animal Kingdom* [qv] was much easier to follow. Despite its raw power, the much praised *Snowtown* hardly offers any fresh insights into such criminals as those depicted here. MS

❥ Lucas Pittaway, Daniel Henshall, Louise Harris, Anthony Groves, Beau Gosling.
❥ *Dir* Justin Kurzel, *Pro* Anna McLeish and Sarah Shaw, *Screenplay* Shaun Grant from a story by him and Kurzel inspired by the books *Killing for Pleasure* and *The Snowtown Murders*, *Ph* Adam Arkapaw, *Pro Des* Fiona Crombie, *Ed* Veronika Jenet, *M* Jed Kurzel, *Cos* Alice Babidge and Crombie.

Screen Australia/Warp Films Australia/Film Victoria etc-Revolver Entertainment.
120 mins. Australia. 2010. Rel: 18 Nov 2011. Cert. 18.

Something Borrowed ★

The fine line between love and friendship is thinly explored in this slack, distasteful comedy, as terminally single lawyer Rachel (Ginnifer Goodwin) falls again for one-time fellow NYU student, rich boy Dex (Colin Egglesfield) now the fiancé of her best friend Darcy (Kate Hudson). Darcy asks Rachel to be her maid of honour, but Rachel's buddy Ethan (John Krasinski) tells her she'll regret it if she doesn't make a move. Though based on a bestseller, this conveyor belt rom-com could have been written by a computer,

while the performances are phoned-in and unappealing. Predictable and cliché-ridden, it's even less complicated than it looks. DW

❥ Kate Hudson, Ginnifer Goodwin, John Krasinski, Colin Egglesfield, Jill Eikenberry.
❥ *Dir* Luke Greenfield, *Pro* Hilary Swank, Molly Mickler Smith, Pamela Schein Murphy, Aaron Lubin, Andrew A Kosove and Broderick Johnson, *Screenplay* Jennie Snyder Urman, based on the novel by Emily Giffin, *Ph* Charles Minsky, *Pro Des* Jane Musky, *Ed* John Axelrad, *M* Alex Wurman, *Cos* Gary Jones.

2S Films/Wild Ocean Films/Alcon Entertainment-Entertainment Film Distributors.
112 mins. USA. 2011. Rel: 6 May 2011. Cert. 12A.

Son of Babylon ★★★★

This second feature from Mohamed Al-Daradji of *Ahlaam* again tells a story conveying the suffering in recent times of ordinary people living in Iraq. Equally committed, this is actually the more compelling and convincing film of the two. The focus is on a 12-year-old boy and his grandmother searching for the child's missing father who had been forced to fight in the Gulf War. It's understandably very downbeat but very sympathetic too. MS

❥ Shehzad Hussen, Yassir Taleeb, Bashir Al-Majed, Salih Abdul Rahman Farhad.
❥ *Dir* Mohamed Al-Daradji, *Pro* Isabelle Stead, Al-Daradji and others, *Screenplay* Jennifer Norridge, Al-Daradji and Mithal Ghazi, *Ph* Al-Daradji and Duraid Munajim, *Pro Des* Alison Jeffrey, *Ed* Pascale Chavance and Mohamed Jbara, *M* Kad Achouri, *Cos* Akhlas Saddam.

Human Film/Iraq Al-Rafidain/CRM-114/UK Film Council etc-Dogwoof Pictures.
92 mins. UK/Iraq/France/USA/UAE/Egypt/Palestine/The Netherlands. 2010. Rel: 11 Feb 2011. Cert. 12A.

On the road to nowhere: Yasser Talib and Shazada Hussein in Mohamed Al-Daradji's compelling and convincing *Son of Babylon*.

Soul Surfer ★★★

It's not often that Jesus Christ gets a mention in the credits. However, he gets a special thank-you here. This is the story of Bethany Hamilton, who was wedded to the Hawaiian surf when a terrible accident befell her. The special effects needed for this physical transition are flawless and AnnaSophia Robb is never less than sincere as Bethany. Bearing in mind the audience that this is aimed for, it is a salutary take on life and the rewards of love, hard work and goddamned determination. *Soul Surfer* is by no means a legendary piece of cinema but it could still change lives. JC-W

▶ AnnaSophia Robb, Helen Hunt, Dennis Quaid, Carrie Underwood, Kevin Sorbo, Jeremy Sumpter, Sonya Balmores Chung, Craig T Nelson.
▶ *Dir* Sean McNamara, *Pro* McNamara, David Brookwell, Douglas Schwartz and Dutch Hofstetter, *Screenplay* McNamara & Deborah Schwartz & Douglas Schwartz & Michael Berk, based on a true story by McNamara, Deborah Schwartz, Douglas Schwartz, Michael Berk, Matt R Allen, Caleb Wilson & Bard Gann, *Ph* John R Leonetti, *Pro Des* Rusty Smith, *Ed* Jeff Canavan, *M* Marco Beltrami, *Cos* Kathe James.

Brookwell-McNamara Entertainment/Enticing Entertainment/Island Film Group/Life's a Beach Entertainment/Mandalay Vision-Buena Vista International. 105 mins. USA. 2011. Rel: 23 Sep 2011. Cert. PG.

Sound It Out ★★★★

Jeanie Finlay's unique documentary celebrates the work of Sound It Out, an independent record shop in Teesside which, thanks to Tom Butchart's commitment and expertise, is still thriving at a time when most record shops around the country are closing. Finlay interviews many of its enthusiastic customers, who proudly show their priceless vinyl collections. One of them declares that he wants to be buried in a coffin made from his records. Finlay never attempts to send up her subjects, however tempting. GS

▶ *Dir, Pro* and *Ph* Jeanie Finlay, *Ed* Barbara Zosel, *Music Supervisor* Graham Langley.

Glimmer Films-Verve Pictures. 75 mins. UK. 2011. Rel: 4 Nov 2011. Cert. 12A.

Source Code ★★★★

Director Duncan Jones proves here that *Moon* (2009) was no flash in the pan. Aided by a fine cast headed by Jake Gyllenhaal and Vera Farmiga, he now handles with panache a story which is contemporary yet also rooted in science fiction. The latter element finds the central character sent back in time to discover who planted a bomb on a train. Technically superb, this drama recalls the mind games of *Inception* (2010) and is also great fun. MS

Close circuit: Jake Gyllenhaal in Duncan Jones' slick, mind-stretching *Source Code.*

▶ Jake Gyllenhaal, Michelle Monaghan, Vera Farmiga, Jeffrey Wright, Michael Arden.
▶ *Dir* Duncan Jones, *Pro* Philippe Rousselot, Mark Gordon and Jordan Wynn, *Screenplay* Ben Ripley, *Ph* Don Burgess, *Pro Des* Barry Chusid, *Ed* Paul Hirsch, *M* Chris Bacon, *Cos* Renée April.

Vendome Pictures/Mark Gordon Company etc-Optimum Releasing.
93 mins. USA/France. 2011. Rel: 1 Apr 2011. Cert. 12A.

Sparrow ★★½

Made in 2008 by the Hong Kong director Johnnie To, this is not one of his action thrillers. Indeed it's a work with interesting echoes of French cinema and he directs it adroitly. Even so, this tale of Hong Kong's underworld ('sparrow' is slang for pickpocket) lacks any emotional core and descends into stupidity. What was initially lightly engaging ends up as a waste of time, style being far superior to content. (Original title: *Man jeuk*) MS

▶ Simon Yam, Kelly Lin, Lam Ka Tung, Lo Hoi Pang, Law Wing Cheong, Kenneth Cheung.
▶ *Dir* and *Pro* Johnnie To, *Screenplay* Chan Kin Chung and Fung Chih Chiang, *Ph* Cheng Siu Keung, *Art Dir* Tony Yu, *Ed* David Richardson, *M* Xavier Jamaux and Fred Avril, *Cos* Stanley Cheung.

Universe Entertainment/Milkyway Image (Hong Kong)/ Newlink Development/Foj Limited-Terracotta Distribution.
88 mins. Hong Kong. 2008. Rel: 15 Apr 2011. Cert. 15.

Special Forces ★★

Stéphane Rybojad's French patriotic drama takes place in Afghanistan. When war correspondent Elsa (Diane Kruger) is taken hostage by the Taliban, a group of French elite soldiers are assigned to bring her back. The superb cinematography, strong production values and glamorous cast are more suited to a glossy commercial than a bleak adventure about the Taliban. The enemy are represented as villainous stereotypes while the gung-ho action brings more that a whiff of propaganda. (Original title: *Forces spéciales*) GS

▶ Diane Kruger, Djimon Hounsou, Benoît Magimel, Denis Menochet.
▶ *Dir* Stéphane Rybojad, *Pro* Thierry Maro and Benoit Ponsaillé, *Screenplay* Rybojad and Michael Cooper, *Ph* David Jankowski, *Ed* Erwan Pecher, *M* Xavier Berthelot, *Cos* Céline El Maouzi.

Easy Company/StudioCanal/Sofica Manon/A Plus Image 2/Canal+ etc-Optimum Releasing.
109 mins. France. 2011. Rel: 18 Nov 2011. Cert. 15.

Spy Kids 4: All the Time in the World ★★

Unbeknown to her family, happily married Marissa (Jessica Alba) is a spy who accidentally involves her stepchildren in an operation to

Criminal interest: a beautiful and mysterious Kelly Lin in Johnny To's virtually wordless *Sparrow*.

stop the megalomaniac Timekeeper (Jeremy Piven) from taking over the world. There are no surprises here, though Robert Rodriguez just about keeps the action flowing in this otherwise tired series, again in 3D but also in Aroma-Scope – the gimmick last used by John Waters in *Polyester*. Waters used it to hilarious effect but here all the scratch-card aromas smell more or less the same – like very sugary sweets. GS

▶ Jessica Alba, Joel McHale, Rowan Blanchard, Mason Cook, Jeremy Piven.
▶ *Dir* and *Screenplay* Robert Rodriguez, *Pro* Rodriguez and Elizabeth Avellan, *Ph* Rodriguez and Jimmy Lindsey, *Ed* Dan Zimmerman, *M* Rodriguez and Carl Thiel, *Cos* Nina Proctor.

Dimension Films/Spy Kids 4 SPV/Troublemaker Studios-Entertainment Film Distributors.
89 mins. USA. 2011. Rel: 19 Aug 2011. Cert. PG.

Stake Land ★★★★

After a vampire epidemic has swept across America, teenager Martin (Connor Paolo) joins forces with a vampire hunter called Mister (Nick Damici) and together these two unlikely characters begin a journey of survival through a hostile environment. Jim Mickle gives the vampire genre a new lease of life with this original and atmospheric tale. The action is well executed, with striking compositions, and it's also good to see Kelly McGillis in a decent role as a devout nun on the run. GS

▶ Connor Paolo, Gregory Jones, Kelly McGillis, Nick Damici, Tim House, Phyllis Bash.
▶ *Dir* and *Ed* Jim Mickle, *Pro* Peter Phok, Brent Kunkle, Derek Curl, Adam Folk and Larry Fessenden,

Screenplay Mickle and Nick Damici, *Ph* Ryan Samul, *Pro Des* Daniel R Kersting, *M* Jeff Grace, *Cos* Elisabeth Vastola.

Bella Donna Productions/Glass Eye Pix/Off Hollywood Pictures-Metrodome.
98 mins. USA. 2010. Rel: 17 June 2011. Cert. 15.

The Story of Lovers Rock ★★★½

Black filmmaker Menelik Shabazz, noted for *Burning an Illusion* (1981) and some television documentaries on black issues, here looks back at the romantic reggae music of the 1970s and '80s by British musicians born to Caribbean families. Their music subsequently influenced many British bands including The Police, UB40 and Culture Club. Through dance, Lovers Rock provided a healing process that allowed young people to cope with the disturbing situations on the streets. The film, which includes recent footage of musicians such as Janet Kay and Brown Sugar in performance, is a useful and memorable guide to a forgotten period of British music. PL

▶ With UB40, Maxi Priest, Angie Le Mar, Janet Kay, Linton Kwesi Johnson, Eddie Nestor, Robbie Gee, Levi Roots, Brown Sugar.
▶ *Dir* Menelik Shabazz, *Pro* Paulette Harris-German, *Ph* Ian Watts, *Ed* Julian Sabath, *Cos* Jackie Lodge-West.

EFM Media/SunRa Pictures-Verve Pictures.
97 mins. UK. 2011. Rel: 30 Sep 2011. Cert. 12A.

Washed out: the excellent Craig Roberts in Richard Ayoade's surprising and very funny *Submarine.*

Straw Dogs ★★

In 1971, Sam Peckinpah's *Straw Dogs* set a new benchmark for gratuitous violence. By today's standards of torture porn (the *Saw* films, *Hostel*, etc) the film seems relatively mild, so it was a fascinating prospect to update it and relocate it from Cornwall to Louisiana. Fascinating but ultimately pointless. The notorious rape scene is played down here (this is a Hollywood film, after all) and because we don't care for – or believe in – the central couple, the violence, when it comes, is barely shocking. JC-W

▶ James Marsden, Kate Bosworth, Alexander Skarsgård, Dominic Purcell, James Woods.
▶ *Dir* and *Screenplay* Rod Lurie, *Pro* Lurie and Marc Frydman, *Ph* Alik Sakharov, *Pro Des* Tony Fanning, *Ed* Sarah Boyd, *M* Larry Groupé, *Cos* Lynn Falconer.

Screen Gems/Battleplan Productions-Sony Pictures.
109 mins. USA. 2011. Rel: 4 Nov 2011. Cert. 18.

Submarine ★★★★

Craig Roberts plays Oliver, a 15-year-old looking for love, or at least a girlfriend, in Swansea. He's a loner, an outsider, but still he hitches up with Jordana (Yasmin Paige), another oddball prone to starting fires. Stone-faced Oliver only breaks his solemn expression on receiving his first kiss. His parents' (Noah Taylor and Sally Hawkins) rocky marriage is under strain as Mum is seeing ex-boyfriend, New Age hippie Graham (Paddy Considine), who has moved in next door. Richard Ayoade's first feature is weird and at times wonderfully funny. It won't appeal to everybody but its quirkiness and cinematic skill make for an impressive debut. MHD

▶ Noah Taylor, Paddy Considine, Craig Roberts, Yasmin Paige, Sally Hawkins, Darren Evans.
▶ *Dir* and *Screenplay* Richard Ayoade, from the novel by Joe Dunthorne, *Pro* Andy Stebbing, Mark Herbert and Mary Burke, *Ph* Erik Alexander Wilson,

Love letter to Spielberg: Kyle Chandler, Joel Courtney, Elle Fanning and Ron Eldard in J J Abrams' cute and entertaining *Super 8*.

Pro Des Gary Williamson, *Ed* Chris Dickens and Nick Fenton, *M* Andrew Hewitt, *Cos* Charlotte Walter.

Film 4/Film Agency for Wales/Red Hour Films/Warp Films etc-Optimum Releasing.
97 mins. UK/USA. 2010. Rel: 18 Mar 2011. Cert. 15.

Sucker Punch ★½

When Babydoll (Emily Browning) is forced by her father into a mental institution she is determined to fight for her freedom, but first she has to convince four other inmates to join her... The opening is strong, while Zack Snyder's clever use of music with sharp editing in the style of a pop video catches attention. But as the action moves into video game territory it becomes boring and loses total credibility. GS

▶ Emily Browning, Abbie Cornish, Jena Malone, Vanessa Hudgens, Jamie Chung, Scott Glenn.
▶ *Dir* Zack Snyder, *Pro* Zack and Deborah Snyder, *Screenplay* Zack Snyder and Steve Shibuya, from a story by Snyder, *Ph* Larry Fong, *Pro Des* Rick Carter, *Ed* William Hoy, *M* Tyler Bates and Marius De Vries, *Cos* Michael Wilkinson.

Warner Bros Pictures/Legendary Pictures/Lennox House Films/Cruel and Unusual-Warner Bros.
110 mins. USA/Canada. 2011. Rel: 1 Apr 2011. Cert. 12A.

SUPER ★★★

Frank D'Arbo (Rainn Wilson) is devastated when his wife (Liv Tyler) is taken from him by a seductive drug dealer (Kevin Bacon). He is determined to get her back but first he decides to become a self-made superhero called Crimson Bolt. He obviously has no super powers but that doesn't stop him acquiring a sidekick. James

Gunn's affectionate satire on superheroes may not be as funny as *Kick-Ass,* but it is still enjoyable. A guilty pleasure, very violent but fun. GS

▶ Rainn Wilson, Liv Tyler, Ellen Page, Kevin Bacon, Gregg Henry, Michael Rooker, Sean Gunn.
▶ *Dir* and *Screenplay* James Gunn, *Pro* Ted Hope and Miranda Bailey, *Ph* Steve Gainer, *Pro Des* Dave Hagen and William A Elliott, *Ed* Cara Silverman, *M* Tyler Bates, *Cos* Mary Matthews.

This Is That Productions/Crimson Bolt/Ambush Entertainment-G2 Pictures.
96 mins. USA. 2010. Rel: 8 July 2011. Cert. 18.

Super 8 ★★★★

Ohio, circa 1979, and young Joe (Joel Courtney) and his pals are filming their own zombie movie on Super 8. When they witness a horrifying train crash, they also see something escape. Could it be an alien? Writer-director J J Abrams pays tribute to his producer-master Steven Spielberg in a kind of *Close Encounters* meets *E.T.* convergence, but it's none the worse for that and indeed turns out to be a good romp both for kids and their parents. The young actors steal all the acting honours from under the grown-ups' noses, under the influence, perhaps, of their co-producer. MHD

▶ Joel Courtney, Kyle Chandler, Riley Griffiths, Elle Fanning, Ryan Lee, Zach Mills, Gabriel Basso.
▶ *Dir* and *Screenplay* J J Abrams, *Pro* Steven Spielberg, Abrams and Bryan Burk, *Ph* Larry Fong, *Pro Des* Martin Whist, *Ed* Maryann Brandon and Mary Jo Markey, *M* Michael Giacchino, *Cos* Ha Nguyen.

Paramount Pictures/Amblin Entertainment/Bad Robot-Paramount Pictures.
112 mins. USA. 2011. Rel: 5 Aug 2011. Cert. 12A.

Interpretation of Dreams: Václav Helsus and Klára Issová in Jan Svankmajer's idiosyncratic *Surviving Life.*

Surviving Life (Theory and Practice) ★★★★

The veteran Czech animator Jan Svankmajer is as idiosyncratic and imaginative as ever in this piece which also features live actors. A married man and the girl who appears in his dreams are central to the film's take on human behaviour. Cleverly it is able both to satirise the ideas of Freud and Jung and to posit a view of life in which a psychoanalyst's notions lie at the root of everything. (Original title: *Prezít svuj zivot (teorie a praxe)*) MS

▶ Václav Helsus, Klára Issová, Zuzana Kronerová, Emília Doseková, Daniela Bakerová.
▶ *Dir, Screenplay* and *Art Dir* Jan Svankmajer, *Pro* Jaromír Kallista, *Ph* Jan Ruzicka and Juraj Galvánek, *Ed* Marie Zemonová, *Cos* Veronika Hrubá, *Animation* Martin Kublák, Eva Jakoubková and Jaroslav Mrázek.
Athanor Film Production Company/C-GA Film/Ceská Televize etc-Verve Pictures/Illuminations.
109 mins. Czech Republic/Japan. 2010. Rel: 2 Dec 2011. Cert. 15.

Sweetgrass ★★★

The visual quality of this documentary renders it a film for cinema viewing. Filmed in Montana, it shows cowboys herding sheep into the mountains for the summer. That's part of a way of life that is passing and the filmmakers come from the fields of anthropology and ethnography. For specialists it may well be fascinating, but the slow pace and absence of any narration may well alienate viewers who lack background information. MS

▶ With John Ahern, Pat Connolly, Elaine Allestad, Lawrence Allestad, Billy Allestad.
▶ *Recorded by* Lucien Castaing-Taylor, *Pro* Ilisa Barbash, *Ed* Barbash and Castaing-Taylor.
Harvard Sensory Ethnography Lab-Dogwoof Pictures.
101 mins. USA. 2009. Rel: 22 Apr 2011. Cert. 15.

Swinging with the Finkels ★

A couple bored with married life begin a search to find another couple for sex... Martin Freeman and Mandy Moore are the Finkels – a likable pair but without any chemistry. Jonathan Newman's lame comedy is practically laugh-free and the dreadful scene with a cucumber is beyond belief. The only exception is the sex clinic scene when the witty black nurse (Andi Osho) tries to reassure her patient by boasting that she is known as Urethra Franklin. GS

▶ Mandy Moore, Martin Freeman, Melissa George, Jerry Stiller, Elizabeth Tan, Jonathan Silverman, Angus Deayton, Beverley Klein, Louis Spence, Andi Osho.
▶ *Dir* and *Screenplay* Jonathan Newman, *Pro* Deepak Nayar, *Ph* Dirk Nel, *Pro Des* James Lewis, *Ed* Eddie Hamilton, *M* Mark Thomas, *Cos* Annie Hardinge.
Starlight Films/Kintop Pictures/Reliance/Filmaka.com-G2 Pictures.
85 mins. UK/USA. 2011. Rel: 17 June 2011. Cert. 15.

Tabloid ★★★½

The famous documentarian Errol Morris here turns to the extraordinary story of Joyce McKinney, who made headlines in 1977 when she was accused of kidnapping a Mormon and forcing him to have sex with her. She insists that his sense of guilt made him portray in that light what was really a great love affair in which he was a willing partner. We hear from her and from others, including journalist Peter Tory, and are free to come to our own conclusions. It's intriguing but arguably more suited to an hour-long television slot. MS

▶ With Joyce McKinney, Peter Tory.
▶ *Dir* Errol Morris, *Pro* Julie Bilson Ahlberg and Mark Lipson, *Ph* Robert Chappell, *Pro Des* Steve Hardie, *Ed* Grant Surmi, *M* John Kusiak.

Airloom Enterprises/Moxie Pictures etc-Dogwoof Pictures. 87 mins. USA. 2010. Rel: 11 Nov 2011. Cert. 15.

Take Me Home Tonight ★

This uneven and unfunny comedy takes place in the 1980s. Matt Franklin (Topher Grace) is a video store employee who claims that he is a banker in order to impress his high-school crush Tori (Teresa Palmer). The set-pieces are extremely loud and incredibly dull while the actors try hard to make an impact but fail miserably without ever gaining any credibility. Even the eccentric presence of Anna Faris as Matt's cynical twin sister can't rescue this one. GS

▶ Topher Grace, Anna Faris, Dan Fogler, Teresa Palmer, Chris Pratt, Michel Biehn, Jeanie Hackett, Lucy Punch.
▶ *Dir* Michael Dowse, *Pro* James Whitaker, Susan Bowen and Ryan Kavanaugh, *Screenplay* Jackie and Jeff Filgo, based on a story by Topher Grace and Gordon Kaywin, *Ph* Terry Stacey, *Pro Des* William Arnold, *Ed* Lee Haxall, *M* Trevor Horn, *Cos* Carol Oditz and Maria Schicker.

Imagine Entertainment/Internationale Filmproduktion Blackbird Dritte-Universal Pictures International. 97 mins. USA/Germany. 2011. Rel: 13 May 2011. Cert. 15.

Take Shelter ★★★

For two thirds of its length this award-winning drama by writer-director Jeff Nichols looks set to equal the impact of his auspicious first feature *Shotgun Stories* (2007). It seems to invite us to identify with a man (the superb Michael Shannon) slipping into paranoia and madness through his visions of an impending apocalypse. Visually the film is outstanding, but very late on it goes off in a quite different direction which, for me at least, undermines the conviction of everything that precedes it. MS

▶ Michael Shannon, Jessica Chastain, Shea Whigham, Katy Mixon, Kathy Baker.
▶ *Dir* and *Screenplay* Jeff Nichols, *Pro* Tyler Davidson and Sophia Lin, *Ph* Adam Stone, *Pro Des* Chad Keith, *Ed* Parke Gregg, *M* David Wingo, *Cos* Karen Malecki.

Hydraulx Entertainment /Rei Capital/Grove Hill Productions/Strange Matter Films etc-The Works. 120 mins. USA. 2011. Rel: 25 Nov 2011. Cert. 15.

Talihina Sky! The Story of Kings of Leon ★★★★

Most documentaries chronicling a popular rock band will be anathema to non-followers. The joy of Stephen C Mitchell's film is that it's about the people involved in this family outfit. Composed of the three brothers Caleb, Jared and Nathan Followill and their cousin, lead guitarist Matthew Followill, the band was raised in the backwoods of Talihina, Oklahoma. It is here that Mitchell visits a family reunion and traces the revivalist Christian ethic that formed the group's outlook. And for the fans there is still some decent live music and studio footage. CB

▶ *Dir* Stephen C Mitchell, *Pro* Casey McGrath and Joshua Levine, *Ed* Paul Greenhouse.

Showtime Networks-Sony Music Entertainment. 87 mins. USA. 2011. Rel: 24 June 2011. Cert. 15.

Tangled ★★★★★

For its 50th animated feature, Disney returns to the wellspring of some of its most enduring successes: the catalogue of the Brothers Grimm. While making a concession to the recent advances in computer animation, the film is in 3D but still mines the enchantment that was so intrinsic in the Disney/Grimm alliances of *Snow White, Cinderella* and *Sleeping Beauty*. Thus we have a captivating tale of spells, princesses and witches perked up by a sparkling script, constant comic invention and the visual miracles that we have come to expect from modern animation. A magical and rewarding gift of escapism. JC-W

▶ Voices of Mandy Moore, Zachary Levi, Donna Murphy, Ron Perlman, Jeffrey Tambor, Richard Kiel.

Hair today: Rapunzel and Flynn Ryder in Nathan Greno and Byron Howard's magical and sparkling *Tangled.*

With forehead villainous low: Djimon Hounsou as Caliban confronts Helen Mirren and Felicity Jones in Julie Taymor's uneven *The Tempest.*

> *Dir* Nathan Greno and Byron Howard, *Pro* Roy Conli, John Lasseter and Glen Keane, *Screenplay* Dan Fogelman, *Pro Des* Douglas Rogers, *Ed* Tim Mertens, *M* Alan Menken.

Walt Disney Animation Studios-Walt Disney. 100 mins. USA. 2010. Rel: 28 Jan 2011. Cert. PG.

Tantric Tourists ★★

A fly-on-the-wall documentary from the English documentarian Alexander Snelling, this is a more miss than hit affair. An American guru specialising in tantra, Laurie Handlers guides a group of uncomfortable Americans on a trip of self-discovery in India. There is plenty of colour and eccentricity, but the film's attempt to find its own inner enlightenment is undermined by a gratingly sardonic voice-over. CB

> *Dir, Ph* and *Ed* Alexander Snelling, *Pro* Snelling and Kirsty Allison, *M* Banco de Gaia, Sirus Severin etc.

Slack Alice Films-Independent Film Company. 80 mins. UK. 2009. Rel: 14 Feb 2011. Cert. 15.

The Taqwacores ★★★½

The subject here is the cultural conflicts confronting young Muslims in modern-day America. It's an example of cheap independent film-making and, while imperfect, deserved a more encouraging critical response than it received in the UK. For a film set in the world of punk and its music, it is at heart a work with a surprisingly gentle spirit and, although taken from a novel, it covers relatively unfamiliar ground. MS

> Bobby Naderi, Noureen Dewulf, Dominic Rians, Nav Mann, Volkan Eryaman, Ian Tran.
> *Dir* and *Pro* Eyad Zahra, *Screenplay* Michael Muhammed Knight and Zahra from Knight's novel, *Ph* J P Perry, *Pro Des* Marwan Kamel, *Ed* Josh Rosenfield, *M* Omar Fadel.

Strand Releasing/Visit Films/Rumanni Filmworks-Network Releasing. 83 mins. USA. 2011. Rel: 12 Aug 2011. Cert. 15.

The Tempest ★★★

Helen Mirren's female Prospero provides an intriguing centre to Julie Taymor's uneven adaptation of Shakespeare's play. At times it suggests a Disneyfied world: there are special effects, excruciating music and an idiosyncratic appearance by Russell Brand in one of the bard's more tiresome comic roles. But some players (Alan Cumming and Tom Conti among them) do well. It's a very mixed bag, but not uninteresting. MS

> Helen Mirren, Djimon Hounsou, Russell Brand, Ben Whishaw, Reeve Carney, Tom Conti, Chris Cooper, Alan Cumming, Felicity Jones, Alfred Molina, David Strathairn.
> *Dir* Julie Taymor, *Pro* Taymor, Robert Chartoff and others, *Screenplay* Taymor from William

Shakespeare's play, *Ph* Stuart Dryburgh, *Pro Des* Mark Friedberg, *Ed* Françoise Bonnot, *M* Elliot Goldenthal, *Cos* Sandy Powell.

Touchstone Pictures/Miramax Films/Miranda Films/ Talkstory Productions/Artemis Films etc-Buena Vista International.

110 mins. USA/UK/India. 2010. Rel: 4 Mar 2011. Cert. PG.

Terry ★

This fake documentary about the gritty life of petty criminal Terry (played by the director Nick Nevern) proves that anyone can make a film these days. Just grab a handheld camera or your mobile phone, shake it about and follow your mates around the estate and there you have it. Consequently the acting is not believable and the inevitable violence at the end fails to make any impact. GS

▶ Nick Nevern, Ian Duck, Daniel Burten-Shaw, Manuel Atkinson, Maximillian Aire, Jason Baptiste, Anita Bravin.
▶ *Dir* and *Screenplay* Nick Nevern, *Pro* Nevern and Jason Maza, *Ph* Manuel Atkinson, *Ed* Steven O'Connell.

Terry the Movie (Production Company)-Stealth Media Group.

90 mins. UK. 2011. Rel: 10 Mar 2011. Cert. 18.

Texas Killing Fields ★★★

Sam Worthington gives his grim macho presence a scalding workout as Mike Souder, a Texas homicide detective who teams up with New York City cop Brian Heigh (Jeffrey Dean Morgan) to track a sadistic serial killer. Soon, the killer starts hunting the cops, teasing them with clues while staying one step ahead. When a local girl, Anne (Chloë Grace Moretz), goes missing, the cops have their hands full trying to save her. The good cast and film noir techniques help paper over credibility cracks in this gritty reworking of an infamous real-life story. The director, Michael Mann's daughter, manages a lot of tension and atmosphere, and plays to her actors' strengths. DW

▶ Sam Worthington, Jeffrey Dean Morgan, Jessica Chastain, Chloë Grace Moretz, Annabeth Gish, Sean Cunningham.
▶ *Dir* Ami Canaan Mann, *Pro* Michael Jaffe and Michael Mann, *Screenplay* Donald F Ferrarone, *Ph* Stuart Dryburgh, *Pro Des* Aran Reo Mann, *Ed* Cindy Mollo, *M* Dickon Hinchliffe, *Cos* Christopher Lawrence.

Forward Pas/Gideon Productions/Watley Entertainment/ Infinity Media/QED International-Anchor Bay Films.

105 mins. USA. 2011. Rel: 14 Oct 2011. Cert. 15.

The Thing ★½

A remake of a remake masquerading as a prequel, this superfluous shape-shifting creature feature follows much the same path as John Carpenter's classic freak-out flick, with a similarly cold, hostile

setting, an identical sombre, paranoid tone and digital effects directly inspired by Rob Bottin's practical make-ups. Although it claims to detail events immediately prior to the 1982 incarnation, said events are largely identical to the beloved, superior '80s instalment, so it's plainly no more than just another derivative, money-making studio ploy. MJ

▶ Mary Elizabeth Winstead, Joel Edgerton, Adewale Akinnuoye-Agbaje, Eric Christian Olsen, Ulrich Thomsen, Trond Espen Seim.
▶ *Dir* Matthijs van Heijningen Jr, *Pro* Eric Newman, *Screenplay* Erich Heisserer, based on John W Campbell Jr's short story *Who Goes There?*, *Ph* Michel Abramowicz, *Pro Des* Sean Howarth, *Ed* Julian Clarke, Jono Griffith and Peter Boyle, *M* Marco Beltrami, *Cos* Luis Sequeira.

Universal Pictures/Morgan Creek Productions/Strike Entertainment-Universal Pictures International.

103 mins. USA/Canada. 2011. Rel: 2 Dec 2011. Cert. 15.

Third Star ★★★

Benedict Cumberbatch makes this heartfelt comedy-drama work with a magnetic turn as terminally ill young Englishman James. He's taken off by his three lifelong buddies (Tom Burke, Adam Robertson, J J Feild) on a risky life-enhancing last trip to his favourite place, the startling Welsh coastline of Barafundle Bay. There are quite a lot of laughs, home truths and touchingly sentimental moments among the tears in the nicely written, literate, thoughtful script, but it's still a bit of a downer. A likable and poignant one, though, for those who enjoy a multi-Kleenex wallow. Hugh Bonneville has a weird cameo as a beachcomber. DW

▶ Benedict Cumberbatch, J J Feild, Rupert Frazer, Tom Burke, Nia Roberts, Hugh Bonneville, Adam Robertson, Eros Vlahos.
▶ *Dir* Hattie Dalton, *Pro* Vaughan Sivell and Kelly Broad, *Screenplay* Sivell, *Ph* Carlos Catalán, *Pro Des*

Rogue trip: J J Feild, Adam Robertson, Benedict Cumberbatch and Tom Burke in Hattie Dalton's touching *Third Star*.

Richard Campling, *Ed* Peter Christelis, *M* Stephen Hilton, *Cos* Marianne Egertoft.

Western Edge Pictures/Matador Pictures/Regent Capital/Cinema One-Independent Distribution. 92 mins. UK. 2010. Rel: 20 May 2011. Cert. 15.

This Our Still Life ★★★

Andrew Kötting's experimental new film revisits his favourite subject, that of his daughter Eden, who was born with a rare neurological disease and is now a young woman of 22. In the 1990 short *Hoi Polloi* Eden was only a baby, and she was seven in Kötting's award-winning *Gallivant*. It is a brave, occasionally uncomfortable piece of filmmaking, not to everybody's taste, mixing experimental sounds and visual effects. GS

▷ Docu-collage from artist Andrew Kötting, with Eden Kötting.
▷ *Dir* Andrew Kötting.

Screen Archive South East/Bognor Regis Film Society/ UCA@Maidstone-British Film Institute. 59 mins. UK. 2011. Rel: 18 Nov 2011. Cert. U.

Hammer horror: Chris Hemsworth in Kenneth Branagh's cartoonish *Thor*.

Thor ★★

Just when you thought that the superhero genre was moving into a higher gear… Strip away the dark drama of *The Dark Knight*, the dry humour of *Iron Man* and the flash iconoclasm of *Kick-Ass* and you have some seriously retrograde genre-subsidence. The trouble with *Thor* is that the depiction of gods in the cinema has always been problematic – cf *Clash of the Titans*. Here, there are two worlds to absorb – the cartoonish CGI realm of Asgard and the relative 'realism' of New Mexico – and the gods can't stop nipping in between the two. Nice shots of the galaxy, though. JC-W

▷ Chris Hemsworth, Natalie Portman, Tom Hiddleston, Stellan Skarsgård, Rene Russo, Anthony Hopkins, Idris Elba, Kat Dennings, Samuel L Jackson, Jeremy Renner.
▷ *Dir* Kenneth Branagh, *Pro* Kevin Feige, *Screenplay* Ashley Edward Miller, Zack Stentz and Don Payne, *Ph* Haris Zambarloukos, *Pro Des* Bo Welch, *Ed* Paul Rubell, *M* Patrick Doyle, *Cos* Alexandra Byrne.

Paramount/Marvel Entertainment-Paramount Pictures. 114 mins. USA. 2011. Rel: 21 Apr 2011. Cert. 12A.

The Three Musketeers 3D ★★

Paul W S Anderson's colourful but unmemorable remake is filmed like a graphic novel with unconvincing dialogue and set-pieces. His lame attempt to put his mark on Dumas' classic falls flat on its face and makes Richard Lester's 1970s version look like a masterpiece. It's over the top and humourless with very basic 3D effects. Thankfully, Christoph Waltz's strong turn as the deliciously nasty Cardinal Richelieu manages to bring some sparkle into an otherwise uninspired film. GS

▷ Matthew Mcfadyen, Luke Evans, Ray Stevenson, Milla Jovovich, Logan Lerman, Orlando Bloom, Christoph Waltz, Mads Mikkelsen, Freddie Fox, James Corden.
▷ *Dir* Paul W S Anderson, *Pro* Anderson, Jeremy Bolt and Robert Kulzer, *Screenplay* Andrew Davies and Alex Litvak, based on the novel by Alexandre Dumas, *Ph* Glen MacPherson, *Pro Des* Paul D Austerberry, *Ed* Alexander Berner, *M* Paul Haslinger, *Cos* Pierre-Yves Gayraud.

Constantin Film/Impact Pictures/New Legacy/Studio Babelsberg/NEF Productions-Entertainment One. 110 mins. Germany/France/UK/USA. 2011. Rel: 12 Oct 2011. Cert. 12A.

Tinker Tailor Soldier Spy ★★★½

It is impossible not to compare this new film with John Irvin's 1979 TV series of the same story. That had Alec Guinness as George Smiley, the spy brought out of retirement to find a double agent among his old senior cronies. Gary

Oldman as Smiley lacks a convincing presence in the role almost to the point of invisibility, while the film generally is mostly drained of colour, at times virtually monochromatic, and is confusing and slow to the point of tedium. Notwithstanding, it does field a great cast, but only spasmodically do they burst into anything approaching life. MHD

❯ Gary Oldman, John Hurt, Benedict Cumberbatch, Colin Firth, Tom Hardy, Mark Strong, Toby Jones, Ciarán Hinds, Kathy Burke.
❯ *Dir* Tomas Alfredson, *Pro* Tim Bevan, Eric Fellner and Robyn Slovo, *Screenplay* Bridget O'Connor and Peter Straughan, based on the novel by John le Carré, *Ph* Hoyte van Hoytema, *Pro Des* Maria Djurkovic, *Ed* Dino Jonsäter, *M* Alberto Iglesias, *Cos* Jacqueline Durran.
StudioCanal/Working Title Films/Karla Films/Paradis Films/Kinowelt Filmproduktion etc-StudioCanal.
127 mins. France/UK/Germany. 2011. Rel: 16 Sep 2011. Cert. 15.

Tomboy ★★★½

This deeply sympathetic film from Céline Sciamma who made *White Lilies* (2007) features a ten-year-old girl played most persuasively by Zoé Héran. She passes herself off as a boy and the one doubtful aspect here lies in the casual response of her parents when they discover this. The viewer in contrast is likely to ask if these are signs that she will in time become either a lesbian or a transsexual, but the film refuses to face any such issue. Nevertheless, it's delicate and sensitive and wholly convincing as a study of pre-adolescence. MS

❯ Zoé Héran, Malonn Lévana, Jeanne Disson, Sophie Cattani, Mathieu Demy.
❯ *Dir* and *Screenplay* Céline Sciamma, *Pro* Bénédicte Couvreur, *Ph* Crystel Fournier, *Art Dir* Thomas Grézaud, *Ed* Julien Lacheray.
Hold Up Films & Productions/Lilies Films/Arte France Cinéma etc-Peccadillo Pictures.
82 mins. France. 2011. Rel: 16 Sep 2011. Cert. U.

Tomorrow, When the War Began ★★★½

Eight high-school friends go on a camping trip to a remote place in the bush called Hell. This lush location turns out to be a kind of paradise, but they discover Hell when they return home to find that everybody has been taken hostage by a mysterious military force. They hide and begin their own war against the invaders. This first of a popular Australian trilogy is an enjoyable adventure despite a weak opening. The action sequences are well staged and the actors are persuasive, particularly Caitlin Stasey as the gutsy heroine Ellie. GS

❯ Caitlin Stasey, Rachel Hurd-Wood, Lincoln Lewis, Deniz Akdenis, Phoebe Tonkin, Chris Pang, Colin Friels.

Cold spies: David Dencik and Gary Oldman in Tomas Alfredson's slow and tedious *Tinker Tailor Soldier Spy*.

Tall story: Michael Peña, Eddie Murphy, Matthew Broderick and Casey Affleck in Brett Ratner's agreeable, all-star *Tower Heist*.

▶ *Dir* and *Screenplay* Stuart Beattie, from the novel by John Marsden, *Pro* Andrew Mason and Michael Boughen, *Ph* Ben Nott, *Pro Des* Robert Webb, *Ed* Marcus D'Arcy, *M* Reinhold Heil and Johnny Klimek, *Cos* Terry Ryan.

Ambience Entertainment/Omnilab Media-Paramount Pictures.

103 mins. Australia. 2010. Rel: 8 Apr 2011. Cert. 12A.

Tower Heist ★★★½

Wall Street megalomaniac Arthur Shaw (Alan Alda) lives in a luxurious New York City penthouse. When he steals two billion from his investors and pension funds the building workers who lost their savings plan to break into his apartment and rob him of his hidden cache of $20 million. But first this unlikely bunch of robbers must get Slide (Eddie Murphy) out of jail... This enjoyable comedy boasts a strong ensemble cast and Murphy proves yet again what a good character actor he can be. GS

▶ Ben Stiller, Eddie Murphy, Casey Affleck, Alan Alda, Matthew Broderick, Judd Hirsch, Téa Leoni, Robert Downey Sr.
▶ *Dir* Brett Ratner, *Pro* Murphy and Brian Grazer, *Screenplay* Ted Griffin and Jeff Nathanson, based on a story by Griffin, Bill Collage and Adam Cooper, *Ph* Dante Spinotti, *Pro Des* Kristi Zea, *Ed* Mark Helfrich, *M* Christophe Beck, *Cos* Sarah Edwards.

Universal Pictures/Imagine Entertainment/Relativity Media/Rat Entertainment-Universal Pictures International.

104 mins. USA. 2011. Rel: 2 Nov 2011. Cert. 12A.

Tracker ★★★

An Afrikaner Boer War veteran (Ray Winstone) arrives in New Zealand and is recruited by the local military commander (Gareth Reeves) to track a Maori whaler (Temuera Morrison) who's gone on the run after being accused of killing a British soldier in a brawl. The reward is 100 sovereigns alive, 25 sovereigns dead. Hunting through the wilderness, Winstone captures Morrison, but then finds he's innocent... Ideally acted by the two tough-guy stars, both on their best mesmerising form, this fascinating action movie tells a compelling yarn grippingly and intelligently – and it always looks a treat too. How couldn't it with those gorgeous New Zealand landscapes? DW

▶ Ray Winstone, Temuera Morrison, Gareth Reeves, Mark Mitchinson, Daniel Musgrove.
▶ *Dir* Ian Sharp, *Pro* Trevor Haysom and David Burns, *Screenplay* Nicolas van Pallandt, *Ph* Harvey Harrison, *Pro Des* Rick Kofoed, *Ed* Sean Barton, *M* David Burns, *Cos* Bob Buck.

Eden Films/T. H. E. Films/Phoenix Wiley-Kaleidoscope. 102 mins. New Zealand/UK. 2010. Rel: 29 Apr 2011. Cert. 12A.

Transformers: Dark of the Moon ★★½

The third in a franchise based on Hasbro toys just about says it all, so what do you expect? Here the Apollo mission discovers an alien spaceship from the planet Cybertron with a weapon that could wipe out Earth, thus beginning a battle between the Autobots, giant shape-shifting robots, and the Decepticons, their enemies on Earth. Shia LaBeouf is yet again Sam, our hero, with new girlfriend Carly (big red-lipped Rosie Huntington-Whiteley), while the likes of John Turturro, John Malkovich and Frances McDormand are simply wasted. The set-pieces of staged destruction by the giant robots are impressive enough, although not enough to curb the boredom of the plot. When you've seen one… MHD

➤ Shia LaBeouf, Rosie Huntington-Whiteley, Tyrese Gibson, Patrick Dempsey, Frances McDormand, John Turturro, John Malkovich, Josh Duhamel, Buzz Aldrin and the voices of Peter Cullen, Leonard Nimoy, Hugo Weaving, James Remar.
➤ *Dir* Michael Bay, *Pro* Lorenzo di Bonaventura, Don Murphy, Ian Bryce and Tom DeSanto, *Screenplay* Ehren Kruger, *Ph* Amir Mokri, *Pro Des* Nigel Phelps, *Ed* Joel Negron, Roger Barton and William Goldenberg, *M* Steve Jablonsky, *Cos* Deborah Lynn Scott.
Paramount Pictures/Hasbro/Di Bonaventura Pictures-Paramount Pictures.
154 mins. USA. 2011. Rel: 1 July 2011. Cert. 12A.

Travellers ★★

Four ageing, city-boy friends set out on a motorcycle adventure weekend and, after a night recalling their misspent youth, investigate a creepy caravan. Then a graffiti prank leads to violence and a fight for survival against angry Irish travellers. First-time director Kris McManus tries hard to put a scary modern-day Brit spin on his earnest throwback to *Deliverance* and *Southern Comfort*. Though this looks a bit murky and is held back by iffy dialogue and uneven pacing, it's still not too bad as a gory, low-budget action thriller. There are no notable performances, but the score, a bare-knuckle boxing fight and Charley Boorman's cameo all spark up the interest. DW

➤ Shane Sweeney, Tom Geoffrey, Alex Edwards, Celia Muir, Dean S Jagger, Ben Richards, Charley Boorman.
➤ *Dir, Screenplay* and *Ph* Kris McManus, *Pro* McManus, Richards and Brian Allen Levine, *Ed* McManus and Phil Eldridge, *M* Adam Langston, Jim Mortimer and Dicken Marshall.
Animus Pictures/Travellers Film/Inroad Pictures/
Delacheroy Films-High Fliers Distribution.
84 mins. UK. 2011. Rel: 13 Jan 2011. Cert. 18.

Treacle Jnr ★★★★

Ignore the off-putting title. In Jamie Thraves' strikingly well-made film, a taciturn, disillusioned man from the Midlands (Tom Fisher) comes to London where, through circumstances and not by choice, he ends up staying with the loquacious Aidan (Aidan Gillen). The latter is portrayed as the kind of person you would do anything to avoid, yet both the visitor and we the audience come to recognise his need for human contact. Admirably unsentimental, this is well worth seeking out, and Gillen is superb. MS

➤ Aidan Gillen, Tom Fisher, Riann Steele, Thomas Murray-Leslie, Elizabeth Murray-Leslie.
➤ *Dir* and *Screenplay* Jamie Thraves, *Pro* Rob Small and Thraves, *Ph* Catherine Derry and Nigel Kinnings, *Pro Des* Steve Ritchie, *Ed* Tom Lindsay and Ross Hallard, *Cos* Jo Thompson.
Golden Rule Films-Soda Pictures.
80 mins. UK. 2010. Rel: 15 July 2011. Cert. 15.

The Tree ★★★½

A young widow bringing up her children in the Australian outback can't put her past and her dead husband behind her. The presence of a tree undermining the family house is to be taken as evidence that this is a symbolic drama. It is beautifully shot but the story line, in itself basically naturalistic, becomes increasingly unconvincing and this mars an interesting film. Charlotte Gainsbourg is the widow. MS

➤ Charlotte Gainsbourg, Marton Csokas, Morgana Davies, Christian Byers, Tom Russell, Aden Young.
➤ *Dir* Julie Bertucelli, *Pro* Yaël Fogiel, Sue Taylor and Laetitia Gonzalez, *Screenplay* Bertucelli based on a screenplay by Elizabeth J Mars from the novel *Our Father Who Art in the Tree* by Judy Pascoe, *Ph* Nigel Bluck, *Pro Des* Steven Jones-Evans, *Ed* François Gédigier, *M* Grégoire Hetzel, *Cos* Joanna Mae Park.
Les Films du Poisson/Taylor Media/ Screen Australia/
Arte France Cinéma etc-Artificial Eye.
101 mins. France/Australia/Belgium/Italy/Germany. 2010. Rel: 5 Aug 2011. Cert. 12A.

Branching out: Charlotte Gainsbourg moves to the Outback in Julie Bertucelli's symbolic, beautifully shot *The Tree.*

The Tree of Life ★★★½

Sometimes reminiscent of Kubrick's *2001: A Space Odyssey* (1968), Terrence Malick's ambitious film is concerned with the history of man, the wonders of nature and the human suffering which can make Christians start to question God's existence. Centred on one family, it is epic, yet at its best when most intimate (as in its evocation of childhood in America in the 1950s). At its worst (as in its concluding sequence) it is utterly banal; at its best it's magnificent. MS

‣ Hunter McCracken, Laramie Eppler, Brad Pitt, Jessica Chastain, Sean Penn, Fiona Shaw.
‣ *Dir* and *Screenplay* Terrence Malick, *Pro* Sarah Green, Bill Pohlad, Brad Pitt and others, *Ph* Emmanuel Lubezki, *Pro Des* Jack Fisk, *Ed* Hank Corwin, Jay Rabinowitz, Daniel Rezende, Billy Weber and Mark Yoshikawa, *M* Alexandre Desplat, *Cos* Jacqueline West.

River Road Entertainment-Icon Film Distribution. 139 mins. USA. 2010. Rel: 8 July 2011. Cert. 12A.

Trespass ★

The meaning of trees: Jessica Chastain in Terrence Malick's epic, banal, magnificent *The Tree of Life*.

Karl Gajdusek's over-wrought screenplay limits credibility and so reduces our concern for a seemingly well-off family menaced in their own home. The result is a movie in which the only appeal is to those who relish seeing characters under threat. It's exactly the kind of voyeuristic piece savagely and brilliantly critiqued by Michael Haneke in *Funny Games* (1997). Nobody emerges with credit. MS

‣ Nicolas Cage, Nicole Kidman, Ben Mendelsohn, Liana Liberato, Cam Gigandet.
‣ *Dir* Joel Schumacher, *Pro* Irwin Winkler, David Winkler and René Besson, *Screenplay* Karl Gajdusek, *Ph* Andrzej Bartkowiak, *Pro Des* Nathan Amondson, *Ed* Bill Pankow, *M* David Buckley, *Cos* Judianna Makovsky.

Millennium Films/Nu Image/Winkler Films etc-Lionsgate. 91 mins. USA. 2011. Rel: 11 Nov 2011. Cert. 15.

Troll Hunter ★★

From America we've had witches, aliens and zombies. Now Norway pitches in with its own hand-held mockumentary chronicling the exploits of three college kids bent on capturing a troll on film. The film's tone of naturalism and Pythonesque black comedy is an odd mix and doesn't really coalesce. If the trolls themselves didn't look like Smurfs the film might have cooked up an iota of suspense. Scarier still would have been to not show them at all. As it is, it's terribly familiar stuff and should really have called itself *The Muppet Troll Project*. However, the frozen, far-flung locations are starkly beautiful. JC-W

‣ Otto Jespersen, Glenn Erland Tosterud, Johanna Mørck.

Wayne's world: Jeff Bridges as Rooster Cogburn with the magnificent Hailee Steinfeld in Ethan and Joel Coen's redundant *True Grit*.

▶ *Dir* and *Screenplay* André Øvredal, *Pro* Sveinung Golimo and John M Jacobsen, *Ph* Hallvard Bræin, *Pro Des* Signe Gerda Landfald, *Ed* Per-Erik Eriksen, *Cos* Stina Lunde.

Filmkameratene A/S/Film Fund FUZZ-Momentum Pictures. 103 mins. Norway. 2010. Rel: 9 Sep 2011. Cert. 15.

True Grit ★★★½

Whatever you may think of John Wayne, he was irreplaceable. Notwithstanding, Jeff Bridges plays Wayne's role of the bad-tempered old cuss Rooster Cogburn in this Coen Brothers remake. Bridges is all right but he's no Wayne, as he may be the first to admit. Hailee Steinfeld does a good job as the teenage Mattie Ross who hires Rooster to seek out her father's killer, Tom Chaney (Josh Brolin), along with Texas Ranger LaBoeuf (Matt Damon). The result passes muster but, as with *Brighton Rock* [qv], why bother to remake a near-classic? Roger Deakins' pellucid cinematography is, as usual, immaculate. MHD

▶ Jeff Bridges, Hailee Steinfeld, Matt Damon, Josh Brolin, Barry Pepper, Domhnall Gleeson.
▶ *Dir* and *Screenplay* Ethan Coen and Joel Coen, from the novel by Charles Portis, *Pro* Ethan and Joel Coen and Scott Rudin, *Ph* Roger Deakins, *Pro Des* Jess Gonchor, *Ed* Roderick Jaynes (the Coens), *M* Carter Burwell, *Cos* Mary Zophres.

Paramount Pictures/Skydance Productions/Scott Rudin/ Mike Zoss-Paramount Pictures. 110 mins. USA. 2010. Rel: 11 Feb 2011. Cert. 15.

Trust ★★★

Central to this drama is the topical theme of the internet being used for grooming and Liana Liberato is very convincing as the 14-year-old who receives sexual initiation at the hands of a man much older than he claimed on line. Set in Chicago, the film is not exploitative, but unfortunately it becomes increasingly unlikely, right down to a reconciliation scene with dad (Clive Owen) which smacks of dialogue better suited to the stage. MS

▶ Clive Owen, Catherine Keener, Liana Liberato, Jason Clarke, Noah Emmerich, Viola Davis.
▶ *Dir* David Schwimmer, *Pro* Tom Hodges, Ed Cathell III, Schwimmer and others, *Screenplay* Andy Bellin and Robert Festinger, *Ph* Andrzej Sekula, *Pro Des* Michael Shaw, *Ed* Douglas Crise, *M* Nathan Larson, *Cos* Ellen Lutter.

Millennium Films/Nu Image/Dark Harbor-Lionsgate. 106 mins. USA. 2010. Rel: 8 July 2011. Cert. 15.

TT3D: Closer to the Edge ★★★½

The famous Isle of Man TT (Tourist Trophy) race, the most dangerous circuit in the world, has claimed many victims in its time. The sometime TV star Guy Martin (of *The Gadget Show* and *The Boat That Guy Built*) is preoccupied with the TT to the point of obsession and, as a motor mechanic, admits to feeling responsible for the fate of some of the riders. Richard De Aragues' documentary not only has thrilling action from the race itself, but also captures the love and the spirit of those taking part and gets to the heart and soul of the speed freak. MHD

▶ With Guy Martin, Ian Hutchinson, John McGuinness, Michael Dunlop, Keith Amor, Bruce Anstey and narrator Jared Leo.

Redneck Dawn:
Alan Tudyk and
Tyler Labine
in Eli Craig's
unexpected and
hilarious *Tucker
and Dale vs Evil.*

▶ *Dir* Richard De Aragues, *Pro* Marc Samuelson and Steve Christian, *Ph* Thomas Kürzl, *Ed* Beverley Mills, *M* Andy Gray.

Isle of Man Film/CinemaNX-CinemaNX.
104 mins. UK. 2011. Rel: 22 Apr 2011. Cert. 15.

Tucker & Dale vs Evil ★★★★

Tucker (Alan Tudyk) and Dale (Tyler Labine) are on their way to their holiday cabin deep in the woods. They hope to relax, drink beer, catch some fish and have a good time. But their Memorial Day weekend becomes a nightmare when their *Deliverance* hillbilly looks cause them to be mistaken for disturbed serial killers by a group of college students... This is the most fun comedy horror since *An American Werewolf in London*. It is hilarious and first-time director Eli Craig is definitely a talent to watch. GS

▶ Tyler Labine, Alan Tudyk, Katrina Bowden, Jesse Moss, Brandon McLaren.
▶ *Dir* Eli Craig, *Pro* Morgan Jurgenson, Albert Klychak, Deepak Nayar and Rosanne Milliken, *Screenplay* Craig and Jurgenson, *Ph* David Gedes, *Pro Des* John Blackie, *Ed* Bridget Durnford, *M* Mike Shields, *Cos* Mary Hyde-Kerr.

Reliance Big Pictures/Loubyloo Productions/Eden Rock Media/Urban Island/Kintop Pictures/Gynormous Pictures etc-Magnolia Pictures/Hillbilly Hero Productions.
89 mins. USA/Canada. 2010. Rel: 23 Sep 2011. Cert. 15.

Turnout ★★★

East London boy George (George Russo) and his girlfriend Sophie (Ophelia Lovibond) are trying to get the money to go on their first holiday together. But, with two weeks left to pay the outstanding balance of £2000, George is broke and uses Sophie's holiday money to fund an ill-judged drugs deal, selling coke to make up the balance. This very lively, amusing slice of London low-life boasts a winning performance by Russo, convincing characters that are fun-to-be-with and a good line in winning dialogue. If the plot's a bit thin and Lovibond doesn't really convince you her character is worth all this trouble, this is still a neat little film, raising a lot of truthful laughs. DW

▶ Ophelia Lovibond, George Russo, Ben Drew, Neil Maskell, Ricci Harnett, Diana Kent, Annie Cooper, Tilly Vosburgh.
▶ *Dir* Lee Sales, *Pro* Nick Barratt and Danny Potts, *Screenplay* Sales, George Russo and Francis Pope, *Ph* James Friend, *Pro Des* Celina Norris and Danny Rogers, *Ed* Kieron Hawkes, *Music Supervisor* Vicki Williams, *Cos* Frances Hounsom.

DP Films/Fulwell 73-Revolver Entertainment.
97 mins. UK. 2011. Rel: 16 Sep 2011. Cert. 18.

A Turtle's Tale: Sammy's Adventures ★★★½

This likable animation feature follows Sammy (Dominic Cooper), a sea turtle born on a

California beach, who begins an odyssey across the globe in search of his missing soulmate Sally (Gemma Arterton). It is a lovely film with a strong message about the environment and global warming, with decent animation and clever 3D effects that will satisfy the whole family. GS

> Voices of Dominic Cooper, Gemma Arterton, Melanie Griffith, Isabelle Fuhrman, Yuri Lowenthal, Ed Begley Jr, Tim Curry, Stacey Keach, Gigi Perreau.
> *Dir* Ben Stassen, *Pro* Stassen, Caroline Van Iseghem, Gina Gallo, Mimi Maynard and Domonic Paris, *Screenplay* Paris, *Art Dir* Jeremy Degruson, *Ed* Julien Ducenne and Aurelia Rosman, *M* Ramin Djawadi.

Illuminata Pictures/nWave Pictures/uFilm-Optimum Releasing.
88 mins. Belgium. 2010. Rel: 25 Mar 2011. Cert. U.

The Twilight Saga: Breaking Dawn Part 1 ★½

A wafer-thin tale is stretched impossibly thinner in this fumbling first half of the final terrible *Twilight* movie. A girl who can't smile (Kristen Stewart) marries a dead vegetarian (Robert Pattinson) while a shirtless werewolf (Taylor Lautner) moons about it. Then, against both nature and supernature, she gets knocked up with a vampire baby that drains her from the inside. Tortuously drawn-out and so far from interesting it's on another continent, this anaemic soapy drama will likewise drain the life out of you. MJ

> Taylor Lautner, Kristen Stewart, Robert Pattinson, Anna Kendrick, Ashley Greene, Billy Burke, Dakota Fanning, Kellan Lutz, Michael Sheen, Peter Facinelli.
> *Dir* Bill Condon, *Pro* Stephenie Meyer, Karen Rosenfelt and Wyck Godfrey, *Screenplay* Melissa Rosenberg, based on Meyer's book *Breaking Dawn*, *Ph* Guillermo Navarro, *Pro Des* Richard Sherman, *Ed* Virginia Katz, *M* Carter Burwell, *Cos* Michael Wilkinson.

Summit Entertainment/Sunswept Entertainment/Temple Hill Entertainment/Total Entertainment/Zohar Entertainment etc-Entertainment One UK.
117 mins. USA. 2011. Rel: 18 Nov 2011. Cert. 12A.

Two in the Wave ★★★½

This unfailingly fascinating documentary concentrates on two of the major figures in the French cinema's Nouvelle Vague: Truffaut and Godard. Their friendship turned to hostility and Jean-Pierre Léaud was torn between two father figures. But neither he nor Godard appears and the film fails to tell the whole story, while many film clips are left unidentified. In short it could easily have been better, but it's not for a moment boring. (Original title: *Deux de la vague*) MS

> With Isild Le Besco. Narrated by Antoine de Baecque.

> *Dir* and *Pro* Emmanuel Laurent, *Written by* Antoine de Baecque, *Ph* Nicholas de Pencier amd Etienne Carton de Grammont, *Ed* Marie-France Cuenot.

Films à Trois etc-New Wave Films.
96 mins. France/Belgium. 2009. Rel: 11 Feb 2011. Cert. 12A.

Tyrannosaur ★★★★

With this grim tale of a woman (superb Olivia Colman) caught between an abusive husband (Eddie Marsan) and a loner who drinks (Peter Mullan) but with whom she unexpectedly establishes a rapport, the actor Paddy Considine makes an impressive feature debut as director. Those who admired Gary Oldman's *Nil By Mouth* (1997) and who now favour the films of Andrea Arnold may well take to this tough, unsentimental and authentically atmospheric work. MS

> Peter Mullan, Olivia Colman, Eddie Marsan, Ned Dennehy, Sally Carman.
> *Dir* and *Screenplay* Paddy Considine, *Pro* Diarmid Scrimshaw, *Ph* Erik Alexander Wilson, *Pro Des* Simon Rogers, *Ed* Pia Di Ciaula, *M* Chris Baldwin and Dan Baker, *Cos* Lance Milligan.

Film4/UK Film Council/Warp X/Inflammable Films etc-StudioCanal.
92 mins. UK. 2010. Rel: 7 Oct 2011. Cert. 18.

Ultrasuede: In Search of Halston ★★½

According to Liza Minnelli, Roy Halston Frowick put American fashion on the map. Besides his urbane demeanour, famous friends and entourage of gorgeous girls, he stamped his elegant, simple imprint on dresses, handbags, sunglasses, luggage, carpets and even police uniforms and aeroplane interiors. He was a phenomenon. This documentary, directed, co-written, produced and presented by Whitney Sudler-Smith, is an odd affair. Anything but slick, it is a low-res home movie in which Sudler-Smith himself undergoes

Charity and the Neanderthal: Olivia Colman and Peter Mullan in Paddy Considine's impressive and authentically atmospheric *Tyrannosaur.*

dramatic changes in appearance, while his interviewees (Liza, Anjelica Huston, Billy Joel, Dianne von Furstenberg, etc) seem to have been caught on the hop. JC-W

▶ *Dir* Whitney Sudler-Smith, *Pro* Sudler-Smith, Adam Bardach, Anne Goursaud and Nicholas Simon, *Screenplay* Sudler-Smith and Goursaud, *Ph* Scott Miller, *Ed* Goursaud and John Paul Horstmann, *M* Christophe Franke and Edgar Rothermich.
Ultrafilms LLC 2010-Verve Pictures.
92 mins. USA. 2010. Rel: 23 Sep 2011. Cert. 15.

Unknown ★★½

When an American botanist (Liam Neeson) survives a car accident in Berlin, he is perplexed that his wife no longer recognises him. Furthermore, she appears to have a new husband… There's something about Neeson running around Europe – not to mention the prospect of a man developing amnesia in a foreign city – that smacks of familiarity. It's like a nexus of old plots rebooted onto a USB stick. This is strictly B-movie fare but it's engagingly done, complete with a few decent pulse-quickening set-pieces. JC-W

▶ Liam Neeson, Diane Kruger, January Jones, Aidan Quinn, Bruno Ganz, Frank Langella, Sebastian Koch.
▶ *Dir* Jaume Collet-Serra, *Pro* Joel Silver, Leonard Goldberg and Andrew Rona, *Screenplay* Oliver Butcher and Stephen Cornwell, *Ph* Flavio Labiano, *Pro Des* Richard Bridgland, *Ed* Tim Alverson, *M* John Ottman and Alexander Rudd, *Cos* Ruth Myers.
Warner Bros/Dark Castle/Panda/Canal+/Horticus UK/Studio Babelsberg/StudioCanal/TF1 Films-Optimum Releasing.
113 mins. UK/USA/Germany/France/Canada/Japan. 2011. Rel: 4 Mar 2011. Cert. 12A.

Upside Down: The Creation Records Story ★★★★

This is a well-researched documentary about Creation Records – one of the world's most successful independent labels. Founder of Creation Alan McGee is still passionate about his work as he reminisces about the glory days of the 1980s and '90s, when he signed The Jesus and Mary Chain and Oasis before everything turned sour. It is an honest and fascinating film about sex and drugs and rock 'n' roll but not just for music lovers. GS

▶ With Alan McGee, Bobby Gillespie, Noel Gallagher, Liam Gallagher, Irvine Welsh, Jim Reid, Gruff Rhys, Paul McGuigan.
▶ *Dir* and *Pro* Danny O'Connor, *Ph* Daryl Chase, *Ed* Jonny Halifax.
Documentary Productions Ltd-Revolver Entertainment.
101 mins. UK. 2010. Rel: 29 Apr 2011. Cert. 15.

A Very Harold & Kumar 3D Christmas ★★★★

Harold (John Cho) and Kumar (Kal Penn) have now grown apart but on Christmas Eve Kumar unexpectedly turns up at Harold's house with a mysterious package. When he accidentally burns down the precious Christmas tree of Harold's stern father-in-law (Danny Trejo), they embark on a new adventure in search of a replacement. It is a very silly premise but hugely enjoyable, with great use of 3D effects. It is, of course, utterly non-PC (there's a running gag with an infant hooked on cocaine), but it's the best Christmas film since *Bad Santa*. GS

▶ John Cho, Kal Penn, Isabella Gielniak, Bobby Lee, Tom Lennon, Amir Blumenfeld, Danny Trejo.
▶ *Dir* Todd Strauss-Schulson, *Pro* Greg Shapiro, *Screenplay* Jon Hurwitz and Hayden Schlossberg, *Ph* Michael Barrett, *Pro Des* Rusty Smith, *Ed* Eric Kissack, *M* William Ross, *Cos* Mary Claire Hannan.
Kingsgate Films/Mandate Pictures-New Line Cinema.
90 mins. USA. 2011. Rel: 9 Dec 2011. Cert. 18.

The Veteran ★½

Ex-soldier Robert Miller (Toby Kebbell) finds it difficult after Afghanistan to re-adjust to society.

Crimble bound: John Cho and Kal Penn in Todd Strauss-Schulson's utterly non-PC A Very Harold & Kumar 3D Christmas.

And his work in the undercover surveillance of suspected terrorists leads him into more turmoil. Kebbell gives a committed performance but struggles to give depth to a one-dimensional character who is a million miles from *Taxi Driver* – to which the producers clearly want their film to be compared. GS

❯ Toby Kebbell, Brian Cox, Tony Curran, Adi Bielski, Tom Brooke, Mem Ferda.
❯ *Dir* Matthew Hope, *Pro* Kim Leggatt and Debbie Shuter, *Screenplay* Hope and Robert Henry Craft, from a story by Hope, *Ph* Philipp Blaubach, *Pro Des* Chris Richmond, *Ed* Emma Gaffney, *M* Bogdan Bondarchuk, *Cos* Emma Fryer.
Veteran Pictures/Premiere Pictures/Media Pro One/ DMK Productions/Local Films/Iconiq Group-Revolver Entertainment.
98 mins. UK. 2011. Rel: 29 Apr 2011. Cert. 15.

Vidal Sassoon: The Movie ★★★★

The late Vidal Sassoon, the celebrity hairdresser from Shepherd's Bush, was an articulate and engaging figure. He's screen centre in this documentary about his life, which is far better than the absurd hyping by the contributors seen at the outset would lead you to expect. Grace Coddington from *The September Issue* (2009) makes an appearance and Roman Polanski features in a fascinating anecdote. (Also known as *Vidal Sassoon: How One Man Changed the World with a Pair of Scissors*) MS

❯ With Vidal Sassoon, Ronnie Sassoon, Mary Quant, Grace Coddington.
❯ *Dir* and *Ed* Craig Teper, *Pro* Michael Gordon and Jackie Gilbert Bauer, *Written by* Heather Campbell Gordon and Teper, *Ph* Saul Gittens and Teper, *M* Steven Griesgraber.
Michael Gordon/Vidal Sassoon The Movie-Verve Pictures. 93 mins. USA. 2010. Rel: 20 May 2011. Cert. PG.

Villain ★★★★

Yuichi (Satoshi Tsumabuki) is a shy construction worker desperate to find love through the internet. His first encounter ends in tragedy while his second date with the equally lonely shop assistant Mitsuyo (Eri Fukatsu) is not much better. But surprisingly these two lonely souls fall for each other despite his violent nature and her blind obsession. This is a gripping story, superbly acted and directed, which keeps you mesmerised till the end, despite the lengthy running time. (Original title: *Akunin*) GS

❯ Satoshi Tsumabuki, Eri Fukatsu, Hikari Mitsushima, Masaki Okada, Akira Emoto, Kirin Kiki.
❯ *Dir* Sang-il Lee, *Pro* Genki Kawamura and Yoshihiro Suzuki, *Screenplay* Shuichi Yoshida and Sang-il Lee, based on the novel by Yoshida, *Ph* Norimichi Kasamatsu, *Pro Des* Yohei Taneda, *Ed* Takeshi Imai, *M* Joe Isaishi, *Cos* Ogawa Kumiko.
Toho Company/Yahoo Japan/Dentsu/Horipro/Sony Music Entertainment etc-Third Window Films. 139 mins. Japan. 2010. Rel: 19 Aug 2011. Cert. 15.

Model weather: tonsorial subjects in Craig Teper's *Vidal Sassoon: The Movie.*

The Violent Kind ★½

Troubled Cody (Cory Knauf) and his biker friends are partying in a farmhouse deep within the redwood forest when Cody's ex-girlfriend Michelle (Tiffany Shepis) is discovered stumbling around covered in blood... The only positive thing to say about this nasty horror is that it is not predictable and, like Cody, we find ourselves trying to make sense of what is going on. It is loud and unpleasant while The Butcher Brothers' direction lives up to their name. GS

▶ Cory Knauf, Taylor Cole, Bret Roberts, Christina Prousalis, Tiffany Shepis, Nick Tagas.
▶ *Dir* The Butcher Brothers (Phil Flores and Mitchell Altieri), *Pro* Jeremy Platt, Andy Gould, Jeffrey Allard, Malek Akkad and Michael Ferris Gibson, *Screenplay* The Butcher Brothers, from a story by them and Adam Weis, *Ph* James Laxton, *Pro Des* Will King, *Ed* Nic Hill, Joel T Pashby and Jesse Spencer , *M* Joshua Myers, *Cos* Alexis Beck.
San Francisco Independent Cinema-Eagle Films.
85 mins. USA. 2010. Rel: 22 July 2011. Cert. 18.

Viva Riva! ★★½

Films from the Congo are rare but one can't welcome this drama set in Kinshasa. That's because its tale of a crook pursued both by a psychopath and by the bandit whose woman he covets plays as pulp fiction. By that I mean that the violence (often) and the sex (occasionally) suggest exploitation fare and it's so overplayed

that it can't be taken seriously. But, should that be what you want, there's enough action and pace to please. MS

▶ Patsha Bay, Manie Malone, Hoji Fortuna, Marlène Longange, Diplome Amekindra, Alex Herabo.
▶ *Dir*, *Pro* and *Screenplay* Djo Tunda Wa Munga, *Ph* Antoine Roch, *Art Dir* Philippe van Herwijnen, *Ed* Yves Langlois, *M* Louis Vyncke Congopunq, *Cos* Ramelle Mulanga and Charlotte Lebourgeois.
Formosa/MG Productions/Canal+/CinéCinéma etc-Metrodome Distribution.
98 mins. France/Belgium/Congo/South Africa/Angola. 2010. Rel: 24 June 2011. Cert. 15.

Wake Wood ★★★★

Grieving couple Patrick (Aidan Gillen) and Louise (Eva Birthistle) move to Wakewood from the city in order to recover from the tragic death of their daughter. But in this rural Irish town they discover that its inhabitants are able to bring a person back from the dead for three days... David Keating's confident film relies heavily on atmosphere and boasts terrific performances. Just when you think this is merely another version of *The Wicker Man* the story takes an unexpected turn before the chilling climax. GS

▶ Aidan Gillen, Eva Birthistle, Timothy Spall, Ella Connolly, Ruth McCabe, Brian Gleeson, Tommy McArdle, John McArdle.
▶ *Dir* David Keating, *Pro* Brendan McCarthy and John McDonnell, *Screenplay* Keating and Brendan

McCarthy, from a story by McCarthy, *Ph* Chris Maris, *Pro Des* John Hand, *Ed* Tim Murrell, *M* Michael Convertino, *Cos* Louise Stanton.

Hammer Film Productions/Fantastic Films/Solid Entertainment-Vertigo Films.
90 mins. Ireland/UK. 2011. Rel: 25 Mar 2011. Cert. 18.

Warrior ★★★★

Irony is what you least expect in a fight movie but… in Pittsburgh ex-Marine Tommy Conlan (Tom Hardy) returns home to see his alcoholic father Paddy (Nick Nolte), hoping to train again in the Mixed Martial Arts ring. Meanwhile his estranged brother Brendan (Joel Edgerton) is also back and, what do you know, they eventually face each other in the MMA tournament final. Fine acting from Hardy, Edgerton and particularly Nolte save this from being just another pugilist picture. If you're into watching fighters – with back stories of emotional trauma – punching seven bells out of each other, this is the one – it's a knockout. MHD

▶ Tom Hardy, Joel Edgerton, Nick Nolte, Jennifer Morrison, Frank Grillo, Kevin Dunn.
▶ *Dir* Gavin O'Connor, *Pro* Gavin O'Connor and Greg O'Connor, *Screenplay* Gavin O'Connor, Anthony Tambakis and Cliff Dorfman, from a story by O'Connor and Dorfman, *Ph* Masanobou Takayanagi, *Pro Des* Dan Leigh, *Ed* Matt Chesse, John Gilroy, Aaron Marshall and Sean Albertson, *M* Mark Isham, *Cos* Abigail Murray.

Lionsgate/Solaris Entertainment/Mimran Schur Pictures/Filmtribe-Lionsgate.
140 mins. USA. 2011. Rel: 23 Sep 2011. Cert. 12A.

Waste Land ★★★★

A documentarian drawn to unusual and intriguing subject matter, Lucy Walker here turns her attention to the Brazilian artist Vik Muniz. The latter's work with found objects led to a project that involved the poor of Rio de Janeiro participating in the creation of art from discarded rubbish. The effect was to add to their sense of self-worth and this is a film of some humanity. MS

▶ With Vik Muniz, Fabio Ghivelder, Isis Rodrigues Garros, Magna De França Santos.
▶ *Dir* Lucy Walker, *Pro* Angus Aynsley and Hank Levine, *Ph* Dudu Miranda, *Ed* Pedro Kos, *M* Moby.

Almega Projects/O2 Filmes-E1 Films.
99 mins. UK/Brazil. 2009. Rel: 25 Feb 2009. Cert. PG.

Water for Elephants ★★

Circuses are pretty surreal and seedy places and this rather stodgy adaptation of Sara Gruen's best-selling novel is anything but. Set during the Depression, the film is a surprisingly glossy affair, failing to capture the grim reality of a continent on the brink. Instead, Francis Lawrence's drama focuses on the star wattage of Reese Witherspoon and Robert Pattinson and the one-dimensional villainy of Christoph Waltz's tyrannical ringmaster. Unfortunately, there's not a quark of chemistry between the romantic leads, leaving this old-fashioned show a rather dull and predictable affair. JC-W

▶ Reese Witherspoon, Robert Pattinson, Christoph Waltz, Paul Schneider, Jim Norton, Hal Holbrook, James Frain.
▶ *Dir* Francis Lawrence, *Pro* Kevin Halloran, Gil Netter, Erwin Stoff and Andrew R Tennenbaum, *Screenplay* Richard LaGravenese, from Sara Gruen's novel, *Ph* Rodrigo Prieto, *Pro Des* Jack Fisk, *Ed* Alan Edward Bell, *M* James Newton Howard, *Cos* Jacqueline West.

Fox 2000 Pictures/3 Arts Entertainment/Flashpoint Entertainment/Crazy Horse Effects-20th Century Fox.
120 mins. USA. 2011. Rel: 4 May 2011. Cert. 12A.

The Way ★★½

Emilio Estevez directs his own father, Martin Sheen, in an initially promising story about a father who, following his son's death, takes the route of pilgrimage across the Pyrenees to Santiago de Compostela in his place. It looks great but sadly the characters met en route are poorly drawn and plot developments unpersuasive. Well intentioned undoubtedly but not, alas, convincing. MS

▶ Martin Sheen, Deborah Kara Unger, Yorick van Wageningen, James Nesbitt, Angela Molina.
▶ *Dir* and *Screenplay* Emilio Estevez, *Pro* Estevez, David Alexanian and Julio Fernández, *Ph* Juan Miguel Azpiroz, *Pro Des* Victor Molero, *Ed* Raúl Davalos, *M* Tyler Bates, *Cos* Tatiana Hernández.

Filmax Animation/Castelao Productions/Elixir Films etc-Icon Film Distribution.
128 mins. USA/Spain/UK. 2010. Rel: 13 May 2011. Cert. 15.

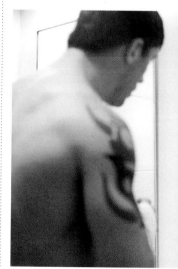

Emotional body blow: Tom Hardy burns up the screen in Gavin O'Connor's endorphin-sparking *Warrior*.

Way of the Morris ★½

It's evident from this redundant documentary that director-writer-actor Tim Plester disagrees with ex-porn star Linzi Drew's statement (borrowed from Sir Thomas Beecham), "Try everything once except incest and Morris dancing." He is adamant that he has not a dance bone in his body but eventually he 'miraculously' follows his family's tradition and joins in the festivities in the small North Oxfordshire village of Adderbury. Plester is determined to prove to the world that Morris dancing is no laughing matter and self-indulgently hammers his point in vain. GS

▶ With Billy Bragg, Chris Leslie, Tim Plester, the Adderbury Village Morris Men, and the voices of MyAnna Buring and Donald Sumpter.
▶ *Dir* and *Pro* Tim Plester and Rob Curry, *Screenplay* Tim Plester, *Ph* Richard Mitchell, *Ed* Jono Griffith, *M* Adrian Corker.

Fifth Column Films-Safecracker Pictures.
64 mins. UK. 2011. Rel: 9 Sep 2011. Cert. 12A.

We Have a Pope ★★★

Meet the parents: Tilda Swinton and John C Reilly in Lynne Ramsey's powerful and chilling *We Need to Talk About Kevin*.

Nanni Moretti's film, in which he appears as a psychoanalyst, is a well-staged comedy that makes fun of how the Church seeks to hide the truth from the faithful when a newly elected pope (Michel Piccoli) backs away, declaring that he is unworthy. The man himself is not mocked and Piccoli is a wonderful central presence, but unfortunately the second half falls away, leaving it all too clear that nobody knew where to take the story. It's good enough initially to be very disappointing ultimately. (Original title: *Habemus Papam*) MS

▶ Michel Piccoli, Nanni Moretti, Renato Scarpa, Jerzy Stuhr, Margherita Buy.
▶ *Dir* Nanni Moretti, *Pro* Moretti and Domenico Procacci, *Screenplay* Moretti, Francesco Piccolo and Federica Pontremoli, *Ph* Alessandro Pesci, *Art Dir* Paola Bizzarri, *Ed* Esmeralda Calabria, *M* Franco Piersanti, *Cos* Lina Nerli Taviani.

Sacher Film/Fandango/Le Pacte/France 3 Cinéma etc-Soda Pictures.
105 mins. Italy/France. 2011. Rel: 2 Dec 2011. Cert. PG.

We Need to Talk About Kevin ★★★½

Kevin (Ezra Miller) was always a little monster and continues to be so in his teen years. He hates his mother (Tilda Swinton) with a passion and does everything he can to unhinge her. His father (John C Reilly) just thinks his son is being boyish. The original novel was written in the form of letters from Kevin's mother to her husband. Here things are spelled out in flashbacks in an effort to explain the catastrophe that Kevin finally brings about. It's a slow-starter but, as Kevin's behaviour worsens, the film takes on powerful, chilling moments. A good cast all round is eclipsed, however, by Miller's creepily strong performance as Kevin. MHD

▶ Tilda Swinton, John C Reilly, Ezra Miller, Ashley Gerasimovich, Siobhan Fallon Hogan.
▶ *Dir* Lynne Ramsay, *Pro* Jennifer Fox, Luc Roeg and Robert Salerno, *Screenplay* Ramsay and Rory Kinnear, from the novel by Lionel Shriver, *Ph* Seamus McGarvey, *Pro Des* Judy Becker, *Ed* Joe Bini, *M* Jonny Greenwood, *Cos* Catherine George.

BBC Films/UK Film Council/Piccadilly Pictures/Lipsync Productions/Artina Films/Rockinghorse Films/Atlantic Swiss Productions-Artificial Eye.
112 mins. UK/USA. 2011. Rel: 21 Oct 2011. Cert. 15.

We Were Here ★★★★

This moving documentary features five people from San Francisco looking back on when the AIDS crisis hit. Historical footage is interwoven with their personal narratives and the film shows the gay community first reacting in shock and then finding solidarity, not unlike that said to have been experienced by Londoners in the Blitz. The film is inevitably harrowing, but so much love is evident (both past and present) that the impact is far from downbeat. MS

▶ With Eileen Glutzer, Paul Boneberg, Ed Wolf, Daniel Goldstein, Guy Clark.
▶ *Dir* David Weissman with Bill Weber, *Pro* Weissman, *Ph* Marsha Kahm, *Ed* Weber, *M* Holcombe Waller.

Funded by California Council for the Humanities/San Francisco Foundation Bay Area Documentary Fund etc-Peccadillo Pictures.
90 mins. USA. 2011. Rel: 25 Nov 2011. No Cert.

Weekend ★★★★½

Andrew Haigh's film is almost a two-hander. Superbly played by Tom Cullen and Chris New, it is about two contrasted gay men in Nottingham and the way in which they influence each other over one weekend following a pick-up. I'm not quite convinced that Haigh knew how to end it, but as an authentic portrayal of gay people today it does for 2011 what Ron Peck's *Nighthawks* did for 1978. Brilliantly characterised, it's a landmark film in British gay cinema. MS

▶ Tom Cullen, Chris New, Jonathan Race, Laura Freeman, Loretto Murray.
▶ *Dir, Screenplay* and *Ed* Andrew Haigh, *Pro* Tristan Goligher, *Ph* Ula Pontikos, *Pro Des* Sarah Finlay.

Glendale Picture Company/The Bureau Film Company/Synchronicity Films/EM Media etc-Peccadillo Pictures.
97 mins. UK. 2011. Rel: 4 Nov 2011. Cert. 18.

Weekender ★★

The time is 1990 and the place is Manchester. Two friends, Matt (Henry Lloyd-Hughes) and Dylan (Jack O'Connell), are fed up with their petty thieving and believe that the only way to

get rich quick is to exploit the rave scene. They find deserted warehouses and factories where they organise rave parties for a massive profit. Their success story takes them to Ibiza and Amsterdam but a group of thugs are on their trail. Karl Golden's likable film boasts a lot of energy but lacks real drama. GS

▶ Henry Lloyd-Hughes, Jack O'Connell, Ben Batt, Sam Hazeldine, Zawe Ashton, Dean Andrews.
▶ *Dir* Karl Golden, *Pro* Ian Brady, Robert Walak and Stephen Salter, *Screenplay* Chris Coghill, *Ph* John Conroy, *Pro Des* Kristian Milsted, *Ed* Martin Brinkler, *M* James Edward Barker, *Cos* Camille Bender.

Benchmark Films-Momentum Pictures.
90 mins. UK. 2011. Rel: 2 Sep 2011. Cert. 15.

Opposite attraction: Tom Cullen and Chris New in Andrew Haigh's brave, funny and spontaneous Weekend.

Welcome to the Rileys ★★½

Welcome, indeed, to the talented cast here (James Gandolfini, Kristen Stewart, Melissa Leo and Ersa Davis all do good work), but not to the screenplay which lets them down. Living in Indianapolis, the Rileys are a couple whose life is overshadowed by the death of their daughter. Fair enough, but what happens in New Orleans when dad treats a teenage stripper like a substitute daughter becomes increasingly implausible. In consequence, what begins promisingly concludes by seriously disappointing us. MS

▶ James Gandolfini, Kristen Stewart, Melissa Leo, Joe Chrest, Ally Sheedy, Ersa Davis.
▶ *Dir* Jake Scott, *Pro* Giovanni Agnelli, Scott Bloom and Michael Costigan, *Screenplay* Ken Hixon, *Ph* Christopher Soos, *Pro Des* Happy Massee, *Ed* Nicholas

Country matters: Daniel Auteuil and Astrid Bergès-Frisbey in *The Well Digger's Daughter*.

Gastner, *M* Marc Streitenfeld, *Cos* Kim Bowen.

Scott Free/Argonaut Pictures/Samuel Goldwyn Films etc-High Fliers Films.
110 mins. USA. 2010. Rel: 18 Nov 2011. Cert. 15.

The Well Digger's Daughter
★★★★

Daniel Auteuil not only stars here but has adapted a lesser known work by Marcel Pagnol and directs it himself. Admirers of *Jean de Florette* and its sequel have been waiting for another film like this for years and will probably not feel let down by this period tale of class distinctions and young love. It's very traditional and rather obvious material, but Auteuil has a feeling for Provence and the right audience will embrace it. (Original title: *La Fille du puisatier*) MS

▶ Daniel Auteuil, Astrid Bergès-Frisbey, Sabine Azema, Kad Merad, Jean-Pierre Darroussin, Nicolas Duvauchelle.
▶ *Dir* and adaptation from Marcel Pagnol's novel by Daniel Auteuil, *Pro* Alain Sarde and Jerôme Seydoux, *Ph* Jean-François Robin, *Art Dir* Bernard Vezat, *Ed* Joelle Hache, *M* Alexandre Desplat, *Cos* Pierre-Yves Gayraud.

A.S. Films/Zack Films/Pathé/TF1 Films/CinéCinéma etc-Pathé Distribution.
109 mins. France. 2011. Rel: 9 Dec 2011. Cert. PG.

West is West ★★★★

Sadly under-rated, this sequel to *East is East* (1999) features the same family but now concentrates on the youngest son (the excellent Aqib Khan) being taken from England to Pakistan by his father (Om Puri) to make him aware of his culture. It's touching as well as amusing and in its mainstream way both heart-warming and not without subtlety. As a feel-good movie of quality it totally outclasses the over-rated *Slumdog Millionaire*. Well worth seeking out. MS

▶ Om Puri, Linda Bassett, Aqib Khan, Jimi Mistry, Lesley Nicol, Ila Arun.
▶ *Dir* Andy De Emmony, *Pro* Leslee Udwin, *Screenplay* Ayub Khan Din, *Ph* Peter Robinson, *Pro Des* Aradhana Seth and Tom Conroy, *Ed* John Gregory and Stephen O'Connell, *M* Rob Lane, *Cos* Louise Stjernsward.

BBC Films/Assassin Films etc-Icon Film Distribution.
103 mins. UK. 2010. Rel: 25 Feb 2011. Cert. 15.

What's Your Number? ★★★

Ally Darling (Anna Faris) looks back at the last 20 men she's had relationships with and comes to the conclusion that she missed the true love of her life. She recruits her attractive neighbour Colin (Chris Evans) to find him and the search begins. Faris is a rare talent – she is very likable and funny and is able to make average material watchable. This is above average and she shares an excellent chemistry with Evans. GS

▷ Anna Faris, Chris Evans, Ari Graynor, Blythe Danner, Ed Begley Jr, Heather Burns, Martin Freeman.
▷ *Dir* Mark Mylod, *Pro* Tripp Vinson and Beau Flynn, *Screenplay* Gabrielle Allan and Jennifer Crittenden, from Karyn Bosnak's novel *Twenty Times a Lady*, *Ph* J Michael Muro, *Pro Des* Jon Billington, *Ed* Julie Monroe, *M* Aaron Zigman, *Cos* Amy Westcott.

Regency Enterprises/New Regency/Contrafilm-20th Century Fox.
106 mins. USA. 2011. Rel: 30 Sep 2011. Cert. 15.

When China Met Africa ★★★½

From the makers of *Black Gold* (2006) comes this view of China's economic links with Zambia, told through a study of three people: Zambia's Minister for Trade, a Chinese company man sent out to manage a new road project and a Chinese farmer who has found a better life in Zambia. The issues involved have generated more heat than one would guess from this film, but it's well made and determinedly unsensational. MS

▷ With Liu Changming, Li Jianguo, Felix Mutati.
▷ *Dir*, *Pro* and *Written by* Marc and Nick Francis, *Ph* Marc Francis, *Ed* Hugh Williams, *M* Florencia Di Concilio.

Speak-It Films/Zeta Productions/ARTE France/BBC/ VPRO etc-Speak-It Media.
75 mins. UK/France/The Netherlands/Switzerland/ Finland/Sweden/Norway/USA. 2010. Rel: 7 Oct 2011. Cert. 12A.

Will ★★½

Eleven-year-old Will (a convincing Perry Eggleton) can't believe his luck when his estranged father (Damian Lewis) buys him tickets for the 2005 Champions League final in Istanbul. But as fate would have it Will has to make his own way across Europe... This is a charming story but not very believable. A similar tale with more style and imagination was told in *Africa United*, but here the one-dimensional script and thinly drawn supporting characters lack credibility. GS

▷ Damian Lewis, Bob Hoskins, Alice Krige, Perry Eggleton, Jane March, Malcolm Storry, Jamie Carragher, Steven Gerrard, Kenny Dalglish.
▷ *Dir* Ellen Perry, *Pro* Perry, Zack Anderson, Timothy J Nicholas, Mark Cooper, Taha Altayli, *Screenplay* Perry and Anderson, *Ph* Oliver Stapleton, *Pro Des* James Merifield, *Ed* Derek Burgess, Lesley Walker and Brenna Rangott, *M* Nigel Clarke and Michael Csányi-Wills, *Cos* Lindsay Pugh.

Galatafilm/Strangelove Films-Premier PR.
102 mins. UK. 2011. Rel: 4 Nov 2011. Cert. PG.

Win Win ★★★★

Tom McCarthy's third feature is certainly not without humour but it is essentially an engaging moral drama about a good man who succumbs to deceit when in financial difficulties. Paul Giamatti is on great form, but so too are Margo Martindale in a cameo role and young newcomer Alex Shaffer. For once we have a film that might have gained from being a bit longer (the conclusion is slightly rushed), but this is a fine character-driven work. MS

▷ Paul Giamatti, Amy Ryan, Alex Shaffer, Bobby Cannavale, Melanie Lynsky, Margo Martindale.
▷ *Dir* Tom McCarthy, *Pro* Mary Jane Skalski, McCarthy and others, *Screenplay* McCarthy from a story by Joe Tiboni and himself *Ph* Oliver Bokelberg, *Pro Des* John Paino, *Ed* Tom McArdle, *M* Lyle Workman, *Cos* Melissa Toth.

Fox Searchlight Pictures/Groundswell /Next Wednesday etc-20th Century Fox.
106 mins. USA. 2011. Rel: 20 May 2011. Cert. 15.

Winnie the Pooh ★★★★

This charming animation feature brings A A Milne's much-loved animals back to the screen. Pooh claims that "My tummy is feeling a little 11 o'clockish" before he has a hallucination that he's swimming in a lake full of honey.

Wherein hangs a tail: Piglet and the gang in Disney's latest incarnation of *Winnie the Pooh*.

Meanwhile, the rest of the gang are looking for Eeyore's missing tail... A lovely story wittily told and charmingly narrated by John Cleese. GS

▶ Voices of Jim Cummings, Bud Luckey, Craig Ferguson, Jack Boulter, Travis Oates, Kristen Anderson-Lopez, Wyatt Dean Hall and narrator John Cleese.
▶ *Dir* Stephen J Anderson and Don Hall, *Pro* Clark Spencer and Peter Del Veco, *Screenplay* Anderson, Hall, Don Dougherty, Jeremy Spears, Clio Chiang etc, based on the books by A A Milne, *Ph* Julio Macat, *Art Dir* Paul Felix and Patrick M Sullivan Jr, *Ed* Lisa Linder, *M* Henry Jackman.

Walt Disney Pictures/Walt Disney Animation Studios-Walt Disney Studios Motion Pictures.
63 mins. USA. 2011. Rel: 15 Apr 2011. Cert. U.

The Woman ★★★★

Lawyer Christopher Cleek (Sean Bridgers) loves hunting near his remote country home but one day instead of a deer he captures a wild woman (Pollyanna McIntosh). He locks her in the shed and tries to tame and civilise her despite his dysfunctional family's objections. The acting is very believable in this darkly humorous and shocking tale. It's one of the most original horror films of recent years, compelling and unpredictable in equal measure. GS

Femme fatale: Pollyanna McIntosh in Lucky McKee's darkly humorous and shocking *The Woman.*

▶ Sean Bridgers, Pollyanna McIntosh, Brandon Gerald Fuller, Lauren Ashley Carter, Chris Krzykowski.
▶ *Dir* Lucky McKee, *Pro* Robert Tonino and Andrew van den Houten, *Screenplay* McKee and Jack Ketchum, *Ph* Alex Vendler, *Pro Des* Krista Gall, *Ed* Zach Passero, *M* Sean Spillane, *Cos* Sandra Alexandre and Michael Bevins.

Moderncné-Revolver Entertainment.
101 mins. USA. 2011. Rel: 30 Sep 2011. Cert. 18.

World of the Dead! The Zombie Diaries ★

Here is yet another zombie movie filmed like an amateur video with uninteresting characters and not much of a plot. A few survivors have managed to escape from the clutches of the flesh-eating living dead and have taken refuge at a rural military barracks... The handheld camera becomes very irritating by the end while the gratuitous violence is unforgivable. GS

▶ Philip Brodie, Alix Wilton Regan, Rob Oldfield, Vicky Araico, Toby Bowman, Russell Jones.
▶ *Dir* Michael Bartlett and Kevin Gates, *Pro* Rob Weston, *Screenplay* Gates, *Ph* George Carpenter, *Pro Des* Michael Bell, *Ed* Drew Cullingham and Mark Tehnsuko, *M* Pete Renton, *Cos* Millie Sloan.

Bleeding Edge Films/Straightwire Films/Off World Films-Metrodome Distribution.
88 mins. UK. 2011. Rel: 24 June 2011. Cert. 15.

Wreckers ★★★½

D R Hood's first feature suffers from some weaknesses in her writing, especially toward the end, yet she is a new British filmmaker of immense promise. The Fenland setting is admirably used and the subject matter intrigues. It's an intimate drama about a wife, her husband and his brother and it investigates tellingly how difficult it can be to know other

people truly, even if they are close to you. Give it a try. MS

▶ Claire Foy, Benedict Cumberbatch, Shaun Evans, Peter McDonald, Sinead Matthews, June Watson.
▶ *Dir* and *Screenplay* D R Hood, *Pro* Simon Onwurah, *Ph* Annemarie Lean-Vercoe, *Pro Des* Beck Rainford, *Ed* Claire Pringle, *M* Andrew Lovett, *Cos* Rebecca Gore.

Likely Story/Non-Aligned Films-Artificial Eye. 85 mins. UK. 2010. Rel: 16 Dec 2011. Cert. 15.

Wuthering Heights ★★★★

As she did in her two previous features, *Red Road* and *Fish Tank,* writer-director Andrea Arnold in her adaptation of Emily Brontë's novel strips things down to bare essentials. No Hollywood phoniness as when Merle Oberon and Laurence Olivier capered about the California hills circa 1939, for here Arnold goes out to the wild, wild dales of Yorkshire itself and the film is all the better for it. Naturalism in acting, wild sound (no incidental music) and a realistically bleak atmosphere of abuse all add up to a fine achievement. Casting a black Heathcliff is another coup and Arnold gets memorably creditable performances out of her largely unknown cast. MHD

▶ Kaya Scodelario, James Howson, Oliver Milburn, Steve Evets, Amy Wren, James Northcote, Paul Hilton, Shannon Beer, Solomon Glave.
▶ *Dir* Andrea Arnold, *Pro* Douglas Rae, Kevin Loader

and Robert Bernstein, *Screenplay* Arnold and Olivia Hetreed, from the novel by Emily Brontë, *Ph* Robbie Ryan, *Pro Des* Helen Scott, *Ed* Nicolas Chaudeurge, *Cos* Steven Noble.

Film 4/Ecosse Films/Goldcrest Pictures/UK Film Council/HanWay Films/Screen Yorkshire-Artificial Eye. 129 mins. UK. 2011. Rel: 11 Nov 2011. Cert. 15.

X-Men: First Class ★★★★

Fresh off his audacious re-imagining of the superhero genre with *Kick-Ass,* Matthew Vaughn liberates the *X-Men* franchise from its comic-book shackles. The result is a younger, snazzier and decidedly more British set of mutants coming to terms with their genetic differences. The premise of the entire franchise – to make a strength of one's uniqueness – still holds true but is given both sex appeal and a youthful bloom, as well as a personal and historical context. This is smart, dry and ingenious comic-book pulp in which the human characteristics of the X-men are just as winning as their CGI-enhanced feats. JC-W

▶ James McAvoy, Michael Fassbender, Rose Byrne, Jennifer Lawrence, January Jones, Kevin Bacon, Oliver Platt, Nicholas Hoult, Zoë Kravitz, Jason Flemyng, Matt Craven, Rade Serbedzija, Michael Ironside, Hugh Jackman.
▶ *Dir* Matthew Vaughn, *Pro* Gregory Goodman, Simon Kinberg, Lauren Shuler Donner and Bryan Singer, *Screenplay* Ashley Edward Miller, Zack Stentz, Jane Goldman and Matthew Vaughn, *Ph* John Mathieson, *Pro Des* Chris Seagers, *Ed* Eddie Hamilton

Valley girl: Solomon Glave and Shannon Beer in Andrea Arnold's creditable *Wuthering Heights.*

and Lee Smith, *M* Henry Jackman, *Cos* Sammy Sheldon.

20th Century Fox/Bad Hat Harry Productions/Donners' Company/Marvel-20th Century Fox.
131 mins. USA. 2011. Rel: 1 June 2011. Cert. 12A.

The Yellow Sea ★★★½

Taxi driver and obsessive gambler Gu-nam (the magnificent Jung-woo Ha) has reached rock bottom in China's Yanji City. He is deeply in debt and desperate to hear from his wife who fled to South Korea six months earlier, so he reluctantly agrees to cross the yellow sea to Korea for a contract killing. The first half of Hong-jin Na's stylish action thriller is simply superb, with amazing set-pieces. But, as the action develops, the labyrinthine subplots become too complicated and the endless car chases and explosions increasingly lose their impact. GS

❧ Jung-woo Ha, Yun-seok Kim, Seong-ha Cho, Chul-min Lee, Jae-hwa Kim.
❧ *Dir* and *Screenplay* Hong-jin Na, *Pro* Sung-goo Han, *Ph* Sung-je Lee, *Pro Des* Hwo-kyoung Lee, *Ed* Sun-min Kim, *M* Young-kyu Jang and Byung-hoon Lee, *Cos* Kyung-hwa Chae.

Popcorn Films/Wellmade Starm/Fox International Productions/Showbox Mediaplex etc-Eureka Entertainment on behalf of Bounty Films.
157 mins. South Korea. 2011. Rel: 21 Oct 2011. Cert. 18.

Yogi Bear 3D ★★★½

The action takes place in Jellystone Park, the home of Yogi Bear (Dan Aykroyd) and Boo Boo (Justin Timberlake), which becomes endangered when Mayor Brown (Andrew Daly) decides to turn it into a building development. So it is now up to Yogi and the animals to save the day... Dan Aykroyd is perfectly cast as the voice of the mischievous bear. The plot is predictable to say the least but this is such a good-natured film that it's guaranteed to put a smile on your face. GS

❧ Voices of Dan Aykroyd, Justin Timberlake, Anna Faris, Andrew Daly, Tom Cavanagh, T J Miller and narrator Josh Robert Thompson.
❧ *Dir* Eric Brevig, *Pro* Donald De Line and Karen Rosenfelt, *Screenplay* Jeffrey Ventimilia, Brad Copeland and Joshua Sternin, *Ph* Peter James, *Pro Des* David Sandefur, *Ed* Kent Beyda, *M* John Debney, *Cos* Liz McGregor.

Warner Bros Pictures/De Line Pictures/Sunswept Entertainment/Rhythm and Hues/Picnic Basket-Warner Bros.
80 mins. USA/New Zealand. 2010. Rel: 11 Feb 2011. Cert. U.

You Instead ★★★

Wonderfully atmospheric, this feature from David Mackenzie tells a story but was shot in five days at Scotland's 'T in the Park' Music Festival. Those who love such events may well love this film, but it's slight stuff right down to its highly predictable love story, although newcomer Natalia Tena as the heroine has an agreeably fresh personality. It's not a patch on Shane Meadows' *Le Donk and Scor-Zay-Zee* (2009), which it brings to mind. MS

❧ Luke Treadaway, Natalia Tena, Matthew Baynton, Ruta Gedmintas, Joseph Mydell.

Mean streets: Jung-woo Ha in Hong-jin Na's flashy, labyrinthine *The Yellow Sea.*

▶ *Dir* David Mackenzie, *Pro* Gillian Berrie, *Screenplay* Thomas Leveritt with contributions from director and cast, *Ph* Giles Nuttgens, *Pro Des* Judi Ritchie, *Ed* Jake Roberts, *Cos* Kelly Cooper Barr.

BBC Films/Sigma Films/Head Gear Films/Creative Scotland etc-Icon Film Distribution.
80 mins. UK. 2011. Rel: 16 Sep 2011. Cert. 15.

You Will Meet a Tall Dark Stranger ★★★½

Woody Allen returns to London to look at romance and the characters riding love's roundabout. Alfie (Anthony Hopkins) leaves his wife Helena (the wonderful Gemma Jones) for the younger, gold-digging Charmaine (Lucy Punch). Helena visits clairvoyant Pauline Collins who tells her to move on. Her daughter Sally (Naomi Watts) and writer son-in-law Roy (Josh Brolin) are also having marital difficulties and decide to look elsewhere for love, Sally to her art gallery boss (Antonio Banderas) and Roy to his neighbour (Freida Pinto), his new-found muse. It's all neatly put together with some fine Woody barbs and finds the filmmaker almost back on form. MHD

▶ Antonio Banderas, Josh Brolin, Anthony Hopkins, Gemma Jones, Freida Pinto, Lucy Punch, Naomi Watts, Pauline Collins, Rupert Frazer, Kelly Harrison, Ewen Bremner.

▶ *Dir* and *Screenplay* Woody Allen, *Pro* Stephen Tenenbaum, Jaume Roures and Letty Aronson, *Ph* Vilmos Zsigmond, *Pro Des* Jim Clay, *Ed* Alisa Lepselter, *Cos* Beatrix Aruna Pastor.

Mediapro/Gravier Productions/Versátil Cinema/ Dippermouth/Antenna 3-Pathé.
98 mins. USA/Spain. 2010. Rel: 18 Mar 2011. Cert. 12A.

Young Hearts Run Free ★★½

The action takes place in a small Northumbrian village in 1974 during a miner's strike. Mark (Andy Black) upsets his community by first falling in love with a girl from London whom nobody likes, but even more so when he becomes a scab in order to pay for his studies. It is a competent but modest first feature from Andy Mark Simpson with likable performances, particularly from Black as the confused young man. GS

▶ Andy Black, Jennifer Bryden, Lyndsey Milne, Danny McCready, Jimmy Carter, Matthew Brown.
▶ *Dir, Pro* and *Screenplay* Andy Mark Simpson, *Ph* David Beaumont, *Pro Des* Richard Reay, *Ed* Mark Waters, *M* Robert Owen, *Costume Consultant* Eric Doughney.

Bede Films-Bede Films Ltd.
93 mins. UK. 2011. Rel: 1 Apr 2011. Cert. 12A.

London calling: Gemma Jones and Naomi Watts in Woody Allen's *You Will Meet a Tall Dark Stranger.*

Fashion police: Yves Saint-Laurent and Pierre Bergé in Pierre Thoretton's engaging *Yves Saint-Laurent: L'Amour Fou.*

Your Highness ★

'Tis a tragedy that a filmsmith of David Gordon Green's calibre should stoop to this balderdash. Following such critically acclaimed films as *George Washington* and *All the Real Girls*, Green has deigned to direct a pantomime co-produced, co-written by and starring Danny McBride. Floundering in the footsteps of *The Princess Bride*, it is a crass, crude and desperately unfunny 'romp' set in a time of valiant princes, awful dragons and wicked wizards. Too often reliant on CGI and obsessed with masturbation, *Your Highness* offers up a rich visual palette distinguished by some noble acting talent sharing their all-time professional lows. JC-W

▶ Danny McBride, James Franco, Natalie Portman, Zooey Deschanel, Justin Theroux, Toby Jones, Charles Dance, Damian Lewis, Rasmus Hardiker, Julian Rhind-Tutt.
▶ *Dir* David Gordon Green, *Pro* Scott Stuber, Jon Mone, Danny McBride, Mark Huffam and Andrew Z. Davis, *Screenplay* McBride and Ben Best, *Ph* Tim Orr, *Pro Des* Mark Tildesley, *Ed* Craig Alpert, *M* Steve Jablonsky, *Cos* Hazel Webb-Crozier.

Universal/Stuber Prods-Entertainment One.
98 mins. USA. 2011. Rel: 13 Apr 2011. Cert. 15.

Yu-Gi-Oh! 3D Bonds Beyond Time ★★

Ken'ichi Takeshita's manga animation of the popular card game and TV series begins with an update of previous adventures before duellists Yugi, Jaden and Yusei start their new futuristic mission. Civilisation is on the brink of extinction but the brave duellists are prepared to travel back in time and face their nemesis, Paradox... The complex plot is aided by fun 3D effects but it is strictly for fans of the genre and the game. GS

▶ Voices of Greg Abbey, Matt Charles, Dan Green, Sean Schemmel, Ted Lewis, Tom Wayland.
▶ *Dir* Ken'ichi Takeshita, *Screenplay* Shin Yoshida, based on the manga by Kazuli Takahashi, *Animation Director* Takahiro Kagami, *M* Hiramitsu Takuya and Elik Alvarez.

NAS/Televi Tôkyô-Manga Entertainment.
61 mins. Japan/USA. 2010. Rel: 14 May 2011. Cert. PG.

Yves Saint-Laurent: L'Amour Fou ★★★★

Pierre Thoretton's engaging documentary not only celebrates Yves Saint-Laurent's remarkable career but also his relationship with his lifelong partner of 50 years, Pierre Bergé. The story is mostly told from Bergé's point of view and, although Yves comes across as a shy man full of joy, Bergé claims that he was a manic depressive, especially towards the end of his life. It is illuminating but sad, with perhaps a few too many lingering shots of their elegant houses in Paris, Marrakech and Normandy. GS

▶ With Pierre Bergé, Betty Catroux, Loulou de la Falaise, Jack Lang, Catherine Deneuve and archive footage of Yves Saint-Laurent.
▶ *Dir* Pierre Thoretton, *Pro* Hugues Charbonneau and Kristina Larsen, *Ph* Léo Hinstin, *Art Dir* Olivier Pacteau, *Ed* Dominique Auvray, *M* Côme Aguiar.

Les Films du Lendemain/Les Films de Pierre/France 3 Cinéma/Canal+/France Télévision-Optimum Releasing.
98 mins. France. 2010. Rel: 7 Nov 2011. No Cert.

Zebra Crossing ★★★

Lee Turnbull is Justin, who cried for a month when he was born 18 years ago in South London's concrete-clad tower block estates – and life's still a vale of tears. With friends like Billy, Sean and Tommy, who are into drink, drugs, fights, crime and killing gays, his only real comfort is his bedridden sister Suzanne. Strikingly filmed in black and white with colour appearing only at the end, this startling, brutal film has an impressively gritty, realist feel. Turnbull leads a clutch of eye-catching performances, with Richard Pryal's demented drug dealer and Greg Wakeham's psycho the other standouts. DW

▶ Lee Turnbull, Greg Wakeham, Aaron White, Richard Pryal, Karl Treslove, Kathryn O'Reilly, Michael Maris.
▶ *Dir* and *Screenplay* Sam Holland, based on his idea, *Pro* Anastasia Atanesyan, *Ph* Holland and Lucio Cremonese, *Pro Des* Ilinka Dumitrescu, *Ed* Holland and Justin Krish, *M* Holley Gray.
Exile Media Group.
93 mins. UK. 2011. Rel: 28 Jan 2011. Cert. 18.

Zombie Undead ★

Dreary and desolate Leicester is the appropriate (and rarely used) setting for this Brit indie zombie flick that starts with a bomb going off. Then follows the tale of Sarah (Ruth King) and her badly wounded father being driven by Steve (Barry Thomas) to a suburban hospital, where it turns out there be zombies! She's saved from a fate worse than death by machete-wielding Jay (Kris Tearse) and the duo find other survivors to join the battle for freedom. Weak acting, poor scripting and a slow pace largely sink this unimaginative, derivative, low-budget effort – though it is quite well made and shot. DW

▶ Ruth King, Kris Tearse, Barry Thomas, Christopher J Herbert, Steven Dolton, Sandra Wildbore.
▶ *Dir* and *Pro* Rhys Davies, *Screenplay* Kris Tearse,

Ph Neil Phillips, *Art Dir* Kit Cox, *Ed* Davies and Tearse, *M* Tearse and David Fellows.
Hive Films-Metrodome Distribution.
79 mins. UK. 2010. Rel: 29 Apr 2011. Cert. 18.

Zookeeper ★★

Franklin Park Zoo caretaker Griffin Keyes (Kevin James) is more comfortable in the company of his animals than he is with women. After a disastrous marriage proposal to the woman of his dreams (Leslie Bibb), he decides to leave the zoo for a more glamorous job. But all the animals, voiced by several movie celebrities, join forces in a desperate attempt to keep their friend. It's a fun idea but the script feels like a first draft, while the cast seem to be having a better time than the audience. GS

▶ Kevin James, Rosario Dawson, Leslie Bibb, Nick Bakay, Donnie Wahlberg and the voices of Adam Sandler, Nick Nolte, Sylvester Stallone, Cher, Judd Apatow, Jon Favreau, Don Rickles.
▶ *Dir* Frank Coraci, *Pro* Adam Sandler, Kevin James, Jack Giarraputo, Todd Garner and Walt Becker, *Screenplay* Nick Bakay, Rock Reuben, Kevin James, Jay Scherick and David Ronn, from a story by Scherick and Ronn, *Ph* Michael Barrett, *Pro Des* Kirk M Petruccelli, *Ed* Scott Hill, *M* Rupert Gregson-Williams, *Cos* Mona May.
Columbia Pictures/Metro-Goldwyn-Mayer Pictures/ Broken Road/Zookeeper Productions/Happy Madison/ Hey Eddie-Sony Pictures Releasing.
102 mins. USA. 2011. Rel: 29 July 2011. Cert. PG.

Naked lunch? Kevin James (right) dines out with simian friend in Frank Coraci's critically eviscerated *Zookeeper.*

Awards and Festivals

The 83rd American Academy of Motion Picture Arts and Sciences Awards ('The Oscars') and Nominations for 2010
27 February 2011

▶▶ **Best Film:** *The King's Speech*. Nominations: *127 Hours*; *Black Swan*; *The Fighter*; *Inception*; *The Kids Are All Right*; *The Social Network*; *Toy Story 3*; *True Grit*; *Winter's Bone*.

▶▶ **Best Director:** Tom Hooper, for *The King's Speech*. Nominations: Darren Aronofsky, for *Black Swan*; Joel and Ethan Coen, for *True Grit*; David Fincher, for *The Social Network*; David O Russell, for *The Fighter*.

▶▶ **Best Actor:** Colin Firth, for *The King's Speech*. Nominations: Javier Bardem, for *Biutiful*; Jeff Bridges, for *True Grit*; Jesse Eisenberg, for *The Social Network*; James Franco, for *127 Hours*.

▶▶ **Best Actress:** Natalie Portman, for *Black Swan*. Nominations: Annette Bening, for *The Kids Are All Right*; Nicole Kidman, for *Rabbit Hole*; Jennifer Lawrence, for *Winter's Bone*; Michelle Williams, for *Blue Valentine*.

▶▶ **Best Supporting Actor:** Christian Bale, for *The Fighter*. Nominations: John Hawkes, for *Winter's Bone*; Jeremy Renner, for *The Town*; Mark Ruffalo, for *The Kids Are All Right*; Geoffrey Rush, for *The King's Speech*.

▶▶ **Best Supporting Actress:** Melissa Leo, for *The Fighter*. Nominations: Amy Adams, for *The Fighter*; Helena Bonham Carter, for *The King's Speech*; Hailee Steinfeld, for *True Grit*; Jacki Weaver, for *Animal Kingdom*.

▶▶ **Best Original Screenplay:** David Seidler, for *The King's Speech*. Nominations: Lisa Cholodenko and Stuart Blumberg, for *The Kids Are All Right*; Scott Silver, Paul Tamasy and Eric Johnson, for *The Fighter*; Mike Leigh, for *Another Year*; Christopher Nolan, for *Inception*.

▶▶ **Best Screenplay Adaptation:** Aaron Sorkin, for *The Social Network*. Nominations: Danny Boyle and Simon Beaufoy, for *127 Hours*; Michael Arndt, for *Toy Story 3*; Joel Coen and Ethan Coen, for *True Grit*; Debra Granik and Anne Rosellini, for *Winter's Bone*.

▶▶ **Best Cinematography:** Wally Pfister, for *Inception*. Nominations: Matthew Libatique, for *Black Swan*; Danny Cohen, for *The King's Speech*; Jeff Cronenweth, for *The Social Network*; Roger Deakins, for *True Grit*.

▶▶ **Best Editing:** Angus Wall and Kirk Baxter, for *The Social Network*. Nominations: Andrew Weisblum, for *Black Swan*; Jon Harris, for *127 Hours*; Pamela Martin, for *The Fighter*; Tariq Anwar, for *The King's Speech*.

▶▶ **Best Original Score:** Trent Reznor and Atticus Ross, for *The Social Network*. Nominations: Alexandre Desplat, for *The King's Speech*; John Powell, for *How to Train Your Dragon*; A R Rahman, for *127 Hours*; Hans Zimmer, for *Inception*.

▶▶ **Best Original Song:** 'We Belong Together', from *Toy Story 3*, music and lyrics by Randy Newman. Nominations: 'I See the Light', from *Tangled*, music by Alan Menken, lyrics by Glenn Slater; 'Coming Home', from *Country Strong*, music and lyrics by Tom Douglas, Hillary Lindsey and Troy Verges; 'If I Rise', from *127 Hours*, music by A R Rahman, lyrics by Dido and Rollo Armstrong.

▶▶ **Best Art Direction:** Robert Stromberg (art direction), and Karen O'Hara (set decoration), for *Alice in Wonderland*. Nominations: Stuart Craig (art) and Stephenie McMillan (set), for *Harry Potter and the Deathly Hallows Part 1*; Guy Hendrix Dyas (art) and Larry Dias and Doug Mowat (set), for *Inception*; Eve Stewart (art) and Judy Farr (set), for *The King's Speech*; Jess Gonchor (art) and Nancy Haigh (set), for *True Grit*.

▶▶ **Best Costume Design:** Colleen Atwood, for *Alice in Wonderland*. Nominations: Antonella Cannarozzi, for *I Am Love*; Jenny Beavan, for *The King's Speech*; Sandy Powell, for *The Tempest*; Mary Zophres, for *True Grit*.

▶▶ **Best Sound Editing:** Richard King, for *Inception*. Nominations: Tom Myers and Michael Silvers, for *Toy Story 3*; Gwendolyn Yates Whittle and Addison Teague, for *Tron: Legacy*; Skip Lievsay and Craig Berkey, for *True Grit*; Mark P Stoeckinger, for *Unstoppable*.

▶▶ **Best Sound Mixing:** Lora Hirschberg, Gary A Rizzo, and Ed Novick, for *Inception*. Nominations: Paul Hamblin, Martin Jensen and John Midgley, for *The King's Speech*; Jeffrey J Haboush, Greg P Russell, Scott

Above: Colin Firth and Helena Bonham Carter in *The King's Speech*.
Opposite: Asa Butterfield in *Hugo*.

Millan and William Sarokin, for *Salt*; Ren Klyce, David Parker, Michael Semanick and Mark Weingarten, for *The Social Network*; Skip Lievsay, Craig Berkey, Greg Orloff and Peter Kurland, for *True Grit*.

▶▶ **Best Make-Up:** Rick Baker and Dave Elsey, for *The Wolfman*. Nominations: Adrien Morot, for *Barney's Version*; Edouard F Henriques, Gregory Funk and Yolanda Toussieng, for *The Way Back*.

▶▶ **Best Visual Effects:** Paul Franklin, Chris Corbould, Andrew Lockley, and Peter Bebb, for *Inception*. Nominations: Ken Ralston, David Schaub, Carey Villegas, and Sean Phillips, for *Alice in Wonderland*; Tim Burke, John Richardson, Christian Manz, and Nicolas Aithadi, for *Harry Potter and the Deathly Hallows Part 1*; Michael Owens, Bryan Grill, Stephan Trojanski, and Joe Farrell, for *Hereafter*; Janek Sirrs, Ben Snow, Ged Wright, and Daniel Sudick, for *Iron Man 2*.

▶▶ **Best Animated Short Film:** *The Lost Thing*. Nominations: *Day & Night*; *The Gruffalo*; *Let's Pollute*; *Madagascar, a Journey Diary*.

Uggie the dog with Jean Dujardin in *The Artist*.

▶▶ **Best Live Action Short Film:** *God of Love*. Nominations: *The Confession*; *The Crush*; *Na Wewe*; *Wish 143*.

▶▶ **Best Animated Feature:** *Toy Story 3*. Nominations: *How to Train Your Dragon*; *The Illusionist*.

▶▶ **Best Documentary Feature:** *Inside Job*. Nominations: *Exit Through the Gift Shop*; *Gasland*; *Restrepo*; *Waste Land*.

▶▶ **Best Documentary Short:** *Strangers No More*. Nominations: *Killing in the Name*; *Poster Girl*; *Sun Come Up*; *The Warriors of Qiugang*.

▶▶ **Best Foreign-Language Film:** *In a Better World* (Denmark). Nominations: *Hors la Loi (Outside the Law)* (Algeria); *Incendies* (Canada); *Dogtooth* (Greece); *Biutiful* (Mexico).

▶▶ **Irving G Thalberg Memorial Award:** Francis Ford Coppola.

▶▶ **Academy Honorary Awards:** Kevin Brownlow, Jean-Luc Godard and Eli Wallach.

The 84th American Academy of Motion Picture Arts and Sciences Awards ('The Oscars') and Nominations for 2011
26 February 2012

▶▶ **Best Film:** *The Artist*. Nominations: *The Descendants*; *Extremely Loud and Incredibly Close*; *The Help*; *Hugo*; *Midnight in Paris*; *Moneyball*; *The Tree of Life*; *War Horse*.

▶▶ **Best Director:** Michel Hazanavicius, for *The Artist*. Nominations: Woody Allen, for *Midnight in Paris*; Terrence Malik, for *The Tree of Life*; Alexander Payne, for *The Descendants*; Martin Scorsese, for *Hugo*.

▶▶ **Best Actor:** Jean Dujardin, for *The Artist*. Nominations: Damian Bichir, for *A Better Life*; George Clooney, for *The Descendants*; Gary Oldman, for *Tinker Tailor Soldier Spy*; Brad Pitt, for *Moneyball*.

▶▶ **Best Actress:** Meryl Streep, for *The Iron Lady*. Nominations: Glenn Close, for *Albert Nobbs*; Viola Davis, for *The Help*; Rooney Mara, for *The Girl with the Dragon Tattoo*; Michelle Williams, for *My Week With Marilyn*.

▶▶ **Best Supporting Actor:** Christopher Plummer, for *Beginners*. Nominations: Kenneth Branagh, for *My Week With Marilyn*; Jonah Hill, for *Moneyball*; Nick Nolte, for *Warrior*; Max Von Sydow, for *Extremely Loud and Incredibly Close*.

▶▶ **Best Supporting Actress:** Octavia Spencer, for *The Help*. Nominations: Bérénice Bejo, for *The Artist*; Jessica Chastain, for *The Help*; Melissa McCarthy, for *Bridesmaids*; Janet McTeer, for *Albert Nobbs*.

▶▶ **Best Original Screenplay:** Woody Allen, for *Midnight in Paris*. Nominations: J C Chandor, for *Margin Call*; Asghar Farhadi, for *A Separation*; Michel Hazanavicius, for *The Artist*; Kristen Wiig and Annie Mumolo, for *Bridesmaids*.

▶▶ **Best Screenplay Adaptation:** Alexander Payne, Nat Faxon, and Jim Rash, for *The Descendants*. Nominations: John Logan, for *Hugo*; George Clooney, Grant Heslov and Beau Willimon, for *The Ides of March*; Steven Zaillian and Aaron Sorkin, for *Moneyball*; Bridget O'Connor and Peter Straughan, for *Tinker Tailor Soldier Spy*.

▶ **Best Cinematography**: Robert Richardson, for *Hugo*. Nominations: Guillaume Schiffman, for *The Artist*; Jeff Cronenweth, for *The Girl with the Dragon Tattoo*; Emmanuel Lubezki, for *The Tree of Life*; Janusz Kami ski, for *War Horse*.

▶ **Best Editing**: Angus Wall and Kirk Baxter, for *The Girl with the Dragon Tattoo*. Nominations: Anne-Sophie Bion and Michel Hazanavicius, for *The Artist*; Kevin Tent, for *The Descendants*; Thelma Schoonmaker, for *Hugo*; Christopher Tellefsen, for *Moneyball*.

▶ **Best Original Score**: Ludovic Bource, for *The Artist*. Nominations: Alberto Iglesias, for *Tinker Tailor Soldier Spy*; Howard Shore, for *Hugo*; John Williams, for *The Adventures of Tintin: The Secret of the Unicorn*; John Williams, for *War Horse*.

▶ **Best Original Song**: 'Man or Muppet', from *The Muppets*, by Bret McKenzie. Nomination: 'Real in Rio', from *Rio*, by Sérgio Mendes, Carlinhos Brown and Siedah Garrett.

▶ **Best Art Direction**: Dante Ferretti (art) and Francesca Lo Schiavo (set), for *Hugo*. Nominations: Laurence Bennett (art direction) and Robert Gould (set decoration), for *The Artist*; Stuart Craig (art) and Stephenie McMillan (set), for *Harry Potter and the Deathly Hallows Part 2*; Anne Seibel (art) and Hélène Dubreuil (set), for *Midnight in Paris*; Rick Carter (art) and Lee Sandales (set), for *War Horse*.

▶ **Best Costume Design**: Mark Bridges, for *The Artist*. Nominations: Lisy Christl, for *Anonymous*; Sandy Powell, for *Hugo*; Michael O'Connor, for *Jane Eyre*; Arianne Phillips, for *W.E.*

▶ **Best Sound Editing**: Eugene Gearty and Philip Stockton, for *Hugo*. Nominations: Lon Bender and Victor Ray Ennis, for *Drive*; Ren Klyce, for *The Girl with the Dragon Tattoo*; Erik Aadahl and Ethan Van der Ryn, for *Transformers: Dark of the Moon*; Richard Hymns and Gary Rydstrom, for *War Horse*.

▶ **Best Sound Mixing**: Tom Fleischman and John Midgley, for *Hugo*. Nominations: David Parker, Michael Semanick, Ren Klyce and Bo Persson, for *The Girl with the Dragon Tattoo*; Deb Adair, Ron Bochar, Dave Giammarco and Ed Novick, for *Moneyball*; Greg P Russell, Gary Summers, Jeffrey J Haboush and Peter J Devlin, for *Transformers: Dark of the Moon*; Gary Rydstrom, Andy Nelson, Tom Johnson and Stuart Wilson, for *War Horse*.

▶ **Best Make-Up**: Mark Coulier and J Roy Helland, for *The Iron Lady*. Nominations: Martial Corneville, Lynn Johnson and Matthew W Mungle, for *Albert Nobbs*; Nick Dudman, Amanda Knight and Lisa Tomblin, for *Harry Potter and the Deathly Hallows Part 2*.

▶ **Best Visual Effects**: Rob Legato, Joss Williams, Ben Grossmann and Alex Henning, for *Hugo*. Nominations: Tim Burke, David Vickery, Greg Butler and John Richardson, for *Harry Potter and the Deathly Hallows Part 2*; Erik Nash, John Rosengrant, Danny Gordon Taylor and Swen Gillberg, for *Real Steel*; Joe Letteri, Dan Lemmon, R Christopher White and Daniel Barrett, for *Rise of the Planet of the Apes*; Scott Farrar, Scott Benza, Matthew E Butler and John Frazier, for *Transformers: Dark of the Moon*.

▶ **Best Animated Short Film**: *The Fantastic Flying Books*

Leila Hatami in *A Separation*.

of Mr Morris Lessmore. Nominations: *Dimanche*; *La Luna*; *A Morning Stroll*; *Wild Life*.

▶ **Best Live Action Short Film**: *The Shore*. Nominations: *Pentecost*; *Raju*; *Time Freak*; *Tuba Atlantic*.

▶ **Best Animated Feature**: *Rango*. Nominations: *A Cat in Paris*; *Chico and Rita*; *Kung Fu Panda 2*; *Puss in Boots*.

▶ **Best Documentary Feature**: *Undefeated*. Nominations: *Hell and Back Again*; *If a Tree Falls: A Story of the Earth Liberation Front*; *Paradise Lost 3: Purgatory*; *Pina*.

▶ **Best Documentary Short**: *Saving Face*. Nominations: *The Barber of Birmingham: Foot Soldier of the Civil Rights Movement*; *God Is the Bigger Elvis*; *Incident in New Baghdad*; *The Tsunami and the Cherry Blossom*.

▶ **Best Foreign Language Film**: *A Separation* (Iran). Nominations: *Bullhead* (Belgium); *Footnote* (Israel); *In Darkness* (Poland); *Monsieur Lazhar* (Canada).

▶ **Jean Hersholt Humanitarian Award**: Oprah Winfrey.

▶ **Academy Honorary Awards**: James Earl Jones and Dick Smith.

Italian convicts rehearse Shakespeare in *Caesar Must Die* (*Cesare deve morire*).

The 62nd Berlin International Film Festival
9-19 February 2012

▶ **Golden Bear for Best Film**: *Caesar Must Die* (Italy), by Paolo and Vittorio Taviani.
▶ **Silver Bear, Jury Grand Prix**: *Just the Wind* (Hungary/Germany/France), by Benedek Fliegauf.
▶ **Silver Bear, Best Director**: Christian Petzold, for *Barbara* (Germany).
▶ **Silver Bear, Best Actress**: Rachel Mwanza, for *War Witch* (Canada).
▶ **Silver Bear, Best Actor**: Mikkel Følsgaard, for *A Royal Affair* (Denmark/Czech Republic/Germany/Sweden).
▶ **Silver Bear for Outstanding Artistic Achievement**: Lutz Reitemeier for the photography in *White Deer Plain* (China).
▶ **Best Screenplay**: Nikolaj Arcel and Rasmus Heisterberg, for *A Royal Affair*.
▶ **Alfred Bauer Prize for a work of particular innovation**: *Tabu* (Portugal/Germany/Brazil/France), by Miguel Gomes.
▶ **Special Award – Silver Bear**: *Sister* (Switzerland/France), by Ursula Meier.
▶ **Honorary Golden Bear**: Meryl Streep.

◆ **FIPRESCI Prizes**
▶ **Competition**: *Tabu*, by Miguel Gomes.
▶ **Panorama**: *Atomic Age* (France), by Héléna Klotz.
▶ **Forum**: *Hemel* (The Netherlands/Spain), by Sacha Polak.
▶ **Golden Bear for Best Short Film**: *Rafa* (Portugal/France), by João Salaviza.

◆ **Jury**: *Mike Leigh* (president), *Anton Corbijn, Asghar Farhadi, Charlotte Gainsbourg, Jake Gyllenhaal, François Ozon, Boualem Sansal* and *Barbara Sukowa*.

The 2010 British Academy of Film and Television Arts Awards ('Baftas')
Royal Opera House, Covent Garden, London, 13 February 2011

▶ **Best Film**: *The King's Speech*.
▶ **Outstanding British Film**: *The King's Speech*.
▶ **Best Director**: David Fincher, for *The Social Network*.
▶ **Best Actor**: Colin Firth, for *The King's Speech*.
▶ **Best Actress**: Natalie Portman, for *Black Swan*.
▶ **Best Supporting Actor**: Geoffrey Rush, for *The King's Speech*.
▶ **Best Supporting Actress**: Helena Bonham Carter, for *The King's Speech*.
▶ **Best Original Screenplay**: David Seidler, for *The King's Speech*.
▶ **Best Adapted Screenplay**: Aaron Sorkin, for *The Social Network*.
▶ **Best Cinematography**: Roger Deakins, for *True Grit*.
▶ **Best Production Design**: Guy Hendrix Dyas, Larry Dias and Doug Mowat, for *Inception*.
▶ **Best Editing**: Angus Wall and Kirk Baxter, for *The Social Network*.
▶ **Best Music**: Alexandre Desplat, for *The King's Speech*.
▶ **Best Costumes**: Colleen Atwood, for *Alice in Wonderland*.
▶ **Best Sound**: Richard King, Lora Hirschberg, Gary A Rizzo and Ed Novick, for *Inception*.
▶ **Best Special Visual Effects**: Chris Corbould, Paul Franklin, Andrew Lockley and Peter Bebb, for *Inception*.
▶ **Best Make-Up/Hair**: Valli O'Reilly and Paul Gooch, for *Alice in Wonderland*.
▶ **Best Non-English Language Film**: *The Girl with the Dragon Tattoo* (Sweden).
▶ **Best Short Film**: *Until the River Runs Red*, by Paul Wright and Poss Kondeatis.

▶ **Best Animated Film**: *Toy Story 3*.
▶ **Best Short Animated Film**: *The Eagleman Stag*, by Michael Please.
▶ **Most Promising Newcomer**: Chris Morris, writer-director of *Four Lions*.
▶ **The Orange Rising Star Award**: Tom Hardy.
▶ **BAFTA Fellowship**: Christopher Lee.
▶ **Outstanding British Contribution to Cinema**: the *Harry Potter* film series.

The 2011 British Academy of Film and Television Arts Awards ('Baftas')
Royal Opera House, Covent Garden, London, 12 February 2012

▶ **Best Film**: *The Artist*.
▶ **Outstanding British Film**: *Tinker Tailor Soldier Spy*.
▶ **Best Director**: Michel Hazanavicius, for *The Artist*.
▶ **Best Actor**: Jean Dujardin, for *The Artist*.
▶ **Best Actress**: Meryl Streep, for *The Iron Lady*.
▶ **Best Supporting Actor**: Christopher Plummer, for *Beginners*.
▶ **Best Supporting Actress**: Octavia Spencer, for *The Help*.
▶ **Best Original Screenplay**: *The Artist*, by Michel Hazanavicius.
▶ **Best Adapted Screenplay**: *Tinker Tailor Soldier Spy*, by Bridget O'Connor and Peter Straughan.
▶ **Best Cinematography**: Guillaume Schiffman, for *The Artist*.
▶ **Best Production Design**: Dante Ferretti and and Francesca Lo Schiavo, for *Hugo*.
▶ **Best Editing**: Gregers Sall and Chris King, for *Senna*.
▶ **Best Music**: Ludovic Bource, for *The Artist*.
▶ **Best Costumes**: Mark Bridges, for *The Artist*.
▶ **Best Sound**: Philip Stockton, Eugene Gearty, Tom Fleischman and John Midgley, for *Hugo*.

▶ **Best Special Visual Effects**: Tim Burke, John Richardson, Greg Butler and David Vickery, for *Harry Potter and the Deathly Hallows Part 2*.
▶ **Best Make-Up/Hair**: Mark Coulier, J Roy Helland and Marese Langan, for *The Iron Lady*.
▶ **Best Non-English Language Film**: *The Skin I Live In* (Spain).
▶ **Best Short Film**: *Pitch Black Heist*, by John Maclean.
▶ **Best Animated Film**: *Rango*.
▶ **Best Short Animated Film**: *A Morning Stroll*, by Grant Orchard and Sue Goffe.
▶ **Most Promising Newcomer**: Paddy Considine, director of *Tyrannosaur*.
▶ **The Orange Rising Star Award**: Adam Deacon.
▶ **BAFTA Fellowship**: Martin Scorsese.
▶ **Outstanding British Contribution to Cinema**: John Hurt.

The 63rd Cannes Film Festival Awards
12-23 May 2010

▶ **Palme d'Or (Golden Palm)**: *Uncle Boonmee Who Can Recall His Past Lives* (Thailand), directed by Apichatpong Weerasethakul.
▶ **Grand Prix du Jury**: *Of Gods and Men* (France), by Xavier Beauvois.
▶ **Jury Prize**: *A Screaming Man* (France), by Mahamat-Saleh Haroun.
▶ **Camera d'Or** (first-time filmmaker): Michael Rowe, for *Año Bisiesto* (Mexico) .
▶ **Best Actor**: Javier Bardem, for *Biutiful* (Mexico); and Elio Germano, for *Our Life* (Italy).
▶ **Best Actress**: Juliette Binoche, for *Certified Copy* (France).
▶ **Best Director**: Mathieu Amalric, for *On Tour* (France).
▶ **Best Screenplay**: Lee Chang-dong, for *Poetry* (South Korea).

Daniel Radcliffe and company in *Harry Potter and the Deathly Hallows*.

▸▸ **Un Certain Regard Prize**: *Hahaha* (South Korea), by Hong Sang-soo.
▸▸ **Special Jury Prize**: *October* (Peru), by Daniel Vega and Diego Vega.
▸▸ **Palme d'Or – Short Film**: *Chienne D'histoire (Barking Island)* (France), by Serge Avédikian.
▸▸ **Jury Prize – Short Film**: *Micky Bader (Bathing Micky)* (Sweden), by Frida Kempff.

❯ **Jury:** *Tim Burton* (president), *Kate Beckinsale, Emmanuel Carrère, Benicio del Toro, Alexandre Desplat, Víctor Erice, Shekhar Kapur* and *Giovanna Mezzogiorno.*

The 64th Cannes Film Festival Awards
11-22 May 2011

▸▸ **Palme d'Or (Golden Palm)**: *The Tree of Life* (USA), directed by Terrence Malick.
▸▸ **Grand Prix du Jury**: *Once Upon A Time in Anatolia* (Turkey), by Nuri Bilge. Ceylan; *The Kid with a Bike* (Belgium), by Jean-Pierre Dardenne and Luc Dardenne
▸▸ **Jury Prize**: *Polisse* (France), by Maïwenn.
▸▸ **Camera d'Or** (first-time filmmaker): Pablo Giorgelli, for *Las Acacias* (Argentina/Spain) (Critics' Week) .
▸▸ **Best Actor**: Jean Dujardin, for *The Artist* (France).
▸▸ **Best Actress**: Kirsten Dunst, for *Melancholia* (Denmark/Sweden/France/Germany).
▸▸ **Best Director**: Nicolas Winding Refn, for *Drive* (USA).
▸▸ **Best Screenplay**: Joseph Cedar, for *Footnote* (Israel).
▸▸ **Un Certain Regard Prize**: *Arirang* (South Korea), by Kim Ki-Duk; *Halt auf freier Strecke (Stopped on Track)* (Germany), by Andreas Dresen.
▸▸ **Special Jury Prize**: *Elena* (Russia), by Andrey Zvyaginstev.

Jessica Chastain in *The Tree of Life*.

▸▸ **Best Director**: Mohammad Rasoulof , for *Bé omid é didar* (*Good Bye*) (Iran).
▸▸ **Palme d'Or – Short Film**: *Cross (Cross – Country)*, by Maryna Vroda (France/Ukraine).
▸▸ **Jury Prize – Short Film**: *Badpakje 46 (Swimsuit 46)* (Belgium), by Wannes Destoop.
▸▸ **Honorary Palme d'Or Award**: Bernardo Bertolucci.

❯ **Jury:** *Robert De Niro* (president), *Jude Law, Uma Thurman, Martina Gusmán, Nansun Shi, Linn Ullmann, Olivier Assayas, Mahamat-Saleh Haroun* and *Johnnie To.*

The 69th Hollywood Foreign Press Association ('Golden Globes') Awards
15 January 2012

▸▸ **Best Motion Picture – Drama**: *The Descendants.*
▸▸ **Best Motion Picture – Musical or Comedy**: *The Artist.*
▸▸ **Best Director**: Martin Scorsese, for *Hugo.*
▸▸ **Best Actor – Drama**: George Clooney, for *The Descendants.*
▸▸ **Best Actress – Drama**: Meryl Streep, for *The Iron Lady.*
▸▸ **Best Actor – Musical or Comedy**: Jean Dujardin, for *The Artist.*
▸▸ **Best Actress – Musical or Comedy**: Michelle Williams, for *My Week with Marilyn.*
▸▸ **Best Supporting Actor**: Christopher Plummer, for *Beginners.*
▸▸ **Best Supporting Actress**: Octavia Spencer, for *The Help.*
▸▸ **Best Foreign Language Film**: *A Separation* (Iran).
▸▸ **Best Animated Feature Film**: *The Adventures of Tintin: The Secret of the Unicorn.*
▸▸ **Best Screenplay**: Woody Allen, for *Midnight in Paris.*
▸▸ **Best Original Score**: Ludovic Bource, for *The Artist.*
▸▸ **Best Original Song**: 'Masterpiece,' music and lyrics by Madonna, Julie Frost and Jimmy Harry, from *W.E.*

The 32nd London Film Critics' Circle Awards 2011
BFI Southbank, London, 19 January 2012

▸▸ **Film of the Year**: *The Artist.*
▸▸ **British Film of the Year**: *We Need to Talk About Kevin.*
▸▸ **Foreign Language Film of the Year**: *A Separation* (Iran).
▸▸ **Documentary of the Year**: *Senna.*
▸▸ **Director of the Year**: Michael Hazanavicius, for *The Artist.*
▸▸ **Breakthrough British Film-Maker**: Andrew Haigh, for *Weekend.*
▸▸ **The Sky 3D Award for Technical Achievement**: Dante Ferretti, production designer on *Hugo.*
▸▸ **Actor of the Year**: Jean Dujardin, for *The Artist.*
▸▸ **Actress of the Year**: Anna Paquin for *Margaret* and Meryl Streep for *The Iron Lady* (tie).
▸▸ **British Actor of the Year**: Michael Fassbender, for *A Dangerous Method* and *Shame.*
▸▸ **British Actress of the Year**: Olivia Colman, for *The Iron Lady* and *Tyrannosaur.*
▸▸ **Supporting Actor of the Year**: Kenneth Branagh, for *My Week with Marilyn.*

Owen Wilson and Rachel McAdams in *Midnight in Paris*.

▷ **Supporting Actress of the Year**: Sareh Bayat, for *A Separation*.
▷ **Screenwriter of the Year**: Asghar Farhadi, for *A Separation*.
▷ **Young British Performer of the Year**: Craig Roberts, for *Submarine*.
▷ **Dilys Powell Award for Excellence in Film**: Nicolas Roeg.

68th Venice International Film Festival
31 August-10 September, 2011

▷ **Golden Lion for Best Film**: *Faust*, by Aleksander Sokurov (Russia).
▷ **Silver Lion for Best Director**: Shangjun Cai, for *Ren Shan Ren Hai* (China/Hong Kong).
▷ **Special Jury Prize**: *Terraferma*, by Emanuele Crialese (Italy).
▷ **Coppa Volpi for Best Actor**: Michael Fassbender, for *Shame* (UK).
▷ **Coppa Volpi for Best Actress**: Deanie Yip, for *Tao jie* (*A Simple Life*) (China/Hong Kong).
▷ **Marcello Mastroianni Award for Best New Young Actor or Actress**: Shôta Sometani and Fumi Nikaidô, for *Himizu* (Japan).
▷ **Osella for the Best Cinematography**: Robbie Ryan, for *Wuthering Heights* (UK).
▷ **Osella for Best Screenplay**: Yorgos Lanthimos and Efthimis Filippou, for *Alpis* (*Alps*) (Greece).
▷ **Lion of the Future – 'Luigi De Laurentiis' Venice Award**

for a Debut Film: *Là-bas*, by Guido Lombardi (Italy).
▷ **Golden Lion for Lifetime Achievement**: Marco Bellocchio.
▷ **Jaeger-LeCoultre Glory to the Filmmaker Award**: Al Pacino.
▷ **Persol 3D Award for the Most Creative Stereoscopic Film (or Filmmakers) of the Year**: Zapruder Filmmakers Group (David Zamagni, Nadia Ranocchi, and Monaldo Moretti).
▷ **L'Oréal Paris Award for Cinema**: Nicole Grimaudo.

⊙ The Orizzonti section of the festival highlights the newest trends in world cinema:
▷ **Orizzonti Award** (full-length films): *Kotoko*, by Shinya Tsukamoto (Japan).
▷ **Special Orizzonti Jury Prize** (full-length films): *Whores' Glory*, by Michael Glawogger (Austria, Germany).
▷ **Orizzonti Award** (medium-length films): *Accidentes Gloriosos*, by Mauro Andrizzi and Marcus Lindeen (Sweden, Denmark, Germany).
▷ **Orizzonti Award** (short films): *In attesa dell'avvento*, by Felice D'Agostino and Arturo Lavorato (Italy).
▷ **Special Mentions**: *O Le Tulafale* (*The Orator*), by Tusi Tamasese (New Zealand/Samoa); *All The Lines Flow Out*, by Charles Lim Yi Yong (Singapore).
▷ **Controcampo Award** (for narrative feature-length films): *Scialla!*, by Francesco Bruni.
▷ **Controcampo Award** (for short films): *A Chjana*, by Jonas Carpignano.
▷ **Controcampo Doc Award** (for documentaries): *Pugni chiusi*, by Fiorella Infascelli.

2011 (Subtitled)

Mansel Stimpson surveys the foreign language releases of the year.

This is a year which has been notable for its surprises in the sphere of foreign language films, the biggest of all being the worldwide success of Michel Hazanavicius' film *The Artist*. That triumph doubtless owed much to Harvey Weinstein, who took up the movie and promoted it with such skill that it dominated both the BAFTAs here and the Oscars in America.

Being a silent film in which the only dialogue heard – and that very briefly – is in English, it has to be admitted that strictly speaking it does not count as a foreign language picture. Even so, the fact remains that *The Artist* is a work of European cinema, a French-Belgian co-production starring French actor Jean Dujardin (BAFTA's and Oscar's Best Actor) and the delightful Bérénice Bejo. Although it was clearly a labour of love, the film did not, I have to say, win me over to the degree that I had expected (largely because I found it ill-judged in its take on the tragic love story of *A Star is Born*), but within these pages you will find a review of it by Michael Darvell which sides with the more positive view of the majority.

But the surprises provided by 2011's foreign films extended far beyond *The Artist*. I would never have guessed in advance that the best subtitled films of the year would in my eyes be *Incendies*, *13 Assassins*, *A Screaming Man* and Nicolas Philibert's *Nénette*, the follow-up to his popular documentary *Être et Avoir*. Although the earlier film had evidenced Philibert's mastery, it appeared unlikely that the seemingly limited subject matter of *Nénette* would yield so much, being a study of an orang-utan in the menagerie of the Jardin des Plantes in Paris. Admittedly, not everyone will like it since this film is unique in inviting the audience to meditate on what they see and hear – in a sense you create your own film.

If the powerful impact of Denis Villeneuve's drama *Incendies* was no less unexpected, that was because what I had seen of his earlier work had left me unprepared for a film which would resonate so profoundly. Similarly the violence so emphatically present in many films by Japan's Miike Takashi hardly suggested a director capable of recapturing the classic qualities of the best samurai movies, yet his *13 Assassins* did just that. As for Mahamat-Saleh Haroun from Chad, his earlier works such as *Abouna* and *Daratt* had invited respect but were weakened by plot contrivances: yet no such flaws appeared in his masterpiece *A Screaming Man*. Its story, centred on a father and son, spoke volumes about life in Chad today but in terms that were universally relevant.

However, when it comes to foreign films with wide appeal one finds that French cinema is way out in front. An obvious example is François Ozon's comedy *Potiche*, offering the star attraction of reuniting Catherine Deneuve and Gérard Depardieu, while Daniel Auteuil stepped into Marcel Pagnol territory as director and writer as well as star with *The Well Digger's Daughter*. Previously filmed by Pagnol himself as *La Fille du puisatier* in 1941, this should have pleased that wide audience who loved *Jean de Florette* and *Manon des sources* but sadly received a rather limited release. That too was the fate of Mona Achache's congenial film *The Hedgehog*. More widely shown was the ensemble piece *Little White Lies* and so too was *Beautiful Lies*, although the latter was mainly for those (and there are many of them) for whom Audrey Tautou can do no wrong.

Meanwhile, those with a sweet tooth will have welcomed *Romantics Anonymous* and for sheer fun there was Luc Besson's engaging fantasy *The Extraordinary Adventures of Adèle Blanc-Sec*. Popular French cinema of a rather different kind was represented by the adroit thriller *Point Blank – À bout portant*, but I was less taken by the Douglas Kennedy adaptation *The Big Picture*.

Opposite: Youssouf Djaoro in Mahamat-Saleh Haroun's masterpiece *A Screaming Man*.

Below: Daniel Auteuil and Astrid Bergès-Frisbey in Auteuil's Pagnol adaptation *The Well Digger's Daughter*.

Mathias Domahidy in *Film Socialisme*, a film for Jean-Luc Godard completists only.

If that suffered from memories of Chabrol's *La Femme infidèle*, Bertrand Tavernier's period drama *The Princess of Montpensier* faded beside memories of Rohmer's *The Lady and the Duke*.

Wide-ranging as the above sounds, French cinema had even more to offer in 2011. *Two in the Wave* was a documentary looking at the links between Truffaut and Godard, while Godard himself, still functioning in his eighties, came up with the uncompromising *Film Socialisme* (which is to say that it is only for the out-and-out admirers of this challenging artist). Echoing earlier Godard was Xavier Dolan's *Heartbeats*, which primarily appealed to an audience of about the same age as the 21-year-old filmmaker. Meanwhile, that idiosyncratic team Benoît Delépine and Gustave Kervern came up with two films, *Mammuth* and *Louise-Michel*: here too there will be a warm welcome from those who embrace their work while others will be left cold.

An actress of exceptional promise: Clara Augarde in *Love Like Poison.*

Far more pleasing to me were two works by female directors: Stéphane Brizé's sensitive love story *Mademoiselle Chambon* and Celine Sciamma's equally sensitive *Tomboy*, dealing with a pre-pubescent girl drawn to passing herself off as a boy. I found Katell Quillévéré's *Love Like Poison* even less clear than *Tomboy* over what it wanted to say about emerging sexuality, but it introduced us to an actress of exceptional promise in Clara Augarde. In addition there were four films looking at historical events of the last century. Christian Carion's *Farewell* (or *L'Affaire Farewell*) was a tale of spying set in the 1980s while two titles dealt with France's involvement in the sending of Jews to the concentration camps in 1942. Of these two I preferred *The Round Up* to *Sarah's Key* (the latter more widely seen because it starred Kristin Scott Thomas), but all three of these titles were marred by introducing fictional improbabilities into their treatment of incidents from history. It was not that which made me uneasy over *Outside the Law*, Rachid Bouchareb's study of the fight for Algerian independence, but the absence of that sense of humanity usually so strong in this director's work.

Looking at other countries one finds that none could match the number of films that reached us from France (in which context I should make it clear that these days the majority of foreign movies are co-productions involving more than one country, but I am here concentrating on whatever country seems crucial to the work). Nevertheless several countries came up with at least two or three titles. Italy fielded three pieces by established directors: Nanni Moretti's *We Have a Pope* (notable for the performance by the veteran Michel Piccoli), Gianni Di Gregorio's *The*

Salt of Life and Michele Placido's *Angels of Evil*. Spain, however, provided four titles: I will reserve one of them for mention in my final paragraph, but the other three were Almodóvar's *The Skin I Live In* and two works by lesser known directors, Daniel Monzón's *Cell 211* and *Julia's Eyes* from Guillem Morales. Portugal came up with two films (Eugène Green's *The Portuguese Nun* and Raúl Ruiz's feature swan song *Mysteries of Lisbon*), as did Germany with the thriller *The Silence* and Wim Wenders' documentary tribute to Pina Bausch, entitled simply *Pina*.

There were also two titles from Norway which were well received, *Troll Hunter* and *Oslo, August 31st*. Denmark offered three titles of which a couple were much discussed, *Melancholia* from Lars von Trier and the Oscar winner *In a Better World* from Susanne Bier. *R: Hit First Hit Hardest* received rather less attention. Poland's Jerzy Skolimowski returned with *Essential Killing* and there were also films from Greece (*Attenberg*), the Czech Republic (Svankmajer's *Surviving Life*), Turkey (*Men on the Bridge*), Russia (*How I Ended This Summer*), Uruguay (*The Silent House*) and Kyrgyzstan (*The Light Thief*). Look elsewhere and contrasting views of life in Africa were to be found in *Life, Above All* and *Viva Riva!* In *Son of Babylon* we had an insider's view of life in Iraq while it took an Irish filmmaker, Juanita Wilson, to confront the horrors of the Bosnian war in *As If I Am Not There*.

Films that reached us from the Far East included *Sparrow* and *Revenge: A Love Story* from Hong Kong, the animated film *Arrietty* from Japan's Studio Ghibli, the largely China-set *Snow Flower and the Secret Fan*, made in association with 20th Century Fox, and the Japanese tale *Norwegian Wood*, filmed in that country with a Japanese cast by Tran Anh Hung. As for South

America, we had *Miss Bala* and *Abel* from Mexico, *Post Mortem* from Chile and the minimalistic *Las Acacias* which charted a road journey from Paraguay to Buenos Aires.

To conclude this wide-ranging if not exhaustive round-up, I turn to three notable films not yet mentioned. One of these, *A Separation* from Iran, was far from featuring in my own list of favourites, but it won countless awards culminating in the Oscar for Best Foreign Language Film and was greatly and widely admired. It certainly gave one insights into life in that country and established Asghar Farhadi as a quintessentially Iranian filmmaker yet one whose work was distinct in character from that of his distinguished compatriots.

Personally I was more impressed by the other two titles which came close to joining my four favourites listed earlier. Alejandro González Iñárritu's *Biutiful* was an immensely powerful piece set in Barcelona and in it the great Javier Bardem gave his best performance to date. As for *Poetry*, this extraordinary work from Korea introduced me to the work of director Lee Chang-Dong. I was enthralled by its wide-ranging tale, which dealt in moral issues linked both to social comment and to attitudes to life touching on art and religion. Furthermore, its elderly lead actress Yoon Jung-Hee was quite outstanding. Surprises like this sustain one's faith in the possibilities of cinema.

Left: Javier Bardem gave his best performance yet in *Biutiful*.

Below: Yoon Jung-Hee shone in the remarkable Korean film *Poetry*.

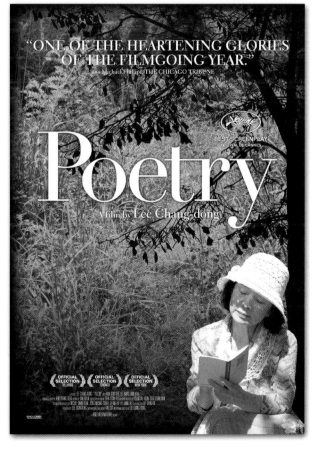

Risen from the Grave

*With the British Horror Revival hitting its tenth birthday, **Jonathan Rigby** takes a look at some of its highs and lows.*

Bring me the head of (horror novelist) Shaun Hutson: Marysia Kay in *Forest of the Damned*.

Something extraordinary happened in 2002. A corpse whose last really noticeable galvanic twitch had occurred in 1987 sprang suddenly into a garish and adrenalin-fuelled afterlife. The corpse was that of the British horror film, the previous twitch had been Clive Barker's sadomasochist fever-dream *Hellraiser*, and the new blood flowed in copious quantities from such 2002 releases as *Dog Soldiers*, *My Little Eye* and *28 Days Later*.

Formerly the jewel in the UK's exploitation crown, at the turn of the 21st century British horror had been in cold storage for something like 25 years, with occasional 1980s titles like *Lifeforce*, *Gothic*, *Dream Demon* and even *Hellraiser* failing to give rise to any kind of consistent revival. (All but one of *Hellraiser*'s numerous sequels were American productions.) "In this country," lamented *Gothic* screenwriter Stephen Volk in 1993, "the film establishment is so intellectually pompous that they wouldn't admit to watching Gothic horror, let alone commissioning it. It's sad. It's one of the few cultural exclusives we could really exploit. But it's so hard to get anybody interested."

When the resurrection came, it was a slow process that originated with a small but powerful item called *Urban Ghost Story*, shot for less than £250,000 in the summer of 1997. The release of Genevieve Jolliffe's film was delayed until 2001, but in the process it became a kind of curtain-raiser for the flood of features that appeared in 2002.

Of these titles, Neil Marshall's *Dog Soldiers* was an exuberant 'squaddies versus werewolves' siege drama set in darkest Scotland (though filmed in Petite-Suisse), with a canny eye on the burgeoning lad's mag demographic. Marc Evans' *My Little Eye* had queasy fun with Reality TV and the rise of the internet, though it played safe by setting the action in a kind of Nova Scotian no-man's-land. And the rough-and-ready DV ferocity of Danny Boyle's *28 Days Later* succeeded in initiating a new vogue (still on-going) for zombie pictures, despite the fact that Boyle's zombies are actually fleet-footed victims of a terrifying 'rage' virus. Other 2002 releases included damp squibs like *Long Time Dead*, *Revelation*, *The Bunker*, *Deathwatch* and the long-delayed *Lighthouse*, while several films that should have come out that year – notably *The Gathering* and *Doctor Sleep* – had to wait for exposure via DVD.

The worldwide success of *28 Days Later*, in particular, ensured that Volk's heartfelt plaint was quickly to become outdated. The revival was assisted to a considerable degree by the availability of inexpensive new formats, which revolutionised independent filmmakers' chances of getting their pictures into production – and made a genre that was traditionally cheap to make cheaper still. The result was an explosion of activity that seemed undaunted by the baleful statistic that a staggering 77 per cent of British films were being routinely shelved, pretty much unseen by anyone.

So, for every fringe success like Johannes Roberts' 'sabre-toothed nudie-cuties' flick *Forest of the Damned*, there was a truckload of unreleased material like Andrew Parkinson's 'Cronenberg in Cromer' curio *Venus Drowning*. (Both films, incidentally, were made in 2004.) But as more and more provincial zombies swarmed forth with no realistic prospect of anyone ever seeing them, hope was kept alive by the freak visibility of oddities like *Colin*, a 'zombie's eye view' apocalypse supposedly made for just 45 quid.

Even so, the tally of new British horrors given cinema releases up to 2010 reached an impressive 40-plus. Early on, Random Harvest sprang a leak with a genre offshoot called Four Horsemen Films, which in 2002 produced a couple of copper-bottomed clinkers (*Octane* and *LD50*) prior to being discontinued. But 2003 saw the production, not only of interesting curiosities like Robert Pratten's *London Voodoo* and Paolo Sedazzari's *The Toybox*, but also Edgar Wright's splendid horror-comic *Shaun of the Dead*. As well as transcending *28 Days Later* in its deft translation of an apparently American sub-genre into a parochial British idiom, Wright's film also proved a sizable international hit.

Also produced in 2003, the Cornwall cop-horror *Cold & Dark* ranks high among the very worst products of the revival. Let's get the others out of the way right now. In the 'approach at your peril' section, and all dating from 2003 to 2010, are such films as *The Witches Hammer* (sic; pathetic *Blade*-style vampire hi-jinks), *Spirit Trap* (Billie Piper and other vacuous teens), *The Dark* (Sean Bean and psychotic sheep), *Puffball* (Irish witchery directed by, sad to say, Nicolas Roeg), *The Sickhouse* (plague doctor still present in Ludgate orphanage), *Credo* (worst false beard in film history), *Reverb* (ghostly voice in ageing record grooves), *Donkey Punch* (nauseatingly meretricious sex drama set on the high seas), and *Psychosis*, a hackneyed retread of the 'is she seeing things or isn't she?' plot.

In addition, the revived Ealing signed its name to the seriously awful *Dorian Gray* and *Burke & Hare*, while *Lesbian Vampire Killers* and several similar horror-comedies made critics wish that their distinguished progenitor – *Shaun of the Dead* – had never existed. There were also painfully threadbare items like *Messages*, *The Spell*, *Basement* and *The Scar Crow*, while Robin Hardy – nearly 40 years after *The Wicker Man* – came up with a fully fledged car crash called *The Wicker Tree*.

After 2002, the next big year for British horror was 2005, which began with a somewhat belated release for the Charing Cross tube shocker *Creep*, a glossy restatement of situations already immortalised in the 1972 classic *Death Line*. The director was Christopher Smith, who became something of a specialist via two other Anglo-German co-productions (*Severance*, 2005; *Black Death*, 2009), interleaving them with the Anglo-Australian *Triangle* (2008). Other 2005 releases included *Snuff*, *The Last Horror Movie* and *The League of Gentlemen's Apocalypse*, all of which were overshadowed by *The Descent*. In this, Neil Marshall progressed from the laddish *Dog Soldiers* to an all-female encounter with hideous troglodyte 'Crawlers' in the Appalachian mountains. The result was so powerful it earned Marshall the back-handed compliment "the Caravaggio of the B-movie" from *Time* magazine. Indeed, he has yet to match it, never mind top it.

Among this slew of horrors, various motifs began to identify themselves, motifs that played on specifically millennial fears. Several films, for example, focused on topical anxieties surrounding animal rights, BSE epidemics and genetic experimentation. The first was common to *28 Days Later*, *Ghost Rig* and *LD50*, while Mad Cow and related diseases were referenced in *Dead Creatures*, *Dead Meat* and *Wild Country*. The best of these films by far was Billy O'Brien's exceptional *Isolation* (2005), a grimly effective Anglo-Irish co-production that cleverly updated the vivisected mutants of *The Island of Doctor Moreau* to a downtrodden farm in County Wicklow.

Harking back to *Deliverance* and *Straw Dogs*, a further recurrent theme was the 'outward bound' sub-genre, which in 2005 yielded the brutal *Wilderness* and skittish *Severance* to match US contemporaries like *Hostel* and *Turistas*. Offering city types a persuasive argument that

Sean Pertwee becomes dog food in *Wilderness*.

The wasteland: Sandra Louise Douglas in the 2008 film *The Dead Outside.*

visiting the country – or, indeed, other countries – is inadvisable, further examples of the type included (deep breath) *Gnaw, Doghouse, Small Town Folk, Backwoods, Dark Nature, Dead Wood, Don't Let Him In, The Fallow Field, The Reeds, Inbred* and *The Hike.*

This sub-genre frequently brought with it another recurring image, that of people being reduced to the inhuman level of their tormentors, a motif at least as old as the words uttered in 1963 by Olivia de Havilland, of all people, in the bizarre 'home invasion' shocker *Lady in a Cage*: "Stone Age, here I come!" Amid Britain's 21st century horrors, the 'reversion to savagery' routine was played out by Cillian Murphy in *28 Days Later*, Andy Serkis in *Deathwatch*, Shauna MacDonald in *The Descent*, Toby Kebbell in *Wilderness*, Laura Harris in *Severance*, Jaime Winstone in *Donkey Punch*, Kelly Reilly in *Eden Lake*, Olga Fedori in *Mum & Dad*, Holly Weston in *Splintered* and Neve McIntosh in *Salvage* – by which time it seemed like a motif in urgent need of retirement.

The breakdown of individuals was frequently mirrored by apocalyptic images of the breakdown of society in general, of which you could get your fill in films like *28 Weeks Later* (the Anglo-Spanish sequel), *The Dead Outside* and the aforementioned *Salvage*. The latter brought societal meltdown to the Merseyside estate familiar from the discontinued soap *Brookside*. Another notable sub-genre took the affordable new formats that enabled the films to be made in the first place and, like *The Blair Witch Project*, made them central to the action. Mock-documentary efforts

included *The Last Horror Movie, Vampire Diary, The Devil's Music, The Tapes, The Zombie Diaries* (which sired a sequel), *Resurrecting "The Street Walker"* and *The Torment.*

There was also a peculiar proliferation of doppelgänger dramas in which young women found themselves trapped in various forms of alternate-reality limbo. The strain was prefigured by the 2003 art-house titles *Kiss of Life* and *Frozen*, after which the stranded female leads ranged from Maria Bello in *The Dark* and Thora Birch in *Dark Corners* to Melissa George in *Triangle* and Lena Headey in *The Brøken* (a disguised remake of *The Man Who Haunted Himself*). Male variants on the theme included *Lie Still, The Deaths of Ian Stone, Mindflesh* and *The Devil's Chair.*

The most pervasive sub-set of 21st century British horror, however, was one that provided an ingenious antidote to the traditional preference of snobbish UK film critics for social realism over fantasy. The answer – obvious, really – was to cross-fertilise the two. Taking their tip from the Glaswegian grime of *Urban Ghost Story* (which in *Variety* had been dubbed "Ken Loach meets *The Exorcist*"), these films offered uniquely cheerless snapshots of Acton (*Dead Creatures*), Shoreditch (*Heartless*), Elephant and Castle (*The Disappeared*), Dalston (*Tony*), the bleak Edinburgh suburbs of Sighthill and Greendykes (*Outcast*) and, perhaps least edifying of all, the shit-smeared toilet bowls of Heathrow Airport (*Mum & Dad*).

So-called 'hoodie horror' also encompassed the inner-city settings of *Wishbaby, Demons Never Die* and *F*, while James Watkins' much-vaunted *Eden Lake* exploited contemporary fears of 'feral youth' with sufficient reactionary zeal to be hailed as a modern masterpiece in the *Daily Mail*. Much the best of these social-realist shockers were Johnny Kevorkian's *The Disappeared* (2007) and Colm McCarthy's *Outcast* (2009), which situated several ghosts and an immortal child killer (Kevorkian), plus Celtic sorcery and adolescent shape-shifting (McCarthy), against a forbidding backdrop of council estate Gothic.

2008 was another big year for Brit horror releases, ranging from the resurrected Nazis of *Outpost* to the demented Aleister Crowley sex farce *Chemical Wedding*. Also on offer were the killer kids of Tom Shankland's *The Children* and Paul Andrew Williams' under-rated horror-comedy *The Cottage*, which charmingly evoked such sub-Carry On extravaganzas as *What a Carve Up!* and *The Big Job*. (Substitute Kenneth Connor for Reece Shearsmith, Sid James for Andy Serkis, Barbara Windsor for Jennifer Ellison…) And in production that year were such impressive entries as the motorway-abduction horror *Hush* and the Clive Barker vignette *Book of Blood*, set, unusually, in up-scale Edinburgh.

A few more potential specialists were becoming identifiable by this stage, among them Black & Blue Films, which made the dreadful

Dead Cert and rather good *Devil's Playground* back-to-back in 2009, later producing the unclassifiable *Elfie Hopkins* and all-too-obvious *Strippers vs Werewolves* in 2011. Among individual filmmakers, writer-director Chris Crow followed the 'Essex lads up against mad Welshman' shocker *Devil's Bridge* (2009) with the much more assured and provocative *Panic Button* (2010), which proposes some very unpleasant consequences for the modern fixation on social networking.

Amid all this activity, the news that many horror fans had long desired but long since despaired of finally came through in May 2007. Britain's greatest horror specialists of all – Hammer Film Productions – were at last back in business, the company having been acquired by a European consortium and "aggressively reinvigorated" with a rumoured infusion of $50 million. The new management's initial aspirations struck horror fans as frustratingly low: *Beyond the Rave* (2007) was a potty-mouthed interactive web serial with vague echoes of *Dracula A.D. 1972*. But in 2008 Hammer backed the thoughtful Anglo-Irish chiller *Wake Wood*, then, in 2009, they shot *The Resident* and *Let Me In* in New Mexico. Despite featuring a Christopher Lee cameo, the first of these was nothing much. *Let Me In*, however, transcended a massive volley of internet sniping to reveal itself as an unusually accomplished remake of the Swedish hit *Let the Right One In*.

In the latter part of 2011, the opposite poles of British horror – ranging from social-realist grot to old-fashioned spectral chills – were handily encapsulated by *Kill List* and *The Awakening*. The first of these combined mutterings about Iraq and the economic recession with gloating violence and an implausible third-act shift into Satanist shenanigans, while *The Awakening* (scripted by Stephen Volk) infused granite-hued Cumbrian gloom into a classy 1920s ghost story. Sandwiched between these two was the bizarre horror-comic absurdity of *Kill Keith*, in which Keith Chegwin, 40 years after fleeing the massacres of Polanski's *Macbeth*, turned mass murderer himself.

Clearly, then, Britain's horror revival is a bona-fide boom by comparison to the miserable lows of the 1980s and '90s. (And, believe me, this brief round-up can only skim the surface of the literally hundreds and hundreds of 21st century horrors produced.) In terms of commercial and cultural impact, however, the new boom is on nothing like the scale achieved by British horror in the late 1950s. Between them, Hammer's *The Curse of Frankenstein* and *Dracula* triggered a worldwide resurrection of a previously moribund genre. Britain's new horrors, by contrast, are the beneficiaries of a millennial resurrection brought about elsewhere (specifically by the US films *The Sixth Sense* and *The Blair Witch Project*, together with a crop of fascinating Asian chillers). And the most successful British horrors of the 21st century's first decade – *28 Days Later, Shaun of the Dead* and *The Descent* – scored international grosses (of $83 million, $30 million and $57 million respectively) that, after adjustment for inflation, are well below the old Hammer level.

Appropriately then, it was the new Hammer that, early in 2012, scored a whopping $130 million (and counting) with *The Woman in Black*. Made in late 2010, James Watkins' film was well worth the wait for all involved. An expertly contrived gazetteer of every haunted house convention known to man, the film gave lurid new life to a story that had already done duty as a successful novel, stage play and TV film. It also proved something that youth-fixated film producers have resisted for a good 20 years or more – that audiences are more than willing to embrace a piece of high Gothic in which the characters wear frock coats and starched collars.

A sequel was announced in no time, of course, and Hammer simultaneously dropped hints that Professor Quatermass might be up for revival and even that blood-lusting overlord of British horror – Count Dracula. So, for all fans of the darker reaches of the Gothic imagination, the future looks paradoxically bright.

Atmospheric advertising for Hammer's money-spinning version of *The Woman in Black*.

Out of the Box

Television has for a long time fed British films with comedians and situation comedies. **Michael Darvell** *looks at how TV has kept cinema box-offices ringing.*

One of British cinema's unexpected successes in 2011 was *The Inbetweeners Movie*, based on the Channel 4 comedy series. It cost around £3.5 million to make but took over £13 million in its opening weekend and one month later had grossed over £41 million.

That's pretty good by anyone's reckoning, a return of 11 times the film's initial cost. Compare that to *Sex and the City* (2008), the film of the successful US television series, which did not recoup its production costs of $65 million until well after its opening weekend. Eventually it grossed $415 million worldwide, which is only between six and seven times its cost. Sadly, *Sex and the City 2* (2010), costing $100 million, took only a little over a third of that on its opening weekend and still hadn't recouped its costs some three months later.

The Inbetweeners Movie deserves its success because it is so good. The first *Sex and the City* movie also warranted success, but the sequel – removing the girls from their NYC comfort zone and sending them to Abu Dhabi – just didn't work. Admittedly, most TV spin-offs have to be opened out, allowing the familiar characters to leave home in order to flesh out the screenplay. *The Inbetweeners Movie* is no exception, with the four heroes heading off for Crete and all the fun they can find. This seems to work, perhaps because in the television series they were not

James Buckley, Blake Harrison, Joe Thomas and Simon Bird, stars of *The Inbetweeners Movie*.

in school all the time anyway, but going off somewhere to escape either their teachers or parents. It hasn't, however, always worked in TV transfers to the big screen, as we shall see.

Comedy performers have long been a staple diet of the film industry the world over. Way back it was the variety theatres in Britain and vaudeville in the US that provided the spotlight for budding film comics. On the home front just think of Will Hay, Tommy Handley, Max Miller, George Formby, Frank Randle, Arthur Askey, Tommy Trinder, Frankie Howerd, Ted Ray, Benny Hill, Bruce Forsyth, Charlie Drake, Arthur Haynes, Eric Sykes, Stanley Baxter, Bob Monkhouse and dear Old Mother Riley: all were products of the variety circuits or pubs and clubs of Britain, and it seemed to be a natural progression to feature them in films.

Later it was radio and television stars who were cast in film comedies. Many of the Carry On team started out that way; in fact, these and other stand-up comedians were usually put into films playing characters based on their own personalities. The classic example is Terry-Thomas, whose pioneering series *How Do You View?* (1949-53) inaugurated most of the conventions of TV comedy – and then propelled him into a dazzling film career.

Rarely did comedians incorporate their stage acts into films. One exception was Sid Field, who was adored on stage by the British public but did

not translate well to the screen. He made only three films before he died at the premature age of 45, and none of them was either a commercial or critical success. Field was allegedly Bob Hope's favourite comic but you had to watch him live to see him at his best.

Norman Wisdom started on stage as a clown and musician but eventually became known mostly for his slapstick comedy films. Even if some of them are hard to watch now, they were immensely popular when first released. Eric Morecambe and Ernie Wise worked together from 1941 but only progressed to films in the mid-1960s – and then disastrously so, because they needed a live audience to get their humour across. Their three films, *The Intelligence Men, That Riviera Touch* and *The Magnificent Two*, really were quite embarrassing to watch both then and now, considering Morecambe and Wise were for a long time the funniest and most popular men on British television.

What was it about Morecambe and Wise that dictated they should try films? Other duos – Little and Large, Hale and Pace – kept to TV and pantomime, although Cannon and Ball made one film, *The Boys in Blue* (1982), loosely based on the Will Hay classic *Ask a Policeman*. Sadly, it was the last feature film of writer-director Val Guest, the grand old man of British cinema whose prolific career covered all genres, including many comedies, most of which he also had a hand in co-writing.

Guest had worked with Will Hay in the 1930s, collaborating later with Arthur Askey, The Crazy Gang and Frankie Howerd. He also teamed up with the American husband-and-wife team Bebe Daniels and Ben Lyon when they moved to London with their popular radio show. He contributed to the film of *Hi Gang!* in 1941 and both co-wrote and directed the films based on the Lyons' BBC radio show, *Life with the Lyons* and *The Lyons in Paris*, in the mid-1950s.

Guest had earlier written for the film of *Band Waggon* (1940), a spin-off from the BBC radio

show with Arthur Askey and Richard Murdoch allegedly living on the roof of Broadcasting House in London. It was a sort of sitcom but the film version was mainly a vehicle for presenting musical acts such as Pat Kirkwood and Bruce Trent. *Life with the Lyons*, therefore, was the first fully fledged sitcom to come to the cinema from radio. It subsequently appeared briefly on television but did not repeat the success of the radio series, which ran from 1950 to 1961.

The Lyons spin-offs were made by Hammer Film Productions, who had previously made three films based on the dashing BBC radio character Dick Barton, the Light Programme's precursor to *The Archers*. Before they found their niche in horror films, Hammer were always willing to capitalise on successful radio or television programmes, also making films of the radio show *The Adventures of PC 49* and the BBC TV *Quatermass* serials.

Whack-O! was a radio and TV comedy series by Frank Muir and Denis Norden with Jimmy Edwards as a headmaster of dubious character; it made it to the cinema as *Bottoms Up!* in 1960. I can think of only one radio show that took the opposite course, coming to the wireless from cinema, and that was *Meet the Huggetts* (1952-61), the BBC radio situation comedy with Jack Warner and Kathleen Harrison that grew out of the films *Holiday Camp, Here Come the Huggetts, Vote for Huggett* and *The Huggetts Abroad*, made between 1947 and 1949.

It's mainly television that has supplied the cinema with many of its sitcom successes. The litany of titles made over the years, however, does not inspire confidence or indeed evoke the best in TV entertainment, popular though the shows were in their day. Remember Granada's *The Army Game* and *Nearest and Dearest*, or ATV's *The Larkins*, with Peggy Mount and David Kossoff, or *Please Sir!* and *On the Buses* (both from London Weekend Television), or *Bless This House*

Left: Before becoming a film star, Terry-Thomas was the mainstay of the innovative TV show *How Do You View?*

Above: Writer-director Val Guest celebrates Barbara Lyon's birthday with her brother Richard and parents Bebe Daniels and Ben Lyon on the set of *Life with the Lyons* (1954).

Above: The Sid James sitcom *Bless This House* became a feature film, with Terry Scott as guest star.

Right: The TV version of *Up Pompeii* (seen here, with Frankie Howerd and assorted handmaidens) was inevitably followed by a big screen adaptation.

Below: Granada's TV hit *The Army Game* gave rise to the feature film *I Only Arsked!* and this tie-in novelisation from 1959.

and *George and Mildred* (from Thames Television), or the BBC's *Are You Being Served?* They're none of them best remembered as the most subtle or witty of comedies, but in their time they all made it to the big screen.

In almost all of them, significantly, the cast has to go away from home. In *I Only Arsked!* (Hammer's 1959 adaptation of *The Army Game*), the squaddies are posted overseas. In *Inn for Trouble* (a spin-off from *The Larkins*, also from 1959) the family take over a pub. In *Please Sir!* (1971) the school kids go on a trip to an outdoor centre for two weeks. In *On the Buses* (1971) there are many more bus-driving exteriors than were possible in the TV version. In the first sequel, *Mutiny on the Buses* (1972), the team end up in Windsor Safari Park, while the second sequel, *Holiday on the Buses* (1973) has Reg Varney and Bob Grant and company going to a holiday camp in Wales. Like the *On the Buses* films, *Nearest and Dearest* (1972) was yet another Hammer project, with Hylda Baker and Jimmy Jewel as brother and sister running a pickle factory and – for the film – taking a holiday in Blackpool.

Admittedly, in *Bless This House* (1972) Sid James and Diana Coupland don't go very far – just out into the garden, in fact. Other sitcom spin-offs that don't go out and about include the film versions of *Love Thy Neighbour*, *Never Mind the Quality Feel the Width*, *Father Dear Father*, *For the Love of Ada* and *Man About the House*, all dating from the peak period of 1972-74. But for *George and Mildred* (1980) Brian Murphy and Yootha Joyce go off to a posh hotel to celebrate their wedding anniversary and get mixed up with a criminal

element. And in *Are You Being Served?* (1977) the staff of Grace Brothers store go on a trip to Spain – the Costa Plonka no less. And that about sums up the general level of humour in these spin-offs.

I have a theory that spin-off movies are only as good as their TV originals. Usually, even after 30 years or more, some of the television episodes are still just as funny as they ever were. A show such as *Dad's Army* (1968-77) never dates because it was always set in period, and it's still transmitted seemingly every week on BBC2. The film version (1971) went back to show how the motley crew of veterans was initially recruited and it retains all the appeal and fun of the original series. Similarly *Up Pompeii* (1971), with Frankie Howerd, is still very enjoyable; indeed, nothing has dated because many of the Carry On-style jokes were already ancient in the first place. As Lurcio, Howerd was in his element and the film spawned two follow-ups shortly afterwards. *Up the Chastity Belt* was set in medieval England and *Up the Front* in World War I, with Howerd playing virtually the same character, suitably renamed Lurkalot and plain Lurk respectively.

The Likely Lads (1976), a spin-off from the original BBC series and its sequel *Whatever Happened to the Likely Lads?*, saw the two Tyneside 'lads', Bob and Terry, now adult but still behaving like kids. In the film they organise a caravanning tour with their respective partners, but of course everything goes wrong. The film is still as funny (and sad) as it ever was. In the 1979 film version of *Porridge* (by *Likely Lads* writers Dick Clement and Ian La Frenais), Fletcher gets unwittingly involved in a jail break and then has to find a way of breaking back in to Slade prison before the governor notices. A good script and Ronnie Barker's classic performance keep this one freshly minted. Likewise *Rising Damp* (1980) makes for a good feature film mainly because of the performance of Leonard Rossiter as Rigsby and writer Eric Chappell's firm grasp on character and situation. It's just a pity that it doesn't have all the original cast members from the TV series, as Richard Beckinsale had died, aged 31, shortly after

making the *Porridge* spin-off. He was also, however, one half of Jack Rosenthal's sitcom *The Lovers*, with Paula Wilcox as his hesitant girlfriend. It was made into a pleasantly funny feature film in 1973.

The BBC series *Steptoe and Son* still raises a laugh whenever it is shown and it spawned two feature films, *Steptoe and Son* (1971) and *Steptoe and Son Ride Again* (1973). In the first Harold actually gets married, something that never happened in the TV series, but, with Steptoe Sr coming along on the honeymoon, matters of romance take a turn for the worse. The scripts by Ray Galton and Alan Simpson were some of the best comedy writing on television and translated well to film. Galton and Simpson also wrote the original *Hancock's Half Hour* radio and television series. *The Rebel*, the 1960 film they wrote for Tony Hancock, is a story about a budding painter that showcases the 'lad 'imself' but not his usual repertory company of Sid James, Bill Kerr, Kenneth Williams and Hattie Jacques. Even so, it works because the screenplay was carefully crafted to Hancock's individual talent.

Benny Hill was a great comic performer and mimic early in his career but, as his humour became broader, his style turned cruder, although he was always a huge TV star. *The Best of Benny Hill* (1981) is a compilation of his TV sketches transferred to film and not very well at that. Ten years earlier, when *Monty Python's Flying Circus* went from television to films, the team had sensibly re-shot some of their funniest sketches for *And Now for Something Completely Different* (1971). They then branched out into more original works such as *Monty Python and the Holy Grail* (1974), *Monty Python's Life of Brian* (1979) and *Monty Python's The Meaning of Life* (1983). Their mentors, The Goons, never made great films because their humour was essentially for radio only. The exception was the delightful short *The Case of the Mukkinese Battlehorn* (1956), a spoof of the Edgar Lustgarten school of Scotland Yard filmmaking.

Recent additions to the genre of TV spin-off movies include *Kevin and Perry Go Large* (2000), with Harry Enfield and Kathy Burke repeating their teenage roles as disaffected youths. It's really only for their closest fans and yes, of course, they go off to Ibiza. Other double-acts have tried to go from telly to film, such as James

Corden and Mathew Horne, of the *Horne & Corden* series, but *Lesbian Vampire Killers* (2009) was not a film destined to further their careers. Similarly, David Mitchell and Robert Webb, of TV's *Peep Show* fame, failed with *Magicians* (2007) to put the requisite magic into their film careers, even with six credited screenwriters. Sacha Baron Cohen, however, made a successful transfer from television to film with *Ali G Indahouse* (2002), *Borat* (2006) and *Brüno* (2009), as well as appearing in many other films and TV shows.

If the likes of *Terry and June*, *Yus My Dear*, *'Allo 'Allo!*, *Father Ted* and *Drop the Dead Donkey* never made it into films, what chance is there for today's sitcoms such as *Outnumbered*, *Not Going Out* or *Friday Night Dinner*? Probably none at all. The days of the regular 'sitcom into filmcom' are probably over. So it's back to where we came in, *The Inbetweeners Movie*, which has done so well that the producers must be tempted to make a sequel. But where can the boys go from here? Not back to school, surely, and hardly to university. They might just get a job, say, on the buses…

In fact, there was once a rumour that Mike (*Austin Powers*) Myers was thinking about an *On the Buses* remake. I can hardly wait to not see it.

The *On the Buses* team – Michael Robbins, Anna Karen, Doris Hare, Bob Grant, Reg Varney and Stephen Lewis.

Documenting the World

Mansel Stimpson reports on the continuing impact of theatrically released documentaries.

Formula One hero Ayrton Senna was the subject of Asif Kapadia's BAFTA-winning *Senna*.

Not so long ago television was seen as the natural home for documentaries. The films of Michael Moore and such works as Kevin Macdonald's *Touching the Void* appeared to be no more than exceptions to the rule. But, while 2010 found more documentaries in cinemas than ever before, it took 2011 to confirm that if this were merely a trend it was at the very least a long-lasting one. Furthermore, it's not just a question of the numbers involved, although they are such that this article cannot mention all of them. The fact is that 2011 saw more documentary films taking their place amongst the best releases of the year than ever before.

2011's prime example of the appeal of documentaries on cinema screens was the notable commercial success of *Senna*. Significantly this was the film which won not only the BAFTA award for Best Documentary but also took the BAFTA for Best Editing, yet its success was no foregone conclusion. On paper the project must have seemed to be one of specialised interest because the film tells the story of the Formula One racing driver Ayrton Senna, who died in 1994. Furthermore, Asif Kapadia's film used only footage that already existed, albeit with comments added on the soundtrack from those who had known Senna. But as soon as the film opened word got about that he came over as such a fascinating figure that the movie was totally involving even for those who found no appeal in motor racing itself. Indeed there's no doubt that this is Kapadia's best film since his 2001 debut with the drama *The Warrior* and amazement has been expressed that *Senna* failed to get nominated for an Oscar.

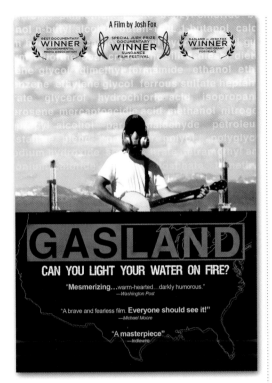

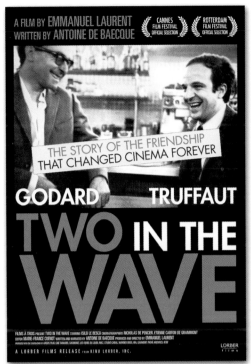

Opposite: Environmental anxieties were the focus in *Gasland*.

Left: The French nouvelle vague was revisited in *Two in the Wave*.

Other works set in the world of sport included the football movie *The Referees* and two films about cricket, *From the Ashes* and *Fire in Babylon*, although the latter's portrayal of the West Indies cricket team was also a social document revealing much about racial attitudes. A rather different game, chess, came up in *Bobby Fischer Against the World*.

Distinguished as the year was for documentaries, there were disappointments. Women in Northern Ireland commented on life in *His & Hers* but it would have been better as radio, while *The Flaw* with its emphasis on talking heads would have been more at home on television. A quite different take on the problems brought about by the banking crisis to that offered in *The Flaw* was handled to much, much better effect in *Inside Job*, one of the few documentaries to gain visual power by being shot in wide screen. Some would disagree, but the really interesting questions were no more than hinted at in the film about The Alternative Miss World, *The British Guide to Showing Off*. The same applies to James Marsh's *Project Nim*, dealing with an experiment involving a chimpanzee brought up in a human environment (but see our review section for a kinder assessment of this work). It was the attempt to dramatise the material so overtly which for me seriously marred such very different films as *My Kidnapper*, set in Colombia, and *Dreams of a Life*, which dealt with a long undiscovered death in London.

Quite a number of films made in recent times have been about what we are doing to the environment. *Gasland* was a very good example. There was also *Planeat* on food issues while two titles carried their own warning, *After the Apocalypse* and Lucy Walker's chilling alert

not to be complacent about the nuclear threat, *Countdown to Zero*. But such subjects were less to the fore in 2011 – and that applied also to portrayals of soldiering, although *Armadillo* featuring Danish troops in Afghanistan was a quality work on a par with 2010's *Restrepo* and Afghanistan also featured in *Hell and Back Again*.

What we did have in 2011 was a whole barrage of films about exceptional individuals. There were interesting if not outstanding pieces about filmmakers (*Two in the Wave* concentrated on Truffaut and Godard while *Great Directors* saw Angela Ismailos talking to ten such), but films about musicians proved more memorable. In the classical sphere there was the insightful *Genius Within: The Inner Life of Glenn Gould*, while Martin Scorsese in a film press-shown but only briefly screened in cinemas devoted three

Canada's virtuoso pianist was celebrated in *Genius Within: The Inner Life of Glenn Gould*.

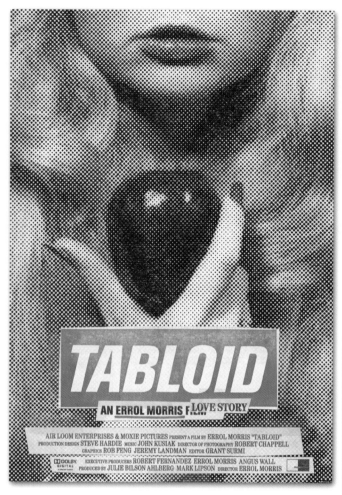

Above: A bizarre 1970s sex scandal was investigated in *Tabloid*.

Right: Steve James, of *Hoop Dreams* fame, returned with *The Interrupters*.

and a half hours to *George Harrison: Living in the Material World*, a work which was clearly a labour of love. Other films about music and dance included *Jig*, *Way of the Morris*, *Upside Down: The Creation Records Story*, *Talihina Sky: The Story of Kings of Leon* and, providing a look at British reggae, *The Story of Lovers Rock*. Yet another film with music at its centre was the widely acclaimed *Benda Bilili!* which showed how poor street performers from Kinshasa found fame and success.

Individuals in other spheres were central in a number of films. If Errol Morris' *Tabloid* turned back to 1977 and the alleged kidnapping by Joyce McKinney of a Mormon for sexual purposes, it was the woman herself who, given plenty of screen time, proved thoroughly intriguing. In contrast the remarkable architect Norman Foster and the most famous of British hairdressers charmed and delighted us in *How Much Does Your Building Weigh, Mr. Foster?* and *Vidal Sassoon: The Movie* respectively. Fashion came up again in both *Ultrasuede: In Search of Halston* and *Yves Saint Laurent: L'Amour Fou*. The individual featured in *Waste Land* is the Brazilian artist Vik Muniz. This is another film from Lucy Walker (who also gave us *Countdown to Zero*) and it looks at the positive effect of creating art,

involving people from the favelas of Rio de Janeiro.

It was also in 2011 that documentary film sought to excite attention by adding an extra ingredient: 3D. It happened most notably in three contrasted films, all much discussed and not least because they adopted the process with some success. Wim Wenders gave us *Pina*, his appreciation of the dance art of the late Pina Bausch, Werner Herzog studied Paleolithic paintings in the south of France in *Cave of Forgotten Dreams* and Richard De Arragues went to the Isle of Man to look at the TT races there in *TT3D: Closer to the Edge*, a very competent piece enhanced by the wholly engaging presence of the driver Guy Martin.

Quite distinct from most of the titles mentioned above are the films which can be viewed as making social comment or being politically concerned or which are, indeed, a mix of the two. *Inside Job*, already noted, belongs to this group beside many other films of distinction. Several of them come from America. Two titles speak for themselves – *Page One: Inside the New York Times* and *Four Days Inside Guantanamo*, the latter dealing with the treatment of Omar Ahmed Khadr who was questioned while imprisoned there in 2003. The rise and fall of the politician Eliot Spitzer is told in *Client 9* and a fascinating New York tale it proves to be. Even more memorable is *The Interrupters*, which sees the return to the cinema of Steve James who made that classic American documentary *Hoop Dreams* in 1995. Filmed in Chicago, it deals with an organisation, Cease Fire, which aims to prevent violence leading on to acts of retaliation. It's unsentimental but heart-warming. Among other titles to be noted here are *An African Election*, *Living in Emergency*, set in Liberia and the Congo, and *Donor Unknown* which featured a frequent sperm donor.

Films of this same genre from outside the USA include an investigation of China's influence in Africa in recent times (*When China Met Africa*), the memorable *Rio Breaks* (superficially about surfing but deeply concerned with the lives of youngsters from the favelas), a weird linking of Japanese culture and insects in *Beetle Queen Conquers Tokyo* and two deeply involving films which rank among the year's best. *Blood in the Mobile* finds the Dane Frank Piasecki Poulsen putting himself at risk to uncover evidence of exploitation in the Congo, the source of minerals used in the production of mobile phones. In *The Green Wave* we are in Iran identifying with the public who hoped that the 2009 election would bring about changes and discovering that would not be allowed by the regime of Mahmoud Ahmadinejad. This film is also notable for its unorthodox but effective use of animation at intervals, an element that reminds one of the fully animated *Waltz with Bashir*.

Also belonging to this genre but looking to past eras are two important historical documents. *Black Power Mix Tape 1967-1975* utilises footage found in Sweden to look afresh at America and its racial history at the time of the Black Panther movement. Even more remarkable is *We Were Here*, a moving yet ultimately uplifting recollection of the emergence of the AIDS crisis in San Francisco and the response to it of the gay community and those who cared for them.

Having picked out the trends I must conclude this survey by mentioning one or two titles among the 2011 releases that exist outside of them. *One Life* from BBC Earth is a reminder that finely photographed nature films continue to appear in cinemas and the same applies to *Born To Be Wild*, although the latter adds 3D to

make a difference. But the others in contrast are unusual one-offs. *Life in a Day* consists of material from YouTube habitués invited to express what life was like for them on 24 July 2010; Italy's *Le Quattro Volte* and the French film about an orang-utan *Nénette*, both touched on in my article on foreign films of the year, redefine what a documentary is capable of – and in doing so will either captivate or bore according to taste. An oddity of a different kind is Morgan Spurlock's comic piece *The Greatest Movie Ever Sold* which comments on product placement in films in a movie itself set up, as we see, by seeking financial backing from those whose product will be featured in it.

I pondered on how to end this article and then the answer leapt out at me. We live in troubled times and many of the films mentioned here inevitably reflect this. That's the case with some of the best of them. But *A Small Act* is a film apart. Made by Jennifer Arnold, it tells the true story of how one act of kindness transformed a life and led in turn to other comparable good acts. The people we meet are memorable and their tale is told without any resort to sentimentality. It's guaranteed to make you feel better about life and to give you a more positive view of human nature.

Left: Set in Iran, the part-animated German film *The Green Wave* was one of the year's best.

Below: The best kind of feel-good film – Jennifer Arnold's delightful *A Small Act*.

Elizabeth Taylor (see page 207)

In Memoriam
2011
by Jonathan Rigby

Given the hundreds of film personalities who died during 2011, the following selection of just 69 is, inevitably, a purely personal one. Pressure of space has excluded numerous important people, over 150 of whom are noted in supplements to the main entries.

DEV ANAND

Born: *26 September 1923, Gurdaspur, Punjab, India.*
Died: *3 December 2011, London, England.*
This legendary figure of Indian cinema started out as a dashingly handsome romantic lead in 1946, earned the sobriquet 'India's Gregory Peck', formed a popular screen partnership with the ill-fated beauty Madhubala, and subsequently diversified into writing, direction and production. In his latter years he garnered an impressive range of Lifetime Achievement awards, adding them to his time-honoured Filmfare gongs for *Kalapani* (Black Water, 1958) and *Guide* (1966). Both of these were products of Navketan Films, the production company he formed with his brother Chetan in 1949, and through which he exercised a Roger Corman-like influence over budding Bollywood stars and technicians. His last film, *Chargesheet* (which, characteristically, he directed, produced and starred in), came out just two months before his death.

❧ Like Anand, **Shammi Kapoor** won two Filmfare awards in his acting prime and then a third for Lifetime Achievement; he died in August, aged 79. Another veteran of Indian cinema, writer-producer **M S Reddy**, died in December at 87.

James Arness

JAMES ARNESS

Born: *26 May 1923, Minneapolis, Minnesota, USA.*
Died: *3 June 2011, Los Angeles, California, USA.*
Boasting Norwegian ancestry on his father's side, this massive (6'7") character star was awarded a Purple Heart during World War II and made his screen debut in *The Farmer's Daughter* (1947). He scored in two 1950s SF classics, as the monstrous title character in *The Thing from Another World* (for which his height came in handy) and as one of the two investigative heroes in *Them!* He also appeared with John Wayne in such films as *Hondo* and *Big Jim McLain*, and in 1955, at Wayne's suggestion, accepted a role in the CBS series *Gunsmoke*. Thereafter, the monolithic Matt Dillon policed Dodge City for two decades, with Arness even reprising the role in his seventies.

GEORGE BAKER

Born: *1 April 1931, Varna, Bulgaria.*
Died: *7 October 2011, West Lavington, Wiltshire, England.*
"With six starring roles behind him," observed the 'Rising Stars' section of this annual's 1957-58 edition, "Associated British contract artiste George Baker is now a force to reckon with in British films." In fact, Baker's dissatisfaction with ABPC rapidly propelled him back to the theatre, though in the meantime this unusually compelling actor had racked up such memorable credits as *The Ship That Died of Shame*, *The Dam Busters*, *The Feminine Touch*, *A Hill in Korea*, *The Moonraker* and *Tread Softly Stranger*. Ahead lay a second string as an award-winning radio and TV playwright, cameos in a couple of James Bond films, plus TV triumphs in *I, Claudius* (1976) and, pre-eminently, as Ruth Rendell's Inspector Wexford (1987-2000).

JOHN BARRY

Born: *3 November 1933, York, Yorkshire, England.*
Died: *30 January 2011, Oyster Bay, New York, USA.*
A true giant among film composers, John Barry began as leader of The John Barry Seven, contributing a hair-raisingly powerful jazz-pop score to *Beat Girl* in 1960 and conjuring from it Britain's first ever soundtrack album. From there he moved on to the swooning, sinister glamour of his James Bond scores (11 in all)

Alfred Burke

and an impressive tally of five Oscars – two for *Born Free* and one each for *The Lion in Winter*, *Out of Africa* and *Dances with Wolves*. His astounding output also encompassed *Zulu*, *The Ipcress File*, *King Rat*, *The Knack*, *The Whisperers*, *Boom*, *Midnight Cowboy*, *The Last Valley*, *Walkabout*, *Murphy's War*, *Robin and Marian*, *The Deep*, *Somewhere in Time*, *Frances*, *The Cotton Club*, *Chaplin*, *Indecent Proposal*, *The Scarlet Letter*, *Mercury Rising* and (his final film) *Enigma*. Not forgetting iconic TV themes like *The Persuaders!* and *Vendetta*. He was awarded an OBE in 1999 and a BAFTA Fellowship in 2005.

⬧ Prolific on US TV but also with features like *The Sweet Ride* and *Foxtrot* to his name, composer **Pete Rugolo** died in October, aged 95. **Hugh Martin** – whose score for *Meet Me in St Louis* (1944) contained the instant standard 'Have Yourself a Merry Little Christmas' – died in March, aged 96.

ROBERTS BLOSSOM

Born: *25 March 1924, New Haven, Connecticut, USA.*
Died: *8 July 2011, Santa Monica, California, USA.*
With his prematurely wizened features, Bartholomew Roberts Blossom proved perfect casting for two iconic, yet starkly contrasted, roles – the Ed Gein-alike necrophile Ezra Cobb in the cult Canadian horror *Deranged* (1973) and the avuncular Old Man Marley in the 1991 hit comedy *Home Alone*. A three-time Obie winner on the New York stage, he made his feature film debut in *The Hospital* (1971) and racked up an impressive roster of eccentrics over a 25-year period, ranging from *Slaughterhouse-Five*, *The Great Gatsby* (as Robert Redford's estranged father) and *Close Encounters of the Third Kind* to *Escape from Alcatraz*, *Christine*, *Doc Hollywood* and *The Quick and the Dead*. Latterly a poet,

he was also the subject of the 2000 documentary *Full Blossom*.

⬧ Other US character actors who died during 2011 included **Paul Picerni** and **Michael Tolan** (both in January, aged 88 and 86 respectively), **Len Lesser** (February, 88), **William Campbell** (April, 87), **Nico Minardos** (August, 81), **Jack Garner** (September, 84), **Ray Aranha** (October, 72), **Paul Kent** (October, 80), **Leonard Stone** (November, 87) and, in December, **Bill McKinney** (80), **Robert Easton** (81) and **William Duell** (88). And **John Sweet**, the real-life US Army Sergeant who in 1944 was ideally cast as the fictional US Army Sergeant in Powell and Pressburger's *A Canterbury Tale*, died in July, aged 95.

ALFRED BURKE

Born: *28 February 1918, London, England.*
Died: *16 February 2011, London, England.*
Alfred Burke's lean and hungry look was seen to best effect as Frank Marker, seedy protagonist of Thames TV's *Public Eye* (1965-75). But he was also a welcome presence in British cinema, starting with *The Constant Husband* in 1954 and ranging across *Bitter Victory*, *The Angry Silence*, *Crooks Anonymous*, *The Night Caller*, even the obscure Hylda Baker vehicle *She Knows Y'Know*. In addition, he more than held his own opposite Bette Davis in the climactic scene of *The Nanny* (1965). He also wrote TV plays and in 1977 was a memorable Long John Silver for the BBC. Though his final film credit was *Harry Potter and the Chamber of Secrets* in 2002, he was still appearing at London's National Theatre in his nineties.

⬧ Two other instantly recognisable British character actors, **Donald Hewlett** (90) and **Richard Pearson** (93), died in June and August respectively. Further nonagenarian actors who departed in 2011 included Argentina's **Osvaldo Miranda** (95, April), Germany's **Friedrich Schoenfelder** (94, August) and **Heinz Bennent** (90, October), and France's **Robert Lamoureux** (91, October) and **Jacques Debary** (97, December).

JOHN BURKE

Born: *8 March 1922, Rye, Sussex, England.*
Died: *20 September 2011, Kirkcudbright, Dumfries and Galloway, Scotland.*
In the 1960s, when tie-in novelisations were among the few merchandising opportunities available to film producers, writer John Burke was the undisputed titan of the format. His progress mirrored that of the British film industry itself, in that he began with novelisations of *Look Back in Anger* and *The Entertainer* and by the 1990s was writing multiple tie-ins for TV's *The Bill* and *London's Burning*. In between, his staggering work-load included *Flame in the Streets*, *The Angry Silence*, *A Hard Day's Night*, *Dr Terror's House of Horrors*, *Maroc 7*, *Privilege*, *Smashing Time*, *Chitty Chitty Bang Bang* and *The Bliss of Mrs Blossom*, plus eight novellas based on Hammer horrors of the period. He also provided the original story for the 1967 cult classic *The Sorcerers*.

MICHAEL CACOYANNIS

Born: *11 June 1921, Limassol, Cyprus.*
Died: *25 July 2011, Athens, Greece.*

A flavour of Greek tragedy broods over much of this director's work, and not just his three full-blown Euripides adaptations, all of them starring Irene Papas – *Electra* (1962), *The Trojan Women* (1971) and *Iphigenia* (1977). Starting out as an actor in London, Mikhalis Kakogiannis gravitated to Athens in the 1950s, showcasing Melina Mercouri in *Stella* and Ellie Lambeti in *A Girl in Black*, *A Matter of Dignity* and *The Wastrel*. The earthy exuberance of his 1964 hit *Zorba the Greek* garnered numerous Oscar nods but brought with it a 'follow that' conundrum that was hardly remedied by the would-be satirical radioactive misfire *The Day the Fish Came Out*. Mainly preoccupied in later years with theatre and opera, Cacoyannis' final film was a suitably autumnal 1998 version of Chekhov's *The Cherry Orchard*.

◈ **Francesco Quinn**, actor son of Cacoyannis' *Zorba* star Anthony Quinn and best known for his 1986 debut in *Platoon*, died in August, aged 48. Greek-born costume designer **Theoni V Aldredge**, who began her screen career with Cacoyannis' *Stella* and was an Oscar winner for *The Great Gatsby*, died in January, aged 88.

LINDA CHRISTIAN

Born: *13 November 1923, Tampico, Tamaulipas, Mexico.*
Died: *22 July 2011, Palm Springs, California, USA.*

Courted by millionaires, married to Tyrone Power, painted by Diego Rivera – Linda Christian had much more going on in her life than a slightly patchy film career. Nevertheless, her exotic beauty lent itself well to

Linda Christian

Diane Cilento

Johnny Weissmuller's final Tarzan outing (*Tarzan and the Mermaids*, 1948) and lurid programmers like *Slaves of Babylon* (1953) and *The Devil's Hand* (1961). Other credits included *The VIPs* (1962) and Francesco Rosi's bullfighting odyssey *Il momento della verità* (1964), in which she effectively played herself. Furthermore, thanks to the CBS television version of *Casino Royale*, she qualified as the first Bond girl eight years in advance of the film series.

◈ **Eve Brent**, who twice played Jane opposite Gordon Scott's Tarzan, died in August at 81.

DIANE CILENTO

Born: *5 October 1933, Mooloolaba, Queensland, Australia.*
Died: *6 October 2011, Cairns, Queensland, Australia.*

This smouldering Antipodean import may have been an anomaly in British cinema of the 1950s but was perfectly suited to such stage roles as Giraudoux' Helen of Troy (on Broadway) and Strindberg's Miss Julie (in London). Her early film credits ranged from *The Angel Who Pawned Her Harp* and *The Woman for Joe* (opposite George Baker, qv) to *The Admirable Crichton* and *Rattle of a Simple Man*, while an earthy, Oscar-nominated turn in *Tom Jones* ensured a mid-'60s Hollywood sojourn, yielding *The Agony and the Ecstasy* and *Hombre*. Subsequent oddball projects included *Negatives*, *ZPG* and, pre-eminently, the 1970s cult favourite *The Wicker Man*. After this she returned to Australia, building a theatre and making only occasional screen appearances.

JACKIE COOPER

Born: *15 September 1922, Los Angeles, California, USA.*
Died: *3 May 2011, Santa Monica, California, USA.*

After an apprenticeship with Our Gang, Jackie Cooper

became a massively popular child star in Paramount's *Skippy* (1931), for which the eight-year-old gained a 'Best Actor' Oscar nomination. At Metro, a winning combination with grizzled father-figure Wallace Beery yielded, among others, *The Champ* (1931) and *Treasure Island* (1934), with Cooper playing Jim Hawkins in the latter. With puberty, however, 'B' pictures prevailed – in one of which, *Glamour Boy* (1940), Cooper pretty much played himself, urging studio bosses to remake *Skippy*. After lots of TV and a spell as a Screen Gems executive, Cooper returned in 1978 as the newspaper editor in *Superman* (and three sequels). He also directed plenty of TV, plus the 1971 'Women's Lib' oddity *Stand Up and Be Counted*.

❖ An earlier Our Gang member, **Billy Naylor**, died in October, aged 95. Also associated with Our Gang, together with major films like *Pennies from Heaven* (1936), was **Edith Fellows**, who died in June at 88. Other child actors who died in 2011 included **Sybil Jason**, Warner Bros' hoped-for answer to Fox's Shirley Temple (in August, aged 83), **John Howard Davies**, who played the title role in David Lean's *Oliver Twist* (also in August, at 72), **Carolyn Lee**, star of *Mrs Wiggs of the Cabbage Patch* in 1942 (September, 76), and **Susan Gordon**, who in 1958 played Tuesday Weld's younger self in *The Five Pennies* (December, 62).

DENISE DARCEL

Born: *8 September 1924, Paris, France.*
Died: *23 December 2011, Los Angeles, California, USA.*
As cover star of the June 1956 issue of 'adult entertainment magazine' *Cabaret*, Denise Darcel was hailed as "France's gift to American men." "French cookie becomes US cabaret favorite," added the copywriter, acknowledging Darcel's impact as smouldering club singers in both *To the Victor* (1948)

and *Young Man with Ideas* (1952), and simultaneously forecasting her post-Hollywood career in cabaret (which sometimes involved stripping as well as singing). In the meantime, she had played opposite Van Johnson in *Battleground*, Lex Barker in *Tarzan and the Slave Girl*, Robert Taylor in *Westward the Women*, Esther Williams in *Dangerous When Wet*, and (her most prominent role) Gary Cooper and Burt Lancaster in *Vera Cruz*. She bowed out in the 1961 POW melodrama *Seven Women from Hell*.

SHELAGH DELANEY

Born: *25 November 1939, Salford, Lancashire, England.*
Died: *20 November 2011, Salford, Lancashire, England.*
Shelagh Delaney was responsible, aged 18, for the landmark play *A Taste of Honey*. Though staged at Stratford East, it was a Royal Court director, Tony Richardson, who turned it into a classic 1961 film, shooting on location in Delaney's native Salford and winning her a BAFTA in the process. Such adulation was hard to sustain, however; her second play, *The Lion in Love*, made few waves and she never wrote another. But her alternative outlets included screenwriting, ranging from Lindsay Anderson's bizarre featurette *The White Bus* (1965) and Albert Finney's directorial debut *Charlie Bubbles* (1967) to Mike Newell's glossy noir *Dance with a Stranger* (1984) and the theatrically released Screen Two production *The Railway Station Man* (1991).

❖ Novelist **Stan Barstow**, whose *A Kind of Loving* became another classic product of British cinema's 1960s new wave, died in August, aged 83. Royal Court playwright **N F Simpson**, whose Absurdist comedy *One Way Pendulum* was filmed in 1964 by Peter Yates [qv], also died in August, aged 92. Another playwright first produced in the late 1950s was **Michael Hastings**, whose films included *The Adventurers*, *The Nightcomers* and *Tom & Viv*; he died in November, aged 73.

ALBERTO DE MENDOZA

Born: *21 January 1923, Buenos Aires, Argentina.*
Died: *12 December 2011, Madrid, Spain.*
Orphaned at five, Alberto de Mendoza was sent to Madrid and made his film debut (in *Alma de Gaucho*) aged seven. Subsequently, he rose to prominence in Spanish theatre and appeared in over 100 further films. He fitted comfortably into Spanish swashbucklers

Denise Darcel

Alberto de Mendoza

Paulette Dubost

(*La máscara de Scaramouche*), Spaghetti Westerns (*A Bullet for Sandoval*), parochial comedy-dramas (*Una abuelita de antes de la guerra*) and Italian gialli like *Lizard in a Woman's Skin*. To English-speaking audiences he probably remains best known for 1970s titles like *And Then There Were None*, *Open Season* and, particularly, for his Rasputin-like mad monk in the Anglo-Spanish chiller *Horror Express*. More recently, he won a new audience through his grandfatherly roles in *Tapas* (2005) and *La mala verdad* (The Awful Truth, 2010).

❥ Among other international character actors who died in 2011, Brazil's **Nildo Parente** and **José Vasconcelos** died in January and October respectively, aged 76 and 85. Poland's **Stanislaw Michalski** died in February, aged 78, and the Italian **Enzo Cannavale** in March, at 82. Spain's **Jorgi Dauder** (73) and **Antonio Molino Rojo** (85) died in September and November respectively, while Uruguay's **Walter Vidarte** and Argentina's **Alberto Anchart** both died at 80 in October. Finally, Mexico lost both **Jorge Lavat** (September, 78) and **Pedro Armendáriz Jr** (December, 71).

PAULETTE DUBOST
Born: *8 October 1910, Paris, France.*
Died: *21 September 2011, Longjumeau, Essonne, France.*
Paulette Dubost began her film career at 20, proving a splendid foil to lugubrious local comedian Fernandel in such films as *Ferdinand le noceur*, and even (in his sole French outing, *Le Roi des Champs-Elysées*) Buster Keaton. She then acquired an international profile in Marcel Carné's *Hôtel du Nord* (1938) and, particularly, as the pert chambermaid in Jean Renoir's masterful *La Règle du jeu* (1939). Having turned down a Hollywood offer, she enjoyed a long post-war career as a character actress, ranging all the way from *Lola Montès* (1955) to *Le dernier métro* (1980) and *Milou en mai* (1990). Her 1992 autobiography was entitled – ironically, given that she would live to be 100 – *C'est court, la vie* (Life is Short).

❥ Other centenarians who died during 2011 included Swedish actress **Ingrid Luterkort** (at 101, in August) and veteran Czech writer-director **Otakar Vávra**

(in September, aged 100). The 101-year-old special effects guru **Harry Redmond Jr**, whose 1930s credits included *King Kong* and *Lost Horizon*, died in May. And glamorous MGM contract player **Louise Henry**, who was also uncredited co-writer of James Whale's *Remember Last Night?* (1935), died in December at 100.

BERND EICHINGER
Born: *11 April 1949, Neuburg an der Donau, Bavaria, Germany.*
Died: *24 January 2011, Los Angeles, California, USA.*
Bernd Eichinger was that apparent oxymoron, a visionary movie mogul. With the shining example of Ufa in mind, he started by founding his own company, Solaris, and producing art-house hits like *Die Konsequenz* (1977) and *Hitler – ein Film aus Deutschland* (both 1977). The gruelling *Christiane F* (1981) gained international attention, but by that time Eichinger had also taken control of Munich's venerable Constantin-Film, through which he produced such English-language hits as *The NeverEnding Story* (1984), *The Name of the Rose* (1986) and *Perfume* (2005). One of his productions, *Nirgendwo in Afrika* (2001), won the Oscar as Best Foreign Film; two others were nominated – *Downfall* (2004) and *The Baader Meinhof Complex* (2008), both of which he co-wrote. In the view of *Der Spiegel*, "Bernd Eichinger made German film what it is today."

PETER FALK
Born: *16 September 1927, New York City, New York, USA.*
Died: *23 June 2011, Beverly Hills, California, USA.*
Peter Falk's trademark glass eye did nothing to compromise his status as a craggy, conflicted American Everyman. He met John Cassavetes in 1967 and,

Peter Falk

also that year, created his signature TV role as the faux-shambolic Lt Columbo. His semi-improvised Cassavetes collaborations included *Husbands* (1970) and *A Woman Under the Influence* (1974), while the Emmy-laden Columbo would continue until 2003. Prior to all this, in the early 1960s Falk gained consecutive Oscar nominations (for *Murder, Inc* and *Pocketful of Miracles*) and was one of several Sinatra satellites in *Robin and the 7 Hoods*. Later he scored in both *The In-Laws* (1979) and *The Princess Bride* (1987), and played himself in Wim Wenders' *Wings of Desire* (1987) and Robert Altman's *The Player* (1991).

ANNE FRANCIS

Born: *16 September 1930, Ossining, New York, USA.*
Died: *2 January 2011, Santa Barbara, California, USA.*
Anne Francis appeared on Broadway (in *Lady in the Dark*) before she hit her teens. Signed up for films, she oscillated from Metro to Fox and back again, playing a reform school girl in *So Young So Bad* (1950), making the most of showy roles in other '50s titles like *Blackboard Jungle* and *The Hired Gun*, and gaining the distinction of being the only woman in two classics of the era, *Bad Day at Black Rock* and *Forbidden Planet*. In 1965 she earned cult status as the sexy star of the ABC detective series *Honey West*, and – rare titles like *More Dead Than Alive* (1968) and *Pancho Villa* (1971) notwithstanding – worked almost exclusively thereafter in television.

BETTY GARRETT

Born: *23 May 1919, St Joseph, Missouri, USA.*
Died: *12 February 2011, Los Angeles, California, USA.*
In April 1946, Betty Garrett starred in the musical revue *Call Me Mister* on Broadway and by the following January had signed with MGM. She quickly racked up credits in *Big City*, *Words and Music* and the Esther Williams vehicles *Neptune's Daughter* and *Take Me Out to the Ball Game*, and in 1949 made her most enduring impact as Frank Sinatra's amorous hijacker in *On the Town*. Along with her husband Larry Parks, she was then frozen out of Hollywood for supposed Communist sympathies, only returning in 1955 for a co-starring role opposite Jack Lemmon and Janet Leigh in *My Sister Eileen*. After that, there was much TV, notably the '70s sitcom *Laverne & Shirley*, and a final Broadway appearance (in *Follies*) in 2001.

❦ **Marilyn Nash**, star of Chaplin's 1947 black comedy *Monsieur Verdoux*, and **Patricia Breslin**, best known for playing the he-she killer in *Homicidal* (1961), both died in October, aged 84 and 80 respectively. Among other US actresses who died in 2011 were **Patricia Smith** (at 80, in January), **Shelby Grant** (74, June), **Leslie Brooks** (88, July), **Patricia Hardy** (78, August), **Phyllis Love** and **Doris Belack**, both of whom died aged 85 in October, **Dorothy Morris** (89, November) and 86-year-old **Doe Avedon** in December.

ANNIE GIRARDOT

Born: *25 October 1931, Paris, France.*
Died: *28 February 2011, Paris, France.*
Alongside Jeanne Moreau, Annie Girardot provided a powerful female counterpoise to such 1960s icons as Alain Delon and Jean-Paul Belmondo. After early experience at the Comédie Française and, from 1955, various minor French films, she became a star (opposite Delon) as an ill-fated Milan prostitute in

Anne Francis

Annie Girardot

Richard Gordon

Michael Gough

Luchino Visconti's *Rocco e i suoi fratelli* (Rocco and His Brothers, 1960). Subsequently, she was called upon repeatedly by directors Philippe de Broca, Claude Lelouch, Marco Ferreri and André Cayatte, and won awards at Venice (*Trois chambres à Manhattan*, 1965) and Berlin (*La vieille fille*, 1972). She also won a César for the 1975 film *Docteur Françoise Gailland*, with two more following much later, for Lelouch's *Les Misérables* (1994) and Michael Haneke's *La Pianiste* (2001).

❥ Other French actors who died in 2011 included, in February, 62-year-old **Catherine Jourdan** (star of Alain Robbe-Grillet's *Eden et après*) and two-time César-winner **Maurice Garrel** (in June, aged 88). The following month, **Jacques Jouanneau**, a regular performer for René Clair and Jean Renoir, died at 84.

RICHARD GORDON
Born: *31 December 1925, London, England.*
Died: *1 November 2011, New York City, New York, USA.*
Working out of New York, Richard Gordon began as Renown Pictures' US distributor and also organised Bela Lugosi's UK stage tour of *Dracula* in 1951. Six years later he set up two British pictures, *Grip of the Strangler* and *Corridors of Blood*, for another boyhood horror hero, Boris Karloff. Thereafter he was the prime mover (though frequently neglecting to take a producer credit) on a string of vibrant British chillers, among them *Fiend Without a Face* (1957), *Devil Doll* (1963), *The Projected Man* (1965), *Tower of Evil* (1971) and *The Cat and the Canary* (1977). He also made possible Antony Balch's two bizarre forays into direction, *Secrets of Sex* (1969) and *Horror Hospital* (1972). Unsympathetic to modern trends in horror, he bowed out with *Inseminoid* (1980).

MICHAEL GOUGH
Born: *23 November 1916, Kuala Lumpur, British Malaya.*
Died: *17 March 2011, London, England.*
Starting in 1958, Michael Gough's outrageous portraits of horror-movie derangement in films like *Horrors of the Black Museum, Konga, Black Zoo, The Corpse, Horror Hospital* and *Satan's Slave* stamped him as a lugubrious, latter-day Lionel Atwill. On stage from 1937, he excelled in Sartre, Anouilh, Ibsen and Ayckbourn, while his non-horror film roles encompassed such titles as *The Man in the White Suit* (1951), *The Go-Between* (1970), *The Dresser* (1982) and *Caravaggio* (1986). Latterly, he was Bruce Wayne's bespectacled butler Alfred in *Batman* (1989) and three sequels. "It's the best way to be," he said of the character actor's lot in 1988. "You don't have the responsibility of a star, you're not as expensive as a star, and you get lovely parts."

❥ Several other well-known British character players died during 2011, among them **Nicholas Courtney** (in February, aged 81), **Terence Longdon** (April, 88), **Edward Hardwicke** (May, 78), **John Wood** (August, 81), **Jonathan Cecil** (September, 72) and **Mark Kingston** (October, 77). Also familiar from British films and TV, the exceptional Irish character star **T P McKenna** died at 81 in February.

Farley Granger

FARLEY GRANGER
Born: *1 July 1925, San Jose, California, USA.*
Died: *27 March 2011, New York City, New York, USA.*
The roster of top-flight directors with whom handsome Farley Granger worked in the 1940s and early '50s was second to none – Lewis Milestone in *The Purple Heart*, Nicholas Ray in *They Live By Night*, Alfred Hitchcock in *Rope* and *Strangers on a Train*, Anthony Mann in *Side Street*, Vincente Minnelli in *The Story of Three Loves*, and, most remarkably, Luchino Visconti in *Senso*. It was a level that Granger seemed unable – and perhaps uninterested – in sustaining. Tiring of studio-mandated efforts to disguise his sexuality, and even of the film-making process itself, he turned to TV and (his favourite) the stage. Enamoured of Rome ever since *Senso*, his latterday credits included several Italian exploitation films, plus the 1981 US slasher *The Prowler*.

DULCIE GRAY
Born: *20 November 1915, Kuala Lumpur, British Malaya.*
Died: *15 November 2011, Northwood, Middlesex, England.*

"I played an awful lot of put-upon wives in those days," said Dulcie Gray of her post-war heyday as a British film star. Starting out in the Gainsborough titles *Madonna of the Seven Moons*, *A Place of One's Own* and *They Were Sisters*, she then made *Wanted for Murder* and *Mine Own Executioner* for other producers prior to beginning a screen partnership with her husband Michael Denison in the most popular British film of 1948, *My Brother Jonathan*. Their other co-starring ventures comprised *The Glass Mountain*, *The Franchise Affair*, *Angels One Five* and, in 1952, *There Was a Young Lady*. They moved thereafter into TV and theatre, and in 1983 were jointly awarded the CBE for Services to Drama.

⦿ Other nonagenarian actresses from the UK included 92-year-old **Georgina Cookson** and 91-year-old **Betty Driver**, both of whom died in October. From the USA, **Claudia Bryar** (93) and **Frances Bay** (92) died in June and September, followed by **Jo Ann Sayers** (93) and **Betty Jane Rhodes** (90) in November and December. Switzerland lost **Stephanie Glaser** (January,

90), Poland **Irena Kwiatkowska** (March, 98), Spain **María Isbert** (April, 94), Norway **Wenche Foss** (March, 93) and **Vibeke Falk** (October, also 93), and Sweden **Annalisa Ericson** (April, 97), **Sif Ruud** (August, 95), **Birgit Rosengren** (October, 98) and **Sickan Carlsson** (November, 96). From Denmark, 94-year-old **Lisbeth Movin** – an indelible presence in Dreyer's 1943 masterwork *Day of Wrath* – died in November.

JILL HAWORTH
Born: *15 August 1945, Hove, Sussex, England.*
Died: *3 January 2011, New York City, New York, USA.*
Discovered by director Otto Preminger, Jill Haworth gave touching teenage performances in three of his sprawling, early 1960s epics – *Exodus*, *The Cardinal* and *In Harm's Way*. She also starred opposite Jean Marais in André Hunebelle's *Les Mystères de Paris*. Then in November 1966 she created the role of Sally Bowles in the original Broadway production of Kander and Ebb's *Cabaret*. Despite remaining in the show for some two years, it was a film made in her home country just prior to her Broadway success – *It!* - that determined the next phase of her career. Several more British shockers followed (*The Haunted House of Horror*, 1968; *Tower of Evil*, 1971; *The Mutations*, 1972), after which she stuck mainly to TV.

❧ Haworth's contemporary **Angela Scoular** – best known for the quintessential 1960s films *Here We Go Round the Mulberry Bush* and *On Her Majesty's Secret Service* – committed suicide in April, also aged 65.

RICKY HUI
Born: *3 August 1946, Panyu, Guangdong, China.*
Died: *8 November 2011, Hong Kong, China.*
A superb deadpan droll during the halcyon years of Hong Kong comedy, Ricky Hui was initially contracted to the Shaw Brothers outfit. He found his true metier, however, when joining his own brothers, Sam and Michael, in such inventive Hui hits as *Ban jin ba liang* (The Private Eyes, 1976), *Modeng baobiao* (Security Unlimited, 1981), *Shen tan zhu gu li* (Inspector Chocolate, 1987) and *San bungan baata* (Front Page, 1990). He also worked for Ronny Yu, Jackie Chan and John Woo, and in later years was still capable of scene-stealing cameos in films like *Wo yaozuo model* (Super Model, 2004). But he remains best known to Western audiences for his delightful performance in the definitive Hong Kong horror-comedy, *Mr Vampire* (1985).

❧ A month Hui's junior and a huge action star in Hong Kong, **Alan Tang** (who, as a producer, sponsored the early films of Wong Kar-wai) died in March, aged 64.

BILL HUNTER
Born: *27 February 1940, Melbourne, Victoria, Australia.*
Died: *21 May 2011, Melbourne, Victoria, Australia.*
In 1959, Bill Hunter was Gregory Peck's swimming double in the Melbourne-shot *On the Beach* and was inspired to enrol at RADA. Having begun his stage career under the patronage of actor-director John Neville [qv], he returned home and became nothing less than an exemplar of Australia for both local and international

Jill Haworth

audiences; in a neat irony, he was the Australian PM in a TV remake of *On the Beach* (2000). His contributions to the local film industry's 1970s renaissance included *Backroads*, *Newsfront* and *Gallipoli* (winning AFI awards for the last two); he was also invaluable during a 1990s resurgence via *Strictly Ballroom*, *Muriel's Wedding* and *The Adventures of Priscilla, Queen of the Desert*. Among his final credits was the posthumously released *Red Dog*.

❧ Another Australian character actor, **Harold Hopkins** – well known for *Don's Party*, *The Club* and *Gallipoli*, among others – died in December, aged 67. AFI award-winning director **Sarah Watt** (*Look Both Ways*, *My Year Without Sex*) died the previous month, aged 53.

PAT JACKSON
Born: *26 March 1916, London, England.*
Died: *3 June 2011, [location unknown], England.*
A key figure in the British documentary movement, Pat Jackson will always be best remembered for his visually stunning impression of the Battle of the Atlantic, *Western Approaches* (1944). A contract with Alexander Korda led, by a circuitous route, to Hollywood, where Jackson directed the low-key noir *Shadow on the Wall* (1949). Back in Britain, he made two films about hospital life, *White Corridors* (1951) and *The Feminine Touch* (1955); he considered the former his best fiction film "because it most happily melded the documentary method with 'big box-office' and made no compromises." His other features included the charming horror-comedy *What a Carve Up!* (1961) and a convincingly creepy 'B' called *Don't Talk to Strange Men* (1962). Thereafter he moved into TV, notably *The Prisoner* and *Arthur of the Britons*.

❧ Also moving from documentary to fiction film, Italy's **Vittorio de Seta** supplemented widescreen Technicolor investigations of Sicilian life with striking features like *Banditi a Orgosolo* (1961); he died in November, aged 88.

CHARLES JARROTT

Born: *16 June 1927, London, England.*
Died: *4 March 2011, Woodland Hills, California, USA.*
Like John Mackenzie [qv], Charles Jarrott began as an actor, became an expert director of groundbreaking BBC dramas, then moved into features and finally TV movies. He won a Golden Globe for his first film, *Anne of the Thousand Days* (1969), and remained in Tudor garb for *Mary, Queen of Scots* (1971). So far so good, but then came a ghastly, beyond-camp musical version of *Lost Horizon* (1972). In the mid-'70s, sea-going romance *The Dove* paired Jarrott with cinematographer Sven Nykvist, *Escape from the Dark* was an atmospheric period drama for Disney, and *The Other Side of Midnight* was an unhappy Hollywood debut for Marie-France Pisier [qv]. Then, after a couple more Disneys, it was mainly back to TV.

❖ Distinguished television director **Peter Hammond** started out as a juvenile lead in numerous post-war British films and directed just one feature, *Spring and Port Wine* (1969); he died at 87 in October. Other British filmmakers who died in 2011 included production designers **Keith Wilson** (*Thunderbirds Are Go*, *International Velvet*) and **Syd Cain** (*Lolita*, *From Russia With Love*) – in July and November, aged 69 and 93 respectively.

MIRIAM KARLIN

Born: *23 June 1925, London, England.*
Died: *3 June 2011, London, England.*
The passionately political nature of this brilliant,

Miriam Karlin

hawk-faced character actress went a great deal deeper than her trademark cry of "Everybody out!" in the classic 1960s sitcom *The Rag Trade*. Schooled in revue and radio (where she formed part of a double-act with Peter Sellers in *Variety Bandbox*), she followed a standard-issue diet of British films (among them, *Fun at St Fanny's*, *The Phantom of the Opera*, *Ladies Who Do* and *The Small World of Sammy Lee*) with stand-out performances in Stanley Kubrick's *A Clockwork Orange* (1971: as 'Catlady') and Ken Russell's *Mahler* (1973: as Gustav's aunt). After much distinguished stage and TV work, she contributed 21st century cameos to *Children of Men* and *Flashbacks of a Fool*.

❖ Among other well-known British character actresses, **Margaret Tyzack**, who died at 79 in June, numbered Kubrick's *2001: A Space Odyssey* among her occasional film appearances. **Sheila Burrell** (*The Man in Black*, *Paranoiac*) died the following month, aged 89, and **Sheila Allen** (*Children of the Damned*, *Venom*) died in October, aged 78.

BARBARA KENT

Born: *16 December 1907, Gadsby, Alberta, Canada.*
Died: *13 October 2011, Palm Desert, California, USA.*
Barbara Kent was the last surviving person to have starred in silent films as an adult. Having earned the title 'Miss Hollywood 1925', the diminutive beauty soon found herself acting opposite Greta Garbo and John Gilbert in *Flesh and the Devil*, Richard Barthelmess in *The Drop Kick*, Douglas Fairbanks Jr in *Modern Mothers*, and Rex the Wonder Horse in *No Man's Law*. Most significantly, she was paired with Glenn Tryon in the dazzling New York odyssey *Lonesome*, directed for Universal in 1928 by the Hungarian visionary Paul Fejös. She entered talkies first as Harold Lloyd's

Barbara Kent

girlfriend in both *Welcome Danger* and *Feet First*, then as Gloria Swanson's younger sister in *Indiscreet*. Among her final credits were early, low-budget versions of *Vanity Fair* and *Oliver Twist*.

❧ Some three months Kent's senior, **Miriam Seegar** – who appeared in three British silents prior to starring in various early talkies in her native America – died in January, also aged 103. Child actor **Douglas Haig**, who played Kent's little brother in *Welcome Danger*, died in February, aged 90.

GEORGE KUCHAR

Born: *31 August 1942, New York City, New York, USA.*
Died: *6 September 2011, San Francisco, California, USA.*
Working with his twin brother Mike, underground filmmaker George Kuchar's prentice efforts included titles like *Pussy on a Hot Tin Roof*, giving notice of the camp sensibility that would reach full bloom when George struck out on his own with the 17-minute vignette *Hold Me While I'm Naked* (1966). Regularly equated with fellow avant-gardistes Stan Brakhage and Kenneth Anger, Kuchar became a professor at the San Francisco Art Institute in 1971 and collaborated with Curt McDowell on mid-'70s films like *The Devil's Cleavage* and the notorious hardcore horror spoof (which Kuchar co-wrote and appeared in) *Thundercrack!* He was the subject of the 2009 documentary *It Came from Kuchar*, as well as collaborating with Mike on a 1997 joint memoir entitled *Reflections from a Cinematic Cesspool*.

ARTHUR LAURENTS

Born: *14 July 1917, New York City, New York, USA.*
Died: *5 May 2011, New York City, New York, USA.*
Arthur Laurents was the Broadway veteran responsible for writing the 'book' of the musicals *West Side Story* and *Gypsy*, both of which would become major 1960s hits on screen. Other dramatic works of his were similarly adapted by other hands, into *Home of the Brave* (1949) and *Summertime* (1955). Conversely, Laurents himself specialised in adapting other writers' plays and novels, yielding *Rope* (1948), *Caught, Anna Lucasta* (both 1949), *Anastasia* (1956) and *Bonjour Tristesse* (1957); the first of these starred his then-lover, Farley Granger [qv]. He later drew on his own experience – of the McCarthy witch-hunts and ballerina Nora Kaye respectively – for the original screenplays *The Way We Were* (1973) and *The Turning Point* (1977), gaining an Oscar nomination for the last.

❧ Other US screenwriters who died during the period under review included **Christopher Trumbo** (in January, aged 70), **Donald S Sanford** (February, 92), **Sidney Michaels** (April, 83), **Kevin Jarre** (April, 56), **David Rayfiel** (June, 87) and **David Zelag Goodman** (September, 80). Comedy specialists **Arthur Marx** and **Hal Kanter** died in April and November, aged 89 and 92 respectively.

RICHARD LEACOCK

Born: *18 July 1921, London, England.*
Died: *23 March 2011, Paris, France.*
For Richard Leacock, "the feeling of being there"

Sue Lloyd

was not only his watchword as a groundbreaking documentarian of the 'Direct Cinema' school but also the title of his posthumously published memoirs. In pursuit of his ideal, Leacock moved from Robert Flaherty's *Louisiana Story* (1948), on which he was cinematographer, to chronicling John F Kennedy both before (*Primary*, 1960) and after (*Crisis*, 1963) he became President. In the countercultural ferment of the late '60s, Leacock collaborated with D A Pennebaker on, among others, the epoch-making *Monterey Pop* and the impenetrable Jean-Luc Godard project *1 P.M.* He later co-founded the film school at the Massachusetts Institute of Technology and finally relocated to Paris; his final film was *A Musical Adventure in Siberia* (2000).

❧ The documentary field also lost jazz specialist and Clint Eastwood collaborator **Bruce Ricker** (in May, aged 68), **Gualtiero Jacopetti**, originator of Italy's 'mondo' shockumentaries (in August, aged 91), and **Tom Daly**, another 'Direct Cinema' innovator and a key figure at Canada's National Film Board (in September, aged 93).

SUE LLOYD

Born: *7 August 1939, Aldeburgh, Suffolk, England.*
Died: *20 October 2011, London, England.*
Sue Lloyd's aquiline hauteur, honed to a fine point by an initial career as a fashion model, propelled her in October 1964 into a co-starring role opposite Michael Caine in Sidney J Furie's classic thriller *The Ipcress File*. On TV, she was then partnered with Steve Forrest in *The Baron* (1966) and Ronald Lewis in *His and Hers*

Sidney Lumet

(1970), with intervening film roles in *Corruption*, *Where's Jack?* and *Twinky*. Subsequent credits included *Innocent Bystanders* (1971), *Spanish Fly* (1975) and *Eat the Rich* (1987); she was also Joan Collins' louche friend in the late-'70s disco duo *The Stud* and *The Bitch*. Her 1998 autobiography was wryly entitled *It Seemed Like a Good Idea at the Time*.

SIDNEY LUMET
Born: *25 June 1924, Philadelphia, Pennsylvania, USA.*
Died: *9 April 2011, New York City, USA.*
Fascinated by questions of morality and social justice, Sidney Lumet was the most prolific, and long-lasting, of the many American directors who came up through 1950s television. His first film, *12 Angry Men* (1957), also marked his first Oscar nomination; three more followed courtesy of *Dog Day Afternoon* (1975), *Network* (1976) and *The Verdict* (1982). Of Lumet's other films, several were stage adaptations, ranging from *Long Day's Journey Into Night* (1962) and *The Sea Gull* (1968) to *The Offence* (1972), *Equus* (1976) and *Deathtrap* (1982). Made mostly in New York (occasionally in Britain but almost never in Hollywood), further important Lumet titles included *Fail-Safe*, *The Pawnbroker*, *The Hill*, *The Deadly Affair*, *The Anderson Tapes*, *Serpico*, *Murder on the Orient Express*, *Prince of the City* and *Running On Empty*. Later years were hit and miss, then at 82 – a year after finally receiving a long-overdue honorary Oscar – he directed the terrific *Before the Devil Knows You're Dead*.

◆ Among other American directors, **Gary Winick** (*Charlotte's Web*, *Letters to Juliet*) died in February, aged 49. **Leonard Kastle**, whose sole credit was the 1968 cult classic *The Honeymoon Killers*, died at 82 in May, and **Gilbert Cates** (*I Never Sang for my Father*, *Summer Wishes Winter Dreams*) died in October, aged 77.

JOHN MACKENZIE
Born: *22 May 1928, Edinburgh, Scotland.*
Died: *8 June 2011, London, England.*
Initially an actor, John Mackenzie became a stalwart of *The Wednesday Play*, *Thirty Minute Theatre* and *Play for Today* as a TV director, diversifying into features in 1969 with *One Brief Summer*, followed by the early 1970s curios *Unman, Wittering and Zigo* and *Made*. In 1979 he made the hard-hitting, blackly comic gangster thriller *The Long Good Friday*, which, when finally released in 1981, was recognised as an 'instant' classic. With tautly sinewed thrillers his forte, he then worked twice with Michael Caine (*The Honorary Consul*, 1983; *The Fourth Protocol*, 1986) and, after the early '90s titles *Blue Heat* and *Ruby*, moved back into TV. His final features were *When the Sky Falls* (1999) and, back with Caine, *Quicksand* (2001).

ANNA MASSEY
Born: *11 August 1937, Thakeham, Sussex, England.*
Died: *3 July 2011, London, England.*
Many filmgoers' enduring image of Anna Massey is that of a gawky 22-year-old, gasping "All this filming

isn't healthy" at the horrifying climax of Michael Powell's 1959 shocker *Peeping Tom*. The previous year, her film debut in *Gideon's Day* involved working with another formidable director, John Ford (who was her godfather); her next film, *Bunny Lake is Missing* (1965), brought yet another – Otto Preminger. And in 1971 she was engaged by Hitchcock for the gruesome *Frenzy*. An actress of rare distinction on stage, she proved to be the same on screen, though her remaining feature film credits were too few. Among them: *A Doll's House* (1972), *Five Days One Summer* (1982), *Another Country* (1983), *Angels and Insects* (1994) and *The Importance of Being Earnest* (2001).

PAUL MASSIE

Born: *7 July 1932, St Catharines, Ontario, Canada.*
Died: *8 June 2011, Liverpool, Nova Scotia, Canada.*
Appearing briefly in the Canadian-shot Rank production *High Tide at Noon*, Paul Massie made sufficient impact to be asked over to the UK. In no time at all, he was starring in the West End premiere of Tennessee Williams' *Cat on a Hot Tin Roof* and received a 'Most Promising Newcomer' BAFTA for his excellently conflicted performance in Anthony Asquith's *Orders to Kill* (1958). For Asquith again, he starred in *Libel*; for Basil Dearden, *Sapphire*; and for Terence Fisher he played the lead(s) in Hammer's *The Two Faces of Dr Jekyll*. In the early 1960s, he appeared in *The Rebel*, *Raising the Wind*, *The Pot Carriers* – and

then, surprisingly, gave it all up, eventually becoming a venerated drama teacher at the University of South Florida.

HARRY MORGAN

Born: *10 April 1915, Detroit, Michigan, USA.*
Died: *7 December 2011, Los Angeles, California, USA.*
Though guaranteed immortality as Colonel Sherman T Potter in the classic CBS series *M*A*S*H* (1975-83), Harry Morgan's wiry and wryly humorous presence also lit up scores of feature films from 1942 to 1997. Among these were *The Ox-Bow Incident* and *The Big Clock* in the 1940s, *High Noon* and *The Glenn Miller Story* in the 1950s, and *How the West Was Won* (as Ulysses S Grant) and *The Flim-Flam Man* in the 1960s. He also played opposite James Garner in the Western comedies *Support Your Local Sheriff!* and *Support Your Local Gunfighter*, John Wayne in the poignant Western lament *The Shootist*, and was memorably matched with Walter Matthau in the 1989 TV movie *The Incident*, plus two sequels.

❧ Other nonagenarian character actors from the USA included **Bruce Gordon** (*Tower of London*, *Piranha*) and **G D Spradlin** (*Apocalypse Now*, *The Lords of Discipline*), who died in January and July respectively, aged 94 and 90.

MARY MURPHY

Born: *26 January 1931, Washington DC, USA.*
Died: *4 May 2011, Los Angeles, California, USA.*
"The new romantic team of blue-eyed Mary Murphy and the controversial Marlon Brando," read a picture caption in this annual's 1954-55 edition, "seen together in Columbia's forthcoming release *The Wild One*." As it turned out, the BBFC ensured that the film only came forth for British audiences in 1968. Precipitated into an acting career by Paramount talent scouts, Mary Murphy

Paul Massie

Harry Morgan

Mary Murphy

John Neville

British, set in schools – *Why Shoot the Teacher?* (1976) and *The Class of Miss MacMichael* (1978). After that, Narizzano returned for the most part to TV.

➲ Another 84-year-old native of Montreal, writer-producer and Cinepix co-founder **John Dunning**, died in September.

JOHN NEVILLE
Born: *2 May 1925, London, England.*
Died: *19 November 2011, Toronto, Ontario, Canada.*
In the 1950s, the chiselled Old Vic heart-throb John Neville was hailed as a new Gielgud pitted against Richard Burton's new Olivier. Later he created the role of *Alfie* on stage; missing out on the film version, he instead played Sherlock Holmes in the 1965 chiller *A Study in Terror*. He was awarded the OBE the same year and in 1972 emigrated to Canada, where he became artistic director of the Stratford Shakespeare Festival. In 1988 he gained his most prominent film role – as the crazily quixotic lead in Terry Gilliam's *The Adventures of Baron Munchausen* – and thereafter enjoyed an Indian summer in such titles as *The Road to Wellville*, *Little Women*, *The Fifth Element*, *The X Files*, *Sunshine* and *Spider*. He was awarded the Order of Canada in 2006.

➲ Actress **Domini Blythe**, whose films ranged from *Vampire Circus* to *Afterglow*, also made the move from Britain to Canada; she died in December, aged 63.

LENA NYMAN
Born: *23 May 1944, Stockholm, Sweden.*
Died: *4 February 2011, Stockholm, Sweden.*
Having made her film debut aged 11, Lena Nyman achieved international notoriety in Vilgot Sjöman's 1967 film *Jag är nyfiken – gul*. With Nyman as an inquisitive sociology student whose sex sessions in trees, ponds and elsewhere were groundbreakingly explicit for the time, Sjöman's vérité piece was

was Laurence Olivier's daughter in *Carrie* (1952) and Fredric March's in *The Desperate Hours* (1955), plus stage assistant to Vincent Price in *The Mad Magician* (1953). Later films included *Escapement* (in Britain, 1957), *Harlow* (1965) and *Junior Bonner* (1971), but her claim on posterity remains that iconic co-starring spot opposite Brando – rather like, though in very different circumstances, Maria Schneider [qv].

➲ **Norma Eberhardt**, Murphy's co-star in the 1958 'bad girl' curio *Live Fast, Die Young* and doe-eyed ingenue of *The Return of Dracula* the same year, died in May, aged 82. A cult classic from earlier in the 1950s, *The Man from Planet X*, starred **Margaret Field** (mother of Sally), who died at 89 in November.

SILVIO NARIZZANO
Born: *8 February 1927, Montreal, Quebec, Canada.*
Died: *26 July 2011, London, England.*
Having won high praise as a director in British television, Silvio Narizzano's first feature film was the magisterial Tallulah Bankhead's last, a skittish Hammer psycho-thriller called *Fanatic* (1964). He then scored mightily with the quintessential Swinging '60s sex comedy *Georgy Girl* (1966), which featured a standout performance from the young Lynn Redgrave and garnered Narizzano an award at the Berlin Film Festival. There followed a patchy roster of hits and misses in various genres – offbeat Western (*Blue*, 1967), black farce (*Loot*, 1969), continental exploitation (*Senza ragione*, 1972) and two films, one Canadian, one

Marie-France Pisier

exported as *I Am Curious (Yellow)* and caused a furore with both the British censor and US Customs. Nyman soon afterwards began a distinguished association with Stockholm's Royal Dramatic Theatre, also scoring on film in Alf Sjöberg's *Fadern* (The Father, 1969), Ingmar Bergman's *Herbstsonate* (Autumn Sonata, 1977) and numerous parochial comedies. Coincidentally, Nyman died the day after another actress indelibly associated with a controversial taboo-buster, Maria Schneider [qv].

MARIE-FRANCE PISIER

Born: *10 May 1944, Dalat, French Indochina.*
Died: *24 April 2011, Saint Cyr-sur-Mer, Var, France.*
The inscrutable beauty of Marie-France Pisier became a touchstone of France's nouvelle vague in the Truffaut film *Antoine et Colette* (part of the portmanteau *L'Amour à vingt ans*, 1962), together with its full-length follow-ups *Baisers volés* (1968) and *L'Amour en fuite* (1979). A two-time César winner, she also did remarkable work for Alain Robbe-Grillet (*Trans-Europ-Express*, 1966), Luis Buñuel (*Le Fantôme de la liberté*, 1974) and André Téchiné (*Barroco*, 1976). Having been central to two of the most beguiling French films of the '70s – *Céline et Julie vont en bateau* (1974) and *Cousin cousine* (1975) – she went to Hollywood for the much less beguiling *The Other Side of Midnight* (1976). Latterly, she directed *Le Bal du gouverneur* (1989), based on her own novel, and, for director Raúl Ruíz [qv], was still luminous in *Le Temps retrouvé* (1999).

❧ In August, **Yekaterina Golubeva**, Russian star of the French cult film *Pola X*, died at the early age of 44. Russia also lost **Lyudmila Gurchenko** (March, 75) and, in August, **Zhanna Prokhorenko** (71) and **Iya Savvina** (75). Other international actresses who died in 2011 included Mexico's **Lilia Michel** (August, 85), Sweden's **Gaby Sternberg** (September, 88) and the Italian-born Mexican star **Rosángela Balbó** (November, 70). Italy's **Dorian Gray** (75) and, from Spain, **Florinda Chico** (84) and former Miss Universe **Amparo Muñoz** (56) all departed in February.

POLLY PLATT

Born: *29 January 1939, Fort Sheridan, Illinois, USA.*
Died: *27 July 2011, New York City, New York, USA.*
Polly Platt was a true Renaissance woman of the 'movie

brat' generation. Working with her then husband Peter Bogdanovich, she was co-writer and production designer on his first feature, the grimly effective *Targets* (1967), then urged him to make a film of Larry McMurtry's novel *The Last Picture Show*; the result was an instant classic. The collaboration survived their 1972 divorce, siring *What's Up, Doc?* and *Paper Moon*, after which Platt added to her design credits such 1980s titles as *Terms of Endearment* and *The Witches of Eastwick*, wrote *Pretty Baby* (1977) and *A Map of the World* (1999), and produced, among others, *Broadcast News* (1987), *The War of the Roses* (1989) and *Bottle Rocket* (1995). Her final film was a 2010 documentary tribute to an early mentor, [Roger] *Corman's World*.

❧ For **Kenneth Mars**, a plum role in Bogdanovich's *What's Up, Doc?* came in between his classic comic performances in Mel Brooks' *The Producers* and *Young Frankenstein*. He died in February, aged 75.

PETE POSTLETHWAITE

Born: *16 February 1946, Warrington, Lancashire, England.*
Died: *2 January 2011, Shrewsbury, Shropshire, England.*
A mainstay of the Liverpool Everyman and the Royal Shakespeare Company in turn, Pete Postlethwaite got his screen break as the ferocious Liverpudlian father in *Distant Voices Still Lives* (1987). From that point on, his beautifully wrought performances lit up a long succession of powerful 1990s films, from *Hamlet*, *The Last of the Mohicans* and *In the Name of the Father* (for which he was Oscar-nominated) to *Romeo + Juliet*, *The Serpent's Kiss* and *Brassed Off*. With major Hollywood projects coming his way in his final decade, he was

Pete Postlethwaite

Cliff Robertson

Painting) and attracted international attention with the beguiling puzzles of *Les trois couronnes du matelot* (Three Crowns of the Sailor, 1982) and *La Ville des pirates* (City of Pirates, 1983). In later years, bigger budgets attracted bigger names, among them Marcello Mastroianni, Isabelle Huppert, John Malkovich and Catherine Deneuve, the last two starring in Ruiz's sumptuous 1999 adaptation of Proust's *Le Temps retrouvé*. In 2010, his penultimate film, *Misterios de Lisboa*, was widely hailed as his masterpiece.

❧ Scotttish critic, novelist and screenwriter **Gilbert Adair**, whose film credits included three collaborations with Ruiz and one with Bernardo Bertolucci, died in December, aged 66. In addition to Ruiz, several other international directors died in the year under review, among them **Fadil Hadžić** (aged 88, in January), **Hysen Hakani** (78, February), **Sachin Bhowmick** (80, April), **Angelino Fons** (74, June), and, in July, **Hideo Tanaka** (77) and **Binka Zhelyazkova** (88). **Janusz Morgenstern** (88), **Jag Mundhra** (62) and **Tatyana Lioznova** (87) all died in September, followed by **Pavlos Tassios** (69) and **Yaropolk Lapshin** (91) in October, **Antonio Eceiza** (76) in November, and **Andrei Blaier** (78) and **Yoshimitsu Morita** (61) in December.

JANE RUSSELL

Born: *21 June 1921, Bemidji, Minnesota, USA.*
Died: *28 February 2011, Santa Maria, California, USA.*
Jane Russell provided as provocative an image of female sexuality as 1940s filmgoers had ever seen. Though begun in 1940, Howard Hughes' *The Outlaw* wasn't properly released until 1946. But Hughes', and by extension America's, breast-fixation followed her ever afterward, even in her films' titles (*Double Dynamite*) and advertising (for *The French Line*: "JR in 3-D. It'll knock *both* your eyes out!"). This was a shame, because she quickly demonstrated – as Bob Hope's smouldering foil in *The Paleface* (1948) – a winning facility for droll, self-aware comedy. She was also perfectly partnered with Robert Mitchum in both *His Kind of Woman* and *Macao*, then reached a personal

awarded the OBE in 2004. Among his last films were *Inception* and *The Town*; for the latter, he not only played one of the most electrifying death scenes in recent memory but also received a fourth BAFTA nomination.

CLIFF ROBERTSON

Born: *9 September 1923, La Jolla, California, USA.*
Died: *10 September 2011, Stony Brook, New York, USA.*
As well as being the actor who, in a Hollywood-rocking late-1970s scandal, exposed Columbia head David Begelman as a common embezzler, Cliff Robertson exemplified two apparently antithetical beacons of Americana, playing John F Kennedy in *PT 109* (1962) and Hugh Hefner in *Star 80* (1983). His early films included *Picnic* (1955), *Autumn Leaves* (1956, as Joan Crawford's deranged husband) and *The Naked and the Dead* (1959). Then, to elude typecasting as a square-jawed war hero, he played a retarded janitor (a role he'd originated on TV) in *Charly* (1968), winning a well-deserved 'Best Actor' Oscar. He was also writer-director-star of the off-beat Western *J W Coop* (1971), and in the 21st century had a recurring role in the phenomenal *Spider-Man* franchise.

RAÚL RUIZ

Born: *25 July 1941, Puerto Montt, Chile.*
Died: *19 August 2011, Paris, France.*
Over a 40-year period, the visually baroque and narratively ambiguous works of Raúl Ruiz made him Chile's most prolific filmmaker. Starting out as a playwright, his earliest films, notably *Tres tristes tigres* (Three Sad Tigers, 1968), bore the stamp of nouvelle vague influence; appropriately then, having fled Chile's 1973 coup d'état, he fetched up in France. There he was lionised by local cinephiles on the 1978 release of *L'Hypothèse du tableau volé* (Hypothesis of the Stolen

Raúl Ruiz

Jane Russell

Ken Russell

Jimmy Sangster

apotheosis when matched with Marilyn Monroe in the luscious 1953 smash *Gentlemen Prefer Blondes*. Later in the decade, she shone, too, in *The Tall Men*, *The Revolt of Mamie Stover* and *The Fuzzy Pink Nightgown*. Her final film, *Darker Than Amber*, appeared in 1970.

KEN RUSSELL
Born: *3 July 1927, Southampton, Hampshire, England.*
Died: *27 November 2011, London, England.*
The premier provocateur of post-war British cinema, Ken Russell underwent a strange transition from 41-year-old enfant terrible, directing the Lawrentian masterwork *Women in Love* in 1968, to a 21st century 'old devil' making self-financed underground films in his own back garden. *French Dressing* (1963) formed a deceptively sunny introduction to his feature work, which – after a string of acclaimed BBC films on famous composers (Elgar, Delius, Debussy) – brought him an Oscar nomination for *Women in Love*. The early 1970s was Russell's most flamboyant period, both lyrically and visually, yielding *The Music Lovers*, the censor-baiting *The Devils*, *The Boy Friend*, *Savage Messiah*, *Mahler* and *Tommy*. In the 1980s there were Hollywood films (*Altered States*, *Crimes of Passion*) and threadbare British ones (*Gothic*, *The Lair of the White Worm*) that suggested his graphic exuberance might be best suited to horror. And then there was a long twilight in which the local industry consigned its most wildly original talent to inexplicable oblivion.

✎ Poet **Christopher Logue** – who scripted Russell's *The Devils* and acted for him in *Savage Messiah* – died in December, aged 85.

JIMMY SANGSTER
Born: *2 December 1927, Kinmel Bay, Wales.*
Died: *19 August 2011, London, England.*
Having been an assistant director and production manager for the fledgling Hammer outfit since 1949,

Jimmy Sangster graduated to screenwriter in 1956 with *X the Unknown*. He then became a crucial contributor to the company's radical reinvention of costume Gothic, scripting their worldwide hits *The Curse of Frankenstein* and *Dracula*, following up with *The Revenge of Frankenstein*, *The Mummy* and *The Brides of Dracula*. In 1960 he changed tack, turning producer as well as writer for such convoluted Hammer thrillers as *Taste of Fear*, *Paranoiac*, *Nightmare* and *The Nanny*. He also directed a few latterday Hammers, notably *Fear in the Night*. In addition to numerous American TV assignments, his non-Hammer screenwriting credits included *Deadlier Than the Male* (1967), *The Legacy* (1978), *Phobia* (1980) and *Flashback* (2000).

✎ Another writer-producer who gained early experience as a Hammer production manager was **Christopher Neame** (*Emily*, 1976; *Feast of July*, 1995), who died in June, aged 68.

MICHAEL SARRAZIN
Born: *22 May 1940, Quebec City, Quebec, Canada.*
Died: *17 April 2011, Montreal, Quebec, Canada.*
Michael Sarrazin signed a Universal contract in his mid-twenties and became the ideal image of a late-flowering beatnik in such movies of the moment as *The Sweet Ride* and *The Pursuit of Happiness*. Between these two, he was contractually prohibited from starring in *Midnight Cowboy* but was rapidly compensated with his most famous role, playing a mercy-killing marathon dancer (opposite Susannah York, qv) in *They Shoot Horses, Don't They?* Other credits included *The Flim-Flam Man*, *For Pete's Sake*, *Harry In Your Pocket* and the forgotten 'past lives' curio *The Reincarnation of Peter Proud*. He was also a highly effective monster in the 1973 TV movie *Frankenstein: The True Story*. Occupied by lower-profile Canadian projects in latter years, his final film, released posthumously, was *On the Road*.

BERT SCHNEIDER

Born: *5 May 1933, New York City, New York, USA.*
Died: *12 December 2011, Los Angeles, California, USA.*
Film producer and political activist Berton Schneider joined with Bob Rafelson in the mid-1960s to form Raybert Productions, manufacturing a pop group for the CBS series *The Monkees* and then providing them with a bizarre feature film showcase called *Head* (1968). Having personally bankrolled Dennis Hopper's counterculture classic *Easy Rider* (1969), Schneider followed up with *Five Easy Pieces* (1970) and *Drive, He Said* (1972), both starring Jack Nicholson (the second directed by him, too). Schneider also produced the period pictures *The Last Picture Show* (1971) and *Days of Heaven* (1978), and won an Oscar for Best Documentary with the anti-Vietnam piece *Hearts and Minds* (1974). Demonstrating the profound gulf between Hollywood old and new, Schneider and Frank Sinatra almost came to blows over that one.

❥ Other Hollywood names who died in December 2011 included 88-year-old casting director **Marion Dougherty**, 63-year-old **Tom Kennedy** (premier producer of US film trailers) and 77-year-old producer-editor **Marion Segal**. Among other American filmmakers, Oscar-nominated cinematographer **Donald Peterman** died at 79 in February, Oscar-winning sound mixers **Bill Varney** (77) and **Gene Cantamessa** (80) in April and November respectively, and BAFTA-winning editor **Peter E Berger** in September, aged 67. Producer **Perry Moore**, driving force behind the *Chronicles of Narnia* films, died in February at the early age of 39, while Italian-born, Oscar-nominated production designer **Bruno Rubeo** died in November, aged 65.

MARIA SCHNEIDER

Born: *27 March 1952, Paris, France.*
Died: *3 February 2011, Paris, France.*
Maria Schneider filmed her scenes in Bernardo

Bertolucci's wildly controversial 1972 film *Last Tango in Paris* shortly before her 20th birthday. Later, she was arrestingly enigmatic in Antonioni's *The Passenger* (1975) and charmingly matched with Joe Dallesandro in Jacques Rivette's improvisational *Merry-Go-Round* (1981). Despite some high-profile walk-outs (from both *Caligula* and Buñuel's *Cet obscur objet du désir*), she kept working reasonably steadily in later years; she was the mad (and mute) Mrs Rochester in Zeffirelli's 1996 *Jane Eyre*, for example. But the unshakable public image of her uninhibited *Last Tango* sex scenes had by then come to define her career, and Schneider herself came to feel she had been exploited.

DON SHARP

Born: *19 April 1921, Hobart, Tasmania, Australia.*
Died: *14 December 2011, Truro, Cornwall, England.*
Initially an actor, this accomplished Australian-born director graduated from Britain's first rock'n'roll movie (*The Golden Disc*, 1958) to the critically lauded romance *Linda* (1960). He then enjoyed a run of colourful Hammer titles – *The Kiss of the Vampire*, *The Devil-Ship Pirates*, *Rasputin the Mad Monk* – together with other highly polished chillers like *Witchcraft* and *The Face of Fu Manchu*. Between the cult curios *A Taste of Excitement* and *Psychomania*, he directed some thrilling chase sequences for Geoffrey Reeve's *Puppet on a Chain* in 1970 and was promoted thereafter to bigger projects like *Callan* (1973), *Hennessy* (1974) and *The Thirty Nine Steps* (1978). Then, after the all-star misfire *Bear Island*, he spent much of the 1980s taking charge of such TV mini-series as *A Woman of Substance*.

JUAN PIQUER SIMÓN

Born: *16 February 1935, Valencia, Spain.*
Died: *8 January 2011, Valencia, Spain.*
Fans of 1980s Euro-exploitation will need no introduction to this Spanish writer-director. They'll recall his occasional use of slumming British actors – Kenneth More in *Viaje al centro de la tierra* (Journey to the Centre of the Earth, 1977), Peter Cushing and Terence Stamp in *Misterio en la isla de los monstruos* (Mystery on Monster Island, 1980) or Frank Finlay in

Michael Sarrazin

Maria Schneider

Juan Piquer Simón

Elaine Stewart

La mansión de los Cthulhu (Cthulhu Mansion, 1990). But they'll remember most vividly his nonsensical slasher *Mil gritos tiene la noche* (Pieces, 1982) – with its memorable tag-line, "You don't have to go to Texas for a chainsaw massacre!" – and the self-explanatory *Slugs, muerte viscosa* (1987), which certainly makes the most of the slime-encrusted fatalities promised in the title.

❧ Other kings of exploitation cinema included 87-year-old **David F Friedman**, sponsor of numerous 'nudie cuties' and pioneering 1960s gore films like *Blood Feast*, who died in February, and 75-year-old **David Hess**, the terrifying gang leader in Wes Craven's *The Last House on the Left* (1971) and its Italian variant *La casa sperduta nel parco* (The House on the Edge of the Park, 1979), who died in October.

ELAINE STEWART
Born: *31 May 1930, Montclair, New Jersey, USA.*
Died: *27 June 2011, Beverly Hills, California, USA.*
"Sultry Miss Stewart," enthused the October 1959 issue of *Playboy*, "made stunning appearances in *The Bad and the Beautiful*, *Take the High Ground*, *Brigadoon*, *Night Passage* and many other films, playing opposite such stalwarts of the cinema as Kirk Douglas, Richard Widmark, James Stewart, Victor Mature." At the time of her (very chaste) *Playboy* pictorial, Stewart's film career was nearing its end; her last notable credit, *The Rise and Fall of Legs Diamond*, came out just six months later. It all began with a sexy cameo in the Martin and Lewis comedy *Sailor Beware* (1951), after which Stewart's trademark sensuality switched seamlessly between absurd MGM exotica (*The Adventures of Hajji Baba*, 1954) and no-nonsense Universal noir (*The Tattered Dress*, 1956).

HUGH STEWART
Born: *14 December 1910, Falmouth, Cornwall, England.*
Died: *31 May 2011, Denham, Buckinghamshire, England.*
Hugh Stewart began his film career as an editor, cutting such 1930s British evergreens as *The Man Who Knew Too Much*, *Q Planes* and *The Spy in Black*. As part of the Army Film and Photographic Unit, he produced the 1944 documentary *Tunisian Victory* with Frank Capra and the following year went over the heads of the War Office by insisting on making a filmed record of the concentration camp at Belsen. Post-war, he became an independent producer under the Rank Organisation banner, starting with the 1948 musical comedy *Trottie True*. He then settled into a long run as producer of ten Norman Wisdom comedies, followed by three for Morecambe and Wise. He bowed out as overseer of several 1970s titles for the Children's Film Foundation.

❧ Living almost as long as Hugh Stewart, **Walter Seltzer** – a production associate of both Marlon Brando (*One-Eyed Jacks*) and Charlton Heston (*The Omega Man*) – died at 96 in February.

MAUREEN SWANSON
Born: *25 November 1932, Glasgow, Scotland.*
Died: *16 November 2011, [location unknown], England.*
Profiling Maureen Swanson on the same page as George Baker [qv], *Film Review 1957-58* pointed out that she had been "placed by the late photographer Baron in a list of the world's ten most beautiful women." After early appearances in *Moulin Rouge* and *Knights of the Round Table*, she made the cover of *Picturegoer* in June 1955. There followed a promising run of Rank Organisation assignments – *A Town Like*

Alice, Jacqueline, The Spanish Gardener, Up in the World and *Robbery Under Arms*. "We're likely to be seeing her on our screens quite a lot in the future," concluded *Film Review*. In fact, she abandoned her career in 1961 on marrying Viscount Ednam, eight years later ascending to the title Countess of Dudley.

ELIZABETH TAYLOR

Born: *27 February 1932, London, England.*
Died: *23 March 2011, Los Angeles, California, USA.*
According to the 'Rising Stars' section of the second *Film Review* annual, "12-year-old Elizabeth Taylor is one of the 1945 screen newcomers who seem destined for big things." Indeed. Having scored as the child star of MGM's *National Velvet*, Taylor passed serenely through early 1950s items like *Father of the Bride* and *A Place in the Sun* prior to showing an aptitude for much meatier roles. The result? Four Oscar nominations in as many years, for *Raintree County*, *Cat on a Hot Tin Roof*, *Suddenly Last Summer* and (winning this one) *BUtterfield 8*. She then followed the elephantine *Cleopatra* with roles in which the early serenity was junked forever, acting up a viperish mid-'60s storm in *The Taming of the Shrew* and (another Oscar-winner) *Who's Afraid of Virginia Woolf?* A film as absurdly self-indulgent as *Boom* was just the ticket for the burgeoning army of Liz cultists, though there was a lot less for them to chew on during the 1970s, and virtually nothing at all after that. Yet she remains arguably the most iconic of all post-war Hollywood stars.

YVETTE VICKERS

Born: *26 August 1928, Kansas City, Missouri, USA.*
Death discovered: *27 April 2011, Beverly Hills, California, USA.*
Making her first film – Billy Wilder's *Sunset Blvd* – in 1949, Yvette Vickers earned cult status via such late-1950s drive-in classics as *Attack of the 50 Foot Woman*, *Reform School Girl* and *Attack of the Giant Leeches*, as well as being the *Playboy* Playmate for July 1959 in a session photographed by Russ Meyer. At the cusp of

the 1960s, she also played opposite Melvyn Douglas in George Roy Hill's Broadway production of *The Gang's All Here*, subsequently appearing briefly in Martin Ritt's Oscar-laden *Hud* (1963) and Curtis Harrington's *What's the Matter with Helen?* (1971). Reclusive in later years, her mummified body lay undiscovered in her Benedict Canyon home for up to 12 months after her death.

➷ Other cult movie queens who died this year include **Dolores Fuller**, muse of Edward D Wood Jr and star of his *Glen or Glenda?* (in May, aged 88), and **Tura Satana**, Amazonian centrepiece of Russ Meyer's *Faster, Pussycat! Kill! Kill!* (in February, aged 72). **Cynthia Myers**, star of Meyer's *Beyond the Valley of the Dolls*, died at 61 in November. Also featured in that film, together with several other Meyer titles, was square-jawed **Charles Napier**, who died in October aged 75. From the more squeaky-clean end of the exploitation spectrum, 1960s beach movie veterans **Aron Kincaid** and **Frank Alesia** died in January and February, aged 70 and 67 respectively.

NICOL WILLIAMSON

Born: *14 September 1936, Hamilton, Lanarkshire, Scotland.*
Died: *16 December 2011, Amsterdam, Netherlands.*
Well known as a latterday hellraiser in the tradition of John Barrymore (whom he played on stage), Nicol Williamson is indelibly associated with the grubby solicitor in John Osborne's 1964 play *Inadmissible Evidence*; like his Brummy *Hamlet* from five years later, the performance is preserved on film. Seemingly too volatile to fulfil the promise of an initially dazzling theatre career, Williamson also hated the process of filming. Even so, it brought him a BAFTA nomination for both the Osborne film and *The Bofors Gun* (1967), together with iconic roles like Little John in *Robin and Marian* (1975) and Merlin in *Excalibur* (1980). And, having rejected the title role in *The Private Life of Sherlock Holmes* in 1969, he essayed an unusual Sherlock six years later in *The Seven-Per-Cent Solution*.

Yvette Vickers

Nicol Williamson

Peter Yates

Googie Withers

Dana Wynter

GOOGIE WITHERS

Born: *12 March 1917, Karachi, British India.*
Died: *15 July 2011, Sydney, New South Wales, Australia.*
Like Dulcie Gray [qv], Googie Withers was known as
part of a husband-and-wife co-starring team; unlike
Gray, she got to play meaty and transgressive roles into
the bargain. She had her first major break in Michael
Powell's *One of Our Aircraft is Missing* (1942) and then
brought her imposing, and apparently 'un-British',
sensuality to bear on the Ealing classics *Pink String and
Sealing Wax*, *The Loves of Joanna Godden* and *It Always
Rains on Sunday*. Certainly no other actress projected
so powerful a female image onto British cinema in its
halcyon period. But after starring in Jules Dassin's
Night and the City and *White Corridors* for Pat Jackson
[qv], she emigrated with her husband, John McCallum,
to his native Australia. Amid much theatre, her final
films were *Country Life* (1994) and *Shine* (1995).

DANA WYNTER

Born: *8 June 1931, Berlin, Germany.*
Died: *5 May 2011, Ojai, California, USA.*
This beautiful British actress began her screen career
for director Pat Jackson [qv] in *White Corridors*. But, as
noted in the 'Rising Stars' section of *Film Review
1956-57*, she was one of many "promising young
British stars lost to Hollywood through lack of
perception on the part of our film producers." In the
US, her films included *Something of Value*, *Fraulein*,
Shake Hands with the Devil, *In Love and War*, *On the
Double*, *The List of Adrian Messenger* and *Airport*, together
with a ton of television. Her enduring claim to fame,
however, remains her desperate flight, alongside Kevin
McCarthy, from the soulless inhabitants of Santa Mira
in the 1955 classic *Invasion of the Body Snatchers*.

PETER YATES

Born: *24 July 1929, Aldershot, Hampshire, England.*
Died: *9 January 2011, London, England.*
Starting out as a director at London's Royal Court
Theatre, Peter Yates made his film debut with the
colourful Cliff Richard vehicle *Summer Holiday* (1962).
He proceeded to a surrealist farce straight out of the

Susannah York

Rosel Zech

Royal Court, *One Way Pendulum* (1964), the gritty crime drama *Robbery* (1967) and, having been snapped up by Hollywood, the electrifying San Francisco-set *Bullitt* (1968). He also crafted engaging showcases for Dustin Hoffman (*John and Mary*, 1969), Peter O'Toole (*Murphy's War*, 1970), Robert Mitchum (*The Friends of Eddie Coyle*, 1973) and Albert Finney (*The Dresser*, 1983). And he had no trouble mastering a wide range of genres, from crazy comedy (*For Pete's Sake*, 1974), sexy aquatic intrigue (*The Deep*, 1977) and poignant 'coming of age' drama (*Breaking Away*, 1979) to the suspenseful convolutions of *Eyewitness* (1981) and *Suspect* (1987).

SUSANNAH YORK

Born: *9 January 1939, London, England.*
Died: *15 January 2011, London, England.*
"This has been a great year for 21-year-old Susannah York," noted F Maurice Speed in this annual's 1964-65 edition, "with her screen career crowned with glory as Tom's true love in the award-laden film *Tom Jones*." She'd already made an impact in *Tunes of Glory* and *The Greengage Summer*, as well as displaying, in *Freud*, some of the neurotic nuance that contradicted her 'English Rose' image. Even more of that febrile quality was on view in subsequent titles like *The Killing of Sister George*, *They Shoot Horses, Don't They?* (for which she won a BAFTA and was Oscar-nominated) and *Images*. Later, she made intriguingly left-field choices like *The Maids* and *The Shout*, and wrote the 1980 film *Falling in Love Again*. Thereafter she focused on theatre and made only occasional film appearances.

ROSEL ZECH

Born: *7 July 1942, Berlin, Germany.*
Died: *31 August 2011, Berlin, Germany.*
Forever remembered as Rainer Werner Fassbinder's fallen Ufa star in *Die Sehnsucht der Veronika Voss*, Rosel

Zech made her stage debut in Bavaria aged 19. Having forged a fruitful theatrical partnership with director Peter Zadek (including an award-winning Hedda Gabler in 1977), she found a similar kindred spirit cinematically in Fassbinder. Initially cast by him in supporting roles, in 1981 she took on Veronika Voss (a character loosely based on Sybille Schmitz) and made an indelible impression. Much of her time subsequently was devoted to TV and (her first love) the stage, but she gave another beautifully nuanced performance in Percy Adlon's Alaskan love story *Salmonberries* (1990), winning a Bayerischer Filmpreis in the process.

❧ Four-time winner of the Bayerischer Filmpreis, 77-year-old writer-director **Peter Schamoni** died in June. **Peter Przygodda**, editor of many Wim Wenders titles, died in October, aged 69.

LAURA ZISKIN

Born: *3 March 1950, San Fernando Valley, California, USA.*
Died: *12 June 2011, Santa Monica, California, USA.*
Laura Ziskin's first producer credit was on the 1978 thriller *Eyes of Laura Mars*; she was assistant to Jon Peters at the time. Soon enough, she scored several successes as a producer in her own right – *Murphy's Romance* (1985), *No Way Out* (1987) and, pre-eminently, *Pretty Woman* (1990). In 1994, making further inroads into traditionally male preserves, she became president of Fox 2000 Pictures, winding up her tenure there five years later with *Fight Club*. In the meantime, she had an executive producer credit on *As Good As It Gets* (1997) and, in the 21st century, produced the phenomenal *Spider-Man* and its three follow-ups. She was also co-founder of Stand Up to Cancer and received both the David O Selznick and Visionary awards from the Producers Guild of America.

❧ **Joe Wizan**, who died at 76 in March, was briefly head of 20th Century Fox and numbered *Junior Bonner* and *Along Came a Spider* among his credits. **John Calley**, who died in September aged 81, headed, by turns, Warners, MGM-UA and Sony, his credits stretching from *The Cincinnati Kid* to *The Da Vinci Code*.

Afterword

by **Mansel Stimpson**

In a sentence that brings together two significant but totally contrasted films, I would describe 2012 thus far as being the year of *The Best Exotic Marigold Hotel* and *Once Upon a Time in Anatolia*.

The success of the former – it has proved to be a film which many cinemagoers see more than once, making it a lesser but still striking example of what could be called the *Mamma Mia!* syndrome – suggests that in some respects the appeal of cinema over the years remains identical. What we have here is a feel-good movie with the star appeal of Judi Dench and Maggie Smith drawing in a public who, in these times of economic woes and of news stories that are full of gloom, seek escape from the world's realities. This new movie is surely serving exactly the same function that Herbert Wilcox's *Spring in Park Lane* did in 1948, when that romantic comedy of gracious living featuring the hugely popular Anna Neagle and Michael Wilding offered the ideal escape route for those living in post-war austerity Britain.

As for the Turkish film, the finest to date from Nuri Bilge Ceylan, *Once Upon a Time in Anatolia* was the critics' darling, receiving more acclaim from those who believe in cinema as an art form than any other release of this period. Even so, one wonders to what extent its audiences appreciated it. Many today who attend art house films have one complaint about them that is more persistent than any other: namely, that they are too slow. This appears to be a reflection of present attitudes and short attention spans, and it leads to some films being under-appreciated by the public. That could certainly apply to Ceylan's film since it is both decidedly slow (little happens in the first three quarters of an hour) and very, very long (157 minutes). Nevertheless, it's a masterpiece, demanding but rewarding and a film best approached with full awareness that, despite beginning with a police search for a dead body, it is not in essence a police procedural. We never learn the truth about the crime because the film goes off in another direction.

There's a definite parallel here with Antonioni's classic *L'avventura* which never resolved the mystery of a girl's disappearance that was its starting point. Back then in 1960 audiences were keen to tackle films that required patience and invited interpretation: indeed, it was even suggested that in intellectual circles of the day it was essential to be able to join in discussions about the latest works of Antonioni, Bergman and Resnais. The restlessness of many

Judi Dench and Celia Imrie in the feel-good smash *The Best Exotic Marigold Hotel*.

audiences today, evidenced by how they always want a film to get a move on, suggests that some attitudes to film very definitely do change. One sees in this a reflection of the age.

There are, of course, filmmakers prepared to go against the grain in this respect. If *Once Upon a Time in Anatolia* ultimately proves to be about the need to understand people's weaknesses and to sympathise rather than condemn, it's a description that applies also to the striking Austrian film *Breathing (Atmen)* and, as an example of even more extreme minimalism, *The Turin Horse*, which Béla Tarr has declared will be his last film. Also bordering on this territory was another Austrian film, *Michael*, an unsensational study of a paedophile. However, the range of subtitled films released during this period has been wide. For example, the French product extended from the underrated Audrey Tautou rom-com *Delicacy* to the sexually explicit *Elles*, which divided opinion over the way it studied female students in Paris willingly supporting themselves by means of prostitution. Meanwhile the Dardenne Brothers scored again with *The Kid with a Bike*, in which Thomas Doret was superb as the troubled 11-year-old at its centre and Ismael Ferroukhi, who made *Le Grand Voyage* in 2004, triumphed too. His new film, *Free Men*, told the true wartime story of how the Paris Mosque helped Jews as well as members of the Resistance during the German occupation of the city.

Before leaving the sphere of foreign films, I should mention some other interesting titles. We have had Agnieszka Holland's *In Darkness*

Above: Long, yes; slow, certainly; but also masterful – *Once Upon a Time in Anatolia.*

Left: Thomas Schubert in the striking Austrian entry *Breathing.*

Below: Juliette Binoche in Malgorzata Szumowska's explicit *Elles.*

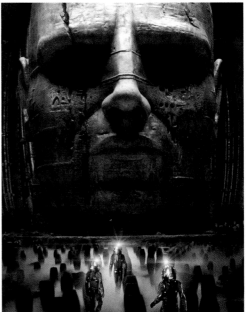

Above: Aksel Hennie in the smooth Norwegian thriller *Headhunters*.

Right: Ridley Scott recalled his 33-year-old hit *Alien* with *Prometheus*.

(another wartime reconstruction, this time from Poland), a contemporary drama set in Buenos Aires (Pablo Trapero's *Carancho*), the highly adventurous *Kosmos* from Turkey (which I regard as a true work of art) and a successful bid to build on the current popularity of Scandinavian thrillers. The latter is *Headhunters*, a slick Norwegian adaptation of a novel by Jo Nesbø.

Furthermore, three works that could be described as documentaries stand out. In *This Is Not a Film* the Iranian director Jafar Panahi is seen at home in Tehran; this is a unique document because it was made as a gesture of defiance after the authorities banned him from

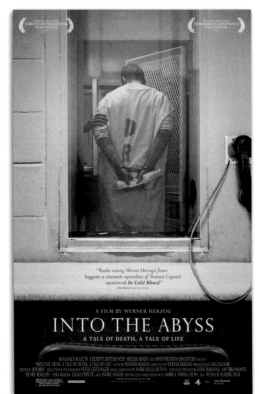

Werner Herzog's latest documentary, *Into the Abyss, A Tale of Death, a Tale of Life*.

filming and at a time when he was appealing against a six-year jail term. In his documentary *Into the Abyss, A Tale of Death, a Tale of Life* Werner Herzog is heard but not seen. Having been shot in Texas, the German filmmaker's latest work is not subtitled, but it seems appropriate to mention it here nevertheless. It deals with a triple killing in 2001, yet this deeply humane work is concerned with the tragedy inherent in any murder – which is to say that the tragedy explored encompasses not only the victims and their families but also the relatives of the killers and, indeed, the murderers themselves. The third work was made in Indonesia by a filmmaker from the Netherlands, Leonard Retel Helmrich. *Position Among the Stars* is centred on one family and in particular on a grandmother leaving her country home to help a grandchild who lives in Jakarta and hopes to study. This caring film may be called a documentary, but it plays like a companion-piece to the classic *Apu Trilogy* and Satyajit Ray, had he lived to see it, would surely have recognised it as a film after his own heart.

Turning to the wider picture and to American films which make it to the multiplexes, one has to conclude that the formula of recent years in which blockbusters predominate has not changed, even if some new franchises are being sought. The response to *The Hunger Games* suggests that it will yield sequels, but only success in non-English speaking territories enabled *John Carter* to get its money back. As I write *Battleship* is the No 1 film at the UK box-office despite a distinct lack of enthusiasm from the critics. Furthermore, it would take serious misjudgments to sink titles such as *Prometheus*, in which Ridley Scott echoes his earlier *Alien*, and *Avengers Assemble,* featuring a whole range of established comic book legends. No less eagerly awaited by the fans are two July releases, *The Amazing Spider-Man* and Christopher Nolan's *The Dark Knight Rises*, the latter perhaps the most keenly anticipated of all. This could mean that 2012 will become a great year for those who favour films in this genre.

Thanks to the promotional flair of Sacha Baron Cohen, the most eagerly awaited comedy has been his new film *The Dictator*, but this May release was still without press screenings at the time of writing. What we have already seen are the Oscar contenders, most of which emerged as ever at the start of the year, but in 2012 the standard was not of the highest. I did like *The Descendants* with George Clooney, but in several cases the performances were more satisfying than the films which contained them (Leonardo DiCaprio in Clint Eastwood's *J. Edgar*, Charlize Theron in *Young Adult*, newcomer Elizabeth Olsen in *Martha Marcy May Marlene*). That applied too to Glenn Close and Janet McTeer in the wonderfully acted *Albert Nobbs*, shot in Ireland and released in April. One other spring movie should be noted since it was underestimated and to my mind misunderstood: I refer to *This Must Be the Place*, made in America (and in Ireland) by Italy's Paolo Sorrentino and starring Sean Penn on top form.

To conclude I turn to British cinema. Despite its British connections and the British talent in the leading roles, Spielberg's *War Horse* was not strictly speaking a British film, while that other hugely successful picture, the Meryl Streep vehicle *The Iron Lady* (another film in which the star outshone the movie), was only part British in that it had French backing. But, even if one ignores these two popular titles, the British contribution has seen a couple of big hits as well as some unusually interesting and even surprising films. One of those hits, *The Best Exotic Marigold Hotel*, I have already mentioned; the other was the ghost story *The Woman in Black*, which made an ideal vehicle for Daniel Radcliffe to go it alone after Harry Potter. Even more to my taste as popular entertainment was *Salmon Fishing in the Yemen*, which was so well played by Ewan McGregor and Emily Blunt that it pulled off the difficult transition halfway through from Ealing-style comedy to romantic drama.

Earlier in the year Ralph Fiennes had successfully turned director with a well-judged modernisation of Shakespeare's *Coriolanus*. Even more adventurous were the Monitor-style documentary about W G Sebald entitled *Patience (After Sebald)* and the avant-garde approach adopted for *The Gospel of Us*, the film version of Michael Sheen's take on the Passion that was staged at Easter last year in and around Port Talbot. As for established directors, Ken Loach's new comedy *The Angels' Share* is on the way as I write, Steve McQueen has daringly followed *Hunger* with his properly disturbing study of sex addiction (*Shame*), the Aardman studio has given us *The Pirates! In an Adventure with Scientists!* and Michael Winterbottom – in *Trishna*, his variation

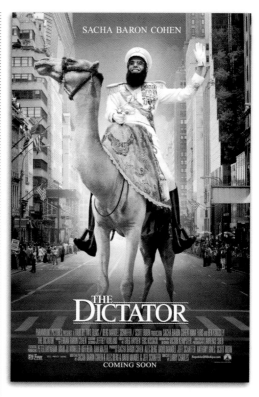

Sacha Baron Cohen strikes again as *The Dictator*.

on Thomas Hardy's novel *Tess of the d'Urbervilles* set in modern India – has given Freida Pinto her best role to date. The diversity of these works is an encouraging sign for cinema in this country at the present time.

Inevitably, this article touches only briefly on the cinema fare available in Britain during the first six months of 2012. If readers continue to support us, however, we hope to cover the year in full and in detail in the next issue of this annual, which is planned to appear in the summer of 2013. We sign off until then with thanks to all of you who purchase *Film Review*.

Emily Blunt and Ewan McGregor, both exceptional in *Salmon Fishing in the Yemen*.

Title Index